MAYA JASANOFF is Coolidge Professor of History at Harvard University. Her first book, *Edge of Empire*, was awarded the 2005 Duff Cooper Prize and was a book of the year selection in numerous publications including the *Economist*, *Guardian* and *Sunday Times*. Her second, *Liberty's Exiles*, won the National Book Critics Circle Award for Non-Fiction and was shortlisted for the 2011 Samuel Johnson Prize (now Baillie Gifford Prize). A 2013 Guggenheim Fellow, Jasanoff won the prestigious 2017 Windham-Campbell Prize for Non-Fiction. Her essays and reviews appear frequently in publications including the *Guardian*, *New York Times*, and *New York Review of Books*.

'*The Dawn Watch* is the most vivid and suggestive biography of Conrad ever written ... [A] beautifully written book'   *Wall Street Journal*

'So well written ... This is a biographer who has done her homework and her legwork for a book that creates a Conrad for our time. Enjoy it – how rarely can one say that about a work of scholarship'   *The Times*

'Fascinating ... [Conrad's] art, which he defined as the capacity to make readers hear, feel and see, was able to capture the contradictions within empires and the resistance to them. This is the Conrad who comes alive in Jasanoff's masterful study. *The Dawn Watch* will become a creative companion to all students of his work. It has made me want to re-establish connections with the Conrad whose written sentences once inspired in me the same joy as a musical phrase'

NGUGI WA THIONG'O, *New York Times Book Review*

'Written with a novelist's flair for vivid detail and a scholar's attention to texts *The Dawn Watch* is by any standard a major contribution to our understanding of Conrad in his time ... what Jasanoff offers the reader is ... a fresh view of a much-scribbled-on writer that enables us to see him in a time in many ways like our own'   *Literary Review*

'Jasanoff's first-rate analysis of the "global compass" of Conrad's fiction, in all its matchless beauty and grave intent' *Evening Standard*

'Skillfully integrates details of Conrad's life and accounts of his four greatest works, linking the challenges and forces that lie behind and within the novels to those of the 21st century ... A powerful encouragement to read his books' *Economist*

'[*The Dawn Watch*] stands out for its vivid and imaginative writing'
Sunday Times

'A strikingly original book ... Jasanoff writes beautifully ... succeeds brilliantly ... an extraordinary and profoundly ambitious book, little short of a masterpiece'

WILLIAM DALRYMPLE, *Guardian*, Book of the Day

'Terrific ... Weaving together biography, history, literature and her own travels, this fascinating, beautifully written work takes one of those literary giants frequently written off these days as a dead white male and reveals how he inhabited and grappled with a world startlingly like our own ... [Jasanoff] explains why it's important that we grapple with figures like Conrad even if we don't share their values. History is like therapy for the present, she writes. It makes us talk about its parents. She's right as well as witty. And reading *The Dawn Watch*, we see how we are in many ways Conrad's children. Even if you hated *Lord Jim* in high school, this book will make you want to pick it up again'

JOHN POWERS, NPR

'Lucid, revelatory and wonderfully concise, *The Dawn Watch* celebrates Conrad's uncanny prescience and shows his continued relevance now in the twenty-first century' WILLIAM BOYD, *TLS*, Books of the Year

'Brilliant ... Jasanoff is an insightful and imaginative historian ... The book comes in the form of a biography of Joseph Conrad, but in fact through Conrad she tells the story of a whole phase in world history ... Boundless curiosity is also an attribute of Maya Jasanoff ... This is the best book on Conrad since [Ian] Watt's. Maya Jasanoff has given us a Conrad for the 21st century' *Los Angeles Review of Books*

'Her historian's eye can untie knots that might baffle the pure critic ... Jasanoff ... steers us securely and stylishly through those latitudes where Conrad witnessed the future scupper the past' *Spectator*

'Gracefully written ... the book is a great pleasure to read, for Jasanoff is driven to understand the world that shaped a writer she loves' ADAM HOCHSCHILD, *Foreign Affairs*

'With wit, nuance, and roving insight, Harvard historian Maya Jasanoff's *The Dawn Watch* maps the massively influential and controversial author's life and work, finding that the themes of his time – dislocation and connection, immigration and xenophobia, power and powerlessness – uncannily mirror our own' MEGAN O'GRADY, *Vogue*

'Jasanoff is a splendid storyteller and stylist' *San Francisco Chronicle*

'A rewarding, richly textured read, sprawling in its reach and full of surprising cross-connections ... Jasanoff ... shares with her subject the knack of capturing human experience in poetic fistfuls of language, although it's sometimes hard to know where Conrad's magic stops and her own starts' *The American Scholar*

'It is Jasanoff's warmth towards her subject that comes through' *Financial Times*

'A great biography of Conrad for our times could never be just a biography of Conrad. *The Dawn Watch* is a scholarly trip to the birthplace of the books themselves, and an extraordinary meditation on Conrad's place in our consciousness. Jasanoff is erudite, passionate and wise: she has it all'
JUAN GABRIEL VÁSQUEZ

'Written with all the immediacy of a fast-moving novel, yet also with all the acuity and scholarship one would expect from one of the most brilliant historians of her generation, *The Dawn Watch* gives us superb new insights into the mind and life of one of the greatest writers in the English tongue. The issues of which Joseph Conrad wrote with such penetrating prescience a century ago – terrorism, racism, interventionism, alienation – are the ones we worry about today, indeed perhaps more so now than at any time since he laid down his pen'
ANDREW ROBERTS

'Jasanoff has done her research on sea and land as well as in the archives, and her book is often thrilling to read as it travels the world with Conrad. An admirable and profoundly meditated biography, worthy of its subject'
CLAIRE TOMALIN

'*The Dawn Watch* lifts Conrad out of the "great tradition" of lit-crit to attempt something larger and more ambitious: demonstrating that his world is ours – and vice-versa. Maya Jasanoff is an eloquent historian and an erudite storyteller'
GEOFF DYER

'In *The Dawn Watch*, Maya Jasanoff has fashioned a singular craft for exploring the rapids and crosscurrents of a newly globalized era. The journey is intellectually exhilarating, and brings us to a richer understanding not only of Conrad's world but our own'
ANTHONY APPIAH

'Enthralling – a major achievement, an unforgettable voyage, an historic circumnavigation of Conrad's whole life. Historical narrative, literary analysis and complex post-colonial argument combined in the most thrilling way … an absolute masterpiece' RICHARD HOLMES

'*The Dawn Watch* takes the reader seamlessly through Joseph Conrad's extraordinary life and voyages, showing us that our globalized world was fundamentally shaped in his lifetime a century ago – and that his pen still illuminates its beating heart. This is a wonder of a book that merges vivid travel, scholarly biography, and sharply observed history. Everyone searching for an understanding of our world today and the voice of one of the 20th century's most evocative writers should set sail with Maya Jasanoff.' ADMIRAL JAMES STAVRIDIS,
former Supreme Allied Commander, NATO

THE

DAWN WATCH

JOSEPH CONRAD
IN A GLOBAL WORLD

MAYA JASANOFF

WILLIAM
COLLINS

William Collins
An imprint of HarperCollins*Publishers*
1 London Bridge Street
London SE1 9GF

www.WilliamCollinsBooks.com

First published in Great Britain by William Collins in 2017
First published in the United States by Penguin Press in 2017
This William Collins paperback edition published in 2018

1

A catalogue record for this book is
available from the British Library

Illustration Credits: Pages 23 (left and right), 35 (left and right), 48, 104, 105, 127, 227 (left and right), 289, 293, 303: Joseph Conrad Collection. General Collection, Beinecke Rare Book and Manuscript Library, Yale University; p. 37: Wikimedia Commons; pp. 45, 59, 61, 77, 97, 128, 139, 172, 183, 188, 190, 193, 196, 212, 299: Widener Library, Harvard University; p. 47: Polona; p. 98: John Oxley Library, State Library of Queensland Neg: 168598; pp. 118 and 131: Royal Netherlands Institute of Southeast Asian and Caribbean Studies and Leiden University Library/Wikimedia Commons; p.119: Wikimedia Commons; pp. 121, 176–177, 265: The David Rumsey Map Collection, www.davidrumsey.com; p. 156: Great Britain Hydrographic Office, "Chart Relating to the Gulf of Siam: Original Navigation Chart Used by Joseph Conrad." General Collection, Beinecke Rare Book and Manuscript Library, Yale University; pp. 163 and 280: Library of Congress Prints and Photographs Division, Washington, D.C.; p.171: By Smithsonian Institution from United States (Carte-de-visite of Henry M. Stanley), Wikimedia Commons; p. 180: By Daderot (Own work) [CC0], Wikimedia Commons; p. 195: MS Eng 46, Houghton Library, Harvard University; p. 242: Print Collection, Miriam and Ira D. Wallach Division of Art, Prints and Photographs, The New York Public Library, Astor, Lenox and Tilden Foundations; p. 287: Biblioteca Digital Trapalanda of the Biblioteca Nacional, Uruguay; p. 287: Author's Collection; p. 308: "Joseph Conrad sitting in a chair," General Collection, Beinecke Rare Book and Manuscript Library, Yale University. Map Credits: The David Rumsey Map Collection, www.davidrumsey.com.

ISBN 978-0-00-755372-3

Printed and bound in Great Britain by
CPI Group (UK) Ltd, Croydon

MIX
Paper from
responsible sources
FSC C007454

This book is produced from independently certified FSC paper
to ensure responsible forest management.

For more information visit: www.harpercollins.co.uk/green

For the friends who have traveled with me.

"I am the world itself, come to pay you a visit."

—JOSEPH CONRAD, *Victory* (1915)

CONTENTS

PART FOUR: EMPIRE

LIST OF

ILLUSTRATIONS

LIST OF

MAPS

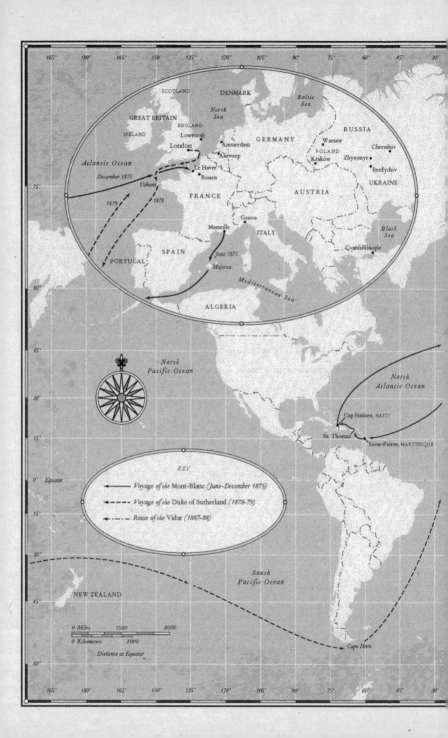

SCOTLAND
DENMARK
Baltic Sea
GREAT BRITAIN
North Sea
ENGLAND
RUSSIA
IRELAND
Lowestoft
GERMANY
Warsaw
Chernihiv
London
Amsterdam
POLAND
Zhytomyr
Antwerp
Kraków
Atlantic Ocean
Le Havre
Berdychiv
December 1875
Rouen
UKRAINE
Ushant
FRANCE
AUSTRIA
1879
1878
Genoa
Marseille
ITALY
Black Sea
Constantinople
SPAIN
June 1875
PORTUGAL
Majorca
Mediterranean Sea
ALGERIA

North Pacific Ocean

North Atlantic Ocean

Cap Haïtien, HAITI

St. Thomas
Saint-Pierre, MARTINIQUE

Equator

KEY

⟵——— *Voyage of the Mont-Blanc (June–December 1875)*

⟵- - - - *Voyage of the Duke of Sutherland (1878–79)*

⟵-·-·-· *Route of the Vidar (1887–88)*

South Pacific Ocean

NEW ZEALAND

0 Miles   1500   3000
0 Kilometers   3000
Distance at Equator

Cape Horn

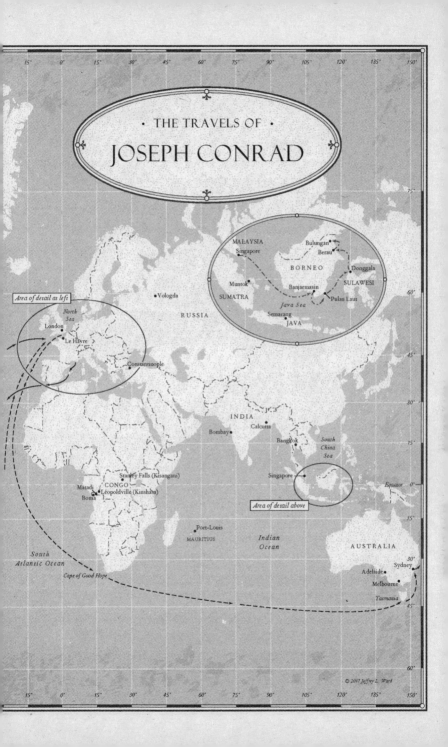

· THE TRAVELS OF ·
JOSEPH CONRAD

Area of detail at left

North
Sea

London

Le Havre

Constantinople

RUSSIA

Vologda

MALAYSIA

Singapore

Bulungan

Berau

BORNEO

Donggala

SULAWESI

Muntok

Banjarmasin

SUMATRA

Pulau Laut

Java Sea

Semarang

JAVA

INDIA

Bombay

Calcutta

Bangkok

South
China
Sea

Singapore

Equator

Area of detail above

Stanley Falls (Kisangani)

Matadi   CONGO

Boma   Léopoldville (Kinshasa)

Port-Louis

MAURITIUS

Indian
Ocean

AUSTRALIA

Sydney

Adelaide

Melbourne

Tasmania

South
Atlantic Ocean

Cape of Good Hope

© 2017 Jeffrey L. Ward

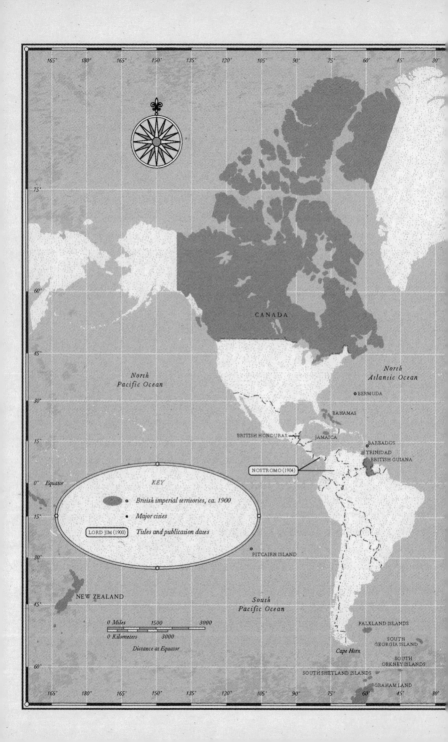

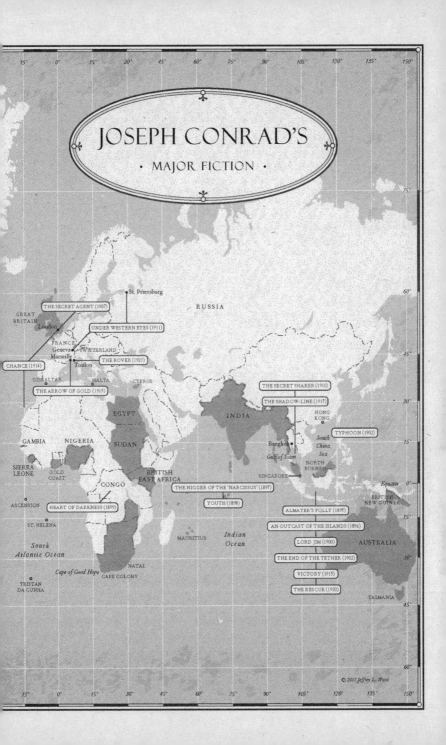

JOSEPH CONRAD'S

· MAJOR FICTION ·

THE SECRET AGENT (1907)

UNDER WESTERN EYES (1911)

CHANCE (1914)

THE ROVER (1923)

THE ARROW OF GOLD (1919)

THE SECRET SHARER (1910)

THE SHADOW-LINE (1917)

TYPHOON (1902)

THE NIGGER OF THE 'NARCISSUS' (1897)

YOUTH (1898)

ALMAYER'S FOLLY (1895)

HEART OF DARKNESS (1899)

AN OUTCAST OF THE ISLANDS (1896)

LORD JIM (1900)

THE END OF THE TETHER (1902)

VICTORY (1915)

THE RESCUE (1920)

St. Petersburg

RUSSIA

GREAT
BRITAIN

London

FRANCE
Geneva
Marseille
Toulon
SWITZERLAND

GIBRALTAR
MALTA
CYPRUS

EGYPT

INDIA

HONG
KONG

GAMBIA
NIGERIA
SUDAN

South
China
Sea

Bangkok
Gulf of Siam

NORTH
BORNEO

SINGAPORE

SIERRA
LEONE
GOLD
COAST
CONGO
BRITISH
EAST AFRICA

Equator

BRITISH
NEW GUINEA

ASCENSION

ST. HELENA

MAURITIUS

Indian
Ocean

AUSTRALIA

South
Atlantic Ocean

Cape of Good Hope
NATAL
CAPE COLONY

TRISTAN
DA CUNHA

TASMANIA

© 2017 Jeffrey L. Ward

ONE OF US

IT WAS HARD TO GET TO CONGO. With ongoing civil war in the east, the south a "shadow state" carved up by international mining companies, and political protest surging in the capital, Kinshasa, the Democratic Republic of the Congo was by many measures one of the world's most dysfunctional states. Though a country of abundant natural resources, it sits near the bottom of the United Nations Human Development Index, and has the second-lowest per capita gross national income in the world.[1] In the words of my guidebook, "This is a huge area of dark corners, both geographically and mentally . . . where man has fought continuously against his own demons and the elements of nature at large."[2] This, in other words, was the heart of darkness. And that's why I wanted to go.

First I needed a visa, and to get that I needed a notarized "*Prise en Charge*," or sponsorship guarantee, from somebody in Congo. Through a fixer in Kinshasa I eventually received a yellow document riddled with stamps and signatures in purple, green, and blue. I counted two dozen in all: from the Ministry of the Interior, the Ministry of Foreign Affairs, the Director General of Immigration, the Public Services Bureau, the Immigration Police, the Mayor's Office, multiple notaries, administrators, and section chiefs. Some had pictures of panthers and spears. I paid more than $500 to get it.

I sent the application for my visa to Washington and booked a plane ticket for more than two months later. I turned to planning what I'd do there. I got in touch with anyone I could think of who had any connection to Congo and contacted everyone they suggested in turn. I arranged an itinerary with an intrepid tour operator that would fly me deep inland to Kisangani, and then travel by boat a thousand miles around the bend of the Congo River, back to Kinshasa. The journey would cost me a lot, despite extremely basic conditions, but that's what I was told it took for a Western female tourist to travel safely (with full-time escorts) in one of the world's least touristed destinations.

At an office in my university called Global Support Services I met a man who sat behind a desk draped in a Zimbabwean flag. He issued me a security briefing and medical evacuation plan. He advised me to waterproof everything twice, keep my money strapped around my ankle, stay vigilant at all times, and expect everything to be stolen. Then he went to a cupboard and came back with a gift: a mosquito net.

Everything was set up. But after months of processing, I still didn't have a visa. The embassy in Washington said it was waiting for approval from the Ministry of Foreign Affairs in Kinshasa; I paid for another stamp. My contacts pressed their contacts. Nothing budged. The delay was deliberate, I was told, and no Americans were getting in.

By the time my visa finally arrived, thanks to a fortuitous link with somebody who worked in the Congolese embassy, it was the first day of the new semester, so I'd have to wait until classes ended before I could go—and in the meantime, Congo was cruising toward political crisis. President Joseph Kabila's term was running out, yet he'd refused to schedule an election. Antigovernment protests roiled Kinshasa; almost fifty people were shot, hacked, and burned to death by security forces.

Taxi drivers refused to go from the airport into the city center for fear of attack. The U.S. State Department ordered family members of government personnel to leave; the European Union planned sanctions.[3] If I was still determined to make the trip, the tour operator advised, I'd have to get out before the president was due to step down—or rather, not step down, triggering worse violence.

That left me exactly three weeks. I packed the mosquito net and guidebook, stuffed cash into my shoes, loaded Congolese rumba (*soukous*) onto my playlist, and headed to the airport.

MORE THAN A HUNDRED YEARS AGO, a Polish sailor named Konrad Korzeniowski also made a trip to Congo that seemed to stall forever, until it happened suddenly all at once. In November 1889 he had interviewed with a Brussels-based company for a job as a steamboat captain on the Congo River. They promised him a position but didn't reply to any of his follow-up letters, and when he inquired again in person, they told him to wait. After six months of uncertain silence, Konrad got word from the company that a job had opened up. He was to leave for Africa within a week.

"If you only knew the devilish haste I had to make!" he wrote to a friend. "If you had only seen all the tin boxes and revolvers, the high boots and the tender farewells . . . all the bottles of medicine and all the affectionate wishes I took away with me."[4] Konrad was supposed to stay in Congo for three years, but after just one trip up and down the river between Kinshasa and Kisangani he quit. He saw in Congo a European regime of appalling greed, violence, and hypocrisy, and left Africa in a state of psychological and moral despair. Nine years later, when he'd settled in England and Anglicized his name to Joseph Conrad, he channeled his experience into a novel called *Heart of Darkness* (1899).

I was going to Congo because I wanted to see whatever I could of what Conrad had seen—because what Conrad had seen shapes what so many other people have seen since. *Heart of Darkness* remains one of the most widely read novels in English; and the movie adaptation *Apocalypse Now* has brought Conrad's story to still more. The very phrase has taken on a life of its own. Conrad's book has become a touchstone for thinking about Africa and Europe, civilization and savagery, imperialism, genocide, insanity—about human nature itself.

It's also become a flash point. In the 1970s, Nigerian novelist Chinua Achebe declared *Heart of Darkness* "an offensive and totally deplorable book," rife with degrading stereotypes of Africa and Africans.[5] Conrad, said Achebe, was "a bloody racist." Not long afterward, a half-American, half-Kenyan college student named Barack Obama was challenged by his friends to explain why he was reading "this racist tract." "Because . . . ," Obama stammered, "because the book teaches me things. . . . About white people, I mean. See, the book's not really about Africa. Or black people. It's about the man who wrote it. The European. The American. A particular way of looking at the world."[6]

When I first read *Heart of Darkness* in my Ithaca high school English class, Conrad's cynical, critical take on European imperialism felt exciting and brave. Later, when I read it and Achebe's essay with my own students at Harvard, I came to value Conrad's perspective for the same reasons Obama did: not just despite its blind spots but because of them. Conrad captured something about the way power operated across continents and races, something that seemed as important to engage with today as it had when he started to write.

And *Heart of Darkness* was just the beginning. As I went on to read more of Conrad's books, I found myself time and again amazed by the prophetic sweep of his "particular way of looking at the world." After 9/11 and the rise of Islamist terrorism, I was startled to remember that the same author who'd condemned imperialism in *Heart of Darkness* had also written *The Secret Agent* (1907), which centers around a terrorist bomb plot in London. After the 2008 financial crisis, I found Conrad in *Nostromo* (1904) portraying multinational capitalism getting up to the same kinds of tricks that I read about in the daily newspaper. As the digital revolution gathered pace, I discovered Conrad writing movingly, in *Lord Jim* (1900) and many other works, about the consequences of technological disruption in the industry he knew best: shipping. As debates about immigration unsettled Europe and the United States, I marveled anew and afresh at how Conrad had produced *any* of these books in English—his third language, which he'd learned only as an adult.

Conrad's pen was like a magic wand, conjuring the spirits of the future.[7] How did he do it? How had Conrad, as the Caribbean writer V. S. Naipaul once observed, somehow "been everywhere before me"? How had he managed, a hundred years ago, to "meditat[e] on my world, a world I recognize today"?[8] If I could figure that out, I'd learn something important about his times—and my own.

I WAS HALFWAY across the Indian Ocean when I realized the answer. I was traveling from Hong Kong to England on board CMA CGM *Christophe Colomb*, a French cargo ship that does an eleven-week circuit between China and northern Europe, carrying up to 13,344 twenty-foot containers. Nowadays, almost no traveler wants to spend four weeks making a trip by boat that could be accomplished in less than fourteen hours by plane. I had decided to make this sea voyage as a deliberate throwback, so I could better understand a central part of Conrad's life and writing.

Born in 1857 to Polish parents in present-day Ukraine, Conrad left the landlocked heart of Europe at the age of sixteen to become a sailor. For the next twenty years, before he ever committed a word to print, Conrad worked as a professional mariner, sailing to the Caribbean, Southeast Asia, Australia, and Africa. These voyages inspired so much of his later fiction that he's often been described as a "sea writer," on a par with Herman Melville.

On *Christophe Colomb* I left behind the speed and connectivity of my twenty-first-century existence—no Internet, no phone, no news—and joined an all-male community not so different from the ones Conrad had been part of. There were about thirty European officers and Asian crew, whose onboard lives were measured out in a round-the-clock rotation of watches, and countdowns to the next port of call. We were following one of the oldest trade routes in the world, swapping yesteryear's cargoes of tea, porcelain, silk, and spice for containers of cheap electronics, plastic-ware, and frozen food. We called at Singapore, where I wandered up and down the river and saw a plaque to Conrad outside the former General Post Office. We whirred gently across the same hot, still ocean at about the same speed as the steamships of a century ago, headed for the Suez Canal, which had opened in 1869. European Union antipiracy patrols cruised off the Horn of Africa, in waters policed in Conrad's day by the Royal Navy.

The more parallels I noted, the more I realized that I had framed things backward. The point wasn't that my voyage on *Christophe Colomb* was an anachronism. It was that Conrad had been in the vanguard. From the deck of a ship, Conrad watched the emergence of the globally inter-related world that I was sailing across today.

History is like therapy for the present: it makes it talk about its parents. Because the term "globalization" was popularized in the 1980s, it's easy to assume that most of the things associated with it date from then or later: an interdependent economy, open borders, ethnically diverse and networked populations, international institutions and standards, shared cultural reference points. But it was in Conrad's youth, not mine, that "three great achievements of the present," as Walt Whitman called them, transformed the speed and range of global connections: "In the Old

World, the east, the Suez canal, / The New by its mighty railroad spann'd, / The seas inlaid with eloquent, gentle wires."[9] Conrad docked alongside the oceangoing steamers that transported emigrants from Europe and Asia on a scale never seen before or since. He cruised over the transoceanic telegraph cables that zapped news, for the first time in history, faster than people. Between voyages, he made his home in London, the center of a global financial market that was more integrated during his lifetime than it would be again until the 1980s.[10]

Conrad wouldn't have known the word "globalization," but with his journey from the provinces of imperial Russia across the high seas to the British home counties, he embodied it. He channeled his global perspective into fiction based overwhelmingly on personal experience and real incidents. Henry James perfectly described Conrad's gift: "No-one has *known*—for intellectual use—the things you know, and you have, as the artist of the whole matter, an authority that no one has approached."[11] That's why a map of Conrad's written world looks so different from that of his contemporaries. Conrad has often been compared to Rudyard Kipling, the informal poet laureate of the British Empire, whose fiction took place in the parts of the world that were colored red on maps, to show British rule. But Conrad didn't set a single novel in a British colony, and even the fiction he placed in Britain or on British ships generally featured non-British characters. Conrad cast his net across Europe, Africa, South America, and the Indian Ocean. Then he wandered through the holes. He took his readers to the places "beyond the end of telegraph cables and mail-boat lines," onto the sailing ships that crept alongside the swift steamers, and among the "human outcasts such as one finds in the lost corners of the world."[12]

The British Empire vanished long ago, and not many people read Kipling anymore. But Conrad's world shimmers beneath the surface of our own. Today Internet cables run along the seafloor beside the

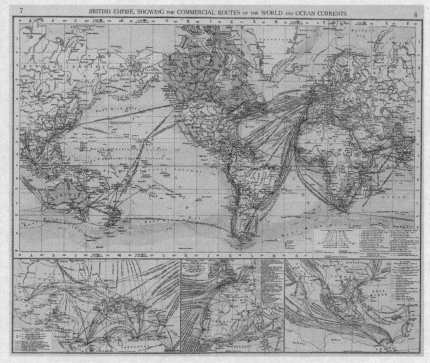

Imperial and global networks in 1900. British colonies are shaded gray.

old telegraph wires. Conrad's characters whisper in the ears of new generations of antiglobalization protesters and champions of free trade, liberal interventionists and radical terrorists, social justice activists and xenophobic nativists. And there's no better emblem of globalization today than the container ship, which has made transport so cheap that it's more cost-efficient to catch a fish in Scotland, send it to China to be filleted, then send it back to Europe for sale, than it is to hire laborers in situ. Ninety percent of world trade travels by sea, which makes ships and sailors more central to the world economy today than ever before.[13]

What I found in Conrad's life and fiction, in short, was a history of globalization seen from the inside out. Next I had to find a way to describe it.

IN THIS BOOK I set out to explore Conrad's world with the compass of a historian, the chart of a biographer, and the navigational sextant of a fiction reader. I tell his life story to link the histories of Europe, Asia, Africa, Latin America, and the oceans in between, and to consider what Conrad said about them in four of his best-known novels: *The Secret Agent*, *Lord Jim*, *Heart of Darkness*, and *Nostromo*.

"Everything about my life in the wide world can be found in my books," Conrad once said.[14] Already in Conrad's lifetime, and with Conrad's blessing, the critics Richard Curle and Gérard Jean-Aubry published accounts of Conrad's early travels and their influence on his work. Conrad's most insightful later critics, Edward Said and Ian Watt, also recognized that the key to interpreting Conrad's fiction was to read it biographically. Not that Conrad made it easy. He let people believe that some stories were autobiographical when they weren't, and he concealed parts of his past that inflected others.[15]

Yet biographers often don't have much more to go on. The *Collected Correspondence of Joseph Conrad* fills nine meticulously edited volumes, totaling some five thousand pages in all. A mere two hundred pages cover the period from Conrad's birth in 1857 until he published his first novel in 1895. That's just 4 percent to document more than 50 percent of his life, and the entirety of that "life in the wide world" that he said inspired his work. The literary historian Norman Sherry did hero's service in the 1960s by hunting down specific sources for Conrad's fiction.[16] But it's little wonder that the many major biographies of Conrad—by Jocelyn Baines, Frederick Karl, Zdzisław Najder, and John Stape—concentrate on the far better-documented details of his literary career: his writing process (tortured), his finances (precarious), his literary friendships (warm), his domestic life (quiet), his relationships with his agent and publishers (mixed), his physical and mental health (dreadful).[17]

To investigate Conrad's "life in the wide world" I've followed a different clue. "History is made by men, but they do not make it in their own heads," says an armchair philosopher in *The Secret Agent*. The line takes a satirical dig at Karl Marx's observation that "man makes his own history, but . . . he does not make it out of conditions chosen by himself."[18] The difference between biography and history is that biographers generally start with the person, while historians generally start with the conditions. If looking at Conrad as a biographical subject opens up a history of globalization from the inside out, approaching him as an object of history has let me shape a biography from the outside in, distinguishing the choices he made from the ones that circumstance made for him.

The difference between fiction and history is usually seen as a matter of facts: novelists make stuff up, historians don't. A better way to characterize the difference might be to consider points of view. Historians don't go where sources don't lead, which means they usually stop at the door to somebody's mind. Even when diaries or letters seem to "tell all," historians typically treat what happened as one thing, and what somebody made of it as another. Novelists walk right in and roam freely through a person's feelings, perceptions, and thoughts. What happened *is* what you make of it. That, Conrad argued, could make fiction the truer record of human experience. "Fiction is history, human history, or it is nothing," he said. "But it is also more than that; it stands on firmer ground, being based on the reality of forms and the observation of social phenomena, whereas history is based on documents . . . —on second-hand impression."[19]

Conrad's novels are also more than that, which is one reason he hated being labeled a sea writer. (He didn't like Melville either, judging *Moby-Dick* "a rather strained rhapsody with whaling for a subject and not a single sincere line in the 3 vols. of it.")[20] "I am something else, and perhaps something more, than a writer of the sea—or even of the tropics," he insisted.[21] In all his writing, wherever it was set, Conrad grappled with the ramifications of living in a global world: the moral and material impact of dislocation, the tension and opportunity of multiethnic societies, the disruption wrought by technological change. In an implicit challenge to the Western liberal ideal of individual freedom, Conrad believed that people can never really escape the constraints of forces bigger than themselves, that even the freest will can be hemmed in by what he would have called fate. His fiction often focuses on characters who confront some critical choice, only to face consequences more far-ranging than they ever imagined. Conrad's novels are ethical injunctions. They meditate on how to behave in a globalizing world, where old rulebooks are becoming obsolete, but nobody's yet written new ones.

Any great writer generates lots of interpretations and reactions, and Conrad is no exception. Whole books have been written on aspects of his life and fiction that I scarcely touch on here—notably his literary influences and relationships. Your Conrad may not be the same as mine. Maybe he's your favorite author, maybe you can't stand him, maybe you've never heard of him, or never read a word.

Often enough I've questioned my own attachment to this dead white man, perpetually depressed, incorrigibly cynical, alarmingly prejudiced by the standards of today. As a woman I balked at spending so much time with an author whose fiction was so short on plausible female characters it seemed like he barely realized that women were people too. As a half-Asian, I winced at Conrad's exoticized and often denigrating portrayals of Asians; as a half-Jew I bridled at his occasional but undeniable anti-Semitism. I lamed myself in Poland following in Conrad's footsteps and got violently seasick on a tall ship sailing in his wake—and that was before whatever awaited me in Congo. I failed spectacularly to read *Nostromo* the first time I tried, and tossed through so many sleepless nights trying to compose this book that I feared the malicious spirit who'd made writing an agony for Conrad had come in turn for me.

Then I recalled the warm, peaceful days I'd spent on *Christophe Colomb*, when the sheer beauty of daybreak over the sea enticed me out of bed early every morning to watch the dawn. I could imagine Conrad on board, smart, witty, erudite, observant, a generous friend, devoted family man, and in places unexpectedly tolerant by the standards of his time. Whether I agreed with Conrad or not, I always found his company worthwhile. He brought to the page a more international and multiethnic assortment of voices than any other writer of his day that I knew. Like me, he was privileged to belong to the middle class of the leading world power of the age, and his books offered thoughtful engagements with the responsibilities and challenges that came with it. He was unafraid to reject truisms and call out exploitation, tyranny, and cant where he saw them. I remembered a phrase repeated mantra-like throughout *Lord Jim*: "He was one of us." For better and for worse, Joseph Conrad was one of us: a citizen of a global world.

PART ONE

NATION

*Partitioned Poland in the
year of Conrad's birth.*

5 Lida R. Niemen Igoumen Staro Bishov The
Grodno 7 Nesvich Bobronisk Korr
rec Bialystok Slonim Rogatchov M. Mi
Protiani Slutzk Glousk Bie
Bielsk Louninetz Retchitza
Kobrin Pinsk R. Pripet Mor
Bug Brezesc-Litovsk M a r s h e s
uskow N Ovroutch D
Kock Kovel L A N Ivanov Ko
L R. Pripet R. Slou R. Dnie
ov Vladimir Novrad Volinsk Kiev
Luck Rovno Ostrog Zytomir Vasilkov
Zaslav 7
Rawa Constantinov Khmiatlinik Bog
Lemberg Tarnopol Letitchev Viuitza
ow I C A Ouman
Sambor Halicz Kaminiek Bracklaw
stry R. Dniester Podhorra Olgopol Balta
an 9.900 Stanislaw Zaleszezyky Mohilev R. Dnie
Munkacs Mons R. Pruth Geriza Tzekinovka nsth

ONE

———·———

NO HOME, NO COUNTRY

THREE WEEKS BEFORE CHRISTMAS, 1857, a friar from the Carmelite monastery in Berdychiv, Ukraine, walked in sandals over the ice-glazed ground to perform the baptism of a firstborn son.[1] He sprinkled the infant three times with holy water, christening the baby with the names of his mother's father Józef, his father's father Teodor, and a hero of Polish patriotic literature, Konrad. God has regenerated you, said the priest to Józef Teodor Konrad Korzeniowski—anointed with a family's history and hopes.[2]

The baby's father, Apollo Korzeniowski, swelled with a sense of occasion. The birth of a first child makes history for any parent, and Apollo experienced it as profoundly political too: a moment to reflect on the destiny of his nation, Poland, which had ceased to exist as a state. Berdychiv had once been part of the independent Polish-Lithuanian Commonwealth, but at the end of the eighteenth century the Commonwealth had been swallowed up by its neighbors in three giant gulps. Now Austria ruled the southern province of Galicia; Prussia governed the northwest; and Russia had snatched everything else, a huge tranche of land encompassing nearly all Lithuania, Belarus, and Ukraine—recovered lands of the Russians, said Catherine the Great; "stolen lands," said the Poles.[3] Almost overnight, Ukraine's Poles became a pebble in the boot of Europe's most autocratic empire.

Apollo was a writer by vocation; he made the political into the poetical. He composed a song for the christening day. "To my son," he began, "born in the 85th year of Muscovite oppression":

> *Baby son, sleep without fear.*
> *Lullaby, the world is dark,*
> *You have no home, no country . . .*

> *Baby son, tell yourself,*
> *You are without land, without love,*
> *Without country, without people,*
> *While* Poland—your Mother *is in her grave.*

Forget about joy, pride, relief, or any of the other happy emotions a parent might express on the safe arrival of a healthy child. Apollo's lullaby was a dirge for a baby orphaned at birth, in mourning before he'd had a chance to live. Apollo approached the future as through a tunnel. There were restricting walls, Russian imperial rule; there was a light at the end, Polish independence; and the challenge was to keep going until you got there. That's why he liked the motto *"ubi crux, ibi poesia"*: where there's a cross, there's poetry—or as he used it, where there's a cause, there's hope. He urged bravery and resilience, devotion and patience. "The time will come, the days will pass," he concluded, and by God's grace, Konrad would see Poland resurrected.[4]

Apollo meant his verses to inspire. Yet as he cradled this warm parcel of balled fingers and buttoned eyes, he couldn't possibly anticipate how these words would resonate—how psychological darkness would torture Konrad, how loneliness would trail him, how far he'd travel into other lands, among distant peoples, before finding some kind of home. Apollo couldn't imagine how his encouragement might read in retrospect like a curse.

THERE'S AN OLD POLISH EXPRESSION about the town where Konrad Korzeniowski was born on December 3, 1857. When you tell someone to "send a letter to Berdychiv," you mean "send a letter to nowhere"—you'll never reach me.[5] The saying plays on Berdychiv's nineteenth-century position as a "somewhere," particularly for the town's then-majority population of Jews. Berdychiv hosted numerous trade fairs every year, making it a routine stop for peddlers with no permanent address. If they said "send a letter to Berdychiv," they meant send a letter to a place I'm going—you'll definitely reach me.

The world is made up of "nowheres" and "somewheres"—but which counts as which depends on what "where" you look from. The story of Konrad's life, and the world in which he lived, was a story of nowheres colliding with somewheres. At the time of his birth, the failure of a bank in Ohio touched off a financial panic that toppled firms in Hamburg.[6] British troops struggled to suppress a rebellion in India. Indian troops sailed to Canton to threaten Chinese imperial officials.[7] Chinese settlers rebelled on a river in Borneo, in a Malay state ruled by a European.[8] European cloth and guns were traded up the Congo basin for ivory by villagers who'd never seen a white person.[9] An American filibuster was booted out of Nicaragua. American-made steamboats plowed up the rivers of South America, and a locomotive built in Leeds pulled the first train out of Buenos Aires.[10]

Though Konrad would grow up to follow quickening, lengthening routes of trade, money, and people, into every continent, his journey started in a place, Poland, that was literally nowhere on a map of Europe, wiped away by the partitions of 1772, 1793, and 1795.[11] But to Konrad's fervently nationalist parents Apollo and Ewa, Poland was the only somewhere that mattered. The worldview they gave their son resembled a kind of tunnel vision.

History sits heavily on some backs. Konrad's family stumbled into the nineteenth century under its weight. They belonged to a privileged class of landed gentry, the *szlachta*, that traced its descent back to the mythical founders of the Polish nation. Encompassing one in ten Poles, *szlachta* might be rich as princes or poor as peasants, but every one of them enjoyed rights ranging from a coat of arms to freedom from arbitrary arrest. Every male *szlachcic* was eligible to hold government office and got to vote for representatives to parliament, which in turn elected the king.[12] Once considered the civic spine of the Polish-Lithuanian Commonwealth, a "republic of nobles," *szlachta* lost their privileges in the Russian Empire, and felt a special responsibility to restore an independent Polish state.

Konrad's parents grew up in the shadow of defeat. In 1830 nationalists launched a major insurrection in the Polish-majority heartland around Warsaw (called the Congress Kingdom) but were beaten back by the Russian army in 1831. The tsar abolished the province's parliament, imposed military occupation, and clamped Russification policies onto education, law, and religion. The regime went on to confiscate the estates of five thousand *szlachta*, deport eighty thousand civilians to Siberia and points east, and force a hundred thousand Polish soldiers into brutal military service in the Caucasus. More fortunate were ten thousand or so insurrectionists who emigrated, swelling the ranks of the Polish nation in exile, capital city Paris. There, politicians plotted their comeback to the resonant cadences of the refugee Adam Mickiewicz's poetry, and the tunes of the émigré Fryderyk Chopin's mazurkas and polonaises.[13]

What do you do when your history has been hijacked, your language suppressed, your religion marginalized, your mode of life scorned and straitened? The two most important men in Konrad's life—his father Apollo Korzeniowski and his maternal uncle Tadeusz Bobrowski—came up with two different answers. On the Bobrowski side of the family, Konrad learned of forebears who tried to make the best of a bad hand. Konrad's maternal grandfather judged the 1830 insurrection "the height of folly" and stayed put in Ukraine while his rasher friends rushed to join.[14] His reward was relative wealth. When he died in 1850 he left six thousand acres and 360 male serfs to offset his debts, as well as a distillery, tavern, mills, and a stable of exceptionally elegant horses.[15] Konrad's uncle Tadeusz, then only twenty-one, took over as head of the Bobrowski family. Tadeusz loathed the Russians as much as anyone, but accepted tsarist rule as a hard truth. He invested his political energy instead in practical questions like land reform and peasant emancipation.[16]

On the Korzeniowski side of the family, Konrad learned of relatives who fought back. Konrad's paternal grandfather, a veteran of the Napoleonic wars, raised a cavalry regiment in 1830 at his own expense and rode off to fight the Russians. His penalty was financial ruin. The family had to move away from their handsome ancestral estate and settle in a different district, where Konrad's grandfather scraped along by working for the government, managing another Pole's confiscated land.

Konrad's father Apollo, just eleven years old when the rebellion failed in 1831, experienced national defeat as personal calamity. He found solace in the verse of Romantics such as Mickiewicz, who sang of Poland as the "Christ of nations" and filled a generation of young *szlachta* with odes to faith, courage, resistance, and love.[17] As a student of languages at St. Petersburg University in his early twenties, Apollo joined a thriving literary underground where Polish students swapped censored texts in smuggled foreign reprints (called "blotting paper"), or manuscripts painstakingly copied by hand.[18] Apollo began to publish himself: a play, a volume of poems, and a translation of his favorite French author, Victor Hugo.[19] Literature gave him what the army had given his father: a place to find meaning, to act on beliefs, to fulfill a sense of duty. If you had no power in politics, you could use the power of poems—and if autocrats wanted to censor your words, you could resist them by speaking into silent pages, passed furtively among friends under false covers.

Tadeusz Bobrowski, ever the pragmatist, detected in Apollo some of the empty-headed utopianism that had ruined Apollo's father, "always ready without a moment's thought to mount his horse and drive the enemy from our land. . . . Everyone knew that some time ago this *szlachcic* had fought well—and few stopped to ask whether he could think well."[20] For Tadeusz, to be a noble was to inherit a political fantasy. One's duty was to get on with reality. He scoffed at Apollo for always trumpeting his *szlachta* status by "rather pretentiously" including his noble clan name, Nałęcz, when he signed his name.[21] But it wasn't mere snobbery that made Apollo do it. To be a noble, for Apollo, was to inherit a tradition of political freedom. One's destiny was to reclaim it.[22]

Apollo returned from St. Petersburg in 1846 to the daily tedium of managing an estate in rural Ukraine. He loathed living among provincial, unpoliticized rustics.[23] "I sometimes think that I have landed in the wild forests of America where hordes of monkeys mock a stray human being," he complained.[24] Two objects of love sustained him.

The first was Ewa Bobrowska, Tadeusz's sister. Born in 1831, she was only sixteen when they met, yet already a great beauty, and "educated at a higher level than was common for our women in her day." He was smitten. She was "his Beatrice, . . . full of charm and intelligence, a refined Ukrainian girl with the heart of an angel."[25] With his sharp conversation, urbane tastes, and striking, some said ugly, looks, Apollo cut a dash in provincial drawing rooms. But it was one thing to have him to tea, quite another to have him court your daughter. Ewa's mother "suspected him of having a frivolous temperament and irregular habits," while her father "found him lacking in practicality and resourcefulness," more likely to be wasting his time "reading, writing and riding than working." To put Apollo off Ewa's scent, her father took him on social calls around the district, hoping he'd fall for another girl, but Apollo "always managed

LEFT: *Ewa Korzeniowska, née Bobrowska.*
RIGHT: *Apollo Korzeniowski.*

things cleverly enough so that either the young woman herself or her parents did not take to him." Though her family didn't yet detect it, Ewa, too, was captivated, and "spurned all other suitors' advances" for Apollo's sake.[26]

Apollo remained equally steadfast in his pursuit of his other great passion, Poland. He wrote, watched, and waited for the moment to rise. Would it be 1848, when democratic revolutions swept across Europe? Not yet. Or 1854, when Britain and France launched a war against Russia in Crimea? Apollo pressed for a *szlachta*-led insurgency in Ukraine, assuming that the serfs would rally behind their Polish landlords. Not yet, ordered the powerful Polish émigrés in Paris.[27]

Years of patience won Apollo his first objective. Ewa Bobrowska had kept her distance in deference to her family's wishes, but by her early twenties she was pining for Apollo so visibly that her mother and brother Tadeusz feared "her health and future were under threat." If she didn't marry Apollo, she'd never marry anyone. They gave Apollo tacit permission to renew his suit, and the couple married in the spring of 1856.[28] He was thirty-six, she was twenty-four, and they'd proven their commitment to each other across nearly a decade of distance. Now they walked hand in hand toward a shared cause, a free Poland.

When their son was born in December 1857, Apollo and Ewa honored their fathers in his first two names, but the baby's third name, Konrad—the one everybody actually called him—signaled their own approach to Russian domination. They drew it from the work of Adam Mickiewicz. His 1828 poem *Konrad Wallenrod* describes how a Lithuanian warrior takes revenge against Teutonic conquerors by infiltrating their highest ranks and deliberately marching them to their deaths.[29] Mickiewicz used the name Konrad again in 1832, in the third section of his play *Dziady*, "The Forefathers' Eve." "Now is my soul incarnate in my country," Konrad sings, "and in my body dwells her soul. / My fatherland and I are one great whole." He looks on Poland "as a son would gaze / Upon his father broken upon the wheel" and cries, "Save us, Lord!"[30]

For the first year or two of Konrad's life, Apollo played the part of *szlachta* landlord by managing an estate he'd leased from a wealthier family. As his brother-in-law Tadeusz had suspected, however, Apollo wasn't much good at it. "Poets," declared Tadeusz, never at a loss for judgments, "men of imagination and ideals, are not capable of clearly formulating concrete plans to live by; they do best not to involve themselves in these matters, but to leave such work to souls less pure and ideal, more aware of the struggles and the needs of mundane life."[31] Money went out, not much revenue came in, more money went out, and by 1859 the Korzeniowskis had lost their entire investment, and some of Ewa's mother's money too.

Apollo moved the family to the town of Zhytomyr, where he tried to earn a living as a writer. "I *must* write, because—for the time being—there is nothing else that I can do."[32] His translations from French to

Polish (more Victor Hugo, and a version of Alfred de Vigny's *Chatterton*) brought in some cash, while he poured his romantic nationalism into poems, plays, and newspaper articles. Under the reform-minded tsar Alexander II, emancipation of the serfs was becoming a major political issue, and *szlachta* seized on the "peasant question" as a possible way to advance Polish interests. Warsaw grandees set up an "Agricultural Society" to discuss questions of land management, which soon became an umbrella organization for *szlachta* nationalists.[33] The connection of agrarian affairs to politics may be why, when Apollo and Tadeusz Bobrowski, in a rare collaboration, proposed publishing a weekly agricultural newsletter for local gentry, the Russian authorities denied them permission.[34]

Apollo was losing faith in rural reform. He despaired at the sight of more and more landlords abandoning farming in favor of industrial beet sugar refineries. "Let us put agriculture and everything related to it forward and ahead of everything," Apollo insisted in an article for a Warsaw paper. "Manufacturing, industry and trade should not overwhelm our agriculture, they should remain its lowly servants."[35] He accused his peers of shamelessly aping the ways of industrial Britain, and predicted mass immiseration and physical and moral degeneration.[36] He channeled his bitterness into a play, *For the Love of Money*, which was produced in Kiev and Zhytomyr, a satire of small-minded, money-grubbing *szlachta*.[37] Apollo began drifting toward more radical solutions to the problem of Polish oppression.

He wasn't alone. In Warsaw, nationalists began to stage big public rallies on Polish historical anniversaries. Crowds chorused patriotic hymns. "Poland Has Not Yet Perished," they sang, and "God Protect Poland," with a new refrain: "Freedom and Fatherland restore to us, O Lord!" In February 1861, as the Agricultural Society held its annual meeting in Warsaw, a mass demonstration formed outside. Russian troops opened fire on the crowd and killed five civilians. Patriots responded by declaring "national mourning" and dressing entirely in black as a sign of protest. Churches across the Polish provinces held memorial services for the victims. Then in April came another rally and another shooting. A hundred civilians—children, women, and men—bled and died on the cobblestones in front of the Royal Castle.[38]

The troubling news from Warsaw resounded across the provinces. In Zhytomyr, Ewa too donned national mourning and encouraged others to do the same. Apollo, by then "a known agitator" among his peers, "certain to be under police surveillance," hosted a political meeting at his house to discuss a petition to the tsar. Students at the high school sang the nationalist hymns. Activists rallied landowners to contribute money for raising an army in the Congress Kingdom, vowing to "mark the borders with blood."[39]

There was a sense of walls closing in, paths narrowing, the light at the end of the tunnel growing ever brighter and more alluring. The Korzeniowskis broke into a run.

KONRAD DARTED AND LOOPED around the garden of his Bobrowski grandmother's manor in Terekhove, five miles into the countryside outside Berdychiv. "I am fine here," he reported to his father, "I run about the garden—but I don't like it much when the mosquitos bite."[40] Granny took him for drives and told him stories. Mama gave him lessons and took him to church, and let him run outside afterward to give alms to the beggars waiting at the door. He chatted with them as long as he could, and on the way home, he told Mama all about it, and all about horses, and all about bears. "I suspect that our dear Konradzio will grow into an exceptional man with a great heart," his doting grandmother declared.[41]

It was the spring of 1861, and at three and a half, Konrad was about the age when a person starts forming memories that stay for life. A child's memory catches things by the corners. It may have been that the strongest perceptions Konrad retained from this time in Terekhove would be the image of a mosquito settling on his peach-soft leg, or playing with the horsewhip a kindly friend gave him, in his new black frock for church.

He probably wouldn't remember the things that his mother took pains to record. She noted how she made that black outfit especially because Konrad kept pleading "to go into mourning," like everyone he saw around him—mourning for murdered Poland. And how every day he asked, "When shall we go see Daddy?"[42]

In May 1861, Apollo was "called to duty in Warsaw by the movement men."[43] His official mission was to publish a magazine called *Dwytygodnik* (*The Biweekly*), inspired by the influential French journal of politics and culture the *Revue des deux mondes*.[44] But "his main goal," remembered one of his closest friends, a fellow patriot and writer named Stefan Buszczyński, was to help coordinate nationalist efforts in Warsaw, "and thus to endow the movement with a common direction."[45]

By now, Poles across the religious and social spectrum had shown support for greater autonomy, but that was where the "common direction" stopped. Apollo descended into a warren of underground organizations, each promoting different visions of national liberation and different means by which to achieve it. Some of his old friends belonged to the "Whites," a moderate group mostly composed of *szlachta* notables, who supported a "moral revolution" rather than a literal one. Apollo favored the "Reds," a radical faction promoting sweeping social revolution alongside independence. He showcased his sympathies by walking around Warsaw in a peasant hat, and won the following of the younger radicals and students who had helped organize the street protests earlier in the year.[46] Consensus didn't come easily, either, among the Reds. Some wanted to participate in upcoming municipal elections, while others wanted to boycott; some wanted to tap into Russian revolutionary networks; others favored terrorist attacks. Apollo stuck to an idealized version of the *szlachta*-led "republic of nobles," in which serfdom would

be abolished, and the historic Polish-Lithuanian Commonwealth re-
stored. "People of Poland," he urged in one of many pamphlets, "remain
in mourning; ask for God's mercy in church; save every penny and amass
funds, so that you have them ready when the time comes."[47]

Ewa and Konrad remained in Ukraine, circulating among the houses
of different relatives until Apollo sent word to come and join him. In letters delivered as often as possible by messengers, to avoid the prying eyes
of postal censors, Ewa updated Apollo on the local political situation.
"Mourning is spreading," she said proudly, and patriotic hymns were
being sung at church. Repression spread too. Russian authorities closed
the Zhytomyr high school for a year and deported troublemaking students to serve in the army. Police harassed clergymen, arrested people on
the spot for so-called seditious speech, and stepped up surveillance of
activists.

If the tsarist police came to search her house, Ewa said, "I am prepared for it, rest assured." From the moment Apollo left, the authorities
had been pestering neighbors and servants to reveal his whereabouts.
The Berdychiv police chief himself "appeared in disguise, without ringing
the bell, at the gate of Terechowa, and questioned people in the stables,"
pretending to be a friend of Apollo's; "finally, explicitly," he asked
"whether you had already returned to Warsaw." Ewa supplied her husband with advice on how to keep his location secret. Use an assumed
name to tell her where he was. Address letters to her via other towns.
Though they both felt the separation like a phantom limb—"you miss
me; and I do not want to speak of my longing for I know that even without
words you must feel it"—he must be patient with her for not writing
to him too often, as "experienced people say that this way it is safer
for you."[48]

Her letters beat with passion and purpose. "Tell me how to love so as
to guard you against misfortune? Tell me how to get my prayers heard so
that you should be inspired and protected by God."[49] She couldn't wait to

join him, to reunite in common cause: "My soul yearns for that 'Young Poland' of our dreams, which you will create, rouse to life, and lead into the future."[50] Days without him fell in a slow drip. "Give me something to do while we are separated," she pleaded. "I tried to set to work on the piano, but thirty strings have been missing for six months. . . . Make me do some translations" (from French), she suggested, "something new and readable."[51] She worked out how to disperse their belongings among friends, so she and Konrad could leave the moment he called.

At the beginning of October 1861, Ewa and Konrad joined Apollo in Warsaw, in a small rented apartment on Nowy Świat. The newspaper, expected to be the voice of the movement, was just a few weeks away from launch. On October 15, demonstrations were staged for the death anniversary of the national hero Tadeusz Kościuszko, who had led Poland's last stand against the partitioning powers in the 1790s. Cossack troops charged into churches to break up the services; they dragged out the worshippers and rounded up more than 1,500 people in a rippling wave of arrests.[52] Apollo assembled a group of about eighteen Red activists in his apartment to discuss their next steps. They formed themselves into a "Committee of Action," declaring themselves ready for an insurrection, "to act as if we were to rise up tomorrow and to rise up when we can be certain of victory; to do much and to speak little."[53]

A few nights later, Ewa and Apollo were up late, reading and writing in the quiet, and Konrad must have been sleeping. It was after midnight. There was a sharp rap at the door. Men in uniform marched into the flat. They accused Apollo of conspiracy, placed him under arrest, and marched back out with him in their custody. "Six minutes after the door-bell had rung he was gone from the house," said Ewa. It felt "like an act of brigandage."[54]

Apollo was arrested on four charges: forming a conspiratorial organization called "The Mierosławski's Reds" with students from the Art School and Gymnasium; stirring up brawls at Café Wedel; publishing an

inflammatory pamphlet called *Nation, Beware!* and agitating in Zhytomyr earlier in the year, where "he had organized . . . communal prayers
for people who had been killed in Warsaw" and "his wife had been
distributing black crape as a sign of mourning." The charges displayed a
curious blend of knowledge and ignorance on the part of the police.
Apollo *had* been plotting with Red student activists, he had published
anonymous nationalist pamphlets, and he had supported national
mourning and prayers in Zhytomyr. But his group wasn't called "The
Mierosławski's Reds," he hadn't been rabble-rousing in a café, he hadn't
written the pamphlet in question, and it's not clear whether he had been
the primary organizer of the Zhytomyr unrest. He denied guilt on all four
counts.[55]

They carried him off to the Warsaw Citadel and locked him into
Pavilion X, the notorious section for political prisoners. "Warsaw Citadel
is the city's ever-ready machine of destruction, and at the same time an
immense dungeon where tzardom buries Polish patriotism," Apollo later
wrote. It "throttles one generation of Polish patriots after another." Just
spending time inside this cold, dank cage turned into a death sentence for
many inmates who fell ill while awaiting a verdict. Periodically Apollo
was yanked out of his cell for interrogation. Yet week after week, he
stayed in jail with no indication of when his case might proceed. Deten-
tion ate into his body. His gums bled, his joints swelled and ached with
rheumatism and scurvy. From his bunk he could hear the clanging of cell
doors, the squeak and thud of iron bolts, the clatter of chains. He could
hear feet trudging in as new political prisoners were rounded up, and
eventually he could hear prisoners trudging out and into exile, to hard
labor in the mines, to death at the gallows, to death by the firing squad—
and, "the worst, because the most infamous of all," to serve in the Russian army, in the enemy's own uniform.[56]

Outside the Citadel, Ewa stayed with Konrad on Nowy Świat and tried to find out what was happening to her husband. The police returned to the apartment and searched it, seizing Apollo's papers and the letters she had written to him from Zhytomyr. They brought Ewa in for questioning too and interrogated her about the content of her letters. It's not my handwriting, she insisted. I never wrote those.[57] Like Apollo, she remained "in complete ignorance of their [family's] fate."[58]

Ewa's mother rushed up from Berdychiv to help. She may have looked after Konrad when Ewa went every day to the Citadel, joining a crowd of women massed at the gates, seeking word of their jailed relatives. Every day, they were refused. "Sometimes we stand there a whole day, in rain and cold, waiting for a short note, for some news, and sometimes we wait in vain. Once, to get warm and to pass the time, we counted ourselves: we were several score more than two hundred." The crowd kept on growing as the arrests continued: priests, rabbis, pastors, "people of all estates, wealth, age and situation; among them several women," all locked away behind the blank brick walls. Unable to see her husband, Ewa pumped the guards for updates about Apollo's health. She delivered clean sheets and food for him, and after much lobbying, was allowed to give him "a prayer-book and Robertson's text-book for learning English." At ten-day intervals she was permitted to write Apollo a short note; if the censors approved it, he got to read it and write her a line back.

Christmas Eve 1861, two months after his arrest. Letters for Apollo had been piling up at home, gifts from friends and relatives, prayers and blessings. Ewa made her way through the city's "sad, black and silent" streets for her daily visit to the fortress. She found the Citadel compound, as usual, crowded with prisoners' relatives, patient, impatient. In the last month or so Ewa had finally been allowed to see Apollo a couple of times, in five-minute snatches through a tight wire mesh, with guards on both sides, guards in ordinary uniforms, guards in fancy uniforms, guards in no particular uniform, all of them shouting "not allowed" when anything of substance got said. Ewa and Apollo used their allotment laughing and joking, because "the sight of tears is not liked," and besides, it was better to keep their spirits up.

Today would be different. As a holiday favor, families were to be granted the chance to meet briefly without a fence between them. Ewa peered around shawled shoulders and scarved heads to spot Apollo coming out. There—there, was that him? He looked so thin, his face blotchy, his beard like a clump of burs. Across the invisible line of freedom they clutched hands. They broke a sacramental wafer, blessed by a priest, and prayed.[59]

Konrad had just turned four. Much later, he would recall that "in the courtyard of this Citadel—characteristically for our nation—my childhood memories begin."[60]

In April 1862, a military tribunal found Apollo Korzeniowski guilty of all charges. There was no trial. Investigators used Ewa's letters from Zhytomyr, where she had warned Apollo of possible arrest, as proof "of his activities and of his alien way of thinking."

Early one morning a couple of weeks later, a warder came into Apollo's cell, escorting a Russian official.

"Please be so kind as to stand up and listen while I read out the sentence," said the official, in Russian. He cleared his throat. "Your name, Sir?"

"Apollo Nałęcz Korzeniowski."

"Even at the Citadel the government may be deceived," the official continued, pompously explaining why he'd asked Apollo for his name. "Somebody else might have been substituted for you and although innocent, subjected to punishment. A just government does not wish it to happen."

"The justice of government is known to all," retorted Apollo, in Polish.

The official unfurled the verdict, many handwritten pages long. He began reading: "The authorities are well aware . . . the principal leader of the entire rebellious movement . . . although the commission of enquiry is not in possession of any evidence . . . bearing in mind the brazen answers . . . that he is a Pole, always has been and always will be striving for Poland's happiness . . . ordered the deportation . . . under constant police surveillance in the place of his exile."

"That's all," he said, stopping abruptly. There were several more pages of the verdict to go. "You have to sign the verdict to show that you've heard it." Apollo protested that he hadn't even heard the whole thing. But one line summed it up: "It has been ordered that Korzeniowski and his wife be sent to settle in the town of Perm under strict police supervision," more than 1,500 miles to the northeast, at the gates of Siberia. The Russian word for his punishment (ссылка) meant exile—or as Apollo later described it in a memoir, "imprisonment in the wilderness, among wild animals and without means of defence."[61]

Exile for the Korzeniowski family became in effect a life sentence of moving and sickness. Perm was a long way to travel, and spring, when roads thawed into sucking, rutted furrows of mud, the worst season for it. The family started east under an escort of Russian gendarmes.[62] The guards "were immensely, despicably polite" as long as they remained in Congress Poland, but the moment they left Polish-majority lands, the gendarmes became just as "despicably impolite."[63] The first victim of the family's sentence was Konrad. Just outside Moscow, he developed a dangerously high fever. A doctor at a coach stop treated him with leeches and advised the Korzeniowskis not to keep traveling "as . . . the child may die if we do so." Yet "just then," the soldiers "start[ed] harnessing the horses" to continue. Panic seized the parents. Apollo refused to budge. Make me, he dared the soldiers. "Save my child, please!" Ewa implored. Their "passive resistance" bought them "about a dozen hours" delay before a local official forced them on, with the chilling verdict that "children are born to die."

The carriage pounded and swung eastward through the mud. Inside the dark cabin Ewa and Apollo prayed over their sick son until the fever broke. "God must have given me His blessing . . . for having kept the boy alive during that hard journey," said Apollo.[64] Then Ewa fell sick. She shivered inside the lurching coach on a makeshift bed. She was so weak when they got to Nizhny Novgorod that the guards had to carry her. Again the Korzeniowskis refused to continue; again the Russians refused to halt the journey. This time the local commanding officer—who turned out to be an acquaintance of one of Ewa's brothers—intervened on their behalf and wired to Moscow for permission to let them rest for a few days. The return telegram delivered further, unexpected relief. It told them that, thanks to a friendly intervention by another acquaintance, their place of exile had been changed to a closer, milder town called Vologda, about three hundred miles northeast of Moscow.

"Vologda is a huge quagmire stretching over three versts, cut up with parallel and intersecting lines of wooden foot-bridges, all rotten and shaky under one's feet," wrote Apollo to some cousins in June 1862, shortly after they arrived. It was notoriously damp and unhealthy; Apollo joked that the river was named Scrofula, for the glandular disease that appeared to be endemic. The town reeked of "mud, birch-tar and whale-oil." "A year here has two seasons: white winter and green winter," he said. "Now is the beginning of the green winter: it has been raining continually for twenty-one days and it will do so till the end." When white winter set in, with Arctic winds whipping down from the White Sea, they stuffed expensive firewood into the stoves in a losing war against creeping frost. They had for company about twenty other Polish exiles, to whom their "arrival was like a few drops of water fallen on quicklime." The Korzeniowskis "founded a chapel" with these other Catholics, "the center of our lives. We pray a lot, earnestly and sincerely."[65]

One of the Poles ran "a photographic atelier developing pictures of local scrofulas."[66] Here, around the time of his fifth birthday, Konrad sat for his

Konrad Korzeniowski in Vologda, and an early piece of his writing.

portrait. His parents combed back his hair, buttoned him into a frogged jacket, and buckled a broad leather belt around his waist. He clambered onto the studio chair, tucked one leg under the other, opened a book on his lap, and looked up at the big black-curtained camera, solemn as a crow. On the back of the photo, a few weeks later, Konrad penned a dedication in large, quivering letters: "To my dear Granny who helped me send pastries to my poor Daddy in prison—grandson, Pole-Catholic and *szlachcic*, Konrad."[67]

Pole, Catholic, *szlachcic*. Those were three labels Apollo and Ewa never wanted their son to forget—especially this winter of 1863, when they told him what to write. They'd just received unbearable news from the Congress Kingdom. After the Korzeniowskis had left Warsaw, the Committee of Action that had met first in their apartment reorganized and grew. Under a new name and leadership, the committee plotted a major uprising for the spring of 1863. But maneuvers by the government (led by a conciliatory "White") forced their hand, and the committee struck early. In January 1863, it declared itself a National Government for Poland and issued a manifesto proclaiming freedom for serfs and calling on the peoples of the historic commonwealth—Jews, Lithuanians, and Ruthenians, as well as Poles—to rise up against the Russians. Ewa's young brother Stefan took charge of the committee in Warsaw and energetically rallied civilians to the cause. From the borders of Prussia to towns deep inside Lithuania, Belarus, and Ukraine, thousands of insurgents launched raids on Russian garrisons.

Again and again, Russian troops beat them back. Despite more than a thousand isolated clashes with Russians, the disorganized, poorly armed insurgents never gained ground. Though the National Government thrived underground—with a sophisticated network of couriers, aliases, and an uncrackable code based on Mickiewicz's poem *Pan Tadeusz*—in the light of day, the uprising never got vital support from France, Britain, or Austria. In the midst of it the tsar also skillfully undercut the chances of peasant backing for the rebels by extending decrees of emancipation for serfs in the Polish provinces, releasing them from forced labor and rents.[68]

In Vologda, Apollo and Ewa opened every bulletin with trembling fingers: "Newspapers are like opium; we know they will kill us and yet we go on reading them." Letters were worse. In the space of a single year Apollo's family was effectively wiped out: his older brother was killed in the fighting; his sister and his younger brother were arrested and exiled; and his father, so often the first to fight, died amid the stress. The Bobrowskis also suffered. Ewa's brother Kazimierz was jailed in Kiev, while Stefan—lovable Stefan, "indescribably" attractive, "full of eloquence and natural wit, of compelling and winsome good-heartedness"—the ringleader of the Warsaw underground, was shot dead in a duel with a political rival.[69] Tadeusz alone, the pragmatist, remained free. It was left to him, like his father before him, to look after the children of friends and relatives involved in the uprising.[70]

Artur Grottger, Mourning News *(1863)*.

"All life within us has come to an end, we are stunned by despair," said Apollo.[71] The Korzeniowskis would have recognized themselves in a drawing by the Polish romantic artist Artur Grottger called *Mourning News*, part of a series illustrating the events of 1863.[72] It shows a group of black-clad figures swooning around a table, on which a newspaper sits like a curse. Women muffle tears in handkerchiefs; a man clutches a letter despairingly over his face. Another man lurks in the corner, fist clenched, brow furrowed, jaw braced for revenge—but that fist dangles from a sling, and beneath his fierce brow, his eyes are shut in grief. Only one person in the frame sees what's going on: a small boy standing amid the mourners with eyes wide open, unsettled, confused.

Apollo vented his fury at what had happened in a pamphlet-length diatribe entitled *Poland and Muscovy*. He juxtaposed his experience in jail against the long history of tsarist oppression. "We Poles have suffered slaughter, conflagration, robbery, rape, and torture in the hands of Muscovy," he began. "We have perished by their sabres, bayonets and guns. We are familiar with their truncheons, knouts and nooses." "The whole of Muscovy is a prison," he continued, hurtling into metaphor. Soon he was spinning images so fast they dissolved into a furious red blur. Muscovy is "a pack of patient jackals." It's "countless swarms" of insects "corrupted and infested with vermin." It's a ravening beast that "chews living Poland as if she were dead." Muscovy is a killing machine, with "cogs and wheels" grinding up Poland, "crushing, smashing, breaking, torturing and robbing." Muscovy is "the most sordid and lethal plague," it's "seas of foul muck poured over the fruits of the earth," it's "barbarism, ignorance, renegation" that devours "civilization, light, faith in God and in the future of mankind."[73] The tunnel collapses. Everything goes black.

NEITHER APOLLO NOR EWA had been well in Vologda, "an hourglass where scrofula runs instead of sand." After repeated petitions to transfer somewhere warmer, for the sake of their health, the authorities let them shift to Chernihiv, Ukraine, less than a hundred miles from Kiev and much closer to home. Ewa, the sicker of the two, also got leave to visit her brother Tadeusz on his estate for three months, bringing five-year-old Konrad with her.[74] She kept insisting that her illness was only "nerves," brought on by "the repeated blows that fall on the members of our joined families," and soon would pass. It never did: she had advancing tuberculosis.

By the winter of 1865, three years into their exile, Ewa, "terribly—gravely ill," had become a wraith. "Despair has been slowly eating like rust into [her] physical constitution," said Apollo, and she "has barely the strength to look at me, to speak with a hollow voice." Apollo "cringed, pleaded, begged" the authorities "to change our place of exile" so they might get better medical care. Their family doctor came all the way from Zhytomyr to treat her, but she was too weak to undergo the operation he recommended. Apollo turned full-time nurse, his own poor health notwithstanding, reading to her, praying with her, lifting her in and out of bed, and acting cheerful all the while so that Ewa could "believe that our parting is inconceivable—otherwise she might not have the strength to bear anything." Yet in his mind he was already composing eulogies. "We have never been blinded by one another; we loved each other not because we were perfect in one another's eyes, but in spite of our short-comings and defects. . . . I believe . . . that until this day we have lived in a superior glow of happiness." This emotional drama had only two roles. "Konradek is of course neglected."[75]

Ewa grew fainter and frailer, and one day in April 1865, she vanished. "Her death was the ultimate, mortal blow for Apollo," said Apollo's old friend Stefan Buszczyński. "There are only a few so well-matched marriages in this world. He adored her and in her eyes he was a man un-matched, an ideal."[76] Apollo buried himself alive in grief. "I spend the greatest part of my days by the grave," he confessed, and nights in a sleepless vigil, questioning his faith, imagining her still by his side, ghost-writing his letters. Apollo assumed that his own death was nigh—and he'd have welcomed it, if it meant being reunited with her.

But there was that "tiny one" who still lived, seven-year-old Konrad. Ewa, his mother, was in her grave. And if—when—Apollo died too, Konrad would need somebody to look after him. "She used to pour out her heart and soul onto the child and now to leave him without any assurance or to dismiss him without any hope would seem to me to be disloyal to Her heart and soul." Apollo pressed an old friend in Warsaw to act as Konrad's guardian, and "arranged for Konradek to have a provision until the end of his schooling, small but sufficient for his upkeep and education. . . . I have made all necessary sacrifices today to ensure his tomorrow."[77]

In the months after Ewa's death, Konrad appeared in Apollo's letters as an interruption from the business of grieving. Apollo asked his Warsaw friend to send a syllabus and schoolbooks, and to sell his old desk to pay for it; "it used to be a favourite of hers, but she will never see me behind it." He knew that he was no fit company for his son. "Poor child . . . he looks at the decrepitude of my sadness and who knows if that sight does not make his young heart wrinkled or his awakening soul grizzled." "The little mite is growing up as though in a cloister; the grave of our Unforgettable is our *memento mori*."[78] He figured that the best thing he could do was to send Konrad away, honoring Ewa's "hope of a sheltered future for her child."[79] "My Konrad will become humanized in human surroundings."[80]

Apollo didn't die, however much he may have wanted to. So he kept on writing. The book Ewa had sent him in jail, Robertson's English lessons, had worked magnificently for Apollo, the onetime St. Petersburg University language student, and he now knew English well enough to translate it into Polish. He couldn't have picked a more evocative title to start: *Hard Times* by Charles Dickens. And gradually, Konrad moved from a lurking worry in the shadows of his bereavement to a new locus of attention, his only reason to go on. "I begin once again to tackle my life, which is, at present, confined solely to Konradek."[81] The boy was growing up "to look very much like his mother."[82] "My dear little mite takes care of me," Apollo remarked proudly. "His heart—he inherited . . . from his mother—but his head is not to be envied—it is mine."[83] Apollo adapted the trusty Robertson method to teaching his son French, "and can marvel now at its excellent results upon my boy."[84]

In the spring of 1866 Apollo sent Konrad to stay with his grandmother and his uncle Tadeusz in the countryside. They could offer him so much more than Apollo: a French governess to teach him, who was "amazed by his knowledge of French after only one year of lessons"; a cousin his own age to play with; and themselves as substitute parents, adoring grandmother and "indulgent uncle who has transferred all his love for his sister on to her son."[85] But Konrad had already suffered from the hardships of exile, and had headaches, sometimes seizures, and a bout of German measles; his relatives took him to Zhytomyr, Kiev, and Odessa for treatment. "I am lonely," Apollo admitted from Chernihiv, where he buried himself in translation work "to make my boy's future more secure financially!"[86] Yet "just imagine," he mused, Konrad "misses me" too, even when "all he saw was my clouded face and where the only diversions of his nine-year-old life were arduous lessons."[87]

Konrad had not seen his father in well over a year when the visitor turned up at Tadeusz Bobrowski's estate, unkempt as a heap of brambles. Apollo had set aside his old jackets and cravats for a simple peasant smock. His once neatly twirled, waxed mustache and beard matted his face like reindeer moss.[88] Deep inside, his lungs were collapsing into pits and pus. He'd been granted a passport to the hotter, healthier climate of Algiers or Madeira—released from exile just when he was too sick to survive long, and too poor to travel far.

Apollo used the visa to get himself and Konrad out of the Russian

Empire at last. Together they traveled to Lviv, in Austrian Galicia, where "that wreck of a human being accompanied by the motherless boy" appeared to one of their neighbors "an image worthy of Grottger's pencil."[89] They moved like a pair of one-legged men, each unable to balance on his own, but when they leaned together they stood. "The two homeless wanderers need one another," said Apollo, "I as his miserable protector, he as the only strength that keeps me on this earth." Father and son spent the summer of 1868 at a health resort in the mountains of the Sambir district, where Konrad was treated for "urinary sand . . . in his bladder causing constant cramps," and Apollo dosed his tuberculosis by "drinking sheep whey . . . with such determination that when the . . . police enquired as to what I was doing in Galicia, I answered with a clear conscience, 'I am drinking sheep whey.'"[90]

Surrounded again by the Polish language, culture, and faith, Apollo felt "roused from my long sleep." Poetry surged within him for the first time in years. In an 1868 verse inspired by his beloved Victor Hugo, Apollo compared the Polish people to the sea. At times they may seem like an ocean at low ebb, flat and quiet—but wait and watch, he urged. The tide will turn, the people will rise again.[91]

Early in 1869, Apollo took a job in Kraków at a magazine called *Kraj*, edited by his old friend and fellow writer Stefan Buszczyński. Kraków was the perfect place, he felt, "to bring up Konradek not as a democrat, aristocrat, demagogue, republican, monarchist, or as a servant and flunkey of those parties—but only as a Pole."[92] Days broadened into spring. Apollo's range of movement narrowed from the apartment, to the bedroom, to the bed. A neighbor's housekeeper helped with the cooking and cleaning. Then came the nursing nuns in stiff white coifs, coasting like swans over the polished wooden floors. Buszczyński visited and found his friend feverishly looking "at his wedding ring and the portrait of his wife." It was time to call for the priest. At the end of May 1869, "surrounded by his dear ones," Apollo Korzeniowski's tide drew out.[93]

His last wishes probably hadn't changed since those hollow months after Ewa's death: "I would not wish for more than to help Konrad stand on firm ground among decent people; to weld his body and awakening soul to the body of our society," he had said, and "to take Her ashes from that alien cemetery to the family grave." For himself, he hoped only "to put my foot on native soil, to breathe its air, to look into the eyes of those I love and to call out: now, please God, receive your servant, for he is very, very weary."[94]

The evening after his death, reported *Kraj*, "huge crowds" gathered on the cobblestones outside the Korzeniowskis' flat "to pay a last tribute to Poland's great son." There were "clergymen, city guildsmen with banners, university professors and school-teachers, students and schoolchildren"—everyone but "what is called high society." In "deep sorrow and reverence," they escorted the hearse across the market square, past the spires of St. Mary's, out the St. Florian Gate and to the Rakowicki Cemetery, where Apollo Korzeniowski was laid to rest as "a victim of Muscovite martyrdom." At the graveside a choir sang *Salve Regina* and the mourners wept and wept.[95]

"At the head of the enormous procession" walked the eleven-year-old orphan Konrad. Afterward, Stefan Buszczyński took Konrad to his house on Floriańska Street and looked after him until his grandmother Teofila Bobrowska arrived from Ukraine. Buszczyński told her how her "beloved orphan" had "surrounded his poor father with the most tender attention and prayed for his soul, in a flood of tears, kneeling between the priest and nuns" at the bedside. Everyone was so overcome by his emotion that it took some time "before they came to their senses and called for Mr. Buszczyński, who took the boy and strained him to his heart."[96]

It was the only contemporary glimpse into Konrad's feelings that anyone provided. It would be more than forty years before he recorded anything about his childhood himself.

TWO

THE POINT OF DEPARTURE

"In accordance with his father's wishes" Teofila Bobrowska placed her grandson Konrad in a small school down Floriańska Street from the Buszczyńskis' house, run by a veteran of the 1863 insurrection. Before Apollo died, he had worried that Konrad "has as yet no taste for learning and lacks stability," though "admittedly he is only eleven. He likes to criticize everything from a sympathetic standpoint. He is also tender and good beyond words."[1] Konrad's unsystematic homeschooling and his "ignorance of the German and Latin languages" meant that he had to stay behind his age-mates, but "the teachers praise his industry, comprehension, and application."[2]

Teofila lived with Konrad in Kraków for most of the next four years. She knew that "for the orphan of a homeless exile there can never be too much human affection," and kept him "close to her heart." Tadeusz Bobrowski (who had no sons of his own) stepped into the role of father and financier.[3] He addressed the first in what became a lifetime of letters to "little Konrad" in September 1869.

"It has pleased God to strike you with the greatest misfortune that can assail a child—the loss of its Parents," he began solemnly. "But in His goodness God has so graciously allowed your very good Grandmother and myself to look after you, your health, your studies and your future destiny." Tadeusz laid down a list of priorities. "Without a thorough education you will be worth nothing in this world," so "maste[r] the beginnings of every subject" with "work and determination." Study "not that which is easy and attractive . . . but that which is useful," however difficult, "for a man . . . who does not know how to work on his own and guide himself, ceases to be a man and becomes a useless puppet." The family would take care of all of Konrad's arrangements and expenses, Tadeusz assured him. "It remains for you to learn and to be healthy and even in that matter . . . if you take heed of the advice of your elders you may become completely well—not giving way to feelings and thoughts which are not really proper to your age."[4]

There was a subtext to these stentorian instructions. Tadeusz wanted to fashion Konrad into a pragmatic Bobrowski, not a dreamy Korzeniowski like his father. To friends, Apollo had been the ideal type of the noble, romantic patriot, who had raised his son first and foremost to "be a *Pole!*"[5] Konrad may not have learned German and Latin, but he could recite reams of Mickiewicz, and no boy (swore Stefan Buszczyński) had "a heart as noble as his." To Tadeusz, Apollo had been feckless, quixotic, and fatally incapable of supporting his family. When Tadeusz had seen Konrad over the years, he'd observed a boy

Tadeusz Bobrowski,
Conrad's uncle and guardian.

too often sick and distracted by moody reveries. Be a Pole? Be practical first.

A man of letters, Apollo had commemorated his son's birth by writing a patriotic poem. A man of numbers, Tadeusz marked his assumption of Konrad's guardianship by opening a ledger. He planned to present it to Konrad "on your reaching maturity." "I want you to know all about the relations of your Parents with the other members of your Family—I want you to know how the small fund was established which is designed to serve you in your future work and independence," and to "know that we all loved your Mother and through her both you and your Father."[6] For the next twenty years, Tadeusz entered every credit and debit on Konrad's account into his "Document," annotated with sardonic assessments of his nephew's behavior.

Tadeusz's "Document" provides the only contemporary record of how and where Konrad spent the next five years of his life. For one year, Konrad remained with the schoolmaster on Floriańska Street, then studied for three years with a private tutor, Adam Pulman, a medical student at Kraków's Jagiellonian University.[7] The fall before Konrad turned sixteen, "because of the cholera which was then prevailing in Cracow," Tadeusz sent Konrad to a cousin's pension in Lviv to "help to harden you, which is something that every man needs in this life." The account book also registered annual trips for the sake of Konrad's health: a visit to "the waters at Wartemberg" with his grandmother in 1869, three summertime stays at the Polish spa Krynica, and a six-week walking trip with Pulman in Switzerland "on doctor's orders," in the spring of 1873.[8]

What the orphan made of any of these measures, not a single word from him survived to tell. There were only hints, between lines written by others, of the persistence of those unsuitable "feelings and thoughts": a cavalcade of ill-defined maladies, headaches, and "nervous attacks."[9] Like soundings off an ocean floor, they suggested depth, but revealed nothing of what things actually looked like below.

Kraków in Konrad's youth: the market square and St. Mary's Church.

When Konrad finally spoke into the record himself, he did so with an action. It was the fall of 1874, and he had just returned to Kraków from his year in Lviv. Mourning had been a habit for the frail, isolated boy who had crossed the main square with his father's funeral cortege several years earlier. Now he was a youth trying on the guise of a man. Konrad slicked back his hair under a glaze of pomade, slipped a monocle into his nappy waistcoat, and walked out of the house. He knew Kraków's grid of high plaster walls and old stones from many corners. The flat where his father died on Poselska Street, the little school on Floriańska Street, the apartment he'd shared with his grandmother on Szpitalna Street, where

Konrad Korzeniowski as a teenager.

he and Stefan Buszczyński's son used to lean out the window and drop water balloons "on the black caftans of passing Jews."[10] From a spire of St. Mary's a solitary bugler trumpeted the *hejnał*, the traditional Kraków serenade that ended abruptly on the fifth note, anthem for a nation stunted.[11]

Crossing one of the parks that girdled the town center, Konrad entered Kraków's best photography studio to sit for his portrait.[12] He posed the way they told him, tilting his face slightly away from the lens. He had that plumpness about his chin and lips that could make adolescents look sullen when they were just trying to be serious. But his eyes belonged to another age, rimmed by dark rings the way a rock in the ocean gets banded by the tide.

Almost seventeen years old and done with school, Konrad was at the perfect age to settle in Kraków and take up Tadeusz's injunction to go into some kind of business. Kraków was also where his father had wanted him to be, to "be a *Pole*!" connected to his heritage. But all that Konrad wanted, and had wanted for years, was to get as far away from there as possible. And miraculously, Tadeusz was prepared to let him.

Tadeusz entered the deed into his ledger for September 1874. "I arrived in Cracow and Lvov in order to send you off to the Merchant Marine which you had been continually badgering me about for two years." Konrad had grown obsessed with the idea of becoming a sailor. It seemed a completely fantastical notion for a young man who'd been raised hundreds of miles from the ocean. Yet Konrad had been adrift his whole life. Going to sea just made it official.

Tadeusz arranged to send his nephew to Marseille, where thanks to the Polish diaspora in France, Tadeusz knew of a Polish man who knew another man who had a cousin who owned a shipping company.[13] (Konrad of course already spoke fluent French.) He paid off Konrad's outstanding expenses in Galicia, the fare for his journey, and "part of the cost of equipping" the budding seaman.

Accounts settled, trunk packed, papers organized, train ticket in hand, Konrad said his goodbyes. To Tadeusz he promised he'd be responsible wherever he was going. To Stefan Buszczyński, his father's closest friend, he promised he'd stay true to where he came from. "I always remember what you said when I was leaving Cracow," he recalled many years later. "'Remember'—you said—'wherever you may sail you are sailing towards Poland!'

"That I have never forgotten, and never will forget!"[14]

. . .

ONCE IN A VERY RARE WHILE, long after Konrad had evolved into Conrad with an English *C*, he turned back the century's page to write about his early years in Poland. A memoir, *A Personal Record*, published in 1908 (when he was fifty), plus an essay or two, applied a mature man's words to the thoughts and feelings of his younger self. In one moving essay Conrad recalled tiptoeing into the "awful stillness" of his father's Kraków sickroom. He'd kiss the prostrate body under the sheets, pad silently out, "and often, not always, cr[y] myself into a good sound sleep." "But when the inevitable" moment of death arrived, Conrad said, "I don't think I found a single tear to shed." Everyone regarded him "as the most callous little wretch on earth."[15]

"I don't know what would have become of me if I had not been a reading boy," Conrad mused. "I suppose that in a futile childish way I would have gone crazy." As against a daily life straitened by exile, isolation, and grief, in books he could travel the world. He read about expeditions in the Arctic and in Africa.[16] He got his "first introduction to the sea in literature" age eight or nine, sitting at the foot of his father's bed and reading aloud the proof pages of Apollo's translation of *Toilers of the Sea* (1866) by Victor Hugo. From there he cruised through the sea stories of Captain Frederick Marryat and into maritime novels by James Fenimore Cooper.[17] He decided he wanted to become a sailor.

Conrad described in *A Personal Record* how the thought matured. I want to become a sailor, he murmured. "At first . . . this declaration passed unperceived" by his family, but "by trying various tones I managed to arouse here and there a surprised momentary attention—the 'What was that funny noise?'—sort of inquiry." I want to become a sailor, he repeated. "Did you hear what that boy said? What an extraordinary outbreak!" "A wave of scandalized astonishment" broke over the family. When the news reached Tadeusz in Ukraine, he made a special trip to Kraków to talk Konrad out of it.

"Think well what it all means in the larger issues—my boy," he advised. "And meantime try to get the best place you can at the yearly examinations."[18]

Conrad went on his walking holiday in the Alps with Adam Pulman. Evidently Pulman had been tasked "with a confidential mission to talk me out of my romantic folly," for "he argued in railway trains, in lake steamboats," and even while they watched the celebrated sunrise over Mount Rigi, one of Switzerland's touristic musts.

"What reward could [you] expect from such a life . . . ?" Pulman asked his pupil. It was "an unanswerable question," Conrad admitted. He felt the "ghostly, unrealized, and desired sea of my dreams" ebb away.

Then suddenly, the tide turned. "Our eyes met and a genuine emotion was visible in his eyes as well as in mine. The end came all at once. He picked up the knapsack suddenly and got on to his feet.

"'You are an incorrigible hopeless Don Quixote. That's what you are,'" said Pulman.

They spoke no more about it. The young men ended their trip in Venice and went out to the Lido. Behind them flickered the lagoon and the skyline of silver domes. Before them gleamed the beach, the breaking waves, and the spreading ocean. Until that moment, said Conrad, "neither he nor I had ever had a single glimpse of the sea in our lives."[19]

Every witness can tell a story differently, and nobody witnesses emotions and ideas like the person who feels them. Yet almost none of what Conrad said lines up with other records. The adults who pulled him sobbing from his father's deathbed described a boy dissolved in grief, the very opposite of a "callous little wretch." He'd first seen the sea in Odessa, not Venice, on a trip with his grandmother in 1866. Tadeusz never mentioned making a special trip to Kraków to dissuade his nephew from going to sea (and knowing him, he would have written it into the ledger if he had). The book that Conrad said inspired him to become a sailor, Hugo's *Toilers of the Sea*, was a curious choice. There's not much actual seafaring in this tale of a social misfit who tries to win the woman he loves, only to drown himself while watching her sail away with another man. The ocean Conrad met on the page was a sea of broken dreams, a sea of suicide.

Memoirs let people fashion themselves into characters they want other people, if not themselves, to accept. Conrad crafted a literary version of his young self as an insouciant dreamer, blithely coasting over childhood turbulence and trauma. The persona portrayed by those who knew him, though, looked nothing like it. It's that more troubled, complicated sort of person who crops up over and over as a figure in Conrad's novels, and "every novel," Conrad conceded in *A Personal Record*, "contains an element of autobiography."[20] His characters struggle with displacement, alienation, and despair. Seventeen of them commit suicide.

Other features of Conrad's early life slipped, unacknowledged, into his oeuvre. He went into adulthood with the idealistic Korzeniowski and the pragmatic Bobrowski tussling for precedence inside him. At first glance, the young Conrad of *A Personal Record* appeared to be very much his father's son, a dreamer and a writer like Apollo. "Those who read me know my conviction that the world . . . rests . . . on the idea of Fidelity," he said in the preface, a value modeled by his parents' undying commitment to Polish independence.

But Conrad disdained the "hard, absolute optimism" of "the revolutionary spirit" as fiercely as any Bobrowski. And when he actually described Poland, he did so in his uncle's voice. It was from Tadeusz's Polish-language memoirs, published in 1900, that Conrad derived the only piece of fiction he ever set in Poland, "Prince Roman," the profile of an 1830 insurrectionist he'd met on a stay at Tadeusz's house.[21] Whole chunks of *A Personal Record* come straight from the same source. It was from Tadeusz that Conrad pulled the description of his Korzeniowski grandfather as "that type of Polish squire whose only ideal of patriotic action was to 'get in the saddle and drive them out.'" It was from Tadeusz that he formed an image of his mother as "the ideal of Polish womanhood," a "loving, wide-browed, silent, protecting presence, whose eyes had a sort of commanding sweetness."[22]

As for his father, the target of Tadeusz's counterprogramming, Conrad described a curious scene a couple of weeks before Apollo's death. He went into the sickroom and found his father "in a deep arm-chair propped up with pillows. This is the last time I saw him out of bed." A nurse knelt by the hearth "feeding the blaze in the fireplace." She was stuffing it— on Apollo's orders—with his manuscripts and letters. Conrad watched aghast. "That act of destruction affected me profoundly by its air of surrender."[23]

Whatever Conrad saw burning, it wasn't Apollo's papers, which survived in the custody of his executors. But the misperception was revealing. Conrad saw his father, at least in the light of retrospect, as "a vanquished man," his words and ideals ultimately unable to fend off the deadly assault by forces so much bigger than himself.

Conrad never forgot or forgave the "oppressive shadow of the great Russian empire" that blighted his childhood. It inspired a fatalistic sense of the world as a realm where, no matter how hard you tried to make your own way, you might never slip the tracks of destiny. Apollo had written of Russia as a machine, its "cogs and wheels" grinding up Poland.[24] Conrad portrayed the world itself as a machine. Life, he wrote to a friend, was like a mechanical loom. "It knits us in and it knits us out. It has knitted time, space, pain, death, corruption, despair and all the illusions—and nothing matters." However much you might wish it to embroider, or weave some brocade, or simply to stop for a while, "you can't interfere with it," "you can't even smash it." You could just "stand appalled" and watch the clacking frames continue their "remorseless process."[25]

Conrad's fiction usually turns on the rare moments when a person gets to make a critical choice. These are the moments when you can cheat fate—or seal it. You can stay on board a sinking ship or jump into a life-boat. You can hurt someone with the truth or comfort them with a lie. You can protect a treasure or steal it. You can blow something up or turn the plotters in.

You could spend your whole life in the place where you were raised or you could leave and never come back.

MARSEILLE, CITY OF OLIVE OIL, orange trees, sweet wine, and sacks of spice, mouth open to the Mediterranean and eye cocked toward the Atlantic, city of Crusaders, revolutionaries, the Count of Monte Cristo. Konrad walked down the hill from his lodgings to the Vieux Port. Masts poked above the roofline like shorn wheat. He walked past cafés of clacking dominoes and twinkling glasses of vermouth, peasant women holding panniers of goat cheese for sale, an old North African cranking his barrel organ over the dissonant screech of trams. In and out of the shipping offices came the captains, faces creased like old papers. Knuckles of sun punched the water in the harbor. "Monsieur Georges!" called a pilot, collapsing "Korzeniowski" in his French mouth.[26]

Konrad had made his escape. He never wrote to Stefan Buszczyński or Adam Pulman, despite nagging from Uncle Tadeusz. A trunk he'd brought from Kraków filled with Polish books and a family photograph disappeared. Tadeusz grudgingly sent him a replacement photo, wrapped in a "dressing-down." "Your disorder and the easy way you take things . . . remind[s] me of the Korzeniowski family," chided Tadeusz, "spoiling and wasting everything—and not my dear Sister, your Mother. . . . Do you need a nanny?"[27]

Money disappeared almost without Konrad's knowing where it went. Eight months' allowance vanished in a matter of weeks, and when pressed he could scarcely account for where he'd spent it: on the daily cost of living, loans to friends, or on other things he really didn't want to talk about. But he needed more, and that meant approaching his uncle yet again. From Ukraine came back a letter spiked with exclamation points and gridded with sums. Uncle Tadeusz criticized his profligacy, his carelessness, even the way he asked for help. "I must say frankly that I did not like the tone in which you refer to what has happened. . . . Certainly, there is no reason for one to take one's life or to go into a Carthusian monastery because of some folly one has committed . . . but a little more contrition would not be amiss." Nevertheless, "*for the first and last time,*" "*only for once,*" Tadeusz sent him the money.[28]

As Konrad neared twenty, it became increasingly urgent—and increasingly more difficult—for him to disappear from the Russians. According to French law, as a foreign national he was supposed to get permission from his consul before he could sign on to a French ship, but the Russian consul would never grant it, because Konrad was at the prime age for military conscription. Until now he'd been able to talk the Marseille port inspector into overlooking the matter, and he'd made three voyages to the West Indies and back. But one day in the summer of 1877, when Russia had just gone to war with Turkey, Konrad turned up to board a ship and the inspectors took a closer look. They saw he didn't have the right papers and refused to let him go. If Konrad wanted to sail again, he'd either have to find a ship that wasn't French—or he'd have to stop being Russian by getting naturalized somewhere else.

Tadeusz ran through the options. There were lots of places he could move to: Switzerland, the United States, Latin America. Konrad had once mentioned meeting the Japanese consul in Marseille, so who knew, "perhaps you will become an Admiral in Japan? Indeed, once you have embarked on a cosmopolitan career such as yours is in the merchant navy—it is unimportant where one is."[29] The only thing Tadeusz counseled against was Konrad's own idea, namely to go to Britain and find work in the world's largest merchant fleet. Was that really practical? "My first question is, do you speak English?"[30]

Despairing of ships, Konrad disappeared even deeper into debt. A serendipitous encounter with the captain of his first ship, the *Mont-Blanc*, promised him a way out. I have a good thing going running contraband over to Spain, the captain confided. Invest with me, he told Konrad, and I'll net you a nice profit. Konrad gave him 1,000 francs and the captain returned with 1,400, so Konrad gave him the rest of his money. The captain returned with nothing. Konrad was wrecked. Unable to face his uncle Tadeusz, he approached one of his friends for a loan, a German named Richard Fecht. He took the money to the casinos of Monte Carlo, hoping to make his fortune back at the gaming tables, but ended up gambling away the lot. Sunk, Konrad returned to Marseille and invited Fecht to tea to break the news.[31]

Tadeusz was at the Kiev trade fair at the end of February 1878 when he received a distressing telegram from France: "*Conrad blessé envoyez argent—arrivez.*"[32] ("Conrad wounded send money—come.") He wrapped up his business and hastened to Marseille, where he found his nephew recovering from a gunshot wound in the chest.

Before Fecht arrived for their tea date, Konrad had taken out a pistol, pointed it at his breast, and pulled the trigger.

To Tadeusz's immense relief, Konrad had missed his heart—on purpose?—and was healing well. As a matter of honor, they agreed to tell others that he'd been wounded in a duel.[33] But Tadeusz knew his nephew enough to sense that this trouble had deep roots. Tadeusz spent two weeks in Marseille to "study the Individual" and set Konrad back on course. He saw too much of the Korzeniowski in Konrad, who seemed romantic, irresponsible, "extremely sensitive, conceited, reserved, and in addition excitable." But he was "not a bad boy" for all that. Unlike most sailors, he didn't drink much, he didn't generally gamble; there were no obvious signs of waywardness with women. He was "able and eloquent," well mannered, "handsome," and "lucky with people." Though "we Poles, particularly when young, have an innate liking for the French and for the Republic," Tadeusz was also happy to see that Konrad was "an imperialist," a supporter of the former regime of Napoleon III.

The obvious thing, as far as Tadeusz could tell, was for Konrad to give up the sea and return to Kraków. This Konrad refused, "maintaining that he loves his profession, does not want to and will not change it." Together uncle and nephew "decided that he should join the English Merchant Marine where there are no such formalities as in France."[34]

Konrad's wounds had only just healed when he signed onto a British-flagged steamer called the *Mavis*. The ship was a poor fit: Konrad didn't like the captain and the crew didn't like him. When the *Mavis* belched toward port on the Norfolk shore, Konrad determined to sign off. There was a quarrel with the captain; he disembarked, forfeiting part of the deposit he'd made for his berth, and sped away to London.[35] He would never write the truth of what happened in Marseille.

THREE

·

AMONG STRANGERS

IN THE FIRST WEEK of AUTUMN, 1878, the biggest city on earth turned around its global axis, getting by and getting ahead, making and spending, investing, inventing, sinning, and selling. Four and a half million strong and growing fast, London was a city settling into its own greatness. Construction crews swept aside the seedy rookeries, grimy courts, and squalid tenements that filled the novels of Charles Dickens and laid down new arteries: Shaftesbury Avenue, Charing Cross Road, Piccadilly Circus. Along the Thames, in Dickens's day a slime-slopped fringe haunted by scavengers and outcasts, engineers eased Cleopatra's Needle into place on the stately Victoria Embankment.[1] Downriver, dockland developers cut the water into a grid of basins and quays. To the north and south, tessellations of terraced houses quilted suburbs with everyman's castles. A burrowing network of Underground trains pumped commuters into and out of the city's heart.

A spider in a worldwide web of somewheres, London caught the world in lines of news. Steamers made ready for Calcutta, Adelaide, Buenos Aires, and Yokohama. Arriving ships brought reports of hurricanes in the West Indies, unrest in southern Peru, a plague of locusts in El

Salvador. Stevedores packed warehouses with American cotton, Australian wool, and Caribbean cocoa. On the money markets prices ticked up and down in Turkish, Brazilian, and Swedish stocks, Latin American mines, Indian tea, and North American railroads. At Woolwich Town Hall, an inquest continued into the disastrous wreck of a crowded passenger ferry in the Thames. At the Crystal Palace, judges gave out prizes at the Fruit Show and International Potato Exhibition. In Newington, seven thousand people heard an American temperance campaigner opine upon the perils of drink. In the West End, full houses delighted in W. S. Gilbert and Arthur Sullivan's new operetta *H.M.S. Pinafore*.

At Liverpool Street Station, a young man stepped off a hissing train from Norfolk. He'd been perusing *The Times*, practicing his beginner's English on its ad-packed pages. Tutors and governesses sought students, cooks and maids sought good households, "the Tall Lady in Black" sought "the gentleman who showed her so much kindness on board the Lyons." One item, set deep amid six columns, seemed to seek *him*:

> SEA.—WANTED, respectable YOUTHS, for voyage or term, in two splendid ships for Australia, and others for India, &c.—W. Sutherland, 11, Fenchurch-buildings, Fenchurch-street, near rail. Established 1851.

An advertisement in The Times, *September 25, 1878.*

Konrad Korzeniowski wanted the job, and he'd come to London to track it down. The ad tucked in his pocket, he consulted a map, took his bearings, and disappeared into the crowd.[2]

"I agreed to your sailing on an English ship but not to your staying in England, not to your traveling to London and wasting my money there!" thundered Konrad's uncle Tadeusz from across the continent when he heard where his errant nephew had washed up. "You travel to London God knows why, being fully aware that you could not manage by yourself, having nothing and knowing nobody."[3] Even if he didn't say it,

Konrad could have sensed why he'd come. London was the best place in the world to disappear. What had happened to him and his parents in the Russian Empire would never have happened here.

London supplied answers without asking questions. There were no restrictions on who could come into the country: no passports or visas required, no need to prove that you had means of support. Nobody could be forced into military service. Nobody could be jailed merely for saying or writing something against the establishment. Nobody got extradited on political grounds. Freedom turned London into Europe's beachcomber, collecting refugees washed up by waves of political change: Poles from the insurrection of 1830-31, Germans and Hungarians from 1848, Italians who'd fought alongside Garibaldi in the 1850s and '60s, French radicals from the Paris Commune of 1871, even France's ex-emperor Napoleon III. Britons took patriotic pride in the country's role as "an asylum of nations," a beacon of liberty. Only Switzerland was so permissive, and Switzerland didn't teem with the possibilities of the world's greatest city.[4]

As he wandered out of the train station, Konrad joined more than fifty thousand continental Europeans living in London—more than all the population of Kraków. Walking east from Liverpool Street, he'd have found some of the city's seven thousand other "Russians and Russian Poles," though most of them were Jews who'd fled tsarist persecution. Heading west, he'd enter "Little Italy" in Clerkenwell, a maze of gray-brick alleys where men and women stocked ice-cream carts and wiped down barrel organs. Italian shaded into French as one continued into Holborn, a veritable Little Paris in the heart of what guidebooks called "Dickensland."[5] From there it was a short walk into Soho, the capital of foreign London—which meant the capital of German London. More than twenty thousand Germans lived in the city, about a quarter of them commercial clerks; others waiters, bakers, butchers, teachers, the occasional royal prince, and a clutch of exiled revolutionaries, like the frizzy-

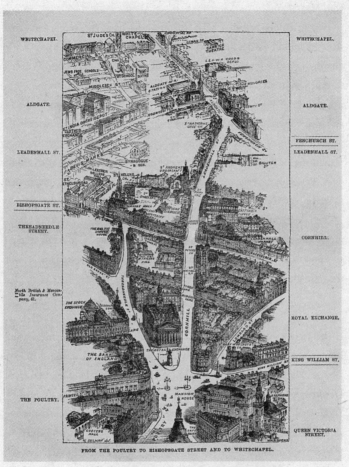

FROM THE POULTRY TO BISHOPSGATE STREET AND TO WHITECHAPEL.

A bird's-eye view of the City of London in 1880.

bearded man you might see scribbling at a desk in the British Library, Karl Marx.[6]

On an avenue banding Soho, rushing with hansoms, traps, and vans, Konrad could board a lurching green omnibus, clamber up to the knife board, and brace himself for a long ride north.[7] The sun in London didn't so much shine as hang a pale scrim behind soot-blackened fronts. From the omnibus's upper deck he'd review the parade of ornamental façades and look down onto costermongers' barrows, boardmen in bowler hats, women in bustle skirts chased by sprays of mud. Beyond the Regent's Canal, the city settled into swatches of pleated roofs pinned with chimneys. Parks and greens breathed free of iron fencing. The bus terminated at Stoke Newington. Konrad would have turned off the main street and walked down Dynevor Road, a long line of cream-silled windows blinking from squat brick faces. At number 6 he'd swing open a small gate, step up to a little portico, open a narrow door, and disappear inside. It was the first address he would consistently give as his "home."

LOOKING BACK ON HIS ARRIVAL in London more than thirty years later, Joseph Conrad described it as if he'd wandered into a novel by Charles Dickens. Everything he knew about London he'd learned from Dickens. As a boy he'd gobbled Dickens in Polish translation, stunned by "how well Mrs. Nickleby could chatter disconnectedly in Polish and the sinister Ralph rage in that language."[8] He stumbled out of Liverpool Street Station to discover his shipping agent in "a Dickensian nook," perched in a "Dickensian" office, eating a mutton chop bought "from some Dickensian eating-house around the corner."[9]

In truth, Dickens's London was already disappearing by the time Konrad Korzeniowski turned up in 1878 (razed for bigger roads and better housing), but that was beside the point. By telling his story through Dickens, Conrad turned a story of arrival into a story of becoming. He lit the way from Konrad Korzeniowski, the bookish son of a Polish writer, to Joseph Conrad, a critically acclaimed English novelist. He also kept parts of his early life conveniently in the shadows: the illnesses and distresses of his unsettled adolescence, the suicide attempt in Marseille.

On the rare occasions that Conrad wrote about his early life, it was these first years in London that he most often recalled. Growing up in the Russian Empire he'd been made constantly aware by his family of the difference between him—Pole, Catholic, *szlachcic*—and the Russians, Jews, and Ukrainian peasantry around him. His identity was sharpened on a blade of difference. As a young foreigner in London, difference became a point of entry. "In a free and hospitable land even the most persecuted of our race may find relative peace and a certain amount of happiness," he wrote—in English—to a Polish acquaintance in Cardiff in 1885. "When speaking, writing or thinking in English the word Home always meant for me the hospitable shores of Great Britain."[10] He filed for (and received) British naturalization in 1886.[11] He never lived more than an hour or two away from London again.

As a mature writer in London, Conrad saw "room enough" in this "enormous town . . . a monstrous town more populous than some continents . . . to place any story, depth enough there for any passion, variety enough there for any setting, darkness enough to bury five millions of lives."[12] Yet he only ever located one novel entirely in London (or in England), and when he did, the story he chose to tell was a story about foreigners. The result was a book, set in London in 1886, published in 1907, that let on more about his life before coming to London than he'd ever done explicitly. He called it *The Secret Agent*.

It opened with a man walking out of a shop in Soho, early one spring morning, under the "bloodshot" eye of a "peculiarly London sun." From a distance, the shop looked like a stationery store, and the man, plump and sleek in a rusty frock coat, looked like the very type of bourgeois respectability. He noted the eccentricity of London street numbering, where number 9 sits next door to number 1, number 37 next door to number 9. You observed such "topographical mysteries" when you were a foreigner, but Adolf Verloc prided himself on being "cosmopolitan enough not to be deceived."[13] It was the first clue that nothing in the world of *The Secret Agent* would be quite what it seemed. What you know depends on how deep you go.

Verloc called himself a "natural-born British subject," but he was of European (French) extraction, and lived for undisclosed periods in unspecified parts of France. He appeared to be a "broad, good-natured" paterfamilias, but his domestic life rested on unspoken compromises. Verloc's young, "steady-eyed" wife Winnie had passed over her sweetheart for Verloc, but only because Verloc could provide a stable home for her gouty mother and her brother Stevie. Fair, sweet-natured Stevie looked "delicate, and in a frail way, good-looking too," but a "vacant droop to his lower lip" signaled some kind of intellectual deficit. The Verlocs' shop appeared to be a stationery store, but when you inspected the window display you found it was a pornography shop, stocked with "photographs of more or less undressed dancing girls" and lascivious books. Men turned up their collars before darting inside.[14]

Often, in the evening, men who looked like pornography customers strode directly up to the counter, raised the flap, and passed through to a back parlor. They huddled around Verloc's grate, flipped their collars back down, and set to talking about revolution. All of them, like Verloc, came from abroad. The group's philosopher prince, Michaelis, had been imprisoned for fifteen years and emerged from jail obese on government food and a favorite of London society hostesses, in whose salons he preached an "optimistic" picture of the fall of capitalism: "The future is as certain as the past—slavery, feudalism, individualism, collectivism." Sometime medical student Alexander Ossipon played propagandist, seducing readers with revolutionary pamphlets, and seducing women with leering, almond-shaped eyes, sandy hair, and florid looks "of the negro type." Then there was bald, scrawny Karl Yundt, a self-described "terrorist" and "veteran of dynamite wars," who championed mass killing through his toothless gums. A fourth, "dingy little man" known as the Professor rounded out the coven. Philosophy didn't count with him at all. "The terrorist and the policeman both come from the same basket. Revolution, legality—counter moves in the same game; forms of idleness at bottom identical." It was the mechanics of revolution that interested him. "I am trying to invent a detonator that would adjust itself to all conditions of action. . . . A really intelligent detonator." He wore explosives under his coat, ready to blow at the squeeze of an India rubber bulb.[15]

As for Adolf Verloc, the public knew him as a shopkeeper. These European "political friends" knew him as an anarchist. At Chesham Square, where he strode "with business-like persistency" that spring morning, rapped on the door of a foreign embassy, and was ushered inside, he was known, simply, as Δ. The embassy belonged to Russia (it wouldn't need saying), and Verloc had been on their payroll as an informant for eleven years.[16]

Verloc had been summoned for an assignment by the embassy's new First Secretary, Vladimir. Vladimir rued the way that Britain, with its "absurd" and "sentimental regard for individual liberty," gave shelter to all kinds of continental troublemakers: anarchists, socialists, revolutionaries. He wanted the British to crack down, and he wanted Verloc to help him. Provoke "a jolly good scare," he ordered Verloc. "The attack must have all the shocking senselessness of gratuitous blasphemy," he mused. "A bomb in the National Gallery would make some noise," but a better choice, it struck him, would be some icon of science and industry, which "they believe . . . is at the source of their material prosperity." "Go for the first meridian" at Greenwich, Vladimir decided, the spot from which the world's longitude and time zones were set. "The whole civilised world has heard of Greenwich," he said, settling happily into his choice. "Nothing better, and nothing easier, I should think."[17]

The explosion happened offstage, in a break between chapters. Ossipon and the Professor were having drinks in a Soho beer hall when Ossipon shared the news. "There's a man blown up in Greenwich Park this morning." He pulled a newspaper out of his pocket. "Enormous hole in the ground under a tree. . . . All round fragments of a man's body blown to pieces. . . . No doubt a wicked attempt to blow up the Observatory, they say."[18]

"H'm," muttered Ossipon. "That's hardly credible." Who could be responsible?

"I will describe him to you in one word," the Professor answered. "Verloc." Verloc had recently gotten some explosives from the Professor. Now it seemed they had gone off by accident, before Verloc could reach his target. The Professor cursed the failure of his detonator. He skulked out of the café brooding about how to make a better bomb. As he turned into an alley, he saw a figure approach. He recognized the man's gait and corn-silk mustache instantly. It was Chief Inspector Heat of Scotland Yard.

Heat had tailed these revolutionaries for years, and could tell you "what each of them is doing hour by hour." When he'd gotten the news about Greenwich that morning, he'd confidently assured his boss that "none of our lot had anything to do with this."[19] But when he went to Greenwich to investigate, the evidence pointed incontrovertibly toward the Verloc circle. Witnesses reported seeing two men coming from the direction of Michaelis's house, and from the scooped-up corpse on the medical examiner's table, Heat picked out clues from what had once been a man: a few fair hairs, a shoe on a severed foot, a calico address label ripped from a coat collar. It read 32 Brett Street. Verloc's shop.

Heat wanted to arrest Michaelis, the ideological ringleader of the group, but his boss at Scotland Yard countermanded him. The assistant commissioner had cut his teeth on police work in tropical Asia, tracking and breaking up criminal gangs. Here was a chance to do the same in London. It was time to flush out "these people in the pay of foreign governments."[20] Verloc was obviously the one to arrest. The assistant commissioner took up the investigation himself and headed into Soho.

He knew that to burrow into the heart of London you'd best disguise yourself as a stranger. He put on humble clothes, adjusted his demeanor, and slid into the streets looking like "he might have been but one more of the queer foreign fish that can be seen . . . flitting round the dark corners" of the neighborhood. He ate a quick supper in "a little Italian restaurant," where "the people were as denationalised as the dishes set before them." "Struck by his foreign appearance" in the reflection of the window, he twirled his mustache and pulled up his collar, and headed to the Verlocs' shop.[21]

Back on Brett Street, the Verloc family had been adjusting to a change. Winnie's mother had decided to move into an almshouse for widows, which left Stevie entirely in Winnie's care. Stevie moped in his mother's absence. Winnie urged Verloc to take him out and cheer him up. "You could do anything with that boy, Adolf. . . . He would go through fire for you." They decided to send Stevie off to stay for a while with Michaelis in the suburbs, hoping the change of scene would do him good. "Might be father and son," thought Winnie, as Verloc and Stevie strolled away.[22]

Verloc came home from visiting Stevie in a sooty rain, hat brim dripping, eyes and nose streaming, teeth rattling. Foul weather, foul mood. He muttered to Winnie. They should withdraw their money. Move to another country. France, California. Winnie prepared his tea and talked him down. "I should like to know who's to make you. You ain't a slave. No one need be a slave in this country—and don't you make yourself one." Unusually, affectionately, she kissed him on the brow. "If I hadn't trusted you, I wouldn't have married you."

The bell rang. Verloc went to answer it. He came back into the parlor looking "bewildered and harassed," and told Winnie he was going out. Winnie didn't recognize the caller, but his pointy mustache and turned-up collar made him look like all her husband's other political friends. "My husband will see you through all right," she assured him, and the men slid out into the filthy night.

The bell rang again. Winnie answered it. This visitor, with the drooping mustache, she did recognize. He was the policeman who was always hanging around on the corner.

"Husband at home, Mrs. Verloc?"

"No, he's gone out."

Know where? No answer.

Know who I am? No answer.

Recognize this? He took out the address label taken from the Greenwich corpse. Of course she did. She'd inked and stitched it herself into Stevie's coat. What was it doing here?

Just as she puzzled over the clue, Verloc returned. Inspector Heat followed him into the parlor. Winnie listened to their conversation at the keyhole.

"Blown to small bits: limbs, gravel, clothing, bones, splinters—all mixed up together. I tell you they had to fetch a shovel to gather him up with."[23] Suddenly, Winnie felt the fragments slot together. It was Stevie who'd been killed. Stevie carried a bomb. Stevie tripped on a tree. Stevie, "poor Stevie," whom she'd practically raised herself, innocent, tender, simple, blown to bits, only a scrap of cloth left to tell who he was.

Verloc insisted that if brought before a judge he'd tell the truth: that the embassy put him up to it as an agent provocateur, that the bomb went off by accident. Heat wanted nothing of the sort: "It would leave Michaelis unscathed; it would drag to light the Professor's home industry; disorganise the whole system of supervision" and "make no end of row in the papers." Again, Heat was preempted by his boss. For the assistant commissioner the beauty of the Greenwich explosion was "that it makes such an excellent starting point for a piece of work which I've felt must be taken in hand—that is, the clearing out of this country of all the foreign political spies, police, and that sort of—of—dogs." Arrest the agents provocateurs, he argued, and make life so uneasy for the foreign diplomats who hired them that they'd never so much as contemplate this kind of thing again.[24]

The assistant commissioner saw the Verlocs as collateral damage. "It is obvious that he did not plan the death of that wretched lad—his brother-in-law," he reported to a government minister. Verloc had "a genuine wife and a genuinely, respectably, marital relation. . . . From a certain point of view we are here in the presence of a domestic drama."[25]

Verloc "was shaken morally to pieces." "I didn't mean any harm to come to the boy," he told Winnie. "You understand I never meant any harm to come to that boy." He was bullied into it by the embassy—forced to take this step after having already sacrificed eleven years of his life to them, having acted the double agent at the risk of "having a knife stuck into me any time these seven years we've been married."[26]

Winnie's thoughts reeled. "This man took the boy away to murder him. He took the boy away from his home to murder him. He took the boy away from me to murder him!" "This man, with whom she had lived . . . —the man to whom she had grown accustomed . . . the man whom she had trusted, took the boy away to kill him!" Verloc "flung himself heavily" onto the sofa, wheezing and worn out. He heard Winnie approach, saw her shadow lengthen on the wall. On the ceiling he saw the shadow of her arm rising. It was holding the carving knife. Before he could move the knife was deep in his chest.[27]

"She had become a free woman with a perfection of freedom which left her nothing to desire and absolutely nothing to do."[28]

Verloc's blood snaked across the floor. All Winnie could think of now was that she'd be caught and hanged. She stumbled into the street afraid, confused, desperate, all "alone in London."[29] Head down she bumped into Alexander Ossipon.

Ossipon had been in a nearby pub for the last two hours, dithering over how to avoid the police. This—a woman in distress—he handled by instinct. "I've been fond of you beyond words ever since I set eyes on your face," he blurted, folding her into his arms. Yet in her scattered confessions he pieced together a story he'd not come close to suspecting. From matron in distress, Winnie morphed in his mind into a madwoman, a murderess, a "degenerate" like her blasted brother. Ossipon promised to whisk her to safety in Paris. He took her onto the boat-train that very night. But as the train pulled out of the station, Ossipon leapt from the carriage, abandoning Winnie. All her money—all Verloc's pay from the embassy—he had tucked in a wallet in his coat.[30]

The novel closes in the Soho beer hall where Ossipon and the Professor met, again, for drinks. Since the Greenwich episode Ossipon had been feeling glum—he couldn't even muster the energy to flirt—so the Professor jollied him along with a toast: "To the destruction of what is." In nervous habit Ossipon fingered a much-creased newspaper in his pocket. Dated ten days earlier, it described the "Suicide of a Lady-Passenger from a Cross-Channel Boat. *An impenetrable mystery seems destined to hang over this act of madness or despair*." A deckhand had found her wedding ring on a bench. Winnie's ring. "Madness or despair" tolled in Ossipon's ears. But the last words of *The Secret Agent* followed the Professor. He ambled into the alleyways of Soho, pondering extermination. Among the city's innocent millions "he passed on unsuspected and deadly, like a pest in the street full of men."[31]

THE SECRET AGENT was Conrad's tribute to his beloved Charles Dickens. Conrad named his characters in nouns and epithets (Heat, the Professor). Like Dickens, he packed personality into physique, larding down Michaelis, wringing out Karl Yundt, beefing up Verloc "in a fat-pig style." Conrad's London, like Dickens's, swallows light, gags on mud, coughs up soot, and chokes in fog. With strokes of Dickensian magic, a character wandering through this swarming metropolis might run up against the very person who moves the plot: the Professor, "lost in the crowd," turning into an alley to find Inspector Heat; Winnie stumbling from the shop "blindly, with an awful dread of falling down," right into Ossipon. Conrad's favorite Dickens novel, *Bleak House*, which he read "innumerable times, both in Polish and English," with "an intense and unreasoning affection," peered between the lines.[32] Dickens's Inspector Bucket, "a stoutly built, steady-looking, sharp-eyed man in black," taps the shoulder of Conrad's Inspector Heat, a "stalwart man . . . in a dark overcoat" whose "eyeballs glimmered piercingly." Dickens's innocent, abused street sweeper Jo might be the cousin of poor, simpleminded Stevie. *Bleak House* features an episode of spontaneous combustion; *The Secret Agent* has its dynamite blast. Konrad Korzeniowski read Dickens; Joseph Conrad rewrote him.[33]

On the face of it, *The Secret Agent* appears to be a detective thriller. Every detective novel is a historical novel: it uses clues in the present to figure out how something happened in the past. Set twenty years before it was written, *The Secret Agent* was explicitly a historical novel, too. Conrad based the plot on a real incident that had taken place in Greenwich in 1894. That incident, in turn, belonged to a lineage of political intrigue, one that loosely connected the Russian Empire Conrad left to the Victorian London he came to consider home.

The true story of *The Secret Agent* started in St. Petersburg in 1881. Tsar Alexander II was riding back to the Winter Palace after attending a weekly military review. Pedestrians squeezed along the sides of the Catherine Canal to let the royal entourage pass. A bystander took a parcel from under his arm and tossed it between the horses' scissoring legs. There was a flash, smoke, screams, whinnies, Cossacks toppled into the snow. The carriage, bulletproof, was intact; the tsar, uninjured, got out to see what had happened. From the opposite side of the street another man hurled something at the tsar's feet. A funnel of smoke and snow lifted to reveal a bleeding stump of the tsar. Legs blown off, abdomen torn, hand shredded by fragments of his own wedding ring, he died a few hours later. The fatal bomb had been thrown by a Polish *szlachcic*, just a year older than Konrad Korzeniowski.[34]

The tsar who'd punished Konrad's parents was dead. Konrad wrote excitedly to his uncle Tadeusz, spinning out his hopes for a Pan-Slavic confederation. "You please me greatly" with "your interest in our national affairs," Tadeusz replied. "True, that is your duty and I counted on your remaining faithful to it, but many people although they live in their own country don't give it a thought."[35]

Conrad's parents were nationalists who had fought to overthrow *a* state—the imperial Russian regime—in order to liberate the Polish nation. The tsar's assassins, a social revolutionary group called the People's Will, belonged to a new generation of radicals who wanted to overthrow *the* state. They emerged from a nexus of radical groups aiming to reorganize society around "the people." Karl Marx championed one vision, namely state ownership of the means of production—that is, communism. His Russian colleague Mikhail Bakunin—a model for the orotund Michaelis of *The Secret Agent*—pushed for more. Any time you had a state, said Bakunin, you'd have "domination of one class by another and, as a result, slavery." Because "the State without slavery is unthinkable," you had to eliminate the state—that is, anarchism.[36] Radical ends required radical means. "We must spread our principles, not with words but with deeds," Bakunin insisted, "for this is the most popular, the most potent, and the most irresistible form of propaganda."[37]

A few months after the tsar's assassination, anarchists from across Europe filed into a pub near London's Euston Station for the first ever

International Anarchist Congress—their answer to the Communist International, which had also first convened in London, in 1864.[38] Keyed up by events in Russia, the congress formally adopted a strategy of "propaganda by deed." "In a few days," said the anarchic political theorist Peter Kropotkin, a single assassination or bomb could "make more propaganda than thousands of pamphlets."[39]

The deeds were dynamite. Patented in 1867, dynamite armed ordinary people with the means of mass destruction. In Vienna in 1848, Warsaw in 1863, and Paris in 1871, revolutionaries had been mowed down by superior numbers of troops wielding superior weapons. Now all you had to do was steal some dynamite sticks from a mine or a factory, or cook up your own in a backroom chemistry lab, and you alone could shock and destroy. The People's Will deliberately chose dynamite instead of pistols for the tsar's assassination because of its dramatic effect.[40] Kropotkin urged anarchists to study chemistry so they could learn to build bombs; the German radical Johann Most went one step further and wrote a bomb-making manual, *The Science of Revolutionary Warfare*.[41] In dynamite's blast, Most saw a new age dawn: "It was within the power of dynamite to destroy the capitalist regime just as it had been within the power of gunpowder and the rifle to wipe feudalism from the face of the earth."[42]

Propaganda by dynamite came to England on a foggy winter evening in 1881: an army barracks bombed in Salford, a little boy killed.[43] The next blasts wrecked a barracks in Chester; then a police station in Liverpool, where agents turned up a cache of "infernal machines formed of clockwork, dynamite, and nitro-glycerine."[44] Once the bombers started attacking London, in 1883, they rarely struck in isolation. In March 1883, coordinated bombs blew up at the headquarters of *The Times* newspaper and a government office building in Whitehall. In October, commuters on a Metropolitan Line train juddered out of Praed Street Station when an explosion shattered the carriages and carpeted the tunnel in splintered glass. Ten minutes later, passengers waiting for the Underground at Charing Cross were knocked to the platform by the force of another explosion.[45] At the end of May 1884, police discovered sixteen dynamite blocks at the base of Nelson's Column in Trafalgar Square. The same evening, not thirty minutes after detectives left work for the night, a bomb demolished a corner of Scotland Yard.[46] A series of attacks in the winter of 1884–85 culminated one January Saturday when simultaneous bomb blasts struck the Tower of London and the crypt beneath Westminster Hall. A third tore into the (empty) chamber of the House of Commons, shredding the leather benches and dousing the room in horsehair stuffing.[47] "At this moment a single wayfarer, with dynamite in his pocket, throws the cities of England in greater terror than would an army of a hundred thousand men landing at Dover," crowed *The Anarchist* newspaper.[48]

Yet not one of these "dynamite outrages" had been planned by anarchists. All were the work of militant Irish nationalists operating out of the United States, known as Fenians.[49] Killing civilians in the course of daily routines, targeting symbolic locations, coordinating attacks to maximize impact, Fenians wrote the script for modern terrorism. The British government pioneered counterterrorism in response. Parliament rushed through an Explosive Substances Act, making it illegal for anyone to possess explosives with intent to injure, and the Metropolitan Police set up a "Special Branch" to investigate political crimes.[50]

Whether thanks to strict policing, as law enforcement agents boasted, or to changes in Anglo-Irish policy, Fenian bombings ceased in 1885.[51] But elsewhere in the world, anarchist and suspected anarchist attacks started to multiply.[52] At Haymarket in Chicago in 1886, a bomb exploded at a workers' demonstration. In Russia there were further assassination attempts; in Rome, there were bombs in a church and piazza. In the Barcelona opera house, an anarchist leaned over the balcony during a performance of Rossini's *William Tell* and dropped a bomb on the audience.[53]

In Paris, a suspected murderer named Ravachol escaped from police custody and planted bombs at the doors of magistrates. When police recaptured him, his followers blew up a restaurant, then a company headquarters, then threw a bomb into the Chamber of Deputies. Terrified French spoke of being *ravacholisé*: killed by dynamite.[54]

Each incident triggered more arrests and expulsions, more European refugees streaming into the safe haven of London. By far the majority were Russian Jews, who by and large had nothing to do with anarchism but had been scapegoated for the tsar's assassination and victimized by pogroms. A small number really were revolutionaries. One French anarchist wrote up a "Practical Guide for a London Exile" for his newly arrived peers, complete with a rudimentary phrase book:[55]

FRENCH	WRITTEN ENGLISH	SPOKEN ENGLISH
Est-il vrai qu'en Angleterre, il y ait eu des hommes politiques honnêtes?	Is it true that in England there have been some honest politicians?	Iz ite trou date ine Ingelen'de der hêve bine some honest politichanese? . . .
Ma jolie fille?	My pretty girl?	Maille prêté guile? . . .
Sacré étranger!	Bloody foreigner!	Bladé forégneur! . . .
Allons boire un verre.	Let us have a drink.	Leteusse hêve é drin'ke.

Radicals found their way to various London hideaways. There was a club for Jewish anarchists on Berners Street in the East End, complete with copies of London's Yiddish revolutionary paper. At the Autonomie Club in Soho, the "regular Anarchist rabbit warren," newcomers slept on couches under pictures of Ravachol and burned their throats on cheap English gin.[56] At a house near Regent's Park, they got a warm welcome from two English teenagers, Olivia and Helen Rossetti. Granddaughters of Italian émigrés (and nieces of the poet Christina Rossetti and the poet and painter Dante Gabriel Rossetti), the sisters had been converted to anarchism by reading a pamphlet by Peter Kropotkin and started an anarchist newspaper in their basement, *The Torch*.[57] The Rossettis' underground newsroom soon became a hub for "foreigners of all tongues . . . Russians, Italians, French, Spaniards, Dutch, Swedes, and before very long they practically swamped the English element. . . . [W]hat genuine Anarchists there are here are mostly foreigners."[58]

The Fenians who actually had thrown bombs heightened British fears about anarchists who talked about throwing bombs. "We are warming a snake in our bosom in harbouring in this country the Anarchical refuse of the world," warned *The Pall Mall Gazette*.[59] It seemed only a matter of time before London itself became a target. Novelists captured the mood of panic. Edward Fawcett's 1893 novel *Hartmann the Anarchist, or, the Doom of the Great City* described a German revolutionary who'd invented an aircraft to bombard London and "pierce the ventricle of the heart of civilization . . . which pumps the blood of capital everywhere, through the arteries of Russia, of Australia, of India, just as through the capillaries of fur companies in North America, planting enterprises in Ecuador, and trading steamers on African rivers." "Paralyze this heart," he said, "and you paralyze credit and the mechanism of finance almost universally."[60] The book's startling frontispiece showed the tower of Big Ben blowing up and pitching into the Thames.[61]

Paranoia fogged London. Detectives and anarchists tailed and dodged. "Every Anarchist learns in time to spot a detective at first sight," claimed some, but they all knew that "the ranks of Anarchy are simply honey-

SHELLING THE HOUSES OF PARLIAMENT.   *See page 147.*

The frontispiece of Edward Fawcett, Hartmann the Anarchist *(1893)*.

combed with spies."[62] Detectives recruited into the Special Branch to track Fenians switched to full-time "Anarchist-hunting."[63] "It became the fashion at this time to regard almost every criminal as an Anarchist," and almost every shady foreigner, too.[64]

It was already dark on a February evening in 1894 when a park keeper at Greenwich heard a loud noise from near the observatory. He rushed up the hill and saw a figure on bent knees. The form resolved into a man, a young man, a delicate, well-dressed young man with light eyes and fair, silky hair, his abdomen gashed open and his bowels spilling out. Fragments of his left hand spackled the grass. "Take me home," he gasped, and died.[65]

The man had been carrying a bottle of explosives, which detonated accidentally. "Blown to Pieces! *Victim an Anarchist (?)*" squealed the tabloids.[66] He was identified as Martial Bourdin, a Frenchman and a member of the Autonomie Club. Obviously, said the police, he had been heading for the Greenwich Observatory to plant a bomb. The Zero Meridian, the center of the world. Others were more skeptical. One anarchist pamphleteer contended that Bourdin had been lured to Greenwich by his brother-in-law, who was working as an agent provocateur. Nobody ever settled on a truth.

Revolutionaries, ideologues, detectives, double agents; a brother-in-law, a bomb, an accident. The mystery at Greenwich pointed an arrow toward *The Secret Agent*. Conrad offered an equally straightforward explanation for his choice of the topic. He got the idea, he said in a 1920 author's note preface, "in the shape of a few words uttered by a friend in a casual conversation about anarchists."[67] The friend was a fellow novelist, Ford Madox Ford, whose first cousins were the young radicals Olivia and Helen Rossetti. Conrad put their newspaper, *The Torch*, in the front window of the Verlocs' shop.[68] And just like that, history entered fiction. Or at least that's what Conrad wanted his readers to think.

. . .

In CONRAD'S LONDON, literary appearances deceived. It might turn out, as in bestsellers by Marie Corelli and Hall Caine, that your rich, suave, impossibly handsome friend was Satan in disguise, or that your visions had been sent by demons instead of God.[69] It might be that you pranced about town as a handsome, ageless cavalier while somewhere in an attic your portrait grew old, ugly, and twisted (Oscar Wilde, *The Picture of Dorian Gray*). It might be that you cooked up a potion to turn into your evil-minded alter ego, but you couldn't retrieve the formula to make yourself good again (Robert Louis Stevenson, *Dr. Jekyll and Mr. Hyde*). You might discover, in *The Strand* magazine, that the dissolute opium smoker or the drunken groom was really Sherlock Holmes, disguised to solve a crime. But if you read the tabloid papers, you knew that Jack the Ripper stalked the East End unknown and uncaught, and could be disguised as anyone. In the world of *The Secret Agent*, nothing was quite what it seemed. What you know depends on how deep you go.

As a historical novel about anarchism, *The Secret Agent* began at the end. Bourdin's bottle was the only suspected anarchist explosive ever to go off in Britain. Immediately after the Greenwich incident, Helen and Olivia Rossetti saw "public feeling" turn "against the Anarchists."[70] Hundreds of protesters mobbed Bourdin's funeral cortege, hissing and yelling "No bombs here!" and "Go back to your own country!" A funeral orator began his eulogy—"Friends and Anarchists"—and got drowned out in calls of "Lynch him!"[71] Police raided the Autonomie Club and shut it down. Special Branch agents arrested two Italians for plotting to build explosives, using Johann Most's bomb-making manual. Soon, onetime champions of "propaganda by deed" such as Peter Kropotkin disavowed a doctrine that seemed little more than an excuse for random malcontents to justify violence. The Rossettis folded *The Torch* and wrote up their adventures in anarchism in a gently critical autobiographical novel called *A Girl Among the Anarchists*.

By the time Conrad started writing *The Secret Agent* in 1906, anarchism in Britain had already become an anachronism. Soho was being transformed from a den of poverty and peril to a trendy hub of bohemian nightlife.[72] Sensation novelists were dramatizing more imminent dangers, like a war with Germany, while G. K. Chesterton spoofed the whole genre of the anarchist thriller in *The Man Who Was Thursday* (1908), in which every member of a secret revolutionary circle turns out to be an undercover policeman. Anarchism delivered more punch line than punch.

"Don't think that I've been satirizing the revolutionary world. All these people are not revolutionaries—they are shams," Conrad told a friend as *The Secret Agent* hit bookstores in 1907.[73] He was annoyed that his American publishers were marketing the book as "A Tale of Diplomatic Intrigue and Anarchist Treachery." "I dont* want the story to be misunderstood as having any sort of social or polemical intention," he complained.[74] "I had no idea to consider Anarchism politically."[75] If anything, it was the complete absence of political significance that made him want to write about Bourdin. He declared the episode "a bloodstained inanity of so fatuous a kind that it was impossible to fathom its origin by any reasonable or even unreasonable process of thought. . . . [O]ne remained faced by the fact of a man blown to bits for nothing even most resembling an idea, anarchistic or other."[76]

"In my eyes," said Conrad, the novel was "a fairly successful (and sincere) piece of ironic treatment applied to a special subject."[77] Irony is to literary style what mystery is to plot. It depends on disguise: a person says one thing and really means another.[78] Irony depends on secrets: readers know things that characters don't.

Every detective novel may be a historical novel. It's just that the inner history of *The Secret Agent* didn't much concern anarchists at all. What looked on the outside like a book about "a secret agent" (Verloc) was actually, Conrad said, "the story of Winnie Verloc." What looked like a book about a political conspiracy was actually, as Conrad's detective observed, "a domestic drama," in which family relationships turn the plot. Verloc agreed to play the agent provocateur to protect his family; Stevie followed his surrogate father Verloc to Greenwich because his mother had moved away; Winnie murdered her husband to avenge her brother. What Conrad presented as a book inspired by "a casual conversation about anarchists" was actually a book written by somebody who needed no informants to tell him how revolutionary politics could upend a family. That's because what looked on the outside like a novel by Joseph Conrad was a novel, also, by Konrad Korzeniowski.

More than anything Conrad would ever write, *The Secret Agent* mapped the contours of his early life. There's a family filling the roles of father, mother, son, and sometimes grandmother: Apollo, Ewa, and Konrad Korzeniowski, sometimes joined by Teofila Bobrowska. There's a coven of revolutionaries in the family home, just as Conrad vaguely remembered having seen "appearing and disappearing in that immense space" of the family's flat on Nowy Świat in 1861, in the weeks before the police came for his father.[79] There are revolutionary organizations, papers, and pamphlets, like his father's Committee of Action, *Dwytygodnik*, and *Kraj*. There's a spectacular event that goes off too soon and kills the wrong person, like the Polish insurrections that backfired in 1863. There's a sinister, autocratic foreign power, manifestly Russia. There's a haven for exiles, namely England. And there's a central figure who lives a double life, like Joseph Conrad Korzeniowski.

"Both at sea and on land my point of view is English," Conrad said of himself, "from which the conclusion should not be drawn that I have become an Englishman. That is not the case. Homo duplex has in my case more than one meaning."[80] He changed his name and nationality. He wrote in English, not Polish. He said his father's papers had been burned, that he'd burned his parents' letters himself.

Yet he couldn't destroy what was burned into his mind. "Living with memories is a cruel business," he mused. "I—who have a double life one of them peopled only by shadows growing more precious as the years pass—know what that is."[81] Now and then when people asked him about his family, he volunteered his recollections. He remembered sitting on his father's sickbed and reading proofs of Apollo's translations. He remembered his father as "a man of great sensibilities; of exalted and dreamy temperament," profoundly religious "and of gloomy disposition." He remembered him as a man with "a terrible gift of irony."[82]

Conrad never wrote explicitly about the failure of his father's political objectives, but the sense that force will crush ideals—and that ideals have victims—recurred throughout his writing. Precisely when he wrote *The Secret Agent*, Conrad could have noted one more casualty of revolutionary enthusiasm. Although in Britain, terror attacks and assassinations came overwhelmingly from British subjects—Fenians, Indian nationalists, and others—the threat of anarchism ramped up nativist hostility toward European immigrants. The number of immigrants had increased exponentially. From 7,000 "Russians and Russian Poles" in London at the time Conrad arrived in the late 1870s, there were more than 100,000 when he wrote *The Secret Agent* in 1906, nearly all of them Jews. If you had a name like "Korzeniowski," Britons weren't going to think first of heroic Polish freedom fighters. They would think of Jews, and they'd think of Jews as poor and grimy, or sleek and grasping, unable and unwilling to fit in. An "alien invasion" was consuming London, warned anti-immigration activists. They claimed (contrary to statistics) that immigrants lowered wages, raised rents, and introduced vice and crime.[83]

When you think a foreigner might take your job, you protest. When you think a foreigner might kill you, you panic. No amount of policing would keep Britain safe, detectives warned, while people "of very unsafe tendencies" were allowed "to land on our shores practically 'with no questions asked.'"[84] Shortly after the Greenwich bomb, the Conservative

Marquess of Salisbury introduced a bill into Parliament to restrict immigration and expel suspicious foreigners. The British "have always loved to consider this island as the asylum of those who are defeated in political struggles," he recognized, but "the course of events has caused an entire change in that idea of the right of asylum." In 1905 Salisbury's colleagues passed an Aliens Act, limiting immigration for the first time in British history. Liberals tried to retain the most capacious provisions for political asylum by admitting anyone confronting "danger to life, limb, and liberty." Didn't almost everyone in the world face danger to liberty, as judged by British standards? rebutted Conservatives. Because Britain couldn't take everyone, the word "liberty" was struck.[85]

A few weeks after the act went into effect, Conrad started writing *The Secret Agent*. The year in which he chose to set the book, 1886—not 1894, when the Greenwich incident took place—was the year he'd become a naturalized British subject.

Conrad sweated over his own duplicity on every page, painful reminders that "English is still for me a foreign language whose handling demands a fearful effort."[86] With pen in hand he struggled to bend the iron bar of language into fiction designed exclusively for "the English," calculating "the effect it will have on an English reader." He knew when he finished *The Secret Agent* that the book marked "a distinctly new departure in my work."[87] Up until then, critics had embraced him as a "sea writer" who'd published a string of insightful novels centered around sailors and ships. Here was a book "with not a drop of water in it—except the rain, which is quite natural since everything takes place in London."[88] He hoped his change of subject would win him more and different readers.

Instead, sales figures were disappointing. All he got for it were reviewers who talked him up "as a sort of freak, an amazing bloody foreigner writing in English."[89] "I suppose there is something in me that is unsympathetic to the general public. . . . Foreignness, I suppose."[90] Not long afterward, an "ass" of a reviewer in *The Daily News* wrote "on god only knows what provocation that I am a man without country and language."[91] The insult got under Conrad's skin like no criticism he'd ever had. "It is like abusing a tongue-tied man. For what can one say. . . . Any answer would involve too many feelings of one's inner life, stir too much secret bitterness and complex loyalty to be even attempted with any hope of being understood."[92] But a few weeks later he did find a way to answer the accusations leveled at him, the "foreign" author of *The Secret Agent*. He started to write his memoir, *A Personal Record*.[93]

The Secret Agent captured the tragic irony of Conrad's life. He had been raised to belong to a country, Poland, he could never truly be in, because it didn't formally exist. He'd adopted a country to which he could never fully belong, because he remained in certain ways an alien, and to some extent by choice. "I have lived amongst strangers but not with strangers, and wandering around the world I have never left 'The Country of Remembrances.'"[94] There's no place that's home.

PART TWO

OCEAN

Shipping routes in the Indian Ocean, 1872.

80 100 120 140 160

50

A S I E N

40

Persien

30

Beludschistan

China

Japanisches Meer

Ochotskisches M.

Kurilen

Japan

GROSSER OCEAN

20

Hinter-China

Formosa

10

Philippinen

Carolinen

Palew J.

0

Süd-Chinesisches Meer

Borneo

Celebes

Sunda

Kleine Sunda

10

Chagos

Cocos Ins.

Christmas

20

Java

Festland von AUSTRALIEN

Neu-Holland

Korallen-Meer

Golf

Mauritius

Rodriguez

Maskarenen

Bourbon

Flaming

Freycinet

Perth

Geographen B.

C. Leeuwin

Austral Golf

und Nordwest-Wind

Amsterdam

St. Paul

v. Cap n. Sydney 60-80 T.

Bei N. O. mit. i. Dbr. u. Jan. v. Cp...

Sydney

Tasmania Van Diemens Land

Hobarton

n. Valpr. 90 T.

Crozet J.

Kerguelens Land

50

60

Südpolar-Wind

Antarktisches Land

80 100 120 140 160

FOUR

FOLLOWING THE SEA

"ALL ON THE STARBOARD WATCH, AHOY!" A shout in the dark, banging on the scuttle. "Do you hear the news there, sleepers?"[1] Ordinary Seaman Konrad Korzeniowski opened sticky eyes to a stack of bunks and slumbering bodies. Faint light dropped from a glass prism overhead. He breathed in the mold and sour breath and registered where he was. On board the *Duke of Sutherland*, six weeks out from London, four days over the Line, seven bells into the morning watch.[2]

He swung his feet over the rim of the bunk and clambered up the companionway, heels tender from the nighttime nibbling of rats.[3] A quick rinse and wipe down with a cloth, then into the galley to scoop a few ladles of gray porridge from the kid. He propped himself against a sail locker to eat, gulping coffee from a tin cup. In the early morning sun the sea blazed white.

Eight bells, eight A.M.: start of the forenoon watch. He took his orders from the bosun, Mayers, a mean, swaggering Barbadian. By now Konrad had just enough seniority not to do the dirtiest of the slopwork—washing the dishes, slushing the masts—but it was up to him and Pitterson, the

Swede, to sweep and swab the deck. He coiled lines in quick flicks over the belaying pins to make them fast, and ran his broom aft.

He'd never been on a ship as large as the *Duke of Sutherland*, or a voyage so long: bound for Australia via the Cape of Good Hope.[4] By now he didn't notice the way the ship hiked gently up to the windward side. Lolling in equatorial calm, it was hard to believe how it had churned and pitched five weeks ago, off Ushant, when they had run into a gale so ferocious it gave even the eldest seamen something to remember. He'd staggered along the sloping deck as waves smacked him in the chest and dragged heavily away. All hands worked frantically to lash down gear, sheet in the sails, and reef the main sail. Raw, burning fingers fumbled with the ratlines. The wind ranted and screeched enough to make a man wish he'd go deaf.[5]

But it had been a slack passage since; no northeasterly trades. The *Duke of Sutherland* sailed slowly into the windless doldrums, waiting for the southeasterlies to pick up. They took down the stout canvas sails meant for strong winds and bent on worn, softer ones, to catch the shallow breaths of hot latitudes. The round of watches cycled through interchangeable days. Near the Azores some larks and starlings flew on board, and a horned owl.[6] The sailors caged them up for company, reminders of land in the shoreless ring of sea.

It had been four years since Konrad's first voyage on the French bark *Mont-Blanc*. That was his first time at sea and it shook his every sense. On a ship you're in motion without moving, in motion in your sleep, in motion in ways you never moved before: swaying, surging, heaving, pitching, rolling, yawing. On high seas you may be tossed till you can't tell down from up, your eyes pulse in your head, salt surges into your mouth, and you hunch vomiting over the leeward rail. He came to know the particular belowdecks stench, clammy and dank, best defeated by smoking a pipe or learning to shut your nose entirely.[7] He settled into the rhythm of a life measured out in shifts. He discovered the infinite qualities of light on water. There's rarely something to look at, there's always something to see. People are always asleep, people are always awake. You're never alone, you're always isolated.

On two more voyages out of Marseille he'd learned the ropes in French. Now he was learning them again in English. A rope was a line, a speed was a knot, and a knot was a hitch. On a calm day like this Konrad could practice his skills with the chafing gear. It was said that the test of a true seaman was what he could do when you put a marlinespike in his hand. A line could be a messy thing when you looked at it up close: frayed, spliced, wound, pointed, foxed. First he wormed, twisting some yarn between the line's fraying strands. Then he parceled, wrapping the line in tarred canvas to clad it against the rain. Last he served, winding yarn around the strands and pulling it taut on a serving board.[8]

Seven bells: dinner for the off-going watch. Yesterday was pork and peas, so today would be beef, bulked up with cracker hash, and a dose of lime juice, sweetened with sugar, to beat the scurvy. There were "no spirits allowed" on board.[9] The only spirits Konrad had seen so far were metaphorical, a few days earlier, when they crossed the Line. According to age-old custom, one of his shipmates dressed up as "King Neptune" and hazed the "pollywogs"—men like him who had never sailed across the Equator before. A rough shave, a boisterous baptism in seawater, and a toast with a mug of grog made a pollywog into a newly hatched "shellback."[10]

Eight bells, twelve P.M.: afternoon watch. He ducked back down the companionway for a patch of what passed for privacy. Some men tumbled into their bunks and straight to sleep; others mended their clothes or carved a souvenir from wood or bone. Konrad got out a book.[11] Books had awakened his interest in the sea, but few sailors had a taste for reading about the sea once they were on it. He packed poetry, himself.

Eight bells, four P.M.: first dogwatch. More coiling lines, stowing gear, sweeping and washing. The off-duty men sprawled out on the foredeck. Many of them had sailed together before, for better or worse, and shared a companionable ease. Officially, there was no talking while on watch, which suited Konrad well enough. He didn't mix well with this crew.[12] It wasn't so much that he wasn't English—half of them weren't either. Of the twenty-five crew there were four Scandinavians, three Canadians, two Heligolanders, two Barbadians, one New Yorker, and one Pole (him). But he felt himself to be of another class, and he showed it. When the crew had signed the register at the shipping office in London, five of them couldn't even write their own names, and just marked an illiterate *X*. He inscribed himself with distinction as "Conrad de Korzeniowski"—inserting an aristocratic "de" to convey his *szlachta* birth. He notched his *d* elegantly above the line and cut the *z* below with a flourish.[13]

The officers kept their own company aft. The chief mate, Baker, trusted the sea to keep him sober—in port, he drowned himself in drink—but he was none the more cheerful for it. Thick-necked and burly, with a shock of black curls, he was always punctual, always correct, yet always sardonic. The second mate, Bastard, was nicer than his name, an old Nova Scotian salt with a wife onshore and retirement in view. Konrad scarcely ever saw the master, John McKay, who spent most of the day shut up in the cabin. McKay had managed the Sydney–London run before in just seventy-two days, and must have railed at the slowness of this passage.[14]

Four bells, six P.M.: second dogwatch. The beginning of a new "day" in sea-keeping time. It was thanks to the dogwatch that one day differed from the next. Two hours long instead of four, they broke the cycle so men didn't repeat the same twenty-four-hour rotation twice running. Konrad had his supper in the twilight and watched the water slice away from the ship in foam-capped strips.

Eight bells, eight P.M.: first night watch. His turn to take a two-hour trick at the helm. He wrapped his palms around handles softened by thousands of grips, feeling the light tension on the tiller. It was easier to stay on course steering by the horizon than the compass, which meant it was harder to steer by night. Keeping awake was another challenge. "Gravy-eyed," they called it.[15] He focused on the compass paper, a bright spot punched through the darkness by the glowing binnacle lamp. His head sagged; he snapped it up. Some men reeled off multiplication tables to stay awake, or sequences of kings and popes.[16] His eyes blurred; he blinked them clear. He recited verses in his head. The poets of his boyhood, Mickiewicz and Słowacki, kept him good company in the still, spangled night of the southern ocean.

The "little one" bell marked midnight: second night watch.[17] He went down to the half-deck and hoisted himself into his bunk. In the dark, men rummaged for caps and shoes. He heard clattering up the ladders, creaking footfalls on deck, and the soft plash of the sea against the hull. Another day done: December 3, 1878, his twenty-first birthday.

"I HAD THOUGHT TO MYSELF that if I was to be a seaman, then I would be a British seaman and no other," Joseph Conrad declared thirty years later. "It was a matter of deliberate choice."[18] He went from the *Duke of Sutherland* to work on a dozen more ships, making his way up the ranks of the British merchant marine to captain, before stepping off his last vessel in 1894—exactly twenty years after he'd left Kraków. (The merchant marine, as distinct from the Royal Navy, consists of commercial ships carrying goods and passengers. Its officers were civilians licensed by the Board of Trade.)

Conrad had pledged to his father's old friend Stefan Buszczyński that he would always "sail towards Poland," honoring his parents' nationalist dream. But if Conrad sailed toward anything during those twenty years, he sailed toward Britain. At sea, Konrad Korzeniowski turned into Joseph Conrad. He learned to speak English on British ships, found a professional niche and social role, became a naturalized British subject, and, sometime toward the end of the 1880s, started to write fiction—the beginning of a lifetime of writing about sailors, ships, and the sea. In the hands of Conrad the author, these matters of biographical fact became the stuff of alchemy. He transformed the British sailing ship into a gold standard for moral conduct. It became for him what Poland had been for his parents, a romantic ideal that served as a guide for life.

In *A Personal Record* Conrad described his connection to Britain the way you might a new romance, as a series of cherished "firsts." In a hotel in the Alps he admired a cohort of burly Scottish engineers, "my first contact with British mankind apart from the tourist kind." He recalled how, just as his tutor was trying one last time to talk him out of becoming a sailor, an "unforgettable Englishman" in a knickerbocker suit, with a "very red face" and very white calves, strode past them like "the ambassador of my future, sent out to turn the scale at a critical moment."[19] He told how he came alongside a big, British, black-hulled cargo steamer in Marseille harbor, and "for the very first time in my life, I heard myself addressed in English—the speech of my secret choice . . . of my very dreams!" What followed thrilled like a consummation: "When I bore against the smooth flank of the first English ship I ever touched in my life, I felt it already throbbing under my open palm." He stared at the British ensign on her mast, "flame-like, intense" and "ardent." "The Red Ensign! . . . The Red Ensign—the symbolic, protecting, warm bit of bunting flung wide upon the seas, and destined for so many years to be the only roof over my head."[20]

Conrad knew, when he presented this story of how he became a British sailor, that he was hiding another one: his "deliberate choice" to leave France after his suicide attempt. He had only just started to find his feet in England in 1878, on board a small coaster doing coal runs from Lowestoft to Newcastle, when he received a stinging letter from his uncle Tadeusz.[21] You're "a lazy-bones and a spendthrift," he read. "You were idling for nearly a whole year—you fell into debt, you deliberately shot yourself. . . . Really, you have exceeded the limits of stupidity permitted to your age!" Absolutely no extra money, Tadeusz vowed. "Find yourself some occupation and earn some money, for you won't get a penny from me." "You set out to be a sailor. . . . You wanted it—you did it—you voluntarily chose it. Submit to the results of your decision. . . . Think of your parents, of your grandmother . . . —remember my sacrifices . . . — reform yourself—work—calculate—be prudent and doggedly pursue your aim and with deeds and not words."[22]

That's when Conrad had answered the ad in *The Times*. The shipping agent he found in London offered poor terms of engagement (a nugatory pay of one shilling per week, as against a twenty-pound retainer) but the all-essential job. On the *Duke of Sutherland* Conrad floated thousands of miles away from Tadeusz's rebuke.

Sometimes decisions that seem very personal—what to do, where to live, whom to live with—can be shaped by conditions remote, if not invisible, to the person making them. Conrad himself may not have known, when he explained why he became "a British seaman and no other," how closely his career aligned with historical conditions that made Britain the best place in the world for a European sailor to find work. It didn't even require a "deliberate choice."

Growing up in the 1860s, Conrad dreamed of going to sea at a time when sailing ships had never been so fast, so glamorous, or so popular— as epitomized by the dashing, rake-masted clippers that raced west from China every year with the season's freshest tea.[23] When Conrad actually went to sea in the 1870s, however, a surge in steamships was disrupting the maritime world. Though at first they were too unreliable and expensive to compete with sailing ships, breakthroughs in engine design in the 1850s started to make oceangoing steamships into a paying proposition.[24] The opening of the Suez Canal in 1869 gave steamships a critical edge over sail on the busy Europe-to-Asia route, thanks to the notoriously adverse prevailing winds in the Red Sea. By the 1870s, steamships had never been so profitable, so comfortable, or so numerous. The tea races under sail ended in 1873; within ten years, steamships carried more international cargo than sail.[25]

Whereas at midcentury, the United States had looked like the up-and-coming maritime power, the rise of steamships played to Britain's considerable competitive advantages: its preeminence in steel production, excellence in engineering, and command of an empire-wide network of coaling stations. Plus, between 1840 and 1880, the implementation of free trade policies practically doubled the importance of global trade to the British economy.[26] By the time Conrad signed on to the *Duke of Sutherland* in 1878, the British merchant marine was by every metric the most powerful commercial force afloat. British ships had five times the registered tonnage capacity of the next-largest merchant fleet.[27] British shipowners controlled about 70 percent of world trade.[28] British shipyards held a dominant position in construction.[29] Almost half the ships in the industrialized world entered the ledgers of *Lloyd's Register* in London, shipping's most important certificatory body.[30] Its annual volumes provided a sort of maritime census, systematically translating each vessel into a code of numbers and symbols. Number 45590, condition "A1" (the most seaworthy), "S F. & Y M.65 c.f." (ship sheathed in felt and yellow metal in 1865, with copper fastenings): the *Duke of Sutherland*.[31]

A sailor didn't need to see the statistics to know that there were more jobs available in Britain than anywhere else, and a wider range of ships to work on. Nor did a sailor need a ledger to tell him how every ship was distinct. A ship might be infected by a "devilish habit of sea-spite that makes her an abode of misery to her crew," infested by rats, or dripping belowdecks all voyage long. Or it might travel in "ways of pleasantness" and ease.[32] If you were lucky you found yourself "a happy ship," fairly well sealed against leaks, without much brass to polish, and with relatively good food: the *Duke of Sutherland*.[33]

No.	Ships.	Masters.	Tons.	DIMENSIONS.			BUILD.		Owners.	Port belonging to.	Port of Survey and Destined Voyage.	Classification.	
				Length.	Breadth.	Depth.	Where.	When.				No. Years first assigned.	Character for Hull&Stores
301	Duchess of Sutherland Bk	R Scaddan W.M.65	349	105·0	26·5	17·0	Sndrl'd Drp.59Srprs61&67	1851	Redway&	Exm'th	Lon.S Leone Ry S.Cr-6yrs	8 C. 8	A 1 1, 6,
2	Dudbrook Bk F.&d.62F.&YM.69	W.Deacon	572	137·1	25·7	20·1	D'ndee w.ptTSdsr.&d.62	1848	W.Deacon	London	Lon. Rest.62–	12 8	A 1 4,63
✠3	Dudley Scw Sr (Iron) M.C.68	T.Robson AP.90H.	696 636	198·5	28·0	16·0	NShlds Drp.66 Smith	1865 10mo.	T.&W.Smith	Nwcstle 3 Blk Hds	Sbl London London (A.&C.P.)	—	A 1 11,06 A 1 4, 07
4	Duke Sw I.B.	J. Bayley	150	77·4	22·6	12·8	Lynn Nd.pt48pt63Drp.54&55Srp	1841 r–63	Bayley&c	Lynn	Lyn. Coaster	9	Æ 1 11,65 Æ 1
✠5	—of Argyll S (Iron)	G.M'Lean	960	199·7	33·2	20·9	Dmbtn Rankin	1865 10mo	Montgmerie	London 2 Blk Hds	Lon. India (A.&C.P.)	—	A 1 10,66 A 1 12,66
✠6	—of Athole S (Iron)	Dlrymple	963 2D.	199·3	33·2	20·9	Dmbtn Rankin	1865 3mo.	Montgmerie	London 2 Blk Hds	Lon. India	—	A 1 11,65 A 1 12,66
✠7	—of Newcastle S ptF.&s 65F.&Y	M'Kenzie M.65ptI.B.	993	170·6	34·9	22·2	Quebec w.F.&s.62 Lee	1861 8mo.	Baines&C.	Liverp'l	Liv. Austral.	7	A 1 6,65
8	—of Northumberland Bk F.&Y	J. Brunton M.62	463	125·0	27·5	19·2	Sndrl'd Srprs53&56Drp.60	1851			Sws. W.Inds	10 C. 3	A 1 2,62
⚓) 9	— (Iron)	S E. Brown	558	130·3	29·0	18·9	Nwcstl Srprs58	1852	Brooks&C	London	Lou.India Rest.62–	6 4	A 1 8,62
310	—of Rothesay Bk ptr &s.62F.&Y	Paschal M.65ptI.B.	575	139·6	30·1	18·7	St. Jhn w.ptF.&s.62	1861	W H Owen	Liverp'l	Liv. India	7	A 1 7,65
✠1	—of Sutherlnd S F.&YM.65c.f.	T.Louttit	1047	201·6	34·2	21·8	Aberdn Smith	1865 6.no.	Louttit&C	Wick	Abn. Austral (A.&C.P.)	9	A 1 7,65

The Duke of Sutherland *as entered into* Lloyd's
Register of British and Foreign Shipping *(1867)*.

The Duke of Sutherland *moored at Sydney's Circular Quay, 1871.*

"EVERY SOUL AFLOAT in Bombay Harbour became aware that new hands were joining the *Narcissus*." They splashed toward the ship in "shore-boats rowed by white-clad Asiatics, who clamoured fiercely for payment" as the tipsy sailors stumbled up the gangway. "In the forecastle the newcomers, upright and swaying amongst corded boxes and bundles of bedding, made friends with the old hands, who sat one above another in the two tiers of bunks, gazing at their future shipmates with glances critical but friendly." A hulking West Indian, "calm, cool, towering, superb," was the last to come aboard. His gear stowed, "shore togs" swapped for "clean working clothes," he sat down on his sea chest to take the measure of his new quarters.

"What kind of ship is this? Pretty fair? Eh?" he asked.

The oldest crewmember leaned in the doorway, catching the cool night air on his back. His chest was "tattooed like a cannibal chief," and "with his spectacles and a venerable white beard, he resembled a learned and savage patriarch."

After a long silence the old man replied, "Ship! . . . Ships are all right. It is the men in them!"[34]

The opening scene of Conrad's 1897 novella *The Nigger of the 'Narcissus'* captured the sailor's sense that what really defined the quality of a voyage was the quality of its crew. But as Britain's maritime dominance increased, who exactly could be found to man all those ships, and what conditions they worked under, became a matter of urgent public interest.

The dark side of British seafaring showed itself in the Board of Trade's annual Wreck Charts, which mapped the shipwrecks that ringed the British Isles like a noose. During the 1860s at least 500 sailors died off the coast annually, hitting a peak of 1,333 fatalities in a single year.[35] The numbers scandalized an activist newspaper editor who challenged the shipping industry for woeful safety standards. An outraged reader alerted her husband to the problem. He, Samuel Plimsoll, Liberal member of Parliament for Derby, hurled himself into a crusade to improve conditions for sailors.[36]

In 1873, Plimsoll published a pamphlet entitled *Our Seamen: An Appeal*, assailing shippers for overloading, undermanning, and improperly maintaining their craft. Plimsoll creatively used illustrations to enhance his case: photographs of sham bolts and corroded iron from shoddily built ships, reproductions of insurance documents scored with so many underwriters' names that no individual could feasibly prosecute suspected wrongdoing. "Oh! My God! My God!" Plimsoll cried. "*Whoever* you are who read this, help the poor sailors, for the love of God. If you refuse . . . before another year has run its course, at least . . . five hundred men!— now in life, will strew the bottom of the sea."[37]

Critics complained that Plimsoll's preaching *Appeal* was riddled with errors, but that didn't stop hundreds of thousands of copies from moving British hearts. In the House of Commons, Plimsoll kept haranguing his colleagues (once even getting thrown out of the chamber for accusing MPs of being personally responsible for killing sailors) until they passed a meaningful reform bill.[38] The Merchant Shipping Act of 1876 required ships to carry a fixed load line—popularly known as a "Plimsoll line"— a mark painted on the hull that showed the maximum depth at which a properly loaded ship could safely sit in the water.[39] The campaign achieved something just as important for sailors' welfare: a recognition that sailors were a laboring population as equally deserving of workplace protections as their peers in factories, mills, and mines.

To Plimsoll, sailors were "the good, true, and brave men we sacrifice by our manslaughtering neglect."[40] But others had a different image. In 1869, the Board of Trade asked British consuls in port cities around the world to report on "the general condition of British seamen who come in under your notice."[41] From Smyrna to Mobile, Montevideo to Riga, the answers ricocheted back. Drunk, illiterate, weak, syphilitic, drunk, dishonest, drunk, incompetent, insubordinate, drunk, the British seaman was widely seen as "a mere drinking and working animal."[42] Who didn't know of the "drunken sailor," "half-seas over" or "three sheets in the wind"? Do-gooders and government alike sought to "improve the character of merchant seamen" with various pieces of "grandmotherly legislation" designed to make Jack (as British seamen were colloquially known) a better boy, like the prohibition of spirits on board and the establishment of a Seaman's Savings Bank to encourage better financial habits.[43]

The risks of poor seamanship were plain. Bad sailors compromised safety and reliability. Bad sailors jeopardized the nation's food supply, which depended on imports.[44] Bad sailors endangered national security, because merchant mariners were in effect the nation's naval reserve, to be drafted in case of war. Bad sailors gave Britain a bad name. "Our ships had been . . . pompously, styled the 'harbingers of peace, Christianity, and civilisation,'" smirked one shipowner, yet "more frequently carried with them to other lands vices previously unknown there."[45]

Harder to pin down was *why* sailors were unfit and what could be done about it. Some blamed changing technology. For generations, young people on Britain's coasts had picked up the rudiments of sailing on coasters like the one Conrad had worked on in Lowestoft in 1878. Twenty years later he fondly remembered the *Skimmer of the Seas* as a "good school for a seaman," its welcoming crew, all hands cousins and brothers, "each built as though to last for ever, and coloured like a Christmas card. Tan and pink—gold hair and blue eyes with that Northern straight-away-there look!"[46] But by then this "nursery for the British seaman" had been closed down by the rise of regional steamers.[47] The government tried to fill the gap by setting up special training ships: two for aspiring officers, and fifteen aimed at poor and delinquent youths, which had the knock-on effect of branding seafaring as "a general and recognised refuge for the destitute."[48]

A more obvious problem was that being a sailor simply didn't pay well. An able seaman setting out in 1880, as Conrad did, on a sailing ship from London to Australia, earned about fifty shillings per month plus food. He might get five or ten shillings per month more on a transatlantic route, and five to fifteen shillings more again on a transoceanic steamship, which was also more comfortable.[49] But if he worked as a coal hewer in Glasgow, or a spinner in a Huddersfield textile mill, he could earn at least twice the wages for a fraction of the working hours—and for all the notorious discomforts of factories and mines, on balance he'd have a better working environment, too.[50] Frankly, admitted the civil lord of the admiralty, "it would have been impossible to obtain men at such low wages, unless the imaginations of boys had been interested by the prospect of a distant travel" and the romantic allure of the sea.[51]

So who could be found to sail Britain's ships? The answer was foreigners like Konrad Korzeniowski. Seafarers' wages might be low by British standards, but they were higher than those on the Continent, and good sailors from poorer parts of Europe such as Scandinavia readily signed on. British captains were equally happy to hire them. One after another attested to foreigners' greater sobriety, competence, and obedience.[52] Over the decades Conrad worked at sea, the number of continental Europeans on British ships climbed from approximately 23,000 to more than 30,000, or about 20 percent of all crewmembers on all British ships. On long-haul sailing ships, which had the lowest wages and worst working conditions, the percentage of foreign sailors was substantially higher, topping 40 percent by 1891.[53] A parallel process on the Indian Ocean saw British ships increasingly manned at the lowest ranks by Asian sailors known as lascars, signed on under special "Asiatic Articles of Agreement."[54]

By the end of the century, it seemed that "scarcely a ship leaves London or any of our great ports without a very considerable percentage of her crew being 'Dutchmen'—the sailor's term for foreigners, of whatever nationality they may be. Swedes, Norwegians, Fins [sic], Danes, Frenchmen, Spaniards, are all Dutchmen to Jack."[55] Whereas other European maritime nations required that a high percentage of crewmembers be citizens (typically two thirds or three quarters, plus 100 percent of officers), Britain had no such quotas. In principle a British ship—owned, registered, and with a home port in Britain—could "be entirely officered and manned by persons not British."[56] Free market enthusiasts applauded. "If British sailors want to hold their own on board British ships they must take care to be not only equal to, but in all respects superior to the foreigner. It is simply a question of the survival of the fittest."[57]

But others feared that the solution to one manning problem just raised another. Foreign crews might be good for British ships, but were they good for Britain? Trade unionists argued that foreigners were taking British jobs and putting downward pressure on wages. They advocated quotas to protect British sailors from wage-cutting owners.[58] Their call was echoed by nativists concerned about national security. Inspired by the American maritime historian Alfred Thayer Mahan's 1890 book *The Influence of Sea Power upon History*, several rising industrial countries—Germany, the United States, Japan—started to build up their fleets, touching off a fresh round of soul-searching in Britain about naval preparedness. Some bemoaned "how insiduously [*sic*] the Asiatic ocean labourer is displacing the European at his own game," but at least lascars were "British subjects" and would (it was assumed) stay loyal to Britain in a war.[59] Not so "Dutchmen," especially Germans. "I want to see the mercantile marine purged of the foreigner," said the popular maritime writer Frank Bullen, "not because I hate the foreigner . . . , but because this peculiarly and particularly maritime nation of ours cannot afford, in the face of the undoubted hatred manifested toward it by practically every Continental people, to allow the life of its citizens to be dependent upon the good will of aliens."[60]

In 1894 a Parliamentary Select Committee convened to consider in detail how best to man British ships. For two years the committee visited ports all over the country and deposed 176 witnesses: union organizers, shipowners, underwriters, and sailors at every rank. Walking a fine line between the interests of labor (largely in favor of quotas) and management (largely against), they folded questions about the number of specifically *British* sailors into a broader query about whether there were enough crewmembers in the first place.

A typical witness was a master with sixteen years' experience in the British service who appeared before the committee at Whitehall in July 1894. Running down a list of the ships he'd served on, the committee wanted to know whether, in each case, he "consider[ed] that that vessel was sufficiently manned?" They invited the captain to elaborate on the appropriate number of crewmembers for a ship, but at no point did they ask him how many crewmembers were foreign, or how well, in his opinion, foreign seamen compared with native Britons. Perhaps it seemed

redundant. The witness was "Mr. J. Conrad Korzeniowski," and he'd
come a long way since landing in England in 1878.[61]

ON PAPER, the transformation of Ordinary Seaman Konrad Korzeniowski into Captain J. Conrad Korzeniowski, "a British seaman," was accomplished in a few simple certificates. In the British merchant marine,
unlike the Royal Navy, any ordinary seaman could move up the ranks to
master (captain) simply by fulfilling minimum service requirements and
passing the qualifying exams administered by the Board of Trade.[62] Conrad got his second mate's certificate in May 1880, his first mate's certificate in December 1884, and his master's certificate in November 1886—a
few months after he'd become a naturalized British subject.[63] Admittedly,
he had fudged his credentials to qualify for the second mate's exam,

Conrad's Certificate of Competency as Master, 1886.

making it look like he'd spent the requisite four years at sea when in fact he'd spent fewer than three. Admittedly, too, he'd passed the exams for first mate and master on the second try each. Still, it was a real accomplishment for someone who hadn't even spoken a word of English two years before he was first certified. "Long live the 'Ordin[ary] Master in the British Merchant Service!!'" Tadeusz Bobrowski cheered from Ukraine. "May he live long! May he be healthy and may every success attend him in every enterprise both on sea and on land!"[64]

Conrad had become, as he put it, "a Polish nobleman cased in British tar."[65] (A "tar," like a "salt," is slang for a sailor.) A photograph captured the officer at work. It was the early 1890s and he was first mate of the *Torrens*, a first-class-only passenger ship known for its swift, comfortable journeys to Australia and back. J. Conrad Korzeniowski, as he'd signed himself, stood on deck surrounded by the ship's apprentices: the cocky one, sprawling like a sports star; the gawky one, all ears; and the kid, tucked into a big, bright-buttoned coat. Sun leathered his cheeks, gray flecked his beard; he'd been sailing longer than some of them had been alive. He wore authority in a whistle around his neck and a peaked cap that made him look taller than he was. He tilted slightly to one side, as if he were pausing on his way to somewhere else.

First Mate Konrad Korzeniowski with the apprentices on board the Torrens, *ca. 1893.*

Once established in his second profession as a writer, Conrad looked back on his maritime career with justifiable pride. "I was conscientious, passing all the necessary examinations, winning the respect of people (in my modest milieu) who, certainly not out of sheer affection, attested to my being a 'good sailor and a trustworthy ship's officer,'" he wrote to a Polish friend. "Which, you must admit," he added, "was not bad for a foreigner without influence. That I never sought, and I have to give the English their due, they never made me feel a foreigner."[66]

But below the surface, rougher currents disturbed Korzeniowski's passage into Conrad. First there were the fights. In 1878, he'd fought with the captain of the ship that brought him to England and quit in a huff. On the *Duke of Sutherland* later that year, he complained that the crew took against him because he didn't speak good English. He judged the captain of his ship after that to be a "madman," and two ships later, on the *Palestine*, he grumbled about the quality of his job.[67] "Is it because being on a 'barque' touches on your honour?" wondered Tadeusz. "Then, of course, £4 a month is disrespectful to your pocket, and, finally, the captain seems to you to be merely a 'creature.'"[68] On the ship after the *Palestine* he quarreled so badly with the disagreeable, drunkard captain that he was dismissed in Madras in 1884 without a character reference.[69] Whatever the provocations, the frequency of his disputes suggested an itchy, bristling soul, loath to settle into place.

Then there was the problem of finding a job in the first place. Judged by tonnage statistics, a young man who joined the British merchant marine when Conrad did was entering an industry enjoying a historic boom. But from a sailor's point of view, the rise of steam mattered less than the fall of sail. Because steamships had so much more cargo capacity than sail, the total *number* of foreign-going ships was falling—by 30 percent, to be precise, over the time in which Conrad served—even as the Board of Trade minted 1,600 fresh officers every year looking for work.[70] Conrad recalled the frustration of "trying to get an officer's berth with nothing much to show but a brand-new certificate. It is surprising how useless you find that piece of ass's skin that you have been putting yourself in such a state about."[71]

Even with the relative fortune of an allowance from Uncle Tadeusz to tide him over between berths, Conrad had hardly been immune to the stress of a tightening job market.[72] In the summer of 1881, he'd again spent through his allowance. He could hear Tadeusz's recriminations. *Find yourself some occupation and earn some money, for you won't get a penny from me.* This time he didn't point a gun at his chest; he took up his pen and spun an elaborate lie. Conrad told Tadeusz that he'd joined a ship called the *Annie Frost*, that it got wrecked, that he lost all his belongings, that he was hospitalized, that the owners refused to pay compensation—and, therefore, that he needed money. Conrad's first foray into fiction paid off. Tadeusz sent him £10 and a warning about wise spending.[73] As if in cosmic quid pro quo, Conrad actually *was* wrecked on his next ship, the *Palestine*.

The plum berths, with the highest wages and best working conditions, were on steamers instead of sailing ships, passenger ships instead of cargo ships, Atlantic crossings instead of weeks'-long hauls across the Pacific or Indian oceans. These usually went to men who had personal ties to owners, charterers, and captains. If, like Conrad, you were a foreigner "with no connexions, contacts, or influential friends," you relied on chance, word of mouth, and more or less dubious brokers like William Sutherland, Conrad's agent, who was prosecuted several times for procuring apprentices without a license.[74] You might have to wait many months onshore, wageless, before you could find another job. You usually had to take jobs below your certified rank, and Conrad almost always did; he captained a ship only once.[75] When you did get berths, they were usually on those long-distance sailing ships, where your crewmates were disproportionately foreigners like you. Fully a third of Conrad's shipmates on British ships were not British.[76] Only in 1894 did

Conrad manage to break into the most sought-after class of ship—a transatlantic steamer—but it wasn't much of an achievement. Although a certified captain, he had to accept the lowly position of second mate, and the *Adowa* was far from a crack British liner. Chartered to carry French emigrants from Rouen to Quebec, its voyage was aborted when it turned out nobody wished to go.[77] Conrad would never work as a sailor again.

Conrad belonged to the last generation of seafarers who worked primarily on sailing ships, and as he navigated the changing labor market, he came to share with his peers the sense that sail and steam represented more than different technologies. They marked different ways of life. Steamships needed engineers in place of sailmakers; firemen who shoveled coal into boilers belowdecks in place of nimble sailors mending rigging high above.[78] Men trained up in sail worried they might (in the words of one of Conrad's characters) have "to chuck going to sea forever and go in a steamer"—because going on a steamship wasn't truly going to sea.[79]

By the early 1900s, maritime authors were writing about the receding age of sail in the sad but fond tones you might use to recall a beloved grandmother. Sensing a commercial opportunity, in 1904 a cash-strapped Conrad started writing a series of meditations-cum-reminiscences about sailing ships, eventually published in 1906 as *The Mirror of the Sea*. He described the book as "a record of a phase, now nearly vanished, of a certain kind of activity, sympathetic to the inhabitants of this Island."[80] Its elegiac tone moved some readers to tears.[81]

Yet for all that he tried to capitalize on the market for sea stories, Conrad always resisted being shut up in a box of genre fiction. Stories set at sea were, for him, stories about life. *The Mirror of the Sea* "is not the sort of book a professed sea-writer would produce," he insisted to his agent. "Even the general public may take to it, for, its interest is not exclusively maritime but largely human."[82] Conrad described sailing vessels as "the aristocracy of ships," operated by skilled artisans, the aristocrats of labor (and in his case, a Polish nobleman cased in British tar).[83] Sailing ships fostered community anchored in shared values of loyalty, determination, courage, and commitment. Sailing ships represented a distinctive—and distinctively British—sense of ethics. Their disappearance marked a moment of profound human, social, and moral significance.

Many of the essays in *The Mirror of the Sea* use metaphor to link aspects of maritime practice to the human condition. "Landfall and Departure," the terms for a voyage's end and beginning, stand in for birth and death. Anchors, associated with stability and homecoming, are "Emblems of Hope." A sailing ship is an ethereal construction of "Cobwebs and Gossamer," and sailing it is "The Fine Art." In his purplest patches, Conrad portrayed the sailing ship as the one place in nature where humans brushed up against the supernatural. A wind-powered ship "seems to draw its strength from the very soul of the world," and glides "mysteriously into a sort of unearthly existence, bordering upon the magic of invisible forces."[84]

But it took more than magic to sail; it took human skill. A sailing ship was, for Conrad, a "craft" in the full sense of the word. To sail it required the ability to observe, interpret, and harness nature. It called for experience, training, courage, perception, creativity, adaptability, and judgment.[85] "The taking of a modern steamship about the world . . . has not the same quality of intimacy with nature," Conrad explained. "It has no great moments of self-confidence, or moments not less great of doubt and heart-searching." It "has not the artistic quality of a single-handed struggle with something much greater than yourself; it is not the laborious, absorbing practice of an art whose ultimate result remains on the knees of the gods."[86]

It's no coincidence that Conrad, a sailor turned writer, characterized sailing as a form of art. Or that the closest thing he ever wrote to a literary manifesto came as a preface to the only book he ever wrote about ordinary seamen "before the mast" (not officers, who berthed aft), *The Nigger of the 'Narcissus.'* In the preface, Conrad described his artistic purpose as trying to awaken "an unavoidable feeling of solidarity" among his readers.[87] The novel represented the ideal sailing ship as a crucible of solidarity—as, literally, a "fellowship." Conrad spoke often of the "fellowship of the craft" forged among men under sail.[88] That they were all men went almost without saying. He countered hints of homosexuality by presenting sailors like the many husbands of a single wife, joined in love for their ship. A ship was always a "she." And because "a ship, though she has female attributes and is loved very unreasonably, is different from a woman," their love for her remained chaste, pure, and safe.[89]

The fellowship's members were ordinary men "who knew toil, privation, violence, debauchery—but knew not fear, and had no desire or spite in their hearts. Men hard to manage, but easy to inspire; voiceless men—but men enough to scorn in their hearts the sentimental voices that bewailed the hardness of their fate."[90] Its dissidents were men like a rabble-rousing malcontent on the fictional *Narcissus*, "the man that cannot steer, that cannot splice, that dodges the work on dark nights. . . . The man who can't do most things and won't do the rest." This kind of man "knows all about his rights, but knows nothing . . . of the unspoken loyalty that knits together a ship's company."[91] Conrad's contempt echoed an enduring distaste for organized labor and radical politics. "Where's the man to stop the rush of social-democratic ideas?" he'd railed in 1885. "England was the only barrier to the pressure of infernal doctrines born in continental back-slums. Now, there is nothing!"[92]

No sailors embodied Conrad's "fellowship of the craft" better than the British. Conrad first invoked this phrase in the short story "Youth," which opens: "This could have occurred nowhere but in England, where men and sea interpenetrate, so to speak—the sea entering into the life of most men, and the men knowing something or everything about the sea."[93] Based on his 1881–83 service as second mate of the *Palestine*, "Youth," Conrad insisted, was barely even fiction but "a feat of memory," "a record of experience."[94] So it was notable that one of the changes Conrad *did* make to the *Palestine* for its fictional counterpart, the *Judea*, was to replace the typically international crew of the *Palestine*—Cornish, Irish, Dutch, Norwegian, West Indian, and Australian—with a crew of "hard cases," "all complete from Liverpool."[95] Whereas the second mate of the *Palestine* was the Polish Konrad Korzeniowski, the role of second mate and narrator on the *Judea* was played by the thoroughly English Charles Marlow, making his first of several appearances in Conrad's fiction.

"To an onlooker they would be a lot of profane scallywags without a redeeming point," Marlow said of his men, but "that crew of Liverpool hard cases had in them the right stuff." They got put to the test when the ship, loaded with coal, spontaneously combusted at sea. Marlow ordered the men to climb the scorching masts and furl the sails. "What made them do it—what made them obey me?" he wondered, when they knew the masts might collapse at any moment? "It wasn't a sense of duty; they all knew well enough how to shirk, and laze, and dodge. . . . Was it the two pounds ten a-month that sent them there? They didn't think their pay half good enough. No; it was something in them, something inborn and subtle and everlasting. I don't say positively that the crew of a French or German merchantman wouldn't have done it, but I doubt whether it would have been done in the same way." *This*, this readiness to sacrifice oneself to a bigger cause, "this could have occurred nowhere but in England." This was the "hidden something," Marlow decided, "that makes racial difference, that shapes the fate of nations."[96] Though Conrad defined "racial difference" as often by ethnicity (Anglo-Saxon, Slavic, etc.) as by skin color, he didn't have to note that sail was, literally if not figuratively, white. Two decades later, almost precisely the same words would turn up in a piece of propaganda Conrad wrote for the Admiralty about the merchant service in the Great War.[97]

Conrad sealed the associations of Britain with sail—and whiteness—at the end of *The Nigger of the 'Narcissus.'* (Whose very title played crudely on black and white; it was initially published in the United States as *The Children of the Sea* to avoid offense.) The book described a crew making a homeward voyage from Asia, whose solidarity got disrupted by the illness—or malingering, many of them suspect—of a West Indian crewmember. Just as the *Narcissus* approached home waters, the West Indian died, a slap of truth in the face of men who'd believed him to be lying. "His death, like the death of an old belief, shook the foundations of our society. A common bond was gone; the strong, effective and respectable bond of a sentimental lie." In that vulnerable moment, their fellowship broken, their patience strained by the long voyage home, the sailors saw Britain itself rising from the waves "like a mighty ship bestarred with vigilant lights." "She towered up immense and strong, guarding priceless traditions and untold suffering, sheltering glorious memories and base forgetfulness, ignoble virtues and splendid transgressions. A great ship! . . . A ship mother of fleets and nations! The great flagship of the race, stronger than the storms! and anchored in the open sea."[98] "Towering" and a bastion of "tradition," this mother ship—this mother country—can be nothing other than a sailing ship, folding up her subjects into nurturing community.

Sail spelled craft. Sail spelled fellowship. Sail spelled Britishness in relation to Europe, whiteness in relation to Asians and blacks. Sail, for Conrad, spelled the best of a world that worked against it, the ideal to be constantly sought if never regained. All these associations explain why, when Conrad wanted to reiterate his attachment to Britain against the critics of *The Secret Agent*, he did so by writing about his career as a sailor in *A Personal Record*. They explain why he crafted a story of his "deliberate choice" to be "a British seaman and no other," in a merchant marine that was in truth less "British" than ever before. And they explain why Conrad made a point, in *A Personal Record*, of stressing a personal attachment to sail in the face of the apparent attractions of steam.

It comes in a long account of his Board of Trade master's exam in 1886, which as a literary device let him demonstrate his command of the craft anew, this time to his reader. (He didn't mention the two times he'd failed his exams.) He described walking up Tower Hill for the test, steeled for his toughest interrogation yet. The rooms were fitted with "paraphernalia of models of ships and tackle, a board for signals on the wall" and "an unrigged mast fixed to the edge" of a table.[99] A chubby, gray-whiskered captain greeted him.

"Let's see. H'm," the examiner began. "Suppose you tell me all you know about charter parties."[100] Conrad thought back to his books. Charter party: "A written contract by which a ship is let and hired for one or more voyages."[101]

"What's your idea of a jury-rudder now?" Conrad had never lost a rudder at sea, but he'd memorized some examples. Start by "tak[ing] sail off the ship" to slow her down. Then rig up a temporary rudder using a spare spar. "One end of a spar should be suspended by a chain down the rudder trunk . . . and the other should have a blade like an oar; weights attached to sink it, a tackle to trice it up . . . , and guys to lead through blocks at the end of the spar across the stern, and thence to the barrel of the wheel."[102]

They ranged over the fine points of ship management, and the examiner reminisced about his adventures "before you were born."

"You are of Polish extraction," the captain observed.

"Born there, sir."

"Not many of your nationality in our service, I should think. . . . An inland people, aren't you?"

"Yes—very much so."[103]

"I don't know what may be your plans," the examiner concluded, "but you ought to go into steam. When a man has his master's certificate it's the proper time. If I were you I would go into steam."[104]

Conrad left the room, he said, sobered by his achievement. "It was a fact, I said to myself, that I was now a British master mariner beyond a doubt. . . . It was an answer to certain outspoken scepticism and even to some not very kind aspersions." He'd crowned his boyhood dreams with success. What next? "You must understand that there was no idea of any sort of 'career' in my call," Conrad assured the reader.[105] Such an unromantic concept that was, not to mention déclassé. If being a certified master meant embracing a professional career as a sailor, and if a career meant going into steam, then it must be time for him to do something else.

That, Conrad explained, was why "I never went into steam—not really. If I only live long enough I shall become a bizarre relic of a dead barbarism, a sort of monstrous antiquity, the only seaman of the dark ages who had never gone into steam—not really."[106] The transition from sail to steam, as he put it, marked his turn from youth to adulthood. It turned him from a sailor into a writer.

It made for tidy rhetoric, but misleading history. Declaring that "I never went into steam—not really," Conrad implied that he turned his back on steam by choice. In point of fact, given the difficulties of finding berths, it might be more accurate to say that steam, at least on state-of-the-art British liners, eschewed him.

And then there was the biographical truth. For after passing his master's exam Conrad *did* go into steam, first in Asia, then in Africa, and he did so as a conscious choice. But if the British sailing ship represented the human, social, and ethical forms he admired most, he'd navigate muddier waters in the steamer's wake.

——— · ———

FIVE

GOING INTO STEAM

KONRAD FOUND AMSTERDAM in February 1887 clutched by a deep freeze. Ice locked the canals. Ships waited for their trapped cargo "like corpses of black vessels in a white world." The captain of the *Highland Forest* hadn't yet arrived, so Konrad was temporarily in charge. He slept on board under a heavy mound of blankets. During the days he took a tram into the city center and settled into the red plush seats of a "gorgeous café," with sparkling gilt ceilings and electric lights. He posted updates to the shipowners in Glasgow, and almost every day got a letter back, "directing me to go to the charterers and clamor for the ship's cargo; . . . to demand that this assortment of varied merchandise, set fast in a land-scape of ice and windmills somewhere up-country, should be put on rail instantly, and fed up to the ship in regular quantities every day." He dutifully called on the charterer, a Mr. Hudig, but before Konrad could start his harangue, the Dutchman silenced him with a good cigar, a roaring fire, and fluent English conversation about the weather.[1]

The ice broke. Barges and schuyts slid down silt-clouded channels bearing cotton goods and provisions for the East Indies. One of a first mate's key responsibilities was to superintend the loading. Each item had to be protected during its long voyage into hot seas, and the cargo as a whole had to be balanced for a safe and speedy passage. Load the weight too high and the ship would get "crank," rolling heavily and running the risk of oversetting under sail; load the weight too low and the ship would grow "stiff," jerking and juddering, and putting too much strain on the masts, rigging, and spars. Konrad knew that every ship had distinctive quirks, but he didn't know the *Highland Forest*, so he loaded it by the book, Robert White Stevens's *On the Stowage of Ships and Their Cargoes.* Wheels of cheese should be "packed in cases with partitions between" and "should not be stowed more than two deep." Beer in bottles should go in the forward, cooler part of the ship; beer in casks should be kept away from anything that might heat it up, to avoid further fermentation. Fabric bales "should be stowed on their *flats* in midships, and on their *edges* in the wings." Oats "should be closely packed, or considerable freightage will be lost; they are usually trodden down by foot."[2]

He'd just finished loading when Captain John McWhir arrived to take command. An Irishman four years older than Konrad, he had captained the *Highland Forest* twice before, and knew her to be an "uncommonly ticklish jade to load." The captain paced up and down the quay studying how she sat in the water. "You have got her pretty well in her fore-and-after trim," said McWhir to his new mate. "Now what about your weights?" Konrad explained that he'd put a third of the cargo near the top of the hold, "above the beams," and two thirds below—per textbook advice.

"Phew!" whistled McWhir. The *Highland Forest* tended toward stiffness, so it needed a lot more cargo stowed high than Konrad had allowed. But it was too late to change anything. "Well," the captain said, chortling, "we shall have a lively time of it this passage, I bet."

They pitched and rolled all the way to Java. Konrad had never experienced anything like it. "Once she began" to roll, "you felt she would never stop. . . . There were days . . . when there was no position where you could fix yourself so as not to feel a constant strain upon all the muscles of your body." They rolled through their work. "Let the blamed hooker knock my brains out if she likes," cursed a crewmember struggling to keep his balance. They rolled at their meals. "That's your one-third above the beams," groaned McWhir, clutching the table for stability. They rolled in their sleep. Spars began to crack and break. "It was only poetic justice" that one spar, flying from the high rigging, struck Konrad hard on the back and flung him across the deck.[3] Sciatic stabs shot down his legs; his dorsal muscles went rubbery.[4] When they reached Semarang, on the Java coast, a European doctor advised him to sign off and recuperate. He nipped across the narrow Strait of Malacca to Singapore and checked into the European hospital.

On bad days in bed he felt hot, damp, hurt, disgruntled. This was supposed to have been a good year. Naturalized a British subject. Certified master in the merchant marine. A new pastime, too. During twelve years at sea he'd stowed away a pile of stories, and when he saw that the magazine *Tit-Bits* ran a competition for stories by sailors, he'd tried his hand at writing one down.[5]

What good was any of it? He was "sick and tired of sailing about for little money and less consideration."[6] He'd kept at this profession for longer than any of his family might have expected, won all the right credentials, and just when it seemed that he had found "the right road" and could "stand on [his] own feet"—*thwack*. "Pas de chance."[7] The Board of Trade examiner advised him to go into steam, but he couldn't get a good berth. His uncle Tadeusz advised him to go into business, but he couldn't save any money. He was a certified master who couldn't find a captaincy, a veteran seaman injured on his own ship, an out-of-work invalid stranded thousands of miles from his soi-disant home. He asked himself: What next?[8]

On better days, Konrad limped around the hospital garden. The hospital was on a hill and he could see straight down into the harbor, scattered with ships "like toys" on a knotted rug.[9] Islands pinched from the sea, the start of an archipelago that reached almost to Australia. "I love the sea," he remembered in these moments. "I love the sea, and if I could just clear my bare living . . . I should be comparatively happy."[10]

When he could walk again with comfort, Konrad checked out of the hospital and ambled down the hill into town. He had been to Singapore before, twice, but on both his past visits he'd stuck close to the Sailors' Home, a bungalow in a "curiously suburban-looking garden," superintended by a sanctimonious temperance campaigner in an office stuffed as full of horsehair furniture and lace as a "respectable parlour in the East End of London."[11] You'd scarcely know you were in Asia but for the Chinese servant halfheartedly flapping a punkah in the living room.[12]

Now he strolled through the city center under the eaves of interlocking shophouses. Their shuttered faces were like the tropical version of the

A Singapore street.

Islington terraces he'd left behind. He passed lintels signed in Chinese and bobbing with red lanterns: teahouses, bankers, tinkers, tailors. Sailors tumbled out of crudely signed taverns, "The Silver Anker" and "The Original Madras Bob." He looked into the forecourt of a Taoist temple hazed in incense; he glimpsed the pea-green minarets of a mosque. Chinese rickshaw pullers trotted past him, and Tamil bearers balanced parcels on their turbans. Here and there he saw a spectral European sheathed in white, from pith helmet down to pipe-clayed shoes.[13] The onion stink of durians followed Konrad down the street.[14]

Arriving at the riverfront, he sized up the stocky profile of British power. The Harbor Office, Post Office, and the Flint Buildings, with its warren of offices, lined the embankment, stout and overdressed in the heat. An iron suspension bridge straddled the canalized river like a policeman with his hands on his hips.

Konrad looked down into the river's inner harbor.[15] Junks with pleated fins of sail, ketch-rigged fishing boats, broad-beamed lighters topped

Boat Quay, on the Singapore River.

with lean-tos, tusk-shaped *perahus* curling from the water with painted eyes that peered over the waterline.[16] Konrad didn't know the names for all these vessels, or the places from which they came, but he could recognize the variety and the promise of a unique maritime world.

MIDWAY BETWEEN INDIA AND CHINA, on the hinge of the Malay Peninsula and Archipelago, Singapore looked geographically predestined to be a cultural crossroads.[17] More Malay than Hong Kong, more Indian than Batavia (Jakarta), more Chinese than Calcutta, more European than Bangkok, it seemed to Westerners the very embodiment of "the East." "Nowhere else can such a mixture of races be seen," said the steel magnate Andrew Carnegie, who spent ten days there in 1879: "one-half . . . Chinese, the remainder Malays, Klings, Javanese, Hindoos, and every other eastern race under the sun, I believe, and a few Europeans. Here the 'survival of the fittest' is being fought out under the protection of the British flag." (Carnegie judged it "only a question of time when the Chinese will drive every other race to the wall.")[18] Conrad always remembered "the brown, bronze, yellow faces, the black eyes, the glitter, the color of an Eastern crowd."[19]

But Singapore's "eastern" blend was in large part the result of European technology and empire. The city had been founded in 1819 by the British East India Company agent Stamford Raffles to break into a market then dominated by the Dutch. To undercut competitors, Raffles designated Singapore a free port, with no tariffs or trade restrictions. That made it a magnet for diasporic populations who had long linked the coasts of the Indian Ocean as merchants and migrants, including Fujians from China, Tamils from south India, Arabs from Hadramawt (in present-day Yemen), and Bugis from the Malay Archipelago.

"The piercing of the Isthmus of Suez," Conrad later wrote, "like the breaking of a dam, had let in upon the East a flood of new ships, new

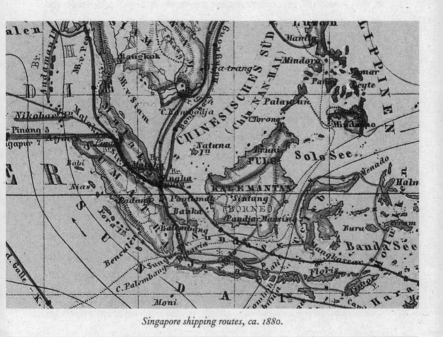

Singapore shipping routes, ca. 1880.

men, new methods of trade."[20] Between 1870 and 1890 the value of exports and imports passing through Singapore nearly tripled.[21] British, Dutch, French, Austrian, and Spanish shipping companies all set up agencies there, of which by far the largest was the British India Steam Navigation Company, which had fifty-seven steamers operating on seventeen different routes.[22] They made Singapore, as an American visitor put it in 1885, into "the great central ganglion of the Malay Archipelago and Southeastern Asia, the hub of the Far East. The spokes are steamship lines running in almost every direction, to Bangkok, Saigon, China and Japan, Manilla, Sarawak, Pontianak, Batavia, Sumatra, Ceylon, Calcutta, Rangoon, and Malacca."[23]

Few ports east of Suez grew so much so fast, and the reason, paradoxically, had to do with a technological limitation. Only steamships could effectively use the canal, but the cost of coal meant that steamers couldn't yet compete with sail on routes longer than 3,500 miles. (One reason Konrad Korzeniowski traveled so often to Australia in the 1870s and 1880s was that, throughout his twenty years at sea, this route remained more cost-effective for sail than for steam.)[24] From northern Europe that meant a steamship could cross the Atlantic or do a circuit around the Mediterranean. From Singapore, the radius of steam encompassed China, India, and the whole of the East Indies, some of the richest trade routes in the world. Singapore boomed as an entrepôt. Half of everything that arrived in the city got off-loaded and put onto different vessels for regional delivery.[25]

Around the "spokes" of long-distance trade, dominated by European firms, turned fleets of small steamers owned by Singapore's Arab and Chinese shippers. In addition to calling at the lesser ports of the Malay Archipelago, they served burgeoning regional passenger markets. The Al Sagoff family, who owned the Singapore Steam Ship Company, the largest local company of the 1880s, acted as brokers for the annual pilgrim traffic to Mecca. Several Chinese shipowners, foremost the Fujian merchant Wee Bin, catered to the booming "coolie trade" in Chinese labor.[26]

The high number of steamers made Singapore a popular spot for mates hoping to rack up experience toward their master's exams—and for Konrad Korzeniowski to find himself a ship.[27] Even with "twice as many men as there are berths going in the local trade," there was less competition for officers' jobs than in Britain, where Konrad had never yet found work at his own rank.[28] What one engineer remembered as a "'hail fellow well met' feeling throughout the whole community of Singapore" made it easy to find out about job opportunities. You might hear about something while you were staying in the Sailors' Home, or over a drink at Emmerson's Tiffin Rooms on the riverfront, "a regular haunt of all and sundry." Or you could just stop by the Harbor Office, a few doors down, the port's central clearinghouse for shipping, and speak to the master attendant Henry Ellis, an Irishman with a fierce sense of self-importance.

On August 22, 1887, a few weeks after he left the hospital, Konrad signed on as the first mate of a 206-ton steamer named the SS *Vidar*. He found the ship berthed at the Tanjong Pagar docks, a squared-off compound of warehouses, coal sheds, and workshops. Sampans and *tongkangs* flitted around the harbor, ferrying goods and people. Coolies streamed in and out of holds; bullock carts heaped with jute sacks lumbered toward town.[29]

The *Vidar* was a British ship insofar as it was built in Tyneside and flew the Red Ensign, but in Konrad's eyes it was "an Eastern ship," too. The owner was a Hadrami Arab called Syed Mohsin bin Salleh al Joof-free, who in his heyday had been one of the richest men in Singapore, with offices in Aden, Jeddah, and Suez.[30] Though now in his seventies, losing his sight and much of his fortune, the "excellent (and picturesque) Arab owner" still commanded respect when he appeared on the quayside, as Konrad would later describe him, "in a snowy robe and yellow

slippers . . . having his hand fiercely kissed by a crowd of Malay pilgrims."
The British turned to Arabs like al Jooffree as go-betweens with the Malay Muslim community, and Konrad judged the shipowner in turn to be
"as loyal a subject of the complex British Empire as you could find east of
the Suez Canal."[31]

Konrad shared the officers' mess with three other Europeans: Captain
James Craig, and engineers James Allen and John Niven, presumably
Scots, like nearly all engineers in the Straits. The ship's thirteen crewmembers were all Asian lascars.[32] European officers tended to rate lascars
by ethnicity. "The best combination I have found to be: Chinese on deck
and as cooks & stewards; Indians in the stoke hole and Malays or Philip-
pinos as quartermasters," pronounced one officer, making the ship into a
microcosm of divide and rule.[33] As a white officer in Asia, Konrad belonged to a minority privileged by race as well as rank. But as a foreigner
on British ships he also knew what it was like not to speak the same language as his officers and shipmates. On board the *Vidar* he picked up
some Malay, to facilitate basic communication with the Malay crew.[34]

The *Vidar* ran a roughly four-week circuit around small ports in Borneo and Sulawesi—the sort of route only a steamship could effectively ply,
nearly oblivious to winds and river currents.[35] The *Vidar* steamed out from
the humid embrace of Singapore harbor and into the South China Sea.

To a sailor, these waters connoted one thing: pirates. They floated out
of coves on Borneo's northern coast, they cruised from the inlets of Sulawesi, they sailed south from the Sulu islands. The British and Dutch
used piracy as a lever against the sultans, forcing them to sign treaties
banning the practice, and then intervening when they didn't. British,
Dutch, and Spanish naval expeditions and patrols had reduced the danger,
but piracy remained too live a threat to have yet become innocent fodder
for storybooks.

The *Vidar*'s first port of call was at Banjarmasin on the southern
coast of Borneo. It was Konrad's first look at a place he'd known only

from books and maps. The size of Britain and France combined, Borneo was populated by dozens of indigenous ethnic groups, called Dayaks; ruled by Malay Muslim sultans ("Borneo" is a corruption of the name of the one sultanate that's still a sovereign state, Brunei); and divided into spheres of influence by British and Dutch agents eager for a piece of the island's economy.[36] It made Borneo into a morass of rebellions, wars of succession, and border squabbles. It also made it a great place for free-booters and smugglers looking for a way to get ahead.

Whatever Konrad knew about Borneo he probably knew from reading about James Brooke, the most famous Briton to make a mark in the islands.[37] In the late 1830s, Brooke had bought himself a schooner and sailed to Southeast Asia looking for a chance to become rich and famous, like his hero Stamford Raffles. He found it in the region of Sarawak, on the northwestern edge of Borneo, where a rebellion threatened to unseat the sultan of Brunei. Brooke helped reinstate the sultan, and was rewarded in 1842 with the title of rajah (king) of Sarawak. As Sarawak's "white rajah," Brooke aimed to "civilize" Sarawak along British lines by stamping out the traditional Dayak practice of head-hunting and by cracking down on the notorious pirates. Brooke recruited Chinese immigrants to mine gold, Anglican missionaries to cultivate souls, and his own English nephews to shore up his personal authority. Though he ultimately didn't achieve his lifelong dream, to transfer Sarawak to Britain as a protectorate, he set up a dynasty instead, and was succeeded as rajah by his nephew Charles in 1868.

The *Vidar* stopped for coal and continued up the Makassar Strait between Borneo and Sulawesi, bound for the port of Donggala. In these narrow waters piracy intersected with smuggling and another illicit practice: slave trading. The Dutch had banned slavery in their colonies in 1863, but unfree labor of various forms remained widespread along the *Vidar*'s route.[38] Sulu pirates seized captives on coastal raids extending from New Guinea to the Philippines and brought them to the East Indies for sale.[39] "The liveliest trader in slaves must be in Donggala"—the *Vidar*'s port of call—reported the Dutch consul general in Singapore. From there "the majority" of slaves were "taken across to the North-East Coast of Borneo." Some would be put to hard labor diving for pearls, mining coal, or collecting jungle produce (birds' nests, wax, and gutta-percha). Others were sold to inland Dayak tribes and met a more sinister fate. The Dayaks tied them up, wrapped them in cloth, and stabbed them to death with spears, as human sacrifices in mourning rituals.[40]

As the British and Dutch tussled for moral and material ascendancy in the East Indies, the British prided themselves on their commitment to fighting piracy and slavery, and accused the Dutch of not doing enough to stop the slave trade. But the Dutch saw things differently. The Dutch consul listed ten different British-flagged steamships involved in illegal gunrunning and slave trading out of Donggala—and one ship most of all. "This transport is almost exclusively carried out at the moment by the SS *Vidar* sailing under the English flag."[41]

It fell to Konrad, as first mate, to supervise the loading and unloading of passengers and cargo from the *Vidar*. He filled out bills of lading stamped with the company's green and red flag, specifying consignments and freight charges, to be countersigned by recipients upon delivery. Ten bags of dates from Singapore to Pulau Laut, fifty-eight bags of resin from Donggala to Singapore: ten dollars, forty dollars; Arabic script and Chinese.[42]

On a sailing ship, as he'd found to his peril on the *Highland Forest*, stowage was a high-risk business requiring care, calculation, and skill. "The modern steamship," he later claimed, was loaded in "a clatter and hurry and racket and heat, in a cloud of steam and a mess of coal-dust."[43] That implied a first mate of a steamship wouldn't have known too much about what was actually getting put into the hold, and *that* implied that, as first mate of the steamship *Vidar*, Konrad may not have known about its contraband cargo of guns and slaves. But he obviously did know

Bill of lading from the SS Vidar.

enough about what the *Vidar* carried to admit, in 1897, that "as late as 1888 arms have been landed on the coast of that island [Borneo]—that to my personal knowledge."[44] As to the slaves—"registered . . . on board" with the harbormaster's collusion "as passengers or servants of passengers"—Konrad said nothing so direct. But he tipped his hand in fiction that portrayed a Malay society permeated by slavery, alongside white characters who appeared largely oblivious to it.[45]

Guns, gunpowder, and slaves hidden among rice, rattan, and passengers, the *Vidar* sailed up the Makassar Strait between Sulawesi and Borneo. Mile upon mile the Borneo coast unspooled alongside them like a frayed green rope. Here and there, rivers cracked the wilderness into "several clean shining fractures." Rivers were lifelines through Borneo's dense forests and mountains, and many of the larger towns lay tucked inside their mouths, some thirty or forty miles upstream. A few days' sail

A river in Borneo in Conrad's time.

out of Donggala, the *Vidar* entered the Berau River to call at the port of Tanjung Redeb. The boat steamed "on through a brown liquid, three parts water and one part black earth, on and on between the low shores, three parts black earth and one part brackish water."[46] The sea receded, the land closed in, the mud thickened, and a kampong (village) climbed out of the river on bamboo poles, supporting rows of houses huddled over the water. Fog slung moist arms around the town's shoulders. Wet, black forest scratched it back. The *Vidar* wheezed to a stop at a rickety jetty.[47]

Estuaries are liminal spaces, between the river and the sea, and up the estuaries of Borneo Konrad encountered liminal figures, living between cultures: a European or two among Asians, clusters of Arabs or Chinese among Malays, refugees from other islands, and "half-castes" of mixed descent. In Berau the *Vidar* traveled in the wake of a British sea captain named William Lingard, whose influence lingered over the settlement.

Lingard had traded in the area for some years when, like James Brooke in Sarawak, he helped the local sultan defeat a rival in a naval battle. The sultan rewarded Lingard in 1862 with the title of Rajah Laut—"King of the Sea"—a grant of land for a trading post in Berau, and an honorific title for his "native housekeeper," a term usually used for a nonwhite wife.

Lingard's frequent appearances "in public in the dress of a native ruler" and his "large influence on the Sultan" worried the Dutch assistant resident in Berau, who "saw in him a second James Brooke."[48] On closer inspection, though, the Dutch realized that the British Lingard wasn't a threat to imperial interests. He just wanted to build his business. Lingard purchased two ships that he used for trade between Singapore and his Berau hideaway. As an old-school mariner, Lingard wanted no part of "a damn steamer instead of the good old sailing-ships." It was the *Vidar*, not the Dutch, that proved to be his nemesis. Lingard's resistance to steam provided an opening to Syed Mohsin al Jooffree, the owner of the *Vidar*. The *Vidar* began calling at Berau in the 1870s, and its speed and regularity gave it the advantage over Lingard's sailing ships. By 1885, Lingard had sold them both off.[49]

On the jetty at Berau in 1887, Konrad met a man who came to embody for him the unexpected cultural convergences of the backwaters. Charles Olmeijer, a Dutchman born in Java, had been Lingard's agent in Berau for nearly twenty years; he'd been joined there in 1876 by Lingard's teenage nephew Jim. For a time Olmeijer had flourished as a local tycoon, but by 1887 the firm's commercial clout had diminished substantially, displaced by the *Vidar*. Olmeijer represented a declining form of commerce, pushed out by steam, and his influence with the Berau sultans had accordingly dwindled. He sought Dutch government permits to go into mining and pearl fishing instead, for which he was eligible as a Dutch subject, unlike his English boss Lingard. But the Dutch colonial government wouldn't grant permits without the approval of the local sultans, and the sultans wouldn't help Olmeijer because he'd lost his economic significance to them, so he found himself trapped between governments, trapped in obsolescence.[50]

However true Konrad was to memory, let alone life, he later described Olmeijer as a tragicomic personification of a misbegotten European notion of "progress." Konrad had heard about Olmeijer at every stop on the *Vidar*'s route, he said, and arrived in Berau excited to meet a man of some importance. The personage he saw shuffling toward the jetty in flimsy pajamas couldn't even pull off faded grandeur, only delusions thereof. Olmeijer had come up to the ship to supervise the unloading of a pony he had ordered from Bali. Konrad couldn't fathom why he had bought the animal, given that "in the whole settlement at which he used to shake daily his impotent fist there was only one path" a pony could feasibly use, and Olmeijer certainly didn't look able to ride him. The best Konrad could figure was that his "ambitious, aiming at the grandiose" purchase played some part in a "hopeful intrigue" to restore his fortunes. The crew strapped the pony into a canvas sling and swung it off the boat with the cargo crane. The moment the horse touched ground, it bolted into the jungle.[51]

Steaming back down the rivers of Borneo, fog dropping behind it, the *Vidar* struck salt water and set course back to Singapore. To come back into the city was to return to a straight-edged, well-ordered world. The *Vidar* docked in a long line of ships holding other goods, other stories. Here was the *Nanshan*, a steamer bringing Chinese coolies from Shantou. There was the *Ranee*, the sole vessel belonging to the Sarawak Steamship Company, arrived from Kuching. Here was the *Sissie*, the steamship that had carried Konrad into Singapore for the first time in 1883, after the wreck of the *Palestine*. There was the *Tilkhurst*, a clipper rig rising above the steam funnels, on which he had come to Singapore the second time, in 1885.[52] And that ship over there was the SS *Celestial*, also on the Dutch consul's list of suspected smugglers, the ship Konrad had taken from

Johnston Quay, Singapore.

Semarang to Singapore the previous month. He "chummed with" its chief officer, a son-in-law of William Lingard, at Emmerson's Tiffin Rooms.[53]

While serving as first mate of the *Vidar*, Konrad Korzeniowski turned thirty, and 1887 turned into 1888. The *Vidar* turned from Banjarmasin to Pulau Laut, Donggala to Berau, Bulungan to Singapore, and back to Banjarmasin and Bulungan and back. Month by month, round on round, from a revelation, to an acquaintance, to a habit. One day Conrad would write about an aging captain "who had served famous firms, who had sailed famous ships . . . who had made famous passages," but now commanded a dinky old steamer like this, on a "monotonous huckster's round, up and down the Straits."

Monotony was that fictional captain's salvation, for secretly he was going blind. He could hide it because he knew the route so well, and when necessary, he could ask his Serang (mate), "an elderly, alert, little Malay," to see and describe for him.[54] For Konrad there would be no such relief. After four times around the loop, in January 1888 Konrad signed off the *Vidar* and checked back into the Sailors' Home. He had seen enough.

SIX

WHEN YOUR SHIP FAILS YOU

MORE THAN FORTY YEARS after Conrad signed off the *Vidar*, his first biographer Gérard Jean-Aubry tracked down the former captain, James Craig, then well into his seventies, who remembered that "when he went down to the cabin to talk to his first mate, he usually found him writing."[1] No letters Conrad wrote on the *Vidar* survived, let alone journals, if he ever kept any. But in one form or another, Konrad Korzeniowski stowed away landscapes, characters, and plots that Joseph Conrad unpacked for decades to come. Altogether, the four and a half months on the *Vidar* inspired more of Conrad's fiction than any other period in his life.

About half of everything Conrad ever published took place in Southeast Asia: six novels, more than a dozen short stories and novellas, chunks of memoirs. His Asian fiction generally took one of two forms. One—beginning with his very first novel, *Almayer's Folly* (1895), and reprised as late as his 1915 novel *Victory*—took place primarily on land, up estuaries like those he'd navigated on the *Vidar*, among the Europeans he glimpsed there, and the Malays and "half-castes" among whom they dwelt. The other—including his celebrated stories "Youth," "The Secret

Sharer," and "Typhoon"—took place primarily on ships in Asian waters, and featured European seamen facing a challenge: how to survive a shipwreck, how to handle a stowaway, how to get through a storm.

On the face of it, Conrad's choice to write so much about Asia looked like a savvy commercial move. Robert Louis Stevenson on the South Seas, H. Rider Haggard on Africa, and the dean of "exotic" writers, Rudyard Kipling on India, had all earned critical and popular success by writing about far-flung locales. With Malaya, Conrad introduced a British audience to a place few would ever have read fiction about. (The best-known novel about the East Indies was the Dutch work *Max Havelaar*, a condemnation of Dutch imperialism, translated into English in 1868.)[2] "Borneo is a new field for English literature," observed a reviewer of *Almayer's Folly*.[3] "Mr. Conrad's readers will proceed to annex his Borneo with the gusto of the Powers partitioning geographical Africa," added another.[4] If he kept up the good work, according to *The Spectator*, Conrad "might become the Kipling of the Malay Archipelago."[5]

Conrad took pains to make his rendition of Malaya accurate, even asking his publisher to send him a Malay-English dictionary to get the vocabulary right, "as I find I've forgotten many words."[6] With the exception of place names, which he generally altered or anonymized (like "an Eastern port" for Singapore), Conrad salted his pages with the names of real ships he'd seen and real men he'd met, like the charterer and captain of the *Highland Forest*, the owner and engineers of the *Vidar*, and the Singapore harbormaster Henry Ellis. In a trio of novels set in Borneo, William Lingard became Tom Lingard, who traded on a little-known river; Charles Olmeijer became Kaspar Almayer, Lingard's washed-up agent; the Donggala trader Babalatchie, who'd consigned goods on the *Vidar*, resurfaced as a canny local courtier. Conrad bridled when a longtime British administrator in Malaya, Hugh Clifford, deemed that these works could "only be called Malay in Mr. Conrad's sense." "Well I never did set up as an authority on Malaysia," Conrad shot back. "All the details about the little characteristic acts and customs . . . I have taken out (to be safe) from undoubted sources—dull, wise books."[7]

Clifford was onto something. His own writing on the "sepia-coloured peoples" of Malaya tried to describe indigenous cultures that he saw disappearing under the influence of British colonial rule.[8] Conrad had seen Asia only at the edges, where Europeans and Asians met. He knew more about Anglo-Dutch rivalry, merchants, pirates, and lascars than he knew about Malay sovereignty, the nature of Islam, or the Dayak societies of Borneo. His fiction rarely ventured outside the heads of European characters.

But Conrad was onto something too. "Facts can bear out my story," he said, "but as I am writing fiction not secret history—facts don't matter."[9] Conrad wrote about the Malay Archipelago the way he'd seen it: from the deck of a steamship. He saw Europeans who'd failed to get rich, industrial schemes that foundered, high-minded objectives run aground. Where the British sailing ship combined all the things Conrad admired most, Asia became the backdrop for a critique of the cruder ways of steam. That's why Conrad's greatest novel set in Asia—*Lord Jim* (1900)— was also a novel about a sailor, and his most challenging novel about a sailor was also a book about a European trying to make it in Asia.

The opening lines of *Lord Jim* introduced a handsome, "powerfully built" Englishman with a look so determined that he "advanced straight at you with . . . a fixed from-under stare which made you think of a charging bull." The son of a country parson, Jim had been inspired by "a course of light holiday literature" to dream of going to sea. He imagined himself leading a "stirring life in the world of adventure," fighting pirates, rescuing castaways, suppressing mutinies, "always an example of devotion to duty, and as unflinching as a hero in a book."[10]

But once he actually became a sailor, "the regions so well known to his imagination" appeared to Jim to be "strangely barren of adventure." "Only once" did he truly feel the raging power of a storm at sea. He promptly got "disabled by a falling spar," and had to disembark at "an Eastern port" to recuperate. As soon as he could walk again, Jim went down to the harbor to look for a homeward passage. Suddenly he changed his mind. Instead he signed on as chief mate on an Indian Ocean steamship called the *Patna*.

The *Patna* ran between Singapore and Jeddah carrying Muslim passengers on the pilgrimage to Mecca. Just by looking at it, you could tell the ship had problems. "The *Patna* was a local steamer as old as the hills, lean like a greyhound, and eaten up by rust worse than a condemned water tank. She was owned by a Chinaman, chartered by an Arab, and commanded by a sort of renegade New South Wales German," a dubious vessel from the hull to the bridge. But a coat of whitewash made the *Patna* look passably seaworthy, and "eight hundred pilgrims (more or less) were driven on board" for the long journey west.

"Into the circular stillness of water and sky" the *Patna* cruised over a flat, hot sea, smoke hissing from the funnels and "the durned, compound, surface-condensing, rotten scrap-heap" of an engine making a "blasted racket down below." Jim plotted the ship's course in a creeping black line across the charts. Families of pilgrims camped out on boxes, mats, and rugs, and dozed under the equatorial sun.[11]

Then one night they were brought up short by a roar "as if thunder had growled deep down in the water." The ship scraped over something beneath it like "a snake crawling over a stick." Jim went belowdecks and saw water pouring in. Somehow, somewhere, something had pierced the hull. Just one rusty bulkhead held back the full force of the sea. His thoughts careened between two terrifying images. In front of him he saw the bulging bulkhead, on the verge of bursting, "the rush of water" ready to "take him at the back and toss him like a chip," and the ship certain to knife to the bottom. Above him he could envision the passengers like a giant "crowd of bodies, laid out for death." "Eight hundred people and seven boats; eight hundred people and seven boats," he chanted. There was no way to get them all off alive.[12]

Jim rushed onto the deck to help however many passengers he could save. He found the captain and engineers struggling to free one of the lifeboats—but it was for themselves, not the pilgrims. Jim shut his eyes and envisioned the pilgrims again, sleeping innocently at the brink of disaster. Here was the chance he'd been waiting for. He could be the sole European to remain on board and steady the ship, rescue the passengers, or die trying. He could be a hero.

Jim opened his eyes and saw the officers clambering into the boat. They cut loose, and shouted up at one of their colleagues to join them. "Jump! Oh, jump!" they cried. Jim recalled the straining bulkhead and surging sea, "eight hundred people and seven boats."[13] He jumped.

FROM HIS BOOK-INDUCED YEN for the sea to his hospital stay in Asia, Jim followed a step or two behind Konrad Korzeniowski. The voyage of the *Patna*, in turn, closely tracked a true tale Konrad would have heard in Singapore.

It was the kind of story that stuck around the dockside bars like stains of red wine. In July 1880, a steamship called the *Jeddah* had left Singapore with 953 pilgrims on board, bound for Mecca. During heavy weather a week out to sea, the engine room boilers shook loose from their moorings and the ship started taking on water. Passengers joined the crew in frantically working the pumps, but on the second day adrift, the captain ordered the crew to ready the lifeboats. There was enough space for only about a quarter of those on board. The captain, his wife, and two engineers hastily climbed into one. When the passengers saw what was going on, they stopped pumping and rushed toward the boats, frantically throwing pots, pans, and boxes into the boats in a desperate bid to prevent the officers from abandoning ship. The first mate, a parson's son named Augustine Williams, hastily lowered the lifeboat to sea, leapt overboard to join it, and the officers cut loose. The *Jeddah* would sink or float without them.[14]

The morning after the officers abandoned the sinking ship, their lifeboat was spotted by a British steamer, the *Scindia*, which hoisted the castaways aboard. They reported that the *Jeddah* had sunk, and that in the melee of its final hours the passengers had murdered the second mate and engineer. The *Scindia* carried them into Aden, from where the captain, Clark, wired the shipowners the terrible news: "*Jeddah* foundered. Self, wife, Syed Omar, 18 others saved." Shocked headlines reported the tragedy to the British public: "Dreadful Disaster at Sea. Loss of Nearly 1000."[15]

The next day, the *Jeddah* arrived in Aden, with 992 passengers and crew on board.

What the rescued officers hadn't known was that in the hours after they abandoned ship, the passengers rallied. Pumping furiously, they managed to get the better of the leaks. The *Jeddah* drifted into calm waters under sail and hoisted a distress signal. Just a few miles offshore it was spotted by a British passenger liner, whose first mate found that "everything on board was in confusion, and all persons on board were panic-stricken," but "organised gangs amongst the pilgrims to pump and bale the vessel," and towed the *Jeddah* safely into Aden.[16]

That the *Jeddah*'s officers had abandoned ship violated the most basic principle of the British seaman's honor code: a captain should go down with his ship. Why hadn't they evacuated more passengers? Why hadn't they told the *Scindia* to go rescue the *Jeddah*? The port authorities in Aden immediately convened an inquiry. The only people to come out well, in the eyes of the court, were the pilgrims, who had shown themselves generally "ready and willing to assist," and became disorderly only

SECOND EDITION, 2 o'clock.

TERRIBLE DISASTER AT SEA.
LOSS OF OVER NINE HUNDRED LIVES.

[REUTER'S TELEGRAM.]

ADEN, August 10.—The steamer *Jeddah*, of Singapore, bound for Jeddah, with 953 pilgrims on board, foundered off Cape Guardafui, on the 8th inst. All on board perished excepting the captain, his wife, the chief engineer, the assistant-engineer, and sixteen natives. The survivors were picked up by the steamer *Scindia* and landed here.

[LLOYD'S TELEGRAM.]

ADEN, August 11, 3.15 A.M.—The *Jeddah*, steamer, from Singapore to Jeddah, with pilgrims, foundered at sea off Guardafui on the 8th of August. Upwards of 1,000 of the crew and passengers drowned.

[The *Jeddah* was a screw steamship, built of iron at Dumbarton in 1872, and was registered in Singapore in 1876 by her owners, the Singapore Steamship Company, Limited. Her dimensions were as follows :—280 feet in length 33 feet in breath, 23 feet depth of hold, her gross tonnage being 1,541, and net tonnage 992, and her engines of 200 horse power.]

A report of the sinking of the Jeddah *in*
The Pall Mall Gazette, *August 11, 1880.*

in a way that "might naturally have been expected from any body of human beings, even Europeans" when placed in such trying circumstances.[17]

Everybody else came in for sharp criticism. The chief engineer had completely misjudged "the extent of the risk and danger" in the engine room. As for Captain Clark, if he had managed to demonstrate an "ordinary display of firmness" and a "little tact in dealing with natives, with whom he is no stranger, he could have ensured their co-operation and gratitude, and saved considerable loss to his owners." Instead, he had "shown a painful want of nerve as well as the most ordinary judgment, and . . . allowed his feelings to master the sense of duty it is the pride of every British shipmaster to vaunt." The authorities suspended Captain Clark's certificate for three years. Williams, the first mate, earned particular rebuke for plying the captain with "officious ill-advice." The court determined that he had "aided and abetted" the disgraceful decision with his "officious behavior and unseamanlike conduct," and (the port's assessor added) "should not be permitted to go in the ship again."[18]

The *Jeddah* scandal reverberated from Singapore to London. *The Daily News*, *The Daily Chronicle*, and *The Globe* trembled with a "feeling of indignation and horror at what seems the cowardly desertion" of the officers. "An indelible stain of discredit" should hang over these "unprincipled and cowardly men who disgrace the traditions of seamanship."[19] Many thought Captain Clark had gotten off far too lightly. Why wasn't he "subjected to penalties more severe than the temporary suspension of his certificate . . . ?" asked an MP in the House of Commons. Joseph Chamberlain, the secretary of the Board of Trade, agreed that Clark's "punishment was altogether inadequate," but deemed a criminal prosecution unfeasible "owing to the absence of witnesses and the fact that the captain had gone on to Singapore, and probably to New Zealand." Chamberlain could only hope that "the stigma attaching to his character" meant that "the captain never could obtain employment as master of a ship again."[20]

Clark's career did indeed suffer; though he was briefly, astonishingly, reappointed to command the *Jeddah*, he stepped down before it sailed. But Williams, the *Jeddah*'s first mate, did successfully find another berth as first mate of a steamship sailing out of Singapore. It was the SS *Vidar*.[21]

"IT WAS AS IF I HAD JUMPED into a well—into an ever-lasting deep hole," said Jim.[22] The *Patna*, like the *Jeddah*, was towed to safety, and its disgraced officers hauled before an official inquiry. Perhaps it was because Conrad sailed in Williams's wake, by succeeding him as chief mate of the *Vidar*, that when he reworked the story of the *Jeddah* in *Lord Jim*, what actually happened on the pilgrim ship was merely a prelude of four short chapters. The bulk of the novel plumbed Jim's shame and his struggle to surface.

To tell Jim's tale, Conrad turned to the veteran English captain Charles Marlow, whom he had introduced in the story "Youth." Marlow was in the "eastern port" where the inquiry took place, and from the moment he saw Jim standing outside the court with the other *Patna* officers, he couldn't fathom how this "upstanding, broad-shouldered youth" could have ended up involved in such a sordid affair. He listened impatiently as the prosecutors grilled Jim about facts. "Facts! They demanded facts from him, as if facts could explain anything!" What Marlow really wanted to figure out was the "fundamental why" beneath the "superficial how." Hoping to find "some profound and redeeming cause, some merciful explanation" for Jim's conduct, Marlow invited him to dinner to explain it for himself.[23]

A trial ends in a sentence: this is what they did. Jim flipped the script.

"What would you have done?" he asked. Marlow had felt instinctively that Jim "was of the right sort; he was one of us." By "us" Marlow meant the sailors' community he revered as the "fellowship of the craft" (as he'd described it in "Youth"), an "obscure body of men held together by a community of inglorious toil and by fidelity to a certain standard of conduct." Yet none of the attributes Marlow admired—white, British, fraternal, hardworking—were to be found among the *Patna*'s nameless, speechless Asian passengers or its horrible, voluble European officers. And the *Patna* was nothing like Marlow's ideal ship. Nobody ever knew precisely what had hit the vessel, but Jim caught the captain murmuring an explanation: "All I heard of it were a few words that sounded like 'confounded steam!' and 'infernal steam!'—something about steam."[24]

"When your ship fails you, your whole world seems to fail you," said Marlow, and so it went for the ethics of the craft in an age of steam. If Jim couldn't keep up the code under such conditions, then who else could? Not the European sailors who made Singapore their home port: men of lazy confidence "always on the verge of dismissal, always on the verge of engagement, serving Chinamen, Arabs, half-castes—would have served the devil himself had he made it easy enough." "They loved short passages, good deck-chairs, large native crews, and the distinction of being white." Not the *Patna*'s German captain, a waddling buffoon who made a mockery of British values: "You English always . . . make a tam' fuss—for any little thing, because I was not born in your tam' country. Take away my certificate. Take it. I don't want the certificate. . . . I shpit on it. . . . I vill an Amerigan citizen begome."[25] Not the *Patna*'s Asian crew, invisible but for two Malay helmsmen.[26] The only person who came close, an assessor at the *Patna* inquiry, was driven to suicide in despair.

At first Marlow "wanted to see [Jim] squirm for the honour of the craft." Yet as he watched Jim desperately "trying to save from the fire his idea of what his moral identity should be," Marlow glimpsed a spark, a "redeeming feature in his abominable case."[27] He arranged a job for Jim in Java, a fresh start.

But news of the scandal soon followed, and Jim ran away. The story caught up with him again; again he ran away. "He retreated in good order towards the rising sun, and the fact followed him casually but inevitably." "I told him the earth wouldn't be big enough to hold his caper," said one employer. At last, with Marlow's help once more, Jim took a job in "a remote district of a native-ruled state," "far from the beaten tracks of the sea and from the ends of submarine cables," where the news couldn't find him.[28]

It was called Patusan, and "it's like something you read of in books," Jim gushed—but it was good that he'd brought the complete works of Shakespeare with him, because he walked into a welter of political intrigues. As soon as Jim arrived he was taken prisoner by the local Malay sultan. "Were the Dutch coming to take the country?" the sultan wanted to know. "Would the white man like to go back down the river? What was the object of coming to such a miserable country?" Jim escaped by jumping over a stockade—"the second desperate leap of his life"—and found shelter among a community of Bugis, refugees from a civil war in Sulawesi. Jim befriended the Bugis' ruler Doramin and his son, and when they in turn got embroiled in a conflict, Jim helped them beat back their enemies. In respectful gratitude they called him "Tuan," or "Lord," Jim—a title of honor.[29]

Everyone in Patusan expected Jim eventually to return to the white man's world. Doramin had seen it all before: "The land remains where God had put it, but white men, they come to us and in a little while they go." But nobody knew that Jim, forever tainted by the *Patna* scandal, could "never go home" again. There, he faced eternal disgrace; here, "his opportunity sat veiled by his side like an Eastern bride, waiting to be uncovered by the hand of the master." Tuan Jim hurled himself into his new life. "He had a mind to try a coffee-plantation. . . . He was going to try ever so many experiments."[30] He fell in love with an actual "Eastern bride," a part Asian and part European woman he dubbed Jewel.

Then one day another Englishman appeared on the river. His name was Brown—"Gentleman Brown," he leered—and he'd robbed, raided, sacked, and dueled his way across the western Pacific. Looking for provisions for his shipload of scoundrels, the menacing Brown "sail[ed] into Jim's history, a blind accomplice of the Dark Powers."[31] Doramin wanted to kill the pirate before he could wreak havoc on Patusan. But Brown claimed he meant no harm, and Jim wanted to believe him. Jim persuaded Doramin to let Brown go in peace.

But as Brown sailed back down the river, past the Bugis settlement, he broke his word and opened fire, just as Doramin had feared. Doramin's own son was killed. Jim's prestige collapsed. "He had retreated from one world, for a small matter of an impulsive jump, and now the other, the work of his own hands, had fallen in ruins upon his head." There was no going back. Jim presented himself to the grieving Doramin in full knowledge of what would follow. Doramin shot him dead in the chest.

"They say that the white man sent right and left . . . a proud and unflinching glance" as he fell—a martyr to "a shadowy ideal of conduct," a hero in a book.[32]

PERIL ON THE HIGH SEAS, war in the jungle, despicable pirates, an alluring maiden, and a young man questing for honor—*Lord Jim* appeared to have all the ingredients of a best-selling imperial adventure novel.[33] Published in serial form in 1899–1900 and in hardcover in 1900, *Lord Jim* was Conrad's most critically successful novel to date, and remained his most popular for so long that, twenty years later, he complained about critics who measured his newer books against it. "I only don't see why I should have Lord Jim thrown at my head at every turn,"

Conrad grumbled to his literary agent. "I couldn't go on writing Lord Jim all my life and I don't think you would have liked me to do so."[34]

Lord Jim appeared at a time when Europe and the United States had colonized virtually all of Africa and Asia. It spoke in a metaphor imperialists could appreciate. White, or light, marked right. White haloed Jim from his first appearance, "apparelled in immaculate white," to his last, through Asian eyes, as "the white man." The *Patna* incident fell "like a shadow in the light." When Marlow visited Jim in Patusan he saw him as the "symbolic" embodiment "of races that have emerged from the gloom," and as he sailed away, he watched Jim dwindle on the shore into "a tiny white speck, that seemed to catch all the light left in a darkened world." Jim's "very dark" servant Tamb' Itam trailed his "'white lord' . . . like a morose shadow." Jim's friend Dain Waris "knew how to fight like a white man" and "had also a European mind"—but he "had not Jim's racial prestige. . . . [H]e was still one of *them*, while Jim was one of *us*." In a Dickensian flourish, Jim's love, a "flitting . . . white form," bore the sparkling name of Jewel—while the white pirate with a "sun-blackened face" was, in fact, Brown.[35]

But *Lord Jim* never was a bestseller. It told of Europeans in Asia not from the veranda of a British colonial bungalow, still less an armchair in a London club—but as Conrad had seen them, from the steamer's deck. Jim was far from the flawless hero of an imperial romp like H. Rider Haggard's *She* (1887): "the handsomest young fellow I have ever seen. He was very tall, very broad, and had a look of power and a grace of bearing that seemed as native to him as it is to a wild stag." If anything, Jim resembled the main character of a book Conrad deeply admired—Stephen Crane's Civil War novel *The Red Badge of Courage* (1895)—who had "dreamed of battles all his life," only to run away from the field the very first time he fought. Rather than projecting the self-confidence of a European-led world order at its height, *Lord Jim* ruminated over values in crisis: the demise of the seafarer's craft in an age of steam.

Nor would *Lord Jim* satisfy readers looking for a piece of "light holiday literature" of the sort that Jim himself enjoyed. One reviewer likened the book's structure to a spider's web, "with side tracks leading, apparently, nowhere, and cross tracks that start back and begin anew and end once more." "*Lord Jim* is tedious, over-elaborated, and more than a little difficult to read," judged another.[36]

The novel's meandering narrative, too, owed much to Conrad's maritime perspective. When you're on a ship at sea, you're cut off from almost everything that gives incident to a day in a life onshore. Rarely in modern human society are so few people so isolated so regularly for so long. There's no separation between workplace and home. There's nobody new to see or talk to, no chance encounters, no passersby. There are no newspapers, no letters. There's no new anything—except, of course, the weather, but even that follows somewhat predictable patterns of season and clime. A ship's logbook captures the peculiar quality of stasis in motion, recording each day in a sequence of digits: dates, degrees, bearings, depths. A flock of birds, a sign of land, can be unusual enough to warrant words.

This gives a sailor at sea a particular relationship to time. Quotidian time passes in a pattern of two- and four-hour blocks, cycling without regard for night and day. Most conversation comes in dogwatch breaks in daylong silences. Shipmates build familiarity in fragments over weeks. With nothing new to talk about in the present, the past and the future become extraordinarily rich imaginative domains. Sailors often speak of how they'll spend their futures: what they'll do onshore, what awaits them at home, what they'll do when they stop sailing altogether. And sailors, famously, spin yarns about adventures and encounters from the past, which—like the lines they coil and mend—come at length, and with twists and turns.

Counting up his months at sea, Conrad spent several years of his life on some of the longest routes that sailing ships regularly plied, with small crews, no passengers, and few port calls along the way. He, like Jim, "knew the magic monotony of existence between sky and water."[37] He learned to see multitudes in the changing colors and contours of the sea and sky—giving him a sensitivity to "atmosphere" that reviewers regularly praised in his fiction. He learned, too, how sailors populated the routinized present with stories from the past, and how they filled their little-varying days by looking forward to different futures. On every ship he'd heard a different group of men's adventures and hopes. He'd heard the same person tell stories spanning a lifetime of adventures—and he'd heard about the same famous incidents from a range of different mouths.

Lord Jim represented the result: a narrative composed in sailor's time. It looped backward and forward, its speakers shifted, it was jammed with embedded tales and texts. Marlow spun, knitted, and snipped: sometimes an actor in Jim's story; sometimes a curator, piecing it together from what other people told him; sometimes an interpreter, teasing out its meaning.[38] None of the story's incidents took place in the present. Everything occurred in collated layers of past, like pages in a file through which Marlow shuffled, pulling different sheets to the front. These deeper and nearer pasts sustained the sense throughout the novel that Jim would always have a future, filled by hopes and dreams.

Conrad believed that "the general effect of a novel must be the general effect that life makes on mankind."[39] A person doesn't process things as "a narration, a report," lining up observations and interpretations like two sides of a zipper. Instead you absorb impressions, feelings, and sensations. Maybe you can spot a pattern, maybe not; maybe you only recognize things much later. As it is, what you see on the face of things may or may not tell you much about what it means—the same way you can be hypnotized by the play of light and shadow on a pool of water without ever knowing how cold or salty it may be.

Lord Jim projected Conrad's ideas about perception onto concepts of "East" and "West." Asia, as Conrad portrayed it, using long-standing

European stereotypes of "the Orient," was a timeless, inscrutable realm of faith and superstition. But in its far reaches, he suggested, "three hundred miles beyond the end of telegraph cables and mail-boat lines," you could find a sort of honest authenticity that the West had long since abandoned.[40] Conrad echoed the German philosopher Arthur Schopenhauer, who drew on Hindu texts to argue that a "veil of Maya"—Sanskrit for "illusion"—hid truth, meaning, and reality from view.[41] "The Western eye, so often concerned with mere surfaces," said Marlow, missed out on "the hidden possibilities of races and lands over which hangs the mystery of unrecorded ages." In Patusan, Marlow saw "the haggard utilitarian lies of our civilisation wither and die." That was why Jim could rediscover his sense of honor there, and foster dreams that, however unrealistic, held "the deep hidden truth of works of art."[42] "Under [Patusan's] obscure surface," Marlow, too, found what he was looking for: "the truth disclosed in a moment of illusion." Jim's self-sacrifice proved to Marlow that he had been right about Jim all along. Jim *was* "one of us." "Patusan," he could have added, is an anagram of *Patna* plus "us."[43]

Even *Lord Jim*'s detractors recognized the novel's "remarkable originality." "If [Conrad] keeps on writing the same sort" of fiction, predicted one American reviewer, "he may arrive at the unique distinction of having few readers in his own generation, and a fair chance of several in the next."[44] Conrad's innovative storytelling inspired younger writers such as Ford Madox Ford (who met Conrad not long before he started *Lord Jim*) to apply the technique of literary impressionism, as he called it, in his 1915 novel *The Good Soldier*.

Of course not everyone was sold. E. M. Forster scored a good point when he complained that Conrad "is always promising to make some general philosophic statement about the universe, and then refraining with a gruff disclaimer." Forster suspected that "the secret casket of his genius contains a vapour rather than a jewel."[45] But for Conrad, the vapor *was* the jewel. From the Polish romantic nationalism he'd absorbed as a boy, to the British sailing ship, to an untouched corner of an imaginary Asia, he treasured a misty ideal of personal honor, commitment to duty, a community of people willing to sacrifice themselves for something bigger.

The tragedy of *Lord Jim* was that what passed for "civilization" was coming for Patusan. The steamship edged out the sailing ship. Hypocrisy, selfishness, and greed triumphed over honesty and hard work. Communities fractured. People broke promises. The tragedy was that the "awful attribute of our nature . . . is not so very far under the surface as we like to think."[46]

PART THREE

CIVILIZATION

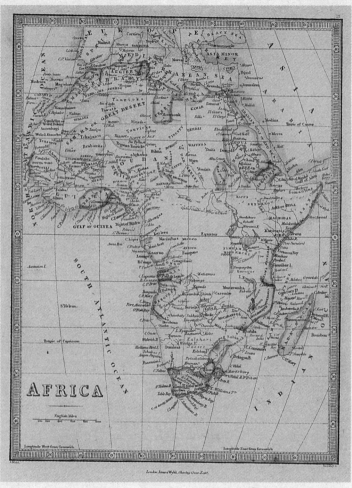

Africa in Conrad's youth, the center a blank.

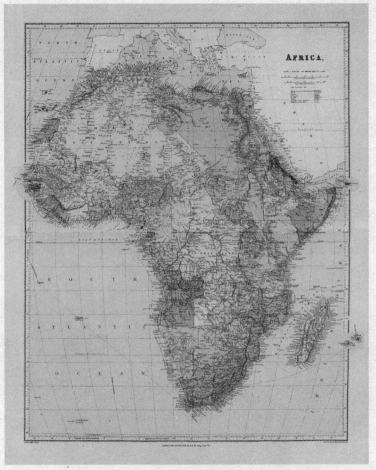

Africa in Conrad's adulthood, carved into European colonies.

SEVEN

—— · ——

HEART TO HEART

AFTER FIFTY-FOUR DAYS from Melbourne via the Torres Strait, the *Otago* reached Mauritius in November 1888, unloaded a cargo of Australian soap, tallow, and fertilizer, and released nine tired crewmembers to enjoy some time onshore. Captain Konrad Korzeniowski had brought his ship here to buy sugar, the island's premier export.

He'd stumbled into this, his first command, just two weeks after signing off the *Vidar* when the Singapore harbormaster Henry Ellis got a telegram from the British consul in Bangkok requesting a captain for a ship whose master had died at sea. Konrad nabbed the post. When he wrote about it later in his novel *The Shadow-Line* (1917), he said none of the other captains had wanted it. "Afraid of the sails. Afraid of a white crew. Too much trouble. Too much work. Too long out here. Easy life and deck-chairs more their mark." His fictionalized self greeted the *Otago* like a lover. "Her hull, her rigging filled my eye with a great content. That feeling of life-emptiness which had made me so restless for the last few months . . . dissolved in a flow of joyous emotion."[1] To show off his mastery of the sea, Konrad deliberately steered the *Otago* to Mauritius by a challenging route.

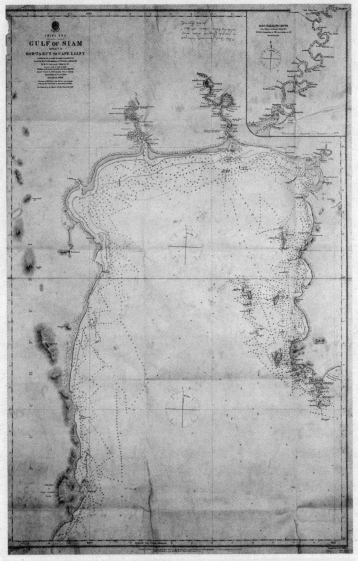

Conrad's navigational chart of the Gulf of Siam.

Many people called Mauritius "the pearl of the ocean." Some said heaven itself was copied from the island.[2] Though a British colony, the island's white population descended chiefly from the French who'd settled the island in the eighteenth century, which meant that for the first time since leaving Marseille, Konrad entered a French-speaking society. He had an entrée through one of his old acquaintances from the French merchant marine, Captain Gabriel Renouf, who introduced Konrad to his brothers and sisters. When it turned out that the jute sacks he'd need to line the ship's hold had been destroyed in a fire, and that he would have to stay several weeks longer than expected, Konrad was actually pleased by the delay.

Every day Konrad went into town to check in with the freight agent about the sacks. He set his bowler hat at a tilt, and punctuated his stride with a gold-knobbed cane. The other captains waiting in the office in their caps and ducks, with grimy, ungloved hands, dismissed him as "the Russian Count," and they were right to see that he came from a different social class.[3] The Renoufs were closer to his kind: professional men and educated, well-mannered women. He took the Renouf sisters on carriage rides down the palm-lined avenues of the Jardin des Pamplemousses, and hosted them for tea on board the *Otago*. Twenty-six-year-old Eugénie, in particular, charmed him. She made him feel light, attractive, uncomplicated, like the man he wanted to be.

One day the ladies suggested a parlor game, a kind of twenty questions. They passed him sheets of paper printed with French questions. He wrote replies on separate leaves—in English, adding to the tease.[4]

"How do you amuse yourself?" the sisters asked.

"By making myself scarce."

"What name makes your heart beat fast?"

"Ready to beat for any name," he demurred.

"What would be your dream of happiness?" A difficult one. "Never dream of it; want reality," he replied.

"Where does the person live, who occupies your thoughts?"

A trap, easily slipped. He wrote, "A castle in Spain."

Your favorite hair color? Favorite eye color? He liked brunettes and blondes equally, and gray eyes the best.

"What would you like to be?"

"Should like not to be," he quipped.

"What country would you like to live in?"

"Do not know. Perhaps Lapland."

"What's your greatest distraction?"

"Chasing wild geese."

"What natural gift do you wish you had had?"

That question hit him in a different place. Sincerity interrupted banter. "Self-confidence."

"Do you think you are loved?"

He blushed inwardly. "Decline to state."

After about six weeks, the jute sacks arrived, and Konrad lined the hold and loaded in five hundred tons of sugar. It was time to get on with business. He took aside one of the Renouf brothers and asked him for permission to propose marriage to Eugénie. The brother looked back at him startled, embarrassed. Don't you know she's already engaged?

Konrad would remember the "pearl of the ocean" as a "crumb of the earth," peopled by provincials keeping up the appearance of gentility in a state of "dull, dignified decay." "The girls are almost always pretty, ignorant of the world, kind and agreeable and generally bilingual; they prattle innocently both in French and English. The emptiness of their existence passes belief," he later wrote.[5]

The Renoufs would remember the unusually cultivated captain who briefly favored their world. He could be wonderful company when he chose, but he had a disconcerting way of falling into deep silences, as if he had suddenly left them.[6]

. . .

"Luckily," mused Captain Charles Marlow, "people, whether mature or not mature (and who really is ever mature?) are for the most part quite incapable of understanding what is happening to them."[7] Marlow—like his creator—had aged a lot by the time he said this in Conrad's 1913 novel *Chance*. He'd seen enough of the world to know that, for all he might think he made decisions about his life course, really he was a billiard ball in a game where fate held the cue. You could make sense of what had happened only after the fact, which was just as well, because if you felt all the hard knocks as they came, you'd never be able to go on living.

Konrad returned to London in May 1889 after an absence of almost two and a half years. He took a room in Pimlico, so close to the Thames that on warm mornings the view out his window was blurred by the river's mist. He never said why he'd come back from Asia, and he had no plan for what to do next.

Konrad's uncle Tadeusz was delighted to have him back in Europe and pressed him to visit. "My sixty-year-old mechanism is constantly falling down on me. Either it is my teeth or my eyes, which have served me faithfully up till now. . . . And my advice to you is to put off reaching this age as long as possible," he wrote. "Anyhow, I hope to God that whether healthy or sick I shall see my beloved Captain at least once more—at home or abroad as the case may be."[8] As a British citizen, Konrad could at last travel to Ukraine without fear of military conscription (or prosecution for avoiding it), though he had to be officially released from his Russian subjecthood first, and then he had to get a visa. It was just a short walk from his lodgings to the Russian embassy in Chesham Square, but it took a very long time to get anything done.

While he waited for his papers to come through, Konrad reconnected with his two oldest friends in London. Adolf "Phil" Krieger, whom he'd known since they had lodged together on Dynevor Road eight years earlier, was a partner in a firm named Barr, Moering & Co. that imported silverware and other consumer goods from Germany.[9] Some years earlier Konrad had invested £350 in the company (with Tadeusz Bobrowski's help), which now generated enough income to tide him over between berths. He'd come to rely on Barr, Moering & Co. as agents for business while he was overseas, even helping himself to their letterhead for his correspondence.[10]

There was also George Fountaine Weare Hope, his first English friend, whom he'd met in his shipping agent's office in 1879. Hope had once sailed on the *Duke of Sutherland* too, and though he'd given up the sea long since for marriage and a desk job, he often stopped by the agency "to see if there was anyone I knew." "Here is a young gentleman who has been in your old ship," said the agent, introducing him to Konrad. Hope sized up the young foreigner in his flat cap and serge suit, "saw at once that he was a Gentleman," and invited him out to lunch. "We met several times before he finally got a ship, and the more I saw of him the more I liked him."[11]

Nowadays Hope, a company director in the City, kept a cruising yawl named the *Nellie* for recreational sailing. One summer weekend, Konrad joined him for a jaunt down the River Medway in Kent. They packed a leg of lamb, a bottle of mint sauce, and a case of beer, and cast off with a fine southwesterly wind at their back. It was a wonderful day to be on the water, and Konrad thought the *Nellie* a "splendid" craft. The first night they joined a bunch of seamen for a drink and a yarn at the Lobster Smack Inn in Hole Haven, Konrad one-upping everyone else with a (tall) tale of gunrunning on the Spanish coast. The next day, they continued on to Chatham. Hope excitedly pointed out the features that made this a bastion of British naval power: stately men-of-war, massive naval dockyards, hilltop castle guarding the approach. To Konrad, though, this was Charles Dickens country above all (Dickens had lived in Chatham as a boy), and he loved seeing spots he'd read about in his favorite novels. Their next port of call was Margate, where they met up with some more of Hope's friends and strolled amid throngs of East End day-trippers, swapping stories about the *Duke of Sutherland*. Bad weather dogged the *Nellie* all the way back to London, but it only added to the sense of adventure and camaraderie. "The fact is that a man must be very fond of the sea to really enjoy such a trip," said Hope—and Konrad enjoyed it thoroughly.

A diversion like this occupied only a few days, though, and with his Russian visa pending from one month to the next, Konrad had lots more time to fill. He found himself looking back on his time on the *Vidar*. Soon he found himself writing about it, too. He conjured "the man Almayer"— Charles Olmeijer of Berau—standing on the jetty as the *Vidar* approached, "clad simply in flapping pajamas of cretonne pattern . . . a thin cotton singlet with short sleeves" and a pair of "straw slippers."[12] He remembered the names of other Europeans he'd heard about in Borneo, like William Lingard, the Rajah Laut, and speculated about what had brought them there, how and with whom they lived. The scene lengthened into two or three chapters, a story about an upriver European agent, his Malay wife, and their daughter. He named the settlement Sambir, after the Galician region where he and his father had enjoyed the last spell of decent health and cheer before Apollo's death.[13]

Many years later Conrad would say that he had been reminded of Borneo by the "opaline mist" on those Pimlico mornings. All writing is an act of translation. It turns something you see or sense into something you say. For Conrad writing fiction would often also be a translation of past experience, a way to find the meaning in all those happenings in life whose significance a person doesn't fully grasp in the moment. Like the fact that the story he started writing in the summer of 1889 would eventually grow into his first published novel, *Almayer's Folly*.

Konrad wrote and waited for the visa to Ukraine that still never came. Money ran tight. He would need to find another job. Konrad asked around among agents and friends, but there were few captaincies going, and more qualified candidates in pursuit of them than ever. At a loss in London, Konrad followed a lead from Phil Krieger to shipping companies in Antwerp with whom Barr, Moering & Co. did business.

Britain and Belgium were two distinct nations, but from a mariner's or merchant's point of view, London and Antwerp were twin cities, separated by only a thin band of sea. When Konrad arrived in Antwerp in November 1889, it had become one of the biggest and fastest-growing ports in Europe. Glamorous transatlantic liners berthed at quays near the city center, where curious tourists could wander on board to gape at sparkling, luxurious interiors. To the north stretched eight vast docks, with more than ten kilometers of quaysides between them. New hydraulic cranes quietly eased cargo from holds and loaded them straight onto railroad cars. Conveyor belts whirred beneath the pavements of the newly opened Africa Dock, carrying sacks of grain. The adjacent America Dock was ringed by storage tanks for an increasingly sought-after commodity, petroleum.

Certain Belgians might have interpreted this maritime power as the culmination of Antwerp's destiny. Local folklore held that in ancient times a giant had blocked the mouth of the River Scheldt, which flowed into the city, and exacted tolls from entering captains. If anyone refused to pay, the giant would cut off his hand and throw it into the river. A fictitious Roman soldier named Silvius Brabo killed the giant, chopped off his hand, and hurled *that* into the sea, liberating the Scheldt and founding the city. The name "Antwerp" was said to derive from "*hand werpen*" ("werpen" means "to throw" in Dutch). Konrad crossed the Grand Place to see a brand-new bronze fountain of Brabo atop the giant's corpse, holding the severed hand aloft. Water spouted from the limb and the open wounds of the body sprawling on the pavement.[14]

In Antwerp Konrad met with a shipping company that had a possible vacancy on a vessel traveling to the West Indies and Mexico.[15] Next he visited Brussels, where he had an entrée to another firm, the Compagnie du Congo pour le Commerce et l'Industrie (CCCI).[16] This was a newly established venture formed to exploit the resources of Belgium's biggest emerging market: the Congo Free State, a vast region in Central Africa that was personally adminis-

Fountain of Silvius Brabo in Antwerp, inaugurated in 1887.

tered by Belgium's King Leopold II. Konrad went to the CCCI headquarters in an ivory-stuccoed office block just behind the iron gates of the Royal Palace.[17] On the office wall he might have seen a map of the company's African field of operations, like a balloon pinched at the Atlantic coast and inflating across the heart of the continent. The Congo River scythed through the territory, one end touching the Atlantic, and the other curving more than a thousand miles inland toward the Great Lakes of East Africa.

Konrad had an interview with the company director, Albert Thys, a military officer with a bristling crew cut and flinty eyes. Thys superintended the CCCI's two subsidiary operations.[18] One was to build a railroad from Matadi, near the Congo's Atlantic outlet, to the river's first navigable point, Léopoldville (present-day Kinshasa), about 250 miles upstream. Another was to run steamboats between Léopoldville and Stanley Falls (present-day Kisangani), 1,068 miles upriver, which stopped at various CCCI stations along the way to collect trade goods, pre-eminently ivory. This arm of the concern, called the Société Anonyme Belge du Commerce du Haut-Congo (SAB), was expanding its steam-boat fleet and looking for captains to command them. If they had a cap-taincy available, Konrad told Thys, he'd be very glad to take it.[19]

Konrad left with a verbal expression of interest from Thys, but no sense of when a job might actually materialize. When he wrote to follow up, he got no reply. Meanwhile, though, the paperwork to visit his uncle in the Russian Empire finally fell into place. On February 4, 1890, Korze-niowski packed his book manuscript into his bag and set out on the multi-stage journey from Pimlico to Ukraine.

He stopped first in Belgium, where he again visited the CCCI office and pressed them for a start date; they told him to check back again in April. He also visited a distant cousin his uncle Tadeusz had just told him about. Aleksander Poradowski had settled in western Europe after the 1863 insurrection. Konrad reached him just in time: Poradowski was seriously ill and not expected to live.

It was in the tense environment of a house waiting for death that Kon-rad met a woman like none he'd ever known, Poradowski's forty-two-year-old wife Marguerite. She came from a scholarly French family (her first cousin, Dr. Paul-Ferdinand Gachet, would treat Vincent van Gogh later that spring), and was herself a noted fiction writer.[20] Her novella *Yaga: A Sketch of Ruthenian Manners*, based on a decade of living in Ukraine with Poradowski, had recently been published in Paris's presti-gious *Revue des deux mondes*. She was glamorous, accomplished, worldly, literate, moving easily through a milieu Konrad admired. Yet she also understood intimately where he'd come from: the landlocked villages of

Ukraine, the European diaspora of Polish cousins, the hereditary pain of unfulfilled patriotism. At just the time he'd started writing fiction himself, she was also the first serious author he'd known, after his own father. Konrad left Brussels with the name of an editor to contact in Warsaw, a copy of Poradowska's novel *Yaga*, and a powerful sense of personal connection to his new "aunt." Aleksander Poradowski died two days later.

Konrad continued east. Three days with relatives in Warsaw, two days with cousins in Lublin, then a train to Kalynivka station and a day-long sleigh ride over the snow to Tadeusz's estate, Kazimierówka.[21] Many years later, Conrad described this moment in *A Personal Record* as a triptych of his life. "The MS. of 'Almayer's Folly' was reposing in the bag under our feet," he remembered, and "I saw again the sun setting on the plains as I saw it in the travels of my childhood. It set, clear and red, as if it were setting on the sea."[22] Into a single image he froze the three parts of his persona: the sailor, the writer, the native-born Pole.

Yet when he actually jogged over the icebound roads in February 1890—uncertain about his next berth, and the shape of his writing—he saw the landscape through the literary images of Marguerite Poradowska. He'd read *Yaga* twice in a matter of days. He wrote to *"ma chère Tante"* from every stop. "I write to you in French because I think of you in French; and these sentiments, so badly expressed, come from the heart, which knows neither the grammar nor the spelling of a studied sympathy."[23] His compassionate condolence letters marked the beginning of an effusive, emotionally charged correspondence between the two. Eight years older, a sort of relative, the new widow was a "safe" repository for Konrad's intimate confessions, and in the coming years he poured them out in sometimes dozens of letters per year. Marguerite became the first woman with whom the adult Konrad formed a sustained emotional relationship.[24]

Konrad spent two months in Ukraine, slipping into the grooves of a society, language, and culture worn soft with age. To be embraced again by family, and folded into familiar surroundings, would have made him aware of what he'd lost when he'd left. Yet to see them all there—Tadeusz's *szlachta* friends with their provincial horizons and unattainable political ideals as if nothing had changed—also reminded him of how happy he was to be gone. People who met him thought he spoke Polish with a foreign accent and had turned into a London snob.[25]

While he was in Ukraine, Konrad at last got word from Brussels: one of the company's Congo steamship captains had been killed, and they needed a replacement immediately. Konrad promised to report in April, and wrote to Marguerite with thanks for making inquiries with the company on his behalf. "With impatience I await the moment when I shall be able to kiss your hands and thank you in person." He hastened back to Brussels, signed a contract to serve the SAB for three years, and was instructed to sail for Africa in less than a week.

Conrad often asserted in later years that he went to Africa because of a boyhood fascination. "It was in 1868," he declared, "when nine years old or thereabouts, that while looking at a map of Africa of the time and putting my finger on the blank space then representing the unsolved mystery of the continent, I said to myself with absolute assurance . . . 'When I grow up, I shall go *there*!'"[26] Marlow made a similar declaration in *Heart of Darkness*. In truth, Conrad never made a point of finding work in Africa. He got the job as a function of chance and personal circumstance. He had links to Belgian shippers via fellow immigrants in London. He had a language—French—in which to communicate with them. He had a newly discovered agent of sorts in Brussels in his socially well-connected "aunt" Marguerite Poradowska. It was the only job he'd ever had that relied on each of his distinctive traits, as a Polish-born, French-speaking, British-certified captain.

Konrad "dashed full tilt" between London and Brussels preparing for his journey, getting supplies, saying his farewells. In early May 1890 he packed up the manuscript of *Almayer's Folly* once more, visited Brussels for a final farewell with Marguerite Poradowska, and continued to Bordeaux, where he boarded the French screw steamer *Ville de Maceio* for the long journey south.

Konrad sailed for Africa with his head and his heart elsewhere: in Borneo with the characters of his emerging novel, and in Brussels with Marguerite. "The screw turns and carries me off to the unknown," he wrote to her from Tenerife, the first stop on his journey. "Happily, there is another me who prowls through Europe, who is with you at this moment. . . . Another me who moves about with great ease; who can even be in two places. Don't laugh! I believe it has happened. So don't laugh!"[27] "You have endowed my life with new interest, new affection," he wrote again some weeks later. "I now look down two avenues cut through the thick and chaotic jungle of noxious weeds. . . . For a long time I have no longer been interested in the goal to which my road leads. I was going along it with my head lowered, cursing the stones. Now I am interested in another traveller; this makes me forget the petty miseries of my own path."[28]

All Konrad knew about what he'd find in Congo was that "I am destined to the command of a steamboat, belonging to M. Delcommune's exploring party. . . . I like this prospect very much, but I know nothing for certain as everything is supposed to be kept secret." He'd heard that "60 per cent. of our Company's employees return to Europe before they have completed even six months' service. Fever and dysentery!"—and he expected homesickness, too.[29] Yet without consciously registering it, Konrad had passed signs on his visits to Belgium—the fountain with the severed hand, the company headquarters at the gates of the Royal Palace, the dead captain—that pointed toward a domain more violent and troubling than he'd ever imagined.

. . .

How Konrad Korzeniowski ended up with a job on a steamer on the Congo River in the 1890s depended on a chain of historical events that, in less than one generation, transformed a vast swath of equatorial Africa from a place scarcely broached by outsiders into one of the most brutally exploited colonies on earth. Seen through the eyes of a villager on the upper Congo River, the steamboat had the character of something supernatural, if not apocalyptic.

Makulo, son of Ahalo and Boheheli of the Turumbu tribe, was born in a rainforest near the fork of the Aruwimi and Congo rivers. He was five or six when the first rumor arrived. Villagers who lived on the river told Makulo's parents that they'd seen a sort of phantom floating on the water. It was a boat that seemed to propel itself, and inside it there was a man as white as an albino, entirely covered except for his head and hands. Five or six years later, Makulo heard another set of rumors. Now there was a whole army coming down the river, questing for ivory and slaves.[30] They came from the east; they wore white cloth, carried no charms or fetishes, and spoke another language. What they did carry, said the neighbors, was "a kind of hollow stick, and when they hit it, you hear a noise, PAM PAM, and shot comes out that hurts and kills people." The weapons gave the raiders their name, "Batambatamba." When they were coming, the only thing to do was to get out of their way.[31]

Makulo and his relatives fled to another village, but one day while they were swimming, the Batambatamba encircled them. They grabbed Makulo's baby cousin from its mother's arms, flung it onto a heap of red ants, and force-marched everyone else to the camp of their chief, Tippu Tib (another echo for the sound of a gun). The hostages' relatives came bearing ivory tusks to buy their family members' freedom. Makulo's uncle was released, his aunt was released, but for a young, healthy boy like Makulo, the slavers demanded two more tusks. Before Makulo's father could return with the payment, the Batambatamba moved the captives by boat to another base, much too far away for Makulo's family to find him. The slaves left their home territory amid "cries, tears, and lamentations." Still, when Makulo arrived in the new camp, he realized he was relatively lucky. He and the other children were taken aside and given lessons in the Koran by a *mwalimu* (Islamic teacher), whereas around them crowded adult slaves, chained by the neck into groups of twenty, reeking with excrement and sweat, beaten and maimed at the Batambatambas' will.[32] Tippu Tib checked in on them sometimes, to make sure they were well, and gave them all new names. Makulo was renamed "Disasi," meaning "cartridge."[33]

Then one day during his lessons, what should Makulo see but the very ghost that had presaged his misfortunes. Up the river glided a big boat that seemed to move by itself. Inside it stood the white man. The local Kele people called him Bosongo, or albino.[34] He came out of the boat and talked at length with Tippu Tib. A little while later, Makulo saw people bring two bales of cloth and sacks of salt from the boat, and Bosongo began cutting the cloth into lengths. Each one would buy a child. Four meters for a young boy, eight meters for a bigger one. The white man purchased Makulo and twenty-two others and took them onto his boat.[35]

On board, Makulo sensed the atmosphere brighten. Everybody felt light and free; they laughed, exchanged stories; there wasn't a chain in sight. Even better, the boats were heading toward the fork in the river where he came from. Familiar places came into view, familiar languages spoken by people on the banks. The children started calling out: they were coming home! But the boats kept going. Why weren't they pulling to shore? The boats didn't stop. The children's spirits dropped like stones in the wake. They were still captives.

Bosongo gathered the children around and addressed them through an interpreter. "I didn't buy you to harm you," he insisted, "but to give you true happiness and prosperity. You've all seen how the Arabs treat your relatives and even you little children. I can't let you go back to your families because I don't want you to become like them, cruel savages, who don't know the Good Lord." The assurances placated Makulo, at least. By the time he disembarked in Kinshasa many weeks later, he had come to regard the white man as a "liberator." He may also by then have learned Bosongo's given name: Henry Morton Stanley.[36] Makulo had been caught, literally, by one of the men most responsible for advancing European colonization in central Africa.

Nominally, at least, the British had stopped coming to Africa for slaves in 1808, well before Makulo was born. Now they came in the name of ending slavery. In eastern Africa, Zanzibaris of Arab descent—the "Batambatamba" of Makulo's recollections—operated a slaving network that reached from the Indian Ocean deep into the Congo basin. Zanzibaris introduced guns and Islam, set up new towns and trade routes, and ravaged local populations along the way. A new wave of European explorers followed on their heels, scouting out avenues for "civilization, commerce, and Christianity," as the celebrated missionary-explorer David Livingstone put it.[37] Europeans aimed to stamp out the slave trade and to introduce a free market economy. But like the Zanzibaris, they carried guns, better ones, and ultimately they devastated the region still more.

Makulo's "liberator" Stanley set the tone. When Livingstone fell out of contact with Europe on an expedition to find the source of the Nile, *The New York Herald* dispatched Stanley as a correspondent to go find him. Stanley tracked Livingstone to a large slave traders' post on the shore of Lake Tanganyika and wrote up his adventures in a best-selling book. It was an extraordinary coup for Stanley, who—though none of his readers knew it—had spent his entire adult life trying to expunge the shame of his origins, born a bastard and raised in a Welsh workhouse. The book sealed his new identity. Fortified by the acclaim, Stanley decided to return to Africa in 1874 as an explorer in his own right. Where, he wondered, did the river system emanating from Lake Tanganyika actually lead? Was it the source of the Nile, as Livingstone thought? Could it be the Niger? Or was it the Congo?

Stanley mounted an expedition to find out. After a year and a half charting the Great Lakes, he proceeded west to the Lualaba River. It was the farthest inland anyone had mapped, and the capital of Tippu Tib's domain. Stanley was received by this "remarkable man," who had "the air of a well-bred Arab and was almost courtier-like in his manner."

Henry Morton Stanley in London after he "found" David Livingstone.

Stanley was an abolitionist, facing perhaps the biggest slave trader in the world. But he knew that he couldn't travel any farther without local assistance. So he cut a deal. He'd pay Tippu Tib to accompany him, with a large armed escort, for the next sixty days' marches.[38] Protection secured, Stanley led his column of about 220 men, women, and children into the "Dark Unknown," swearing to follow the Lualaba "to the ocean—or to death."[39]

For more than a hundred of Stanley's companions, the journey would be to the death: by smallpox, dysentery, scurvy, ulcers, malaria, pneumonia, typhoid. The survivors contended with snakes, hippos, croco-

Tippu Tib (right) *in Congo.*

diles, and red ants, suffocating dampness, strangling vegetation, constant hunger, and frequent human assault. Stanley reported being attacked no fewer than thirty-two times by villagers along the Lualaba. "Savages before you, savages behind you, savages on either side of you." Against this succession of "fierce cannibals" armed with arrows and spears, Stanley trained his guns to wreak "terrible execution." "It is a murderous world," he said after one battle—with Makulo's neighbors on the Aruwimi—"and we feel for the first time that we hate the filthy, vulturous ghouls who inhabit it."[40] The people of Congo, though, had far better reason to hate the white invaders.

In August 1877, Stanley lurched into the European settlement at Boma, on the Atlantic coast, with a train of "haggard, woe-begone invalids." He had come 7,000 miles in two and a half years; hundreds were dead, killed, traumatized; but he'd followed the river as he vowed, to "the broad portal into the Ocean, the blue domain of civilization!" The

Lualaba flowed into the Congo, he had verified, and swept all the way from the Great Lakes region to the Atlantic. The merchants of Boma received and congratulated him "with a great warmth of feeling." "Very moved," Stanley solemnly shook their hands, thanking them in English and "very bad French."[41]

News of Stanley's successful crossing of central Africa electrified the Western newspaper-reading public, and his two-volume account of his journey, *Through the Dark Continent*—1,092 pages written in eighty days—became another bestseller. The book established an image of central Africa in Western minds as an area of "darkness," populated by savages and cannibals, "human beasts of prey," to be subdued by force.[42]

Stanley hoped that the British government would seize upon his discoveries to promote the commercial development of the Congo basin. But his candid reports of mowing down African opposition, to say nothing of his negotiations with the slave trader Tippu Tib, shocked liberal sensibilities. An official inquiry by the British vice-consul in Zanzibar condemned his "atrocities" and put paid to any British government support. So when Stanley got an invitation from King Leopold II of Belgium to dine at the Royal Palace and discuss developing the Congo, he was happy to accept.[43]

King Leopold had been looking for someone like Stanley for years. The king was an outsized man, usually the tallest in a room, with a nose like a mountain slope and a beard like a waterfall foaming over his chest, and he was determined to play an outsized role in the world.[44] But he was king of one of the smallest, most constrained states in Europe. Formed in 1830 to reconcile French and Dutch interests, Belgium was a nation ratified by committee. The terms of its founding treaty established a constitutional monarchy that limited the king's authority and committed Belgium to permanent neutrality to preserve the European balance of power.

As heir to Belgium's modest throne, Leopold became obsessed with bursting the nation's bounds. When he looked north, he saw the Dutch managing the far-flung East Indies. When he looked south, he saw a French Empire reaching into Africa. When he looked west, he saw his first cousin Queen Victoria (married to another of his first cousins, Prince Albert of Saxe-Coburg) presiding over an empire that spanned the entire globe. Leopold wanted a piece of the world for Belgium too. He traveled to Egypt, India, and China, scoping for colonies. In the 1860s, he especially liked his chances in Southeast Asia. He investigated options in Tonkin, pressed the queen of Spain to grant him the Philippines, and approached the British adventurer James Brooke about making the Borneo province of Sarawak into a Belgian colony.[45] If a few transactions had gone differently, Konrad Korzeniowski might have found himself sailing among Belgians around Southeast Asia and never have visited Africa at all.

In the 1870s, King Leopold II turned his attention to Africa. Highly publicized European explorations made Africa the next big thing for colonial investors. In 1876 the king convened a group of academics, diplomats, entrepreneurs, and explorers in Brussels for a "Geographical Conference" on Africa. The aim, Leopold told the delegates, was to figure out how "to open up to civilisation the only part of the globe which it has not yet penetrated, to pierce the darkness in which entire populations are enveloped."[46] Leopold and his peers used "civilization" as a synonym for industrialized, Christian, white-majority societies. When they spoke of bringing "civilization" to Africa, they usually meant three things: introducing a market economy, ending slavery and slave trading, and expanding Christianity. Leopold used "darkness"—as Stanley had—as a catchall for everything he found uncivilized about African society: cannibalism, slavery, polygamy, animism, nudity—and, of course, Africans' dark skins. The more he and his followers invoked "civilization" as the opposite of "darkness," the more racist its connotations.

The conference yielded an organization called the African International Association, charged with establishing stations in tropical Africa dedicated to research, trade, and "diffusing the light of civilisation among the natives."[47] Under Leopold as president, it had chapters across Europe and the United States, chaired by princes, dukes, and generals. What it required next was a location in which to get started. When Leopold learned that Stanley had successfully followed the Congo to the Atlantic, he wanted the river basin to be the place. You couldn't get bigger than that.

Stanley arrived at the Royal Palace in Brussels on a June evening in 1878 to find "various persons of more or less note in the commercial and monetary world, from England, Germany, France, Belgium, and Holland" gathered "to consider the best way of . . . studying what might be made of the Congo River and its basin."[48] They formed another organization for the purpose, the Committee for the Study of the Upper Congo, and Stanley agreed to return to Africa to work for it, on King Leopold's payroll.

He returned to the mouth of the Congo in 1879, with the mandate of "sowing along its banks civilised settlements," as he put it, "to peacefully conquer and subdue it, to remould it in harmony with modern ideas into Nation States, within whose limits the European merchant shall go hand in hand with the dark African trader, and justice and law and order shall prevail, and murder and lawlessness and the cruel barter of slaves shall for ever cease."[49]

The single sentence contained every one of the project's keywords. "civilised," "modern," and "peaceful" versus "dark," "cruel," and "lawless." And it excluded some other notable terms. The polity imagined along the banks of the Congo would not be an *empire*, but a host of nation-states. Not a *colony* to be exploited, but a market to be developed. Not a *Belgian* project, promoting national interests, but an international effort, promoting civilization writ large. King Leopold II's masterstroke was to use Belgium's neutral position in Europe as the basis for a new vision of colonialism. In the Congo Free State he promoted a concept of "civilization" as an international ideal able to transcend parochial, protectionist nationalism.[50]

Stanley got to work founding stations. By far the hardest part of the Congo to traverse was the rapids-filled 250-mile stretch between Matadi, near the Atlantic, and Léopoldville. He spent three years supervising a road-building project between these points, earning the nickname Bula Matari—"breaker of rocks"—which went on to become a general tag for the colonial government. On the king's orders, he then proceeded a thousand miles upriver, back into the slave traders' domains, to set up a station at Stanley Falls. (It was probably on this journey that he purchased Makulo and the other children from Tippu Tib.) Wherever Stanley and the association's agents went, they held palavers (negotiations) with local chiefs and handed them treaties to "sign" with an X. By many of these

documents, the chiefs agreed "freely of their own accord, for themselves and their heirs and successors for ever" to "give up . . . the sovereignty and all sovereign and governing rights to all their territories." They also "promise[d] to assist the said Association in its work of governing and civilising this country . . . and to assist by labour or otherwise, any works, improvements, or expeditions" it undertook. All told, the agents gathered some four hundred treaties in four years.

Meanwhile in Europe, King Leopold II and his agents conferred with representatives from the great powers, seeking diplomatic recognition of the budding state. He placated the French with a "right of first refusal" to the territory should the association fail financially, and thereby also

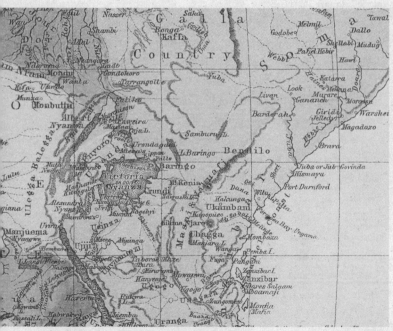

Map of the Congo Free State.

secured Britain's interest in making sure it didn't. He hired a former American diplomat to lobby Congress, and in April 1884 the United States became the first nation to recognize the association as a sovereign entity. The king's diplomatic agenda culminated at Berlin in November of that year when German chancellor Otto von Bismarck invited representatives from the great powers to discuss territorial claims in Africa. Stanley returned from Congo with his clutch of treaties just in time to attend the Berlin Conference as the "technical adviser" to the American delegation. The conference approved Leopold's claim to Congo, and, with it, endorsed his civilizing mission as an international principle. In May 1885, Leopold named the territory—seventy-five times bigger than Belgium—the Congo Free State, and declared himself its "King-Sovereign." He'd made his mark on the map.[51]

Like Belgium itself, the Congo Free State was a domain ratified by committee. Acquired peacefully by treaty, open for free trade and investment, dedicated to the highest standards of what would later be called "human rights," backed by the leaders of the emerging international community and the conventions of international law, on paper it looked as correct and appealing as could be.

Yet those who endorsed King Leopold's project had no accurate idea of what exactly they were approving. For his European and American audience, the king cast the Congo initiative as a philanthropic exercise, transcending nationalist imperialism in favor of broad humanitarian goals. It was headquartered in Brussels, he said, precisely because of Belgium's neutral status.[52] But in truth, he used a shell game of organizations to mask a massive personal power grab. The African International Association became the Committee for the Study of the Upper Congo, which became the International Association of the Congo, which became the Congo Free State. Along the way, what had started as a loosely philanthropic project underwritten by European grandees morphed into a personally administered state, with no constitutional oversight from

Belgium, nor even a board of directors or accountability to shareholders.[53] The result, noted a contemporary critic, was "an anomaly and a monstrosity from an international point of view."[54] The only thing "free" about the Congo Free State was the hand it gave Leopold II to run it however he liked.

In Africa, the duplicity was predictable, and predictably worse. None of the chiefs who put their X on the bottom of the association's treaties could read them. Even if they could have, they wouldn't have shared an understanding of "sovereignty" or "governing rights."[55] They certainly didn't share a scale of economic value, which was how Europeans could hand over jugs of gin, bolts of cloth, and *mitakos* (brass or copper wire doled out as currency) in exchange for land and resource concessions they knew to be worth vastly more on the international market.

As for the chiefs signing "freely of their own accord," the association had ways of ensuring compliance. Europeans in equatorial Africa were intrinsically vulnerable, a small, disease-prone population entirely dependent on locals for food. They played to their technological advantages to get ahead. A Belgian merchant near Boma, facing down a chief who tried to impose conditions on trade, said, "I'll put your head in the same condition as the bottle you see there," raised his gun, and blasted it to smithereens.[56] An agent of the association might hide a battery in his palm, so that when he shook hands with an African he'd deliver an electric shock, showing "that the white man could pull up trees and perform the most prodigious feats of strength." He might use a magnifying glass to light a cigar, and then tell the audience that "his intimate relation to the sun" would let him burn up the whole village if he wanted. He might pretend to load a rifle and ask an African to shoot at him—then pull out a bullet hidden up his sleeve and claim to be superhuman.[57]

Already by 1885 one association employee and accomplished amateur artist, Édouard Manduau, had figured out what "civilization" in Congo really looked like. He painted a scene on the Léopoldville waterfront of a

Édouard Manduau, La Civilisation au Congo *(1884–85)*.

white man casually noting something in a ledger, while an African deputy thrashes another African across the bare back with a _chicotte_, a sharp, rhinoceros-hide whip. Manduau entitled his picture _La Civilisation au Congo_.[58]

KONRAD KORZENIOWSKI was on the _Vidar_ in Borneo at the end of May 1887 when another boat docked at Boma, bearing consequences for his future. On board the _Vlaanderen_ was a thirty-one-year-old Franco-Belgian named Alexandre Delcommune, who had been commissioned to establish CCCI stations on the upper reaches of the Congo River. Delcommune had first come out to Africa as a teenager in 1874, lured to adventure, he said—like his contemporary Konrad—by fiction, in his case the novels of James Fenimore Cooper and Walter Scott. At just twenty-one, Delcommune had become manager for the French trading station at Boma, and he'd stayed there ever since.

To execute his mission, Delcommune needed a boat capable of pushing against the river's strong current. The CCCI had commissioned a twenty-one-meter-long stern-wheel paddle steamer of the kind used on the Mississippi. It was called the _Roi des Belges_, and it sat in pieces in the _Vlaanderen_'s hold. Steel sheets for the hull, wood fittings for the cabin, panels for the roof, nuts, bolts, washers, rivets, hoses—most of it had been packed into bundles that a single strong man could lift. The 4000-kilogram boiler was divided into six parts; the condenser and the paddle wheel were strapped onto specially designed carts. A team of mechanics from the engineering firm traveled with the _Roi des Belges_ to put it all together once they got to Stanley Pool. But first, every single one of these loads had to be ported up the rapids to Léopoldville.[59]

Delcommune liked to boast about his strength and cunning, and he hurled himself energetically into the task of figuring out how to transport this vessel. First he dispatched a convoy of 250 African porters to carry all the lighter packaged parts of the *Roi des Belges* over the wagon road that Stanley had built from Matadi to Léopoldville. Every morning he sent a deputy ahead, with a team of servants, to set up the night's camp. Next crept the long line of porters, inching through the "torrid heat" like so many snails under steel shells. Delcommune brought up the rear, riding a big Spanish mule, rounding up the stragglers. For twenty-three days they traveled this way, scrabbling up hills, skidding down escarpments, trudging through marshes and riverbeds.

That was the easy part. Moving the engine, the paddle wheel, and other heavy machinery posed challenges on another scale. On five huge carriages sat steel components weighing up to 4,500 kilograms each, strapped into place by cables and chains, which needed to be taken to Léopoldville too. Delcommune assigned teams of three hundred men to each carriage. They lined up along thick cables attached to the sides, and on a signal grasped the cables and pulled. The carriages creaked perceptibly forward. They pulled some more; the carts slid another few inches. Musicians danced around the work teams, calling refrains. The laborers responded in unison, pulled in harmony, and the engines crawled a little farther. It was really something to see, marveled Delcommune— muscle power moving steam.

It took seventeen days for the teams to cover a distance that would normally take one. Every day brought new tests: broken shafts, jammed wheels, and the constant leaching away of laborers, who had enough of the back-straining work. On the eighteenth day, the caravan had to negotiate a steep decline. Delcommune reorganized the porters to stand behind the carriages, tugging backward to slow their descent, but the brakes on one carriage failed and it hurtled out of control down into a riverbed. One man was crushed to death, two others badly wounded. Within a few hours, nearly the whole workforce walked away from the job and disappeared into the bush.

For a week, Delcommune went from village to village in the "slow and fastidious" task of recruiting more workers while waiting for reinforcements from Léopoldville. With a new workforce in place, he traded in the big carriages in favor of smaller loads suspended on poles, to be carried in relay. Four weeks later the caravan reached Léopoldville, "brightened by the happy songs of our porters," and the engineers started putting all the pieces together. In March 1888, with injuries, death, and toil and sweat beyond measure in its wake, the *Roi des Belges* steamed into the Congo River. Delcommune hosted the European officers of

The Roi des Belges.

the station for an inaugural cruise around Stanley Pool, then steamed away to chart different branches of the river basin and put new trading posts on the map.

The Congo Free State may have begun in King Leopold II's grandiose imagination, but Delcommune's feat showed how translating the king's scheme into a tangible, functional state depended on committed on-the-ground operatives like him. Between 1890 and 1898, the number of Europeans in the Free State tripled to about 1,700, of whom more and more (about two thirds) were Belgian.[60] Behind the veil of philanthropic ideals, these men (and they were all men) drove the daily, violent work of imposing order and seeking profit. Ideals didn't take them far when it came to finding, organizing, and disciplining labor; supplying, operating, and protecting their facilities; and, ultimately, making the Congo Free State pay. For that, they needed persuasion, trade goods, and force.

The sheer toil of constructing the state fell to Africans pressed into labor. Europeans had initially imported teams of Zanzibari and West African workers, but as the range and extent of projects expanded, so did the need for manpower. The chiefs who had signed Stanley's treaties agreeing "to assist" the association "by labour or otherwise" discovered that what this meant, in practice, didn't look so different from slavery. Agents moved from village to village rounding up workers. Delcommune spoke candidly about how he ensured compliance: beating laborers' hands with a "palmatoria," whipping them with the *chicotte*, or binding them into chain gangs.[61] In 1888, the government formalized its own military, called the Force Publique, which took the role of chief enforcer, and soon began to draw its manpower primarily from conscripts.[62] The Force Publique introduced a grotesque form of reckoning into its policing: soldiers had to provide severed hands from corpses to prove that bullets hadn't gone to waste, an uncanny echo of the founding legend of Antwerp.

Things had changed a lot since Makulo's childhood in the 1870s, when a boat moving by itself on the water looked unearthly. By 1890, there were twenty-nine steamers on the Congo River, nineteen of which belonged to the CCCI or the state.[63] They collected ivory from the string of stations between Léopoldville and Stanley Falls and stopped often elsewhere for food and firewood. Makulo himself was becoming a paragon of the civilizing project as its European champions envisioned it. After Stanley bought him from Tippu Tib, he passed Makulo on to one of his favorite agents in Léopoldville, and when that agent died, Makulo became the student of a Baptist missionary, George Grenfell. He converted to Christianity himself, embracing a life framed by catechism and capitalism. Makulo was relatively lucky. At the same time that he was being "civilized," the state began to set up "children's colonies" dedicated to training "liberated" children like him for the Force Publique.[64] The residents of the Congo basin arguably had more reason than ever to fear steamships and their white officers—and to resist.

In January 1890, the SAB boat *Florida* stopped at Tshumbiri, a large village where the Congo River narrows into a one-hundred-mile channel that flows down toward Kinshasa. While the crew were bartering for provisions and cutting firewood, a scuffle broke out and one of the crewmembers was wounded. The captain, a Dane named Johannes Freiesleben, went ashore to investigate and seek compensation. "I don't want any strangers in my village," declared the chief. "You have probably arrived here to plunder, return to your vessel or you will all be killed."[65] Freiesleben seized the chief as a captive, and a villager shot him with a musket in the gut. The ship's engineer stoked the boiler and sped the *Florida* away. Freiesleben died where he fell. For weeks, a witness told Grenfell, the missionary, his body remained unburied. His hands and feet were cut off. Villagers were seen wearing the dead man's coat, slippers, and watch. "The security of the white man demands that outrages of this kind be vigorously repressed," proclaimed the *Bulletin Officiel* of the Free State.[66] Seven weeks later, two steamers advanced on Tshumbiri carrying 370 soldiers. They gunned down resistance, reclaimed the body, and burned the offending town to the ground.

Not long afterward, Freiesleben's replacement, Konrad Korzeniowski, received his orders to sail.

EIGHT

THE DARK PLACES

Tumbling down the rapids from Kinshasa to the Atlantic, the Congo River bursts out of Africa with such force that you can see its sediment churning into the sea for hundreds of miles offshore, tinting the blue ocean brown. That's the first violence Konrad would have witnessed as he approached the Congo Free State on the *Ville de Maceio* in June 1890. Even before they landed, one of his shipmates, a Belgian company agent named Prosper Harou, returning to Congo after a nasty bout of dysentery the year before, would have told him about the many dangers Europeans feared: the diseases, the climate, the savages, the snakes.[1]

The *Ville de Maceio* docked at Boma, just inside the river's lip. The old European slave-trading station now had the distinction of being a national capital, and here and there flew the flag of the Congo Free State, a yellow star on a blue ground. Company and government offices faced the water, propped up on iron pilings to protect them from ants and rot. There was a post office, where Konrad could dispatch his letters to Europe, and a small Catholic chapel, gloriously styled as a cathedral, built out of prefabricated iron sheets. The governor and company directors lived on a slightly cooler plateau above the docks, connected by a narrow-gauge steam trolley.[2] It was an impressive spread considering there were no more than eight hundred Europeans in the entire Congo Free State.[3]

"Temperature very bearable here and health very good," Konrad wrote cheerfully to Marguerite Poradowska from Matadi, where he and Harou proceeded the next day. This was the last point you could reach on the river before hitting impassable rapids, so the next leg of their journey would be on foot to Léopoldville. Konrad began recording his impressions in a journal, the only one he'd ever kept.[4] Though he was speaking French with his colleagues in Congo, he made his notes in English—the language of the other manuscript he carried with him, the novel *Almayer's Folly*. Perhaps Konrad already had some sense that this journey might find its way into fiction too. What he didn't know was that the trip would be the hardest he'd ever make—and that just about every detail he noted down would find its way into his literary indictment of the whole Free State enterprise, *Heart of Darkness*.

The Société Anonyme Belge station chief hosted Konrad and Harou pending their journey up the Congo rapids. For "some reason of his own," the agent kept them waiting in Matadi for a week, then two, which gave Konrad plenty of time to size up the town and its residents. It was scarcely even a town, he found, just "four or five houses and the workshops for the railroad," which was just starting to be built.[5] The residents also struck him as a work-in-progress. Leaving aside a handful of idealistic missionaries and hardy explorers like Alexandre Delcommune, who was preparing an expedition to Katanga (the one Konrad had thought he'd be assigned to), most were ivory traders, government agents, railway engineers, Force Publique officers: hard characters in hard jobs, ambitious, aggressive, carping. "Think just now that my life amongst the people (white) around here cannot be very comfortable," Konrad noted. "Intend avoid acquaintances as much as possible. . . . Prominent characteristic of the social life here: people speaking ill of each other."

The exception was a lanky young Irishman named Roger Casement,

Construction of the railroad near Matadi.

who worked as a supervisor on the Matadi–Léopoldville railway. Meeting him, Konrad said, "I should consider a great pleasure under any circumstances and now it becomes a positive piece of luck. Thinks, speaks well, most intelligent and very sympathetic." Casement showed Konrad the shed and barracks that had just been built by a thousand laborers brought in from West Africa and Zanzibar. Konrad heard them dynamiting the hills not far from Matadi. The project was expected to take four years.[6]

In Matadi, Konrad also handled ivory for the first time. The tusks came down on steamers from the interior; their weights were measured and prices marked, then they were packed into casks to be sent down to Boma and on to Europe. Konrad found it an "idiotic employment."[7] But he wouldn't have been there without it. Ivory was far and away the most valuable export from the Congo, and the demand seemed limitless. In 1890, the ivory exchange in Antwerp surpassed that of Liverpool with a little over 75,000 kilograms. Five years later, it had almost quadrupled to become the world's largest.[8] That represented the tusks of several thousand elephants, and ivory traders had increasing trouble finding more to get.

On June 28, 1890, Konrad started the trek for Léopoldville with Harou. It was a grueling three-week march along and around the Congo River rapids. The "so-called caravan road is merely a bridle path a few inches in width"; it wound around hillsides, raked up, declined, and climbed again, through grasses that might be twice a person's height.[9] Stanley had grandiloquently proclaimed this stretch of river valley the most beautiful in the world, the passionate expression of "some wild earth-dance."[10] Albert Thys, though, probably captured the view of most Europeans trudging over the hills: "One thinks oneself in a cursed land, a veritable barrier which seems to have been created by nature to halt progress."[11] At least Konrad had it easier than the team of thirty-one African porters with whom he marched. Absent pack animals, Europeans enlisted Bakongo men and boys, sometimes just eight or nine years old, as human "beasts of burden." Toting loads of up to a hundred pounds each, as much as twenty miles a day, porters carried more than fifty thousand bundles per year back and forth between Matadi and Léopoldville.[12]

Konrad had only made long land journeys by rail, and had never moved so steadily or slowly over the earth the way he had on the sea. His journal entries showed him registering the tropical landscape with a seaman's eye. He paid attention to the air and the weather: "White mists on the hills up about halfway. Water effects very beautiful this morning. Mists generally raising before sky clears."[13] He took bearings of mountains and recorded the direction of the wind, as if by habit. He noted whether they walked up or down, through closed-in woods or open valleys, as if he were tracing currents or steering around shoals.

After a mere two days, exhaustion showed: "Harou giving up. Bother. Camp bad. Water far. Dirty." Konrad's temper shortened. The only words he had for the Africans who got and made their food, pitched camp,

Porters on the road from Matadi to Léopoldville.

carried their luggage—and sometimes carried them—were angry and irritated. "Fell into a muddy puddle," he grumbled one day. "Beastly. The fault of the man that carried me. . . . Getting jolly well sick of this fun."

Both he and Harou fell so ill they had to break the journey at a village about halfway called Manianga, where they ended up spending two weeks. Harou remained so weak he had to be toted through the final stages of the trek in a hammock, which provoked a "row with carriers all the way." "Expecting lots of bother with carriers tomorrow," Konrad "had them all called and made a speech which they did not understand. They promise good behaviour."[14] The kindest words Konrad spared on the trip were for a Baptist mission, "eminently civilized and very refreshing to see after lots of tumble-down hovels in which the State and Company agents are content to live." They had a "hospitable reception by Mrs. Comber," the only white woman he'd meet in Africa. Whatever he saw of African life, beyond the porters, made only a faint trace.

"Villages quite invisible. Infer their existence from cal[a]bashes suspended to palm trees for the 'malafu'" (palm wine). One night he was kept up by the sound of "shouts and drumming in distant villages."[15]

On top of all the physical strains, Konrad's diary captured something more sinister, entirely outside his experience to date. On day six: "Saw at a camp[in]g place the dead body of a Backongo. Shot? Horrid smell." The next day: "Saw another dead body lying by the path in an attitude of meditative repose." Later: "Passed a skeleton tied up to a post. Also white man's grave—no name. Heap of stones in the form of a cross."[16] He said nothing more than that, but the juxtapositions were startling in themselves. Each one paired a sign of violence—a stench, a corpse, a skeleton—with an emblem of civility: a campsite, a consciousness, a cross.

By the last day of his trek, at a government rest house near Kinshasa, there was little left in Konrad's journal but violence and disgust. Konrad saw a "row between carriers and a man stating himself in Gov[ernmen]t employ, about a mat. Blows with sticks raining hard," and stepped in to stop it. The same day, a "chief came with a youth about 13 suffering from a gunshot wound in the head." He examined the wound and gave the boy "a little glycerine to put on the wound made by the bullet on coming out." The journey, and the journal, concluded tersely. "Mosquitos. Frogs. Beastly. Glad to see the end of this stupid tramp."[17]

The extended stay at Manianga meant that Konrad reported to duty much later than expected. The SAB deputy director, Camille Delcommune (Alexandre's younger brother), scolded him for the delay. Konrad immediately disliked Delcommune. From Léopoldville he wrote a bitter and disgruntled letter to Tadeusz. He was lucky, given his state of mind, that he wouldn't receive his uncle's "told-you-so" response for months: "I see . . . that you feel a deep resentment towards the Belgians for exploiting you so mercilessly. . . . You can say to yourself: 'You wanted it . . .'; and if you had paid any attention to my opinion on the subject when discussing it with me, you would have certainly detected a lack of enthusiasm in me for this project."[18]

Konrad had been hired to replace the captain of the *Florida*, but he discovered that the ship was laid up for repairs. Instead, he was told to board another company steamer, the *Roi des Belges*, so that he could learn the route to Stanley Falls. For all the effort it had cost to transport and build it, the *Roi des Belges* was a tiny, tinny box compared with anything he'd sailed on before. A mere fifteen tons, with a rectangular hull and flimsy awning of a roof, open on all sides, it looked about as seaworthy as an orange crate. Konrad shared its minimal cabin space with three company agents and—to his chagrin—the deputy director Delcommune, plus a crew of about twenty-five Africans, a Belgian engineer, and the young Danish captain, Ludvig Koch.[19]

They steamed out of Léopoldville on August 3, 1890. The journey started up the channel, pushing against a strong current between high hills. At Tshumbiri, about one hundred miles upriver, the Congo broadened and sprouted islands, hemmed in by grassy banks. Up ahead the water ran like quicksilver; up close, it churned up so much silt as to lay a gritty film over the bottom of the washing buckets. Sometimes great black fronts of rain advanced toward the boat, trampled over it like ten thousand jackboots, and marched swiftly away. You could practically set your watch by the equatorial sunset, which dropped its shutter on the day at six P.M. Konrad fell asleep to the chirp and rattle of frogs and bugs.

Konrad noted just six villages in the first five hundred miles: clusters of thatch and poles, maybe some pirogues (dugout canoes). If any pirogues approached them—as they had when Alexandre Delcommune sailed on the *Roi des Belges* eighteen months before—or if they slipped away at the steamer's approach, Konrad never said. If he had any interactions with people on the banks, or even the African crew on board, he noted not a word. Later, he'd express in fiction the European paranoia

Pirogues alongside the Roi des Belges.

that any bit of jungle might hide a set of attackers, that even the crew might be cannibals.

In actual fact, the rhythms of river life required daily interaction between boat and bank, white and black. The boat frequently stopped so the crew could cut wood on the shore to feed the ravenous boiler. Here and there they'd need food for themselves, too, as tins could only take them so far; they'd have acquired bananas, perhaps, or fish, though Konrad couldn't make sense of the cassava staple *chikwangue* he saw the African crewmembers eating, which looked to him like "half-cooked dough, of a dirty lavender colour . . . wrapped in leaves."[20]

Though you might think a river would be the easiest thing a sailor could navigate—a line from here to there—every river had tricks and traps. The Congo's strength, width, and variation put it in another league from the rivers Konrad had known in Borneo. (In fact, the *Roi des Belges* was speeding off to help another steamer that had gotten caught on a snag.) All day long Konrad stood in the wheelhouse with Koch to watch and learn the waterway. He opened a new journal, printed "Up-River Book" in large letters on the first page, and entered his navigation notes as they went. The entries would have looked like code to someone who didn't know what they were, but to someone who did, they were a key to navigating the river.

Konrad identified landmarks, recorded bearings, distances, and depths, observed where to cut firewood for the engine, and sketched a few channels to indicate shape and soundings. "Steering for a little square white patch. Stick on it. Pass close to the sands—Cautiously!" "A remarkable clump of trees as per chart and many palm trees on the low shore." "Hills on left shore present a reddish appearance. All the right bank fringed with trees." "Snags along but not much off. After passing two little islands you sight a dead trunk of a tree and villages begin." He used description only when it served a navigational function. "2 islets in the bend. One of them has a thin tall dead tree with one green branch on it. It looks like a flagstaff with a bough tied up to it at right angles."[21]

Over a bridge of years, Konrad would render what he saw in majestic descriptive prose: "Going up that river was like travelling back to the earliest beginnings of the world, when vegetation rioted on the earth and the big trees were kings."[22] His journal didn't record anything of what he made of the landscape at the time. Instead, his observations crept into the other manuscript he carried, *Almayer's Folly*. A river ran through this text, too. The novel was four chapters long by the time Konrad arrived in Africa. The fifth chapter rang with echoes of the "Up-River Book." "Where the water palms end

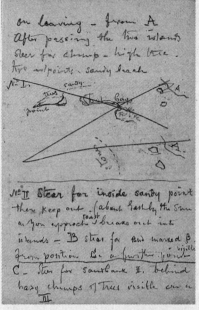

A page from Conrad's "Up-River Book."

and the twigs hang down under the leaning tree," Konrad wrote of his fictional river in Borneo. "Steer for the big green branch." Moor where "a great log had stranded . . . at right angles to the bank, forming a kind of jetty." Reach up to a big hanging branch and push under "a low archway of thickly matted creepers giving access to a miniature bay." He noted a sunrise breaking through the "white canopy of mist . . . disclosing the wrinkled surface of the river sparkling," and observed "black clouds and heavy showers" rolling in from a distance, "the angry river under the lash of the thunderstorm, sweeping onward towards the sea."[23]

The paddle wheel slapped and dripped, the smokestack puffed its ribbon into the sky, the water peeled away from the sides of the boat. The river was wider in its upper reaches than it was in the channel near

Léopoldville; in places it resembled a lake. But the higher upriver they went, the fuller and taller the trees: frothy bamboo and bearded palms, ebony and mahogany with canopies glorious enough to vault a cathedral. He'd never forget those "trees, trees, millions of trees, massive, immense, running up high," whose regal stature and grace dwarfed the panting little *Roi des Belges*.[24]

The steamer made very good time, covering one thousand miles to Stanley Falls in four weeks.[25] This was the farthest you could go before hitting another set of rapids; the farthest into "the dark continent" that European "civilization" had come. Konrad spent most of his one week at the settlement sick, but even so, it wouldn't have taken him long to get the measure of the place and its ways of doing business. The station had been sacked by Zanzibari Arabs as recently as 1886.[26] In a bid to keep the peace, Stanley had named none other than Tippu Tib the new governor of the district, as long as he promised to keep slaving out of the immediate

Fishermen at Stanley Falls.

vicinity. Tippu Tib lived in a grand mud house "fitted in true Oriental style, . . . surrounded by a high palisading, with a remarkably fine garden attached."[27] As against such structures of Eastern splendor (which would almost certainly have included a mosque, the first Konrad would have seen outside Asia), a new team of Belgian administrators had been busy setting up the architecture of Western power: company offices, dwellings for Europeans and the African "boys" who attended them, a jail, powder magazine, and barracks.[28]

Stanley Falls was the epicenter of the ivory trade, and although that trade was "free" in one sense—open to anyone who wanted to engage in it—it was also subject to hefty taxes, recently imposed by the Free State government.[29] That gave Europeans more incentive than ever to hunt down elephant tusks at the lowest prices possible. Given the challenges of traveling deep into the forest, European ivory agents did good business buying instead through a middleman: Tippu Tib. It was an excellent arrangement on both sides, as long as nobody asked too many questions about how the ivory was actually procured.[30]

However much Konrad knew of the deals cut by Europeans and Zanzibaris at Congolese expense, he would always remember one thing about Stanley Falls. All over the town you could hear the rapids crashing in the background, like the drumroll of a distant army, reminding you that the river was in charge.[31]

Konrad may not have fully recovered by the time the *Roi des Belges* sailed again, but the local SAB agent, who was due to travel with them back to Léopoldville, was much sicker, as was Captain Koch. The captain was so sick, in fact, that Camille Delcommune deputized Konrad to command the *Roi des Belges* in the interim, writing out a formal letter of appointment: "Captain: I have the honour of requesting you to take command of the steamer *Roi des Belges*, from this day forward until Captain Koch's recovery."[32]

Konrad took the helm and turned the *Roi des Belges* downstream.

They hastened back to Léopoldville at twice the speed of the upriver passage, riding the brown current between the high fences of trees. In due course Captain Koch recovered enough to resume his command, though the SAB agent did not. Ten days or so after leaving Stanley Falls he died on board, just twenty-seven years old. They buried him at Tshumbiri, the same spot where Freiesleben had been killed earlier in the year.[33]

Konrad returned to Léopoldville on September 24, 1890, to the refreshing sight of a packet of letters, including three from Marguerite Poradowska. "Poor Conrad," she wrote, "I hope you do not think you have to answer all my letters—and at length. I know you are a sailor—that it is hot and that writing is boring. As for me . . . first, it is my profession, and in addition to wanting to please you I feel a great satisfaction in adding a word to this little notebook when the urge takes me. Reply only when your kind heart speaks, and when you, too, are prompted to chat with your aunt."[34] Konrad of course wanted to write back immediately, and at great length. "In reading your dear letters I have forgotten Africa, the Congo, the black savages and the white slaves (of whom I am one) who inhabit it," he told her. "Before whom can I ease my heart if not before you?!" Out poured the pent-up anger, and anguish, of his three months in the Congo Free State.

"Decidedly I regret having come here," he began. "I even regret it bitterly. . . . Everything here is repellent to me. Men and things, but men above all," he fumed. "And I am repellent to them, also. . . . The manager [Delcommune] is a common ivory dealer with base instincts who considers himself a merchant although he is only a kind of African shop-keeper." Even worse, Konrad had learned that he wasn't going to get the promised job as a captain—there weren't, in fact, sufficient vacancies—which put him back in the familiar position of working beneath his rank, only this time with his hands tied by a three-year contract. He blamed Delcommune, who "detests the English, and out here I am naturally regarded as such. I cannot hope for either promotion or salary increases while he is here." Finally, adding injury to insult, he'd been plagued by dysentery and depression throughout his time in Africa. "My health is far from good . . . I feel somewhat weak physically and not a little demoralized; and then, really I believe that I feel homesick for the sea," for the "level expanse of salt water which has so often lulled me," and "a swirl of white foam whipped by the wind under the dark December sky." "When will we meet again?" he wondered plaintively. "Alas meeting leads to parting— and the more one meets, the more painful the separations become."[35]

The weaker, sicker, more depressed he felt, the greater Konrad's determination to find some way out. After just a couple of weeks in Léopoldville, he resolved to break his contract, having served only five months of its three-year term. This was a big step, as Uncle Tadeusz would be the first to point out: "You would expose yourself to considerable financial loss, and you would certainly lay yourself open to an accusation of irresponsibility which may be harmful to your further career."[36] But it had become for Konrad almost a matter of life or death.

In early October 1890, he wrote to Tadeusz to say he was leaving. His hand trembled with illness and strain. Back over the caravan route to Matadi he trekked, "continually sick with dysentery and fever," probably carried part of the way in a hammock—by all accounts an even more harrowing way to travel than doing the journey on foot.[37] In Boma in December 1890 or January 1891, he found a Europe-bound steamship and sailed north.

It may have been at Boma that Konrad received a letter from Tadeusz, which had been written during his outbound voyage, when he'd looked forward to Congo with more or less innocent anticipation. "You are probably looking around at people and things as well as at the 'civilizing' (confound it) affair in the machinery of which you are a cog—before you feel able to acquire and express your own opinion. Don't wait . . . until it all crystallizes into clear sentences," Tadeusz urged him, "but tell me something of your health and your first impressions."[38]

It would end up taking another eight years for the African experience to coalesce into a coherent narrative in Konrad's mind. By then both he and the Congo Free State had aged and changed form. Yet when it did, he gave it a title that captured his emotional state during those final weeks in Congo.

A RIVER IS NATURE'S PLOTLINE: it carries you from here to there. When Conrad started to write a story based on his Congo trip, *Heart of Darkness* flowed straight out. Started in December 1898, it took him less than seven weeks to finish—near record time for Conrad—the same amount of time it had taken to go up and down the river itself.

In basic outline *Heart of Darkness* matched Conrad's personal experience virtually step-by-step. But the novella was anything but basic. Conrad put the story of the African river journey into the mouth of Charles Marlow, fresh from the six-month-old story "Youth," who tells it to an anonymous group of friends in London, one of whom tells it in turn to the reader. Whereas Conrad's upriver journey had no objective but to help another boat off the shoals at Stanley Falls, in *Heart of Darkness* Conrad gave Marlow's a dramatic goal: to fetch a rogue company agent named Kurtz. The result was a text that generated an urgent sense of purpose while simultaneously veiling its meaning, a narrative as tricky to navigate as the Congo River itself.

The story opened on the Thames estuary on the deck of "the *Nellie*, a cruising yawl," the name of the boat that belonged to Conrad's friend G. F. W. Hope. Everyone on board the fictional *Nellie* had been mariners once, but only Marlow "still 'followed the sea.'" As dusk settled over the Thames, one of them found himself musing about the majesty of the river, its glorious tradition of ships and explorers setting out into the world. Marlow broke the silence. "'And this also,' said Marlow suddenly, 'has been one of the dark places of the earth.'" He described how Roman invaders had come up the river to penetrate "the savagery, the utter savagery" of ancient Britain. It reminded him of his only stint as a "freshwater sailor," some years before.

Knocking around in London "after a lot of Indian Ocean, Pacific, China Seas" and unable to find a good berth, Marlow decided to follow a childhood urge to visit Africa. Maps showed a river resembling "an immense snake uncoiled, with its head in the sea, its body at rest curving afar over a vast country, and its tail lost in the depths of the land." A continental European company had recently started trading on that river, and Marlow pressed "an aunt, a dear enthusiastic soul" living on the Continent—like Marguerite Poradowska—to help him get a captaincy on one of its steamships. "The Company had received news that one of their captains," a Dane called Fresleven (i.e., Freiesleben), "had been killed in a scuffle with the natives." Marlow dashed "like mad to get ready," met up with the company director, "an impression of pale plumpness in a frock-coat," and signed a contract agreeing "amongst other things not to disclose any trade secrets."[39]

He disembarked at a rudimentary company station at "the mouth of the big river," littered with "pieces of decaying machinery." In the distance he heard workers dynamiting cliffs to build a railway. Closer to hand he saw a group of laborers literally worked to death: "They were dying slowly—it was clear. . . . [N]othing but black shadows of disease and starvation, lying in the greenish gloom." In a warehouse he saw, as Conrad had, the company's raison d'être: "a stream of manufactured goods, rubbishy cottons, beads, and brass-wire sent into the depths of darkness, and in return came a precious trickle of ivory." He started to loathe the white men around him who had come "to tear treasure out of the bowels of the land . . . with no more moral purpose at the back of it than there is in a burglar breaking into a safe."[40]

Marlow, like Conrad, set off on the trek up the rapids with a fat, sickly white colleague, trudging "through long grass, through burnt grass, through thickets, down and up chilly ravines, up and down stony hills ablaze with heat." "I had no end of rows with the carriers," he recalled, and spotted grisly memorials, drawn almost word for word from Conrad's journal: "A carrier dead in harness at rest in the long grass near the path." "The body of a middle-aged negro, with a bullet-hole in the forehead." He arrived at the Central Station only to find that his steamer had been wrecked on a shoal, and he'd have to wait for several months among the "backbiting and intriguing" whites who lived there until rivets arrived to fix it.[41]

While he waited, Marlow heard more about the "very remarkable" Mr. Kurtz, the agent at the Inner Station whom he was supposed to retrieve. Part English, part French, "all Europe contributed to the making of Kurtz." A champion trader, who "sends in as much ivory as all the others put together," Kurtz was also more: "an emissary of pity, and science, and progress," "a 'universal genius,'" the embodiment of the European civilizing mission. But Marlow heard other things too. Kurtz was doing "more harm than good to the Company," said some; he had adopted an "unsound method." Whether he'd gone rogue, he'd gone mad, he'd gotten sick, or all three, the downriver officials wanted him removed. Marlow proceeded upriver agog to meet him.

Navigating the river called upon all Marlow's skills as a seaman, as it had Conrad's. What had in Conrad's journal been a search for routes became, as retold in *Heart of Darkness*, a search for meaning. "You lost your way on that river as you would in a desert, and butted all day long against shoals, trying to find the channel, till you thought yourself bewitched. . . . I had to keep guessing at the channel; I had to discern, mostly by inspiration, the signs of hidden banks; I watched for sunken stones."[42] To make matters worse, far from the "fellowship of the craft" Marlow had enjoyed at sea, for company he had only vulgar white passengers, and African crew whom he scarcely recognized as fellow humans.

Though Conrad had seen for himself how the Congo River widened considerably on the way up to Stanley Falls, Marlow described his passage as if walls of jungle were closing in, funneling the travelers back in time. "Deeper and deeper into the heart of darkness" the ship steamed with its crew, "wanderers on a prehistoric earth."[43] Fifty miles before reaching the Inner Station, it arrived at "a hut of reeds" on the bank, fronted by a wobbly flagpole. Inside, Marlow "could see a white man had lived there not very long ago." The telltale item was a book. "It was an extraordinary find. Its title was, 'An Inquiry into Some Points of Seamanship,' by a man Tower, Towson—some such name—Master in his Majesty's Navy," and it "was sixty years old," which made it a relic from the age of sail.[44] Marlow found in it "the shelter of an old and solid friendship" that "made me forget the jungle . . . in a delicious sensation of having come upon something unmistakably real."[45] It spoke the language of sail within a mad, savage world of steam.

A few miles below the Inner Station, fog enveloped the boat. It was like being trapped inside a pearl. From the unseen banks they heard a "complaining clamor" of human voices. Then came an attack. Arrows flew at the boat; a spear pinned the helmsman through the chest. Marlow saw the "tangled gloom" of the bank "swarming" with "naked breasts, arms, legs, glaring eyes."[46] He pulled the steam whistle and sped away. Kurtz's compound lay just ahead.

Marlow spotted the house through his binoculars. It sat in a clearing on a hill, ringed by a row of posts, "ornamented with round carved balls." Marlow hoped that meeting Kurtz, this "extraordinary creature," would redeem his journey, if not the whole European enterprise in Africa. Kurtz had laid out his civilizing vision in a report written for a European humanitarian association, the "Society for the Suppression of Savage Customs." It was a marvel of eloquence, a paean to "august Benevolence," "a moving appeal to every altruistic sentiment." But the closer Marlow got, the more he discerned.

A white man hailed Marlow from the bank, dressed in a suit made of "bright patches, blue, red, and yellow," as if he were dressed in a map of colonial Africa.[47] He was a young Russian disciple of Kurtz's; the seamanship manual Marlow had found belonged to him, and marginalia Marlow had thought to be "in cipher" were actually just Cyrillic. When Marlow looked more closely at the "ornamental" knobs around Kurtz's house, he discovered that they were actually shrunken heads, "black, dried, sunken, with closed eyelids."[48]

As to Kurtz, Marlow discovered that this prophet of civilization had become a savage lord. He was surrounded by a devilish throng of painted, masked "scarlet bodies" with "horned heads," and accompanied by a "wild and gorgeous apparition of a woman," evidently his mistress, "savage and superb," wearing "the value of several elephant tusks" in wire anklets and bracelets, and slung with "bizarre things, charms, gifts of witch-men." Even Kurtz's white skin had gone native: he looked "carved out of old ivory." At the bottom of his visionary pamphlet Kurtz had scrawled a crazed injunction: "Exterminate all the brutes!"[49]

The mighty Kurtz harbored fantasies of himself "on the threshold of great things," yet he was wasting away, obviously dying. Marlow persuaded him to leave on the steamboat by appealing to his vanity: "Your success in Europe is assured in any case." They sped downriver hastened by the current, Kurtz's life ebbing as they went. Delirious, he recalled his achievements and imagined grandiose scenes of homecoming. But in his final moments, his face seized up with terror and despair. With his last gasp Kurtz forced out "a cry that was no more than a breath—

"'The horror! The horror!'"[50]

The words hung as epitaphs over Kurtz's contradictions: the champion agent who'd promised civilization while snatching ivory; the white man who pursued "savage customs"—and "savage" women—while pressing to "exterminate all the brutes!"

Marlow left Africa, as Conrad had, sick and worn out. Back in "the sepulchral city" in Europe he disposed of Kurtz's written remains: official documents to a company agent; family letters to a cousin; Kurtz's "famous Report" to a curious journalist; and, finally, a packet of letters and a photograph to Kurtz's fiancée.

She received Marlow dressed in mourning, in an apartment that resembled "a sombre and polished sarcophagus." She pressed Marlow to tell her Kurtz's last words. Marlow remembered the timbre of Kurtz's voice from the darkness, whispering "The horror! The horror!" He couldn't bring himself to reveal the truth.

"The last word he pronounced was—your name."[51]

Marlow fell silent. On the deck of the *Nellie*, the tide had run out. Upstream lurked the great and monstrous city under its "brooding gloom." Downstream the river ran "into the heart of an immense darkness." With no wind, no tide, the *Nellie* couldn't move either way.[52]

HEART OF DARKNESS was published in the literary periodical *Blackwood's Magazine* in 1899, and in book form in 1902. It appeared on the face of it to be the quintessential river story, running from here to there: a journey from Europe to Africa, overlaid by metaphorical journeys from present to past, light to dark, civilization to savagery, sanity to madness. *Heart of Darkness* also looked in some ways like a clear passage from truth into fiction. As a matter of biographical fact, none of Conrad's other works of fiction could be so closely pegged to contemporary records of his experience. And to its early readers, the book's portrayal of Congo as a "heart of darkness" that drove white men mad also seemed to tell a true story. For in the years between Conrad's visit and the publication of *Heart of Darkness*, the Congo Free State had become a "horror" of imperial exploitation, its idealistic principles in tatters over the most nakedly abusive colonial regime in the world.

King Leopold II had been pumping cash into the Congo Free State since its inception—building stations, setting up the Force Publique, underwriting the Matadi–Léopoldville railway—but with scant return. For 1890, the year Conrad visited, revenues covered less than 15 percent of expenditures.[53] In late 1891, the king hit upon a novel solution to his debt problem: he declared huge tracts of Congo territory to be a *domaine privé*, on which the government alone could reap and export products. In a stroke, he had substituted the free trade ethos of Congo for a near-feudal system of royal prerogative. Conrad's employer Albert Thys, among others, fumed at a policy "diametrically opposed" to the Free State's founding principles.[54] But the king got lawyers to craft juridical defenses of his claim (based on the idea of *terra nullius*, or "vacant lands") and found a fresh clutch of financiers to invest, in exchange for monopoly rights.[55]

The king and his agents set about wringing profit from their concessions by several methods. First, they seized more territory. Conrad himself had been in Congo when Alexandre Delcommune set out on an expedition for Katanga in 1890, an expedition that resulted in the region's annexation. The Force Publique made forays into southern Sudan and, in eastern Congo, launched a campaign to unseat the Zanzibari Arabs. The capture of the Arabs' capital Nyangwé in 1893 was heralded by Belgian propagandists as the triumphant fulfillment of Europe's promise to "substitut[e] the benefits of civilization for the horrors of slavery and cannibalism."[56] To those in the armies' tracks, however, the fighting brought "horrors scarcely recorded since the worst days of the Spaniard in Central America, or the Englishman or Dutchman in Southern Asia."[57] Congolese like Disasi Makulo could have drawn a parallel closer to home: the Force Publique seemed like the second coming of the marauding Batambatambas it had displaced.[58]

A second way the king's men took more out of Congo was by collecting more tax revenue from the populace. Congolese couldn't pay taxes with money because there was still, deliberately, no cash economy in the Free State: Europeans traded imports like bolts of cloth, *mitakos*, guns, and alcohol for food, ivory, and rubber. But because, under the *domaine privé*, all "fruits of the land" already belonged to the state, the Congo's indigenous owners had been stripped of commodity wealth, too. So how could they pay? The government proposed an answer. Congolese could work off their tax burden instead.[59]

An extensive system of forced labor took shape. State agents traveled from village to village to draft people into work, equipped with censuses of able-bodied men, *chicottes*, and guns. Along the route between Matadi and Léopoldville, men ran into the bush to avoid conscription as porters, so the state adopted a novel method to enforce compliance, by taking women and children hostage until the men returned.[60] In some areas agents encouraged people to raid their neighbors' villages and deliver up the captives to the government.[61] The Force Publique, originally manned by recruits from West Africa, also filled its ranks by coercion. Many of its "volunteers" were *libérés* acquired from Arabs, like Disasi Makulo, and essentially shunted into another form of captivity.[62]

Makulo, for his part, had a rare positive experience with white colonizers, who educated and clothed him and converted him to Christianity. He was baptized in 1894 and returned to his native village for the first time since he had been kidnapped about a decade before. His own father couldn't believe that this strange, trouser-wearing man was truly his son; Makulo proved his identity by reciting his ancestry and showing his scars. The village erupted in celebration. They slaughtered goats and dogs for a feast in his honor, and suggested killing and roasting two slaves as well. Makulo recoiled. Don't do it! he insisted, horrified by "barbarous customs of slavery and cannibalism." He tried to preach the Gospel to them—but his compatriots weren't interested. "We don't want whites to come and set themselves up here," they said. "They're evil people. Don't show them the way here; otherwise they'll enslave and kill us. Just look at the example of the Batambatamba who committed atrocities everywhere, killing men, women and children, and capturing others, like you!"[63] It had been bad enough to face Arab marauders. Then came the whites, who resembled the Arabs, and if anything were worse. Now here was a black man who talked like the whites. A circle of violence closed around Congo like a python, poised to constrict.

Leopold and his agents had discovered a third way to squeeze profit from Congo. They found a new natural resource to extract. If you were a late-nineteenth-century European lady or gentleman of leisure, passing your hands over the piano keys or clicking balls on a billiard table, you might have touched a piece of Congo ivory. If you were one of the millions all over the world who started riding a bicycle in the 1890s "bicycle craze," you may have coasted on a cushion of Congo rubber. The pneumatic bicycle tire, patented by John Boyd Dunlop in 1888, contributed to a massive global demand for rubber. The best places to satisfy it lay deep in the tropical rainforests of the Amazon and Africa, where rubber trees and vines grew wild. Almost overnight, rubber became the Congo's most sought-after export. In 1890, the year Conrad traveled in Congo, the state exported a modest 133,666 kilograms of rubber. By 1896, it exported ten times as much (1,317,346 kilos), enough to be the biggest rubber producer in Africa. Profits from rubber sales surpassed those of ivory on the Antwerp exchange, netting 6.9 million francs.[64]

The rubber boom couldn't have come at a better time for King Leopold. In 1895, still on the verge of bankruptcy, he had briefly urged Belgium to annex the state outright, and ended up bailing himself out with another loan to the Congo Free State from the Belgian government, shrouded in murky backroom deals.[65] Ivory supplies were dwindling. Now, just one year later, rubber proceeds were well on the way to making the Congo a paying proposition.[66] The king had no more reason to give up the Free State than to abdicate the throne. Instead, he and his associates wanted to get as much out as quickly as possible.

Rubber grew in the jungle for the taking, but extracting it was a beastly business. You had to go into the rainforest, your feet squelching deep into mud and standing water, hoping not to step on a snake, ears pricked for the rustle of leopards a pounce away. You had to pick out a rubber vine in the vegetable tangle, then shimmy up its stalk to a point soft enough that you could slice into it to release the sap. It was faster just to cut a vine in half, but because that killed the vine, the state forbade it. You had to wait for the creamy liquid to drip into your pot, then wait for it to thicken and gum into latex. The easiest way was to smear the sap over your body. Once it dried, you could tear it off your skin (taking your hair or skin with it, if needed) and roll it up into balls. It could take days to fill your basket with enough tough, gray pellets to satisfy the state or company agent.[67]

This was slow, painful, dangerous work, and nobody volunteered to do it. So European agents developed an arsenal of coercive methods. Henceforth, the state required Africans to collect rubber in lieu of paying taxes. District officers set quotas for each region and dispatched the Force Publique into villages to round men up to work. In the concession territories, European agents fixed posts every hundred kilometers or so, made lists of all the men in the villages in their district, and used teams of armed sentries to push them into the forests at gunpoint. These (usually African) soldiers-cum-tax-collectors got paid for delivering rubber to their white bosses, so they had an incentive to use whatever means were necessary to make people go get it. If you refused to work, you would be punished. If you didn't make your quota (and even full-time tapping might not yield enough), you would be punished.[68] If you were caught cutting down vines, you would be punished. If you tried to run away, you would be punished. "Everywhere I hear the same news of the doings of the Congo Free State," reported one of Stanley's former associates, "rubber and murder, slavery in its worst form."[69]

From the Équateur district in central Congo came reports of a particularly gruesome form of reckoning. A Swedish missionary was about to start his Sunday sermon when a sentry barged in to seize a man who'd failed to go out for rubber. The sentry shot him point-blank. Then he ordered "a little boy . . . to go and cut off the right hand of the man who had been shot. The man was not quite dead, and when he felt the knife he tried to drag his hand away. The boy, after some labour, cut the hand off." Around the district, sentries were gathering severed hands from their victims so they could take them "as trophies to the [European] commissary. . . . These hands—the hands of men, women, and children—are placed in rows before the commissary, who counts them to see the soldiers have not wasted the cartridges." To prevent the hands from rotting, agents "put these hands on a little kiln, and after they had been smoked, they by-and-by put them on the top of the rubber baskets." Severed hands became a way for sentries to justify collection shortfalls. If enough rubber hadn't been gathered, soldiers would kill natives merely to cut off their hands. Sometimes, to spare bullets, they just cut off the hands of the living instead.[70]

This disgusting method might have sounded to contemporary Europeans like just the sort of thing you'd expect from a cannibal soldier. But it wasn't the Africans' idea. The habit chimed uneasily with that founding legend of Antwerp, which had been recently revived by Belgian nationalists. Only the terrifying, tax-collecting giant on the Congo River was the Belgian-run government itself.

When *Heart of Darkness* first appeared in *Blackwood's Magazine* in 1899, vanishingly few Europeans knew of "the horror" unfolding in central Africa. They saw only what King Leopold showed them, and he was busy setting his profits in stone: a palace to outdo Versailles, a triumphal arch to trump the Brandenburg Gate, a seaside promenade to make Ostend into the Cannes of the north. For the Brussels Exposition in 1897, he spent £300,000 on an African pavilion in Tervuren. Inside, Belgium's finest designers fashioned an Art Nouveau jungle in wood, recalling the twist of rubber vines and elephant tusks and trunks. They called their new look "whiplash style," naively oblivious about the lacerating terror of the *chicotte*.[71]

But by the time *Heart of Darkness* was republished in the volume *Youth—and Two Other Stories* in 1902, a young Anglo-French shipping clerk named Edmund Dene Morel had almost single-handedly raised public awareness about what was going on in the Congo Free State. Puzzled by company account books that showed tons of imports from Congo yet virtually no exports, Morel had stumbled across the extent of forced labor in what he suddenly realized was the "Congo *Slave* State." He threw himself into a campaign to end Congo's regime of "red rubber," stained in African blood. In May 1903, six months after the volume containing *Heart of Darkness* appeared in bookshops, the House of Commons passed a motion agreeing to strive "to abate the evils" in Congo. The Foreign Office dispatched its consul in Congo to gather evidence.

That consul was none other than Roger Casement, the railroad surveyor Conrad had met in Matadi in 1890.[72] Casement returned to Britain from his mission with notebooks ablaze with damning testimony, ready to write up his own report on the suppression of savage (European) customs. One of the first people he contacted to support the cause was his old acquaintance Joseph Conrad.

Because hadn't *Heart of Darkness* seen and said it all? As a reviewer had recently pointed out, "The 'going Fantee' of civilised man, has been treated often enough in fiction . . . but never has the 'why of it' been appreciated by any author as Mr. Conrad here appreciates it, and never . . . has any writer till now succeeded in bringing . . . it all home to sheltered folk."[73] Here was Conrad calling out "the conquest of the earth" for what it was: "the taking of it from those who have a different complexion or slightly flatter noses than ourselves."[74] He saw through the hypocrisy of Africa's would-be civilizers, granting a pass only to British domains, "because one knows that some real work is being done in there." He even

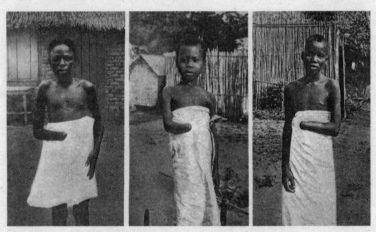

Atrocities in Congo from E. D. Morel, King Leopold's Rule in Africa *(1904).*

captured the Europeans' "unsound method" in sadistic detail—right down to the heads on posts around Kurtz's house, which Conrad may have based on a report of the Belgian station chief of Stanley Falls, who had placed "twenty-one heads" of African victims "as a decoration round a flower bed in front of his house!"[75]

Casement gave Conrad one of Morel's pamphlets, detailing the latest abuses. "It is as if the moral clock had been put back many hours," Conrad said, aghast. "And the fact remains that . . . seventy five years or so after the abolition of the slave trade (because it was cruel) there exists in Africa a Congo State, created by the act of European Powers where ruthless, systematic cruelty towards the blacks is the basis of administration."[76]

Yet for all that Conrad had seen and written of "the horror" in Congo, he never joined the Congo Reform Association founded by Casement and Morel. "It is not in me," he admitted. "I am only a wretched novelist inventing wretched stories and not even up to that miserable game."[77] He'd been raised, after all, in the shadow of an idealistic crusade against savagery that went nowhere but an early grave: his parents' struggle against tsarist Russia.[78] Casement had misread his man.

Casement had also potentially misread his book. To the extent that *Heart of Darkness* was a precise description of what was going on in Congo, it presented the Congo that Conrad had visited in 1890, not the Congo of 1898. In 1890 there was no government monopoly. There was no tax collection. There was no Force Publique. There was no rubber. There were no severed hands. ("During my sojourn in the interior, keeping my eyes and ears well open too, I've never heard of the alleged custom of cutting off hands amongst the natives," he told Casement. "I am convinced that no such custom ever existed along the whole course of the main river to which my experience is limited.")[79] Casement and others believed there was a way to clean up Congo and do civilizing right. But Conrad had detected "the horror" even in the Congo Free State of

1890 partly because, for him, the problem wasn't a hypocritical betrayal of civilization—it was the European notion of civilization as a good in itself.

In rejecting Casement's appeal, Conrad also reasserted the imaginative compass of his work. *Heart of Darkness* was more than a protest pamphlet. Marlow's listener on the *Nellie* warned the reader against literalism when he pointed out that, to Marlow, "the meaning of an episode was not inside like a kernel but outside like a haze."[80] Conrad had used the details of his own journey as stepping-stones into what he called the "foggishness of H of D." He skirted proper names for almost everything in the book (the river, the state, even Africa itself), veiled his meaning in imprecise adjectives—"inscrutable," "inconceivable," "impenetrable," "impalpable"—and twisted the narrative line of a river journey into a spiral no one voice could contain.[81] Marlow was constantly seeing things but only later managing to figure out what they meant.[82] "The horror" was deliberately enigmatic, and could be as plausibly interpreted as a condemnation of "civilization" as it could be a reckoning with the primal, universal capacity for "savagery." The meaning of *Heart of Darkness* had to be sought not only in the specific realities of Congo and Conrad's journey there, but in the experiences and thoughts that surrounded its making.

NINE

WHITE SAVAGES

KONRAD KORZENIOWSKI RETURNED to London from Congo in early 1891 carrying injuries and ghosts. His legs swelled up so badly—probably with gout, the beginning of a lifelong affliction—that his old friend Phil Krieger checked him into the German hospital in Dalston for treatment. Worse, his mind was steeped in despair. "I have been in bed a month," he wrote to Marguerite Poradowska from the hospital, "and I think it has been the longest month of my life." "I see everything with such despondency—all in black." Two weeks later: "The fact is that my nerves are disordered, which results in palpitations of the heart and attacks of breathlessness." Ten days later: "I am still plunged in densest night and my dreams are only nightmares."[1] In Konrad's mental world depression was synonymous with darkness. This was the worst bout of it he had described since his 1878 crisis in Marseille.

Tadeusz Bobrowski, who remembered Konrad's suicide attempt well, winced at his nephew's letters. "From your description, which you try to make comic, I see that you are still very enfeebled and very exhausted. . . . I have reason to suppose (you hinted this indirectly) that you have overtaxed your strength during your stay in Africa."[2] "Tormented" by a letter from Konrad "full of sadness and despondency," Tadeusz offered to send money for "a month's stay in a Maison de Santé" in Switzerland, where Konrad could take a hydropathic cure.[3] "You know me not to be over-generous, but if there is need for it I shall draw what's necessary to save your health."[4]

Three weeks in a Swiss spa did Konrad some good, but no sooner did he return to London than he was hit with a bout of malaria, and depression clawed him back. Too unwell to find a berth, he worked as a warehouse manager for his friends at Barr, Moering & Co. He found the job as tedious as "penal servitude" without "even the consolation of thinking of the pleasure you had in committing the crime." "In the evening, after returning home, I feel so lazy that I look at pens with horror," so he snatched what time he could "in the vast (and dusty) solitude of this warehouse" to write.[5]

"It seemed to him that for many years he had been falling into a deep precipice," Konrad wrote. "Day after day, month after month, year after year he had been falling, falling, falling; it was a smooth, round, black thing and the black walls had been rushing upwards with wearisome rapidity."[6] The rhythm and repetition of his prose captured the sucking, tail-chasing hopelessness of depression. Konrad wasn't writing explicitly of himself, but of Almayer, the title character of the novel he'd carried to Africa and back. In the hollow hours of his warehouse days he edited what he'd written, and added another two or three chapters.

Konrad had gone up the Congo River with Borneo on his mind. Now, he returned to the manuscript of *Almayer's Folly* with memories of Congo fresh. He described Almayer's desire to tap a secret source of inland treasure, a "mountain of gold."[7] The promise of untold wealth in the interior echoed the economy of the Congo Free State, where the richest supplies of ivory lay the farthest upriver. The same way Europeans in Congo were prepared to suspend their principles for profit, by trading with the notorious slaver Tippu Tib, Konrad had Almayer cut a deal with an old rival in Borneo, the local Malay rajah.

He also deepened the novel's portrayal of slavery, which persisted in both Congo and Borneo, even though it was officially forbidden. In *Almayer's Folly* every wealthy character owned slaves. In one of the chapters Konrad wrote shortly after his return from Africa, he attempted to enter the mind of a slave herself, a "half formed and savage mind, the slave of her body—as her body was the slave of another's will." Through her eyes he sketched a fatalistic view of life that echoed his own depressed outlook. "The slave had no hope and knew of no change. —She knew of no other sky, no other water, no other forest, no other world, no other life."[8]

Konrad had come back from Congo more embittered than ever about the tension between "civilization" and "savagery." Well before he wrote about it in *Heart of Darkness*, he put his musings about the divide into *Almayer's Folly*. "There are some situations where the barbarian and the so-called civilized man meet upon the same ground," Konrad wrote. Though Almayer had been born in Java and never visited Europe himself, he lived in hopes of retiring to Europe with his "half-caste" daughter Nina and marrying her off to a white man. Instead, she fell in love with a dashing Malay prince—and, with her mother's blessing, intended to settle with him in Bali. Almayer cursed the long years "of work, of disappointment, of humiliation amongst those savages" in Borneo.[9] His dreams of civilization vanished.

For himself, Konrad continued to draw strength from one source, his relationship with Marguerite Poradowska. He wrote to her often and intimately: "[I]f there is someone in the world to console broken hearts, it is indeed you. . . . I admire you and love you more and more."[10] He also wrote regularly to his uncle Tadeusz. Reassured by what seemed to be an improvement in his nephew's mood, Tadeusz resumed his long-standing gripe about Konrad's lack of direction in life, pointing out "certain defects" in his nephew's character. Konrad bridled at the insinuation and insisted that Tadeusz clarify.

"Well then," said Tadeusz, seizing the opening, "I consider that you have always lacked endurance and perseverance in decisions, which is the result of your instability in your aims and desires. You lack endurance, Panie Bracie [literally Sir Brother, a form of address among *szlachta*], in the face of facts—and, I suppose, in the face of people too?" Tadeusz, a maternal uncle, blamed Konrad's disposition on his father, "an idealistic dreamer." The Korzeniowski men were "always involved in various projects, most diverse in nature," Tadeusz grumbled, "they hatched them in their imagination and were even offended when anyone criticized them— considering their opponents to be 'idiots,' but the facts most often gave the lie to their dreams."

One dream, in particular, Tadeusz advised his nephew to abandon: that of Konrad's beloved "Tante Margot." Tadeusz received letters from her also, and they gave him pause. "It seems to me that you both fail to see that you are only flirting with each other . . . —as an old sparrow friendly to you both I advise you to give up this game, which will end in nothing sensible." He dismissed the widow as "a worn-out female" who would be better off accepting a proposal from an old suitor, Charles Buls, mayor of Brussels, "who would give her a position and love." For Konrad to marry Marguerite "would be a stone round your neck for you—and for her as well. If you are wise you will leave this amusement alone and part simply as friends: if not, however you have been warned!—and you will not be able to say later on that you were not warned!"[11]

Konrad wrote promptly back to Tadeusz, hoping to deflect his concern. He failed profusely. If "'speech (in this case the written word) was given to us to conceal our thoughts', then, Panie Bracie, you have coped most efficiently with the task," Tadeusz replied, "telling me on five whole pages about all the young and old, ugly or beautiful, English women you know, who importune you to flirt with them successfully or unsuccessfully . . . and all this to omit The Only One whom I suspect of such practices with you:—and she not a flat-footed Englishwoman but a certain Margaret well known to me!!" The "old bird" Tadeusz wasn't fooled. "I have got eyes to see with (this time for reading with) and ears for hearing with, and I know what I have read and it is there to stay."[12]

But perhaps Konrad's more considered response would come from Marlow's mouth, many years later, in *Heart of Darkness*, when, frustrated by the impossibility of explaining an experience to those who haven't shared it, Marlow resigns himself to the idea that "we live, as we dream, alone."[13] Though Konrad went on flirting with Marguerite—"This evening I seem to be in a corner, spine cracked, nose in the dust. Would you kindly scrape together the poor devil, put him tenderly in your apron, introduce him to your dolls, make him join the dinner party with the others?"—his uncle's words had an impact.[14] Konrad admitted to Marguerite that he lacked "perseverance, and fidelity, and constancy," and avoided visiting her.[15] He started to look for another job at sea.

In November 1891, Konrad took a position as first mate of the *Torrens*, a handsome clipper ship that carried first-class passengers to Australia. The berth fell below his certified rank of master, but it was a well-known vessel and the captain was a friend of Konrad's friend G. F. W. Hope. Konrad wrote immediately to Marguerite, counting out the days until he'd have a chance to write to her again. "During this time, remember me kindly; reserve a little corner of your heart, and on my return (within 9 to 10 months) if you are willing we shall try to meet. But what is the use of plans? Destiny is our master!"[16] He signed off, as he now often did, under the name "J. Conrad."

CONRAD MADE TWO ROUND-TRIP voyages to Australia and back on the *Torrens*. It was the finest ship he'd ever worked on, and as first mate he socialized with its well-educated, well-heeled passengers. One of them, a recent Cambridge graduate, became the first person ever to read Conrad's fiction, still in manuscript, and encouraged him to keep at it. Two others became lifelong friends: a prep school master named Edward ("Ted") Sanderson, and a young lawyer named John Galsworthy. "The first mate is a Pole called Conrad and is a capital chap, though queer to look at," Galsworthy wrote to his parents. "He is a man of travel and experience in many parts of the world, and has a fund of yarns on which I draw freely. He has been right up the Congo and all around Malacca and Borneo and other out of the way parts, to say nothing of a little smuggling in the days of his youth."[17] Neither passenger nor mate had any inkling that the other would go on to become a major novelist.

But first mate of the *Torrens* was a dead-end job as long as the captain showed no sign of retiring. In July 1893, Conrad signed off the ship and paid a four-week visit to his uncle Tadeusz in Ukraine, back on the first frontier between civilization and savagery he'd ever known. When he returned to London, the best job he could find was as second mate on an old pilgrim trade steamer. It had been chartered to carry emigrants from Rouen to Quebec, but the charterers fought with the shipowners, and no passengers materialized.[18] Conrad idled through Christmas 1893 and the New Year afloat in Rouen harbor, tinkering with *Almayer's Folly*, waiting to steam back to England and sign off. With a justice whose poetry he'd recognize in retrospect, this ship going nowhere sealed off his maritime career. He would never work as a sailor again.

Conrad had only been back in London a few weeks when a telegram arrived from Ukraine. He opened it and read. Regret to inform you . . . "the sad and painful news of the death of your uncle . . . the late Tadeusz Bobrowski."[19]

Conrad's anchor chain snapped. The man he was closest to in life was gone. He had nobody to help him, counsel him, chide him and nag him, love him like a son. Nobody to call him Konradek, "Panie Bracie," "My dear boy." "It seems as if everything has died in me. He seems to have carried my soul away with him."[20]

Tadeusz Bobrowski left Conrad an inheritance of about £1,600, enough to support him for many years, but Conrad felt only the void. The best relief he could find was to hurl himself once more into the manuscript of *Almayer's Folly*, determined to finish. It is "a struggle to the death . . . !" he told Marguerite Poradowska. "If I let go, I am lost!"[21] Death stalked the final chapters. Nina Almayer prepared to follow her lover over the enchanting, deadly ocean whose "surface was for ever changing . . . while its depths were for ever the same, cold and cruel, and full of the wisdom of destroyed life. . . . [I]t held men slaves of its charm for a lifetime and then regardless of their devotion swallowed them up." Almayer watched his daughter leave, then buried her footsteps in the sand, making "a line of miniature graves right down to the water."[22] The last pages described his desperate efforts to forget her. He burned down his house, retreated into opium, and died.

"I regret to inform you of the death of Mr Kaspar Almayer, which occurred this morning at 3 o'clock," Conrad wrote with faux solemnity to Marguerite in April 1894. "It's finished! . . . [S]uddenly this entire company of people who have spoken into my ear, gesticulated before my eyes, lived with me for so many years, becomes a band of phantoms. . . . It seems to me I have buried a part of myself in the pages which lie here before my eyes. And yet I am—just a little—happy."[23] He got the manuscript typed, bore it triumphantly to his friend Hope's office, parceled it up, and sent it, without a cover note, to the publisher T. Fisher Unwin. He chose Unwin because he liked a series Unwin was publishing under authors' pseudonyms; for himself he'd picked the name Kamudi, "a Malay word meaning 'rudder.'"[24]

Yet Conrad had rarely been so rudderless. Book finished, no berth in sight, mourning his uncle, "my nervous disorder tortures me, makes me wretched, and paralyses action, thought, everything! I ask myself why I exist. It is a frightful condition."[25] He looked for berths and failed to find one. He tried another cure in Switzerland, improving just enough to joke that "as I evidently cannot die, I must apply to living—which is very tedious." Therapeutically, he started writing a new novel, a prequel to *Almayer's Folly* using some of the same characters and revolving around "two human outcasts such as one finds in the lost corners of the world. A white man and a Malay. You see how Malays cling to me! I am devoted to Borneo."[26]

Depression dogged his days. "The work goes very slowly. I am discouraged. Ideas don't come," he wrote to Marguerite. "I feel inclined to burn what there is. It is very poor!" Still, he added a few days later, "one talks like that, but then one lacks the courage. There are those who talk like that of suicide." "Good God! How black, black, black everything is!"[27]

He leaned on her for intimacy and comfort. "My dear Aunt," "my very dear and very charming Aunt," "dear and kind Marguerite," he would write. "You cannot know how precious your affection is to me!" "Your letter . . . makes me want to be near you. . . . To be so completely understood is a blessing, and you have understood me from beginning to end." "You are the only one in the world to whom I can tell everything— and your sympathy is, therefore, even more precious." "I think of you so often! Every day." "I kiss you—on both cheeks. . . . I wait for a letter from you each day." "Yours with all my heart," he would sign off, "ever yours," "your J. Conrad."[28]

One piece of news broke through Conrad's despair. In October 1894, Unwin offered to publish *Almayer's Folly* and pay £20—a paltry advance (less than three weeks' wages on the *Torrens*), but "the mere fact of publication is of great importance." "Now, I need only a ship in order to be almost happy."[29] Conrad went to meet his new publishers and was greeted so warmly by the readers who'd vetted his manuscript that he feared they were making fun of him; but on the contrary, one of them, Edward Garnett, would instantly become a close friend. They ushered him into the presence of "the great man" Unwin himself, who greeted his new author with breezy authority. We'll give you critical attention and "a handsome volume at six shillings," Unwin promised. "Write something shorter—same type of thing—for our Pseudonym Library," he added, "and if it suits us, we shall be very happy to be able to give you a much better cheque."[30] But of course, "Joseph Conrad" was already a pseudonym of sorts, translating Captain Konrad Korzeniowski into an English novelist.

Almayer's Folly: The Story of an Eastern River went on sale in April 1895. It was dedicated "to the Memory of T.B."—hiding Bobrowski's Polish name under initials, as "Joseph Conrad" hid "Konrad Korzeniowski." The novel's title may have masked something too. Though Conrad set the book on an "eastern river," he took pains to distance it from specific real-life sources. Yes, he told his publishers, the novel took place in Borneo, but "river and people have nothing true about them—in the vulgar sense—but the names." What's a novel, after all, but a work of the imagination? "Any criticism that would look for real description of places and events would be disastrous to that particle of the universe, which is nobody and nothing in the world but myself."[31] Besides, he pointed out, he was writing about something broader. "Could you not say something about being a 'civilized story in savage surroundings?' Something in that sense if not in those words."[32]

Conrad developed his ideas of civilization and savagery in an "Author's Note" to the book.[33] It responded to an essay that had recently attacked all books set in "exotic" locations as "de-civilized," and "the strange people and the far-off countries" they described as "de-civilized" too.[34] "The critic . . . seems to think that in all those distant lands all joy is a yell and a war dance," Conrad retorted, "all pathos is a howl and a ghastly grin of filed teeth, and that the solution of all problems is found in the barrel of a revolver or on the point of an assegai." The images were striking given that Conrad's book was set in Asia: an assegai is a southern African spear, and a "ghastly grin of filed teeth" would immediately evoke racist caricatures of Africans, particularly those Congolese who practiced tooth sharpening.[35] Conrad concluded with a defense of the essential kinship of all humankind. "There is a bond between us and that humanity so far away," he asserted, and "I am content to sympathize with common mortals no matter where they live; in houses or in tents, in the streets under a fog, or in the forests behind the dark line of dismal mangroves that fringe the vast solitude of the sea."

In the book Conrad later wrote *about* Congo, he put the sentiment from the book he'd written partly *in* Congo to the test. Marlow described a group of Africans in crude racist stereotypes, as "a whirl of black limbs, a mass of hands clapping, of feet stamping, of bodies swaying, of eyes rolling." It was inconceivable to Marlow that there might be a Disasi Makulo among them—that Africans might have a consciousness, let alone a history, society, or faith. (All of which Marlow granted to Asians, albeit in equally stereotyped terms.) Even so, a sense of recognition pulled Marlow up short. "No, they were not inhuman," he realized. "[W]hat thrilled you was just the thought of their humanity—like yours—the thought of your remote kinship with this wild and passionate uproar."[36] He did a similar double take when he discovered that some of his crewmembers were cannibals: shocked not by the fact that these people ate other people, but that these people didn't eat *him*.[37] Marlow "looked at them as you would on any human being, with a curiosity of their impulses, motives, capacities, weaknesses." They had, he realized, a sense of restraint, a sense of ethics. They had the very thing that "civilization" was supposed to imbue—while Kurtz, by implication, did not.

Conrad's slippage between Borneo and Congo, between realms visited and imagined, and his recognition of humanity across a line of savagery that he'd first encountered, himself, in Russia, had the effect of binding his racist language to a potentially radical suggestion. What made the difference between savagery and civilization, Conrad was saying, transcended skin color; it even transcended place. The issue for Conrad wasn't that "savages" were inhuman. It was that any human could be a savage.

WITHIN MARLOW'S SENSE of "thrilled . . . kinship" with "wild and passionate" Africans there coursed another current, less acknowledged, if no less challenging to the idea that savagery and civilization inhabited distinct and separate realms. That was the pull of sexual desire. In Conrad's "exotic" fiction, sexual attraction appeared where what passed for "civilization" did not. It was there in the allure of the feminized sailing ship, as against the sterile machinery of steam. It was there in Patusan, beyond the range of telegraphs and steamships, where Jim fell in love with Jewel. It was there in the central plotline of *Almayer's Folly*, in Almayer's tussle with his own Asian wife over their daughter's marriage— their reproductive future. And it was vividly present in *Heart of Darkness*, in Kurtz's "savage and superb" and sexually desirable mistress, a black woman clothed in the profits of ivory, contrasted with Kurtz's frigid fiancée, a white woman wearing mourning in the "sepulchral city." By ingeniously substituting "your name" for "the horror," Conrad linked the two women through the novel's subterranean channels of desire. Marlow explained the lie by telling his listeners that "the women . . . should be out of it. We must help them to stay in that beautiful world of theirs, lest ours get worse."[38] It sounds in itself like a piece of unexamined sexism, but as with Marlow's racist descriptions of Africans, Conrad embedded it in a story that subverted prejudices as much as it reinforced them.

This undercurrent of yearning—for the noncivilized, for the other, for the forbidden—stood in tantalizing relation to Conrad's own love life. Whether he had any sexual relationships with any women at all, in

Europe or beyond, there was never the slightest contemporary clue. It's tempting to read that silence more as a reflection of secrecy, shame, or simply discretion than as the reality of his experience. But there was abundant evidence of Conrad's fervent platonic attachment to his widowed "aunt" in Brussels. Formed on the eve of his trip to Congo, it entered an unexpected new chapter in the immediate aftermath of his becoming a published author.[39]

The day after *Almayer's Folly* was officially released, Conrad decided to go back to the spa in Switzerland "to repair my wretched nerves with cold water and pure air."[40] His spirits improved in the mountains, so much so that he soon found himself flirting with another guest: a young Frenchwoman named Emilie Briquel. Conrad told the Briquel family that he was English, masking his Polish origins by speaking with them in French. Emilie was enchanted by the captain, whose fine manners were burnished by the sheen of tropical adventure. He found her charming in turn—charming enough not to mention to Marguerite Poradowska, whom he promised to visit in Paris on his way home.

But Conrad left Switzerland without making any romantic overtures to Emilie. He came back to London in June 1895 musing openly, unusually, about love. Love could give him a much-needed reason to live, he wrote to his new friend Edward Garnett. "Still, one must have some object to hang his affections on—and I haven't."[41]

And Marguerite Poradowska? He wrote her a short note a few days later. "I carried away such a good and charming memory of you, of you gay and tranquil in your nest among the birds," he said, evidently referring to a recent meeting, and signed off, as usual, with a warm "embrace."[42] The letter matters less for what it said than for what it didn't. After dozens of letters from Conrad since 1890—effusive, confessional, throbbing with platonic love—this was the last that Marguerite would preserve, and perhaps receive, for another five years. What happened? Had Conrad seen her in Paris? Had he avoided her? Did one of them go too far? Did one of them not go far enough? The mystery gained intrigue given what happened next.

In March 1896, Conrad learned that Emilie Briquel was engaged to be married and wrote to her mother with congratulations. "For her I wish landscapes bathed in sunlight, cool and untroubled shade on the pathways of her life, and the mild breezes of an eternal spring." Then he dropped a bomb. "I also am getting married," he concluded. "But this is a long story which, if you will allow me, I shall relate in my next letter."[43]

The news shocked everyone who knew him. He explained more to a cousin in Poland. "I announce solemnly . . . that I am getting married. No one can be more surprised at it than myself. However, I am not frightened at all, for as you know, I am accustomed to an adventurous life and to facing terrible dangers." Still more astonishing was the person that he'd

LEFT: *Jessie George on the day of her marriage to Joseph Conrad.*
RIGHT: *Joseph Conrad on the day of his marriage to Jessie George.*

chosen. "Jessie is her name; George her surname. She is a small, not at all striking-looking person (to tell the truth alas—rather plain!) who nevertheless is very dear to me. When I met her a year and a half ago she was earning her living in the City as a 'Typewriter' in an American business office of the 'Caligraph' company." After their wedding, which was scheduled for two weeks hence, he intended to move to Brittany and "start working on my third opus, for one has to write in order to live. A few days ago I was offered the command of a sailing vessel—the idea had pleased my Jessie (who likes the sea) but the terms were so unsatisfactory that in the end I refused. The literary profession is therefore my sole means of support."[44]

On March 24, 1896, Joseph Conrad and Jessie George went to the registry office at St. George Hanover Square to "join our two humble fortunes and face together the heat and dust of the road."[45] He was Catholic and she was Protestant, so a civil wedding tidied up the difference. Conrad had no relatives, and was manned only by his old friends Phil Krieger and G. F. W. Hope. Jessie's sprawling family—she had eight siblings—attended en masse. The new Mrs. Conrad puzzled all day over her husband's peculiar behavior. He was standoffish with her family, and when they were alone that night, he sat up late writing letters, which he insisted on going out to post at two A.M. The next day, the newlyweds withdrew (in his words) "from the sights and sounds of civilization and into the wilds of Brittany."[46] As the train hurtled through a tunnel, Jessie was startled by a flash of light. With a jolt of terror she thought her strange new husband had hurled a bomb—like the terrifying anarchists from the Continent.[47]

Who actually was this man to whom Jessie George was now suddenly bound? Conrad (as she called him) was utterly unlike anybody she'd ever met, not merely the first foreigner she knew well, but "the first grown man who appeared to take a particular interest in me." He was "complex," "hyper-sensitive and broodingly reserved," and she didn't expect she would ever really understand him. His strangeness could be disconcerting. For instance, when he proposed. They'd spent the morning at the National Gallery. As they left, he turned to her and said, look. I don't have very long to live, and I don't plan to have children. But for whatever it's worth, he shrugged, I think we could spend a few happy years together? She agreed. Engaged. Done. They took themselves to lunch to celebrate. Muffled by awkwardness, they ate in near silence. Conrad darted away with an "expression of acute suffering" and made no contact for several days, leaving his stunned fiancée to fear that "he had already repented of his offer."[48]

Strangeness can be attractive. There were his wide-set almond eyes, the spellbinding stories he told, each time slightly, dynamically different. She was pulled toward "something restless in him, . . . a sort of inward fire that robbed me of nearly all my powers of speech." She required no words to read his inner neediness. She responded instantly with a "maternal feeling for that lonely man, who had hardly known anything of a mother's care, and had no experience of any sort of home life."[49] And she sensed early, rightly, that he would care for her too. When she got sick in the very first week of their honeymoon, he fluttered attentively around her. A cycle of sickness and care—her illness, his nursing, his illness, her nursing—would shape their shared life.

Who was this woman with whom Conrad now suddenly lived? He had met her in 1894, probably when he was getting *Almayer's Folly* typed for publication, and he'd seen her maybe five more times before proposing in 1896. Every other woman in his life had been a genteel, French-speaking lady of leisure. Jessie was a working-class girl from Peckham. She was eighteen years old. Her father, a warehouseman, died young, so she worked as a typist to help support her bevy of younger siblings.[50] She had never been abroad. She didn't speak French. Their courtship had no flirtatious parlor games, coquetting around the billiard table, or languid carriage rides in botanic gardens. If he'd shared any professions and confessions in letters from Switzerland, he wanted them erased. Before the wedding he told her to burn all his letters, and watched as she obeyed.[51]

Conrad's friends couldn't believe he had married such an uneducated, unrefined person; his uncle Tadeusz, had he been alive, would surely have been horrified. Conrad had evidently sensed, though, that Jessie had qualities that he needed and craved: an even temper, good humor, patience, an impulse to nurture. She would be happy to make her life out of caring for his. He wrote cheerfully to Edward Garnett from his honeymoon that she was "a very good comrade and no bother at all. As a matter of fact I like to have her with me."[52] She respected his silences and moods, she took care of his daily necessities. If Tadeusz had been alive, he ought to have congratulated his nephew on giving up romantic dreams at last and settling into a union that worked. "We live, as we dream, alone," Marlow would say in *Heart of Darkness*. After years of dreaming alone, Conrad chose to live with somebody else.

The newlyweds rented a stone cottage on the peninsula of Île Grande, "actually a whole house!!"—the first that Conrad had had since childhood. From one side of the house, he could see the coast stretching along the water, "rocky, sandy, wild and full of mournful expressiveness," and out the other he looked to the horizon, "green and smiling and sunny." Downstairs there was a big, flagstoned kitchen, where "the fire place alone is big enough for [Jessie] to live in." Upstairs there were two bedrooms. Of these Conrad never said a word, but Jessie chafed at the coarse linen sheets that clothed the canopy bed, with roughly stitched seams down the middle.[53]

The rhythms of a marriage gained pace. Mr. and Mrs. Conrad hired a four-ton cutter named *La Pervenche* (Periwinkle). Conrad taught his wife how to man the tiller, and they cruised around spires of rock with her alternating as helmsman and lookout. Some days they took long walks. In a field of yellow wildflowers, Jessie stooped to gather a bouquet. Conrad pulled out his new cigarette case, a wedding present from Ted Sanderson, and smoked a pungent French cigarette. They went back to their cottage, laid their caps and sticks in the kitchen, and Jessie made supper. Conrad got to work on his third novel, *The Rescuer*, another chapter in the adventures of Captain Lingard in Malaya. When he finished his pages, he handed them over to Jessie to type.

"It was a happy time," Jessie remembered in her memoirs. "There is no doubt in my mind that it was a happy time."[54] But Conrad's demons descended. Two months into their stay, he confessed to Edward Garnett that "I have long fits of depression, that in a lunatic asylum would be called madness. . . . It springs from nothing. It is ghastly. It lasts an hour or a day; and when it departs it leaves a fear."[55] Rheumatism swelled and stiffened his hand, making it painful to write. The novel he was working on ran aground. "It is as if something in my head had given way to let in a cold grey mist. I knock about blindly in it till I am positively, physically sick. . . . I ask myself whether I am breaking up mentally. I am afraid of it."[56]

He found an escape hatch from the novel by writing a story.[57] "It is a story of the Congo," he said. "All the bitterness of those days, all my puzzled wonder as to the meaning of all I saw—all my indignation at masquerading philanthropy—have been with me again, while I wrote." He called it "An Outpost of Progress," and a few of its details showed that he had read Henry Morton Stanley's paean to the civilizing mission, *The Congo and the Founding of Its Free State*.[58] It described a remote trading station in Africa, run by two Europeans named Carlier and Kayerts (the name of somebody he'd traveled with in Congo), with "a Sierra Leone nigger" named Makola as bookkeeper. They bought their food and ivory from the local chief, "a grey-headed savage" whom they greeted with the fond question: "'How goes it, you old image?'"[59]

After a few months in the station, some outsiders arrived, armed with "percussion muskets." They were "bad fellows," Makola explained to his employers. "They fight with people, and catch women and children.

They are bad men and got guns." But they also had ivory. On Kayerts's authorization, Makola bartered away ten Africans who worked at the station in exchange for "six splendid tusks." But the slavers also seized some of the villagers, and the chief cut off food to the station in retaliation. Stranded, suspended in the midst of "pure unmitigated savagery," Kayerts and Carlier descended into starvation and madness. They "talked about the necessity of exterminating all the niggers before the country could be made habitable"; they "cursed the Company, all Africa, and the day they were born." In time they began to fight with each other. In a scuffle over a few sugar cubes, Kayerts shot Carlier dead, then killed himself. When "the Managing Director of the Great Civilizing Company" finally showed up to check on them, he discovered Kayerts's corpse hanging from the cross on a white man's grave. From a puffed purple face his "swollen tongue" stuck out "irreverently" at his boss.[60]

It was the most cynical, despairing thing Conrad had ever written. Jessie recalled how, on mornings when "he happened to be in a good mood," Conrad would greet her with a line from the story: "'How goes it, you old image?'" But she knew he was "in a somewhat savage mood" when he wrote "An Outpost of Progress." It was the only story he didn't let her read until it was completely finished. He handed the final manuscript to her to type. Do it fast, he ordered. "I want it out of the house!"[61]

Why did Conrad imagine his way back to Congo in the middle of his honeymoon? One answer may have lain within the metal travel trunk Conrad had brought to France. Rummaging around inside it Jessie found "two little sixpenny notebooks with shiny black covers" containing his Congo journals. Conrad wanted to burn them straightaway, she said, but got distracted before he could do it.[62]

Another may have lodged within his own, depressed outlook, as a sense of hopelessness and nihilism pushed him to write about a place where he'd felt the same way. "An Outpost of Progress" speaks from an emotional universe in which pain is the only truth. "We talk about oppression, cruelty, crime, devotion, self-sacrifice, virtue, and we know nothing real beyond the words. Nobody knows what suffering or sacrifice mean—except, perhaps, the victims."[63]

ON JULY 1, 1898, the Matadi–Léopoldville railway, whose first stages of construction Conrad had seen in 1890, was declared officially open "to the humanitarian and commercial enterprises of the civilized world."[64] Among the VIP delegation who'd traveled to Africa to see it was Charles Buls, the mayor of Brussels—and the longtime suitor of Marguerite Poradowska.[65] Eight years in the making instead of the projected four, costing 82 million francs instead of the budgeted 25 million, the railroad project had become a hell within a hell. One in five workers had died of exhaustion and sickness in the first two years, "desertions multiplied, revolts broke out, and there was total demoralisation among the ranks." The railroad company imported Barbadian and Chinese coolies to fill out the labor force, who ended up dying or fleeing in even greater numbers. A thousand kilometers into the bush, people stumbled across the corpses of Chinese workers who'd fallen on a desperate flight "toward the rising sun," east, toward home.[66]

After the ceremony, Buls traveled by steamer to Stanley Falls and back, following "the enormous liquid serpent that spans four thousand kilometers with its sinuous folds," just as Conrad had done in 1890.[67] He wrote up his impressions in a short book called *Congo Sketches*. It was a notable companion piece to Conrad's journey, not only because it showed how the Congo Free State had changed materially since 1890. Buls was the first in a long line of outsiders to see the Congo in part through Conrad's eyes. Encouraged by Marguerite Poradowska, their mutual connection, Conrad had sent Buls a copy of *Almayer's Folly*. The mayor read it "at a single sitting" and wrote back to congratulate the author. "I now imagine perfectly" the Borneo jungles, and "the *yellow race's* inner life. . . .

With you one gradually fathoms their character and grasps the profound differences that exist between their way and ours of contemplating life's ideal."[68] When Buls described the Congo forest he echoed one of the passages he most admired in *Almayer's Folly*—a passage, in turn, that Conrad wrote during or shortly after his trip to Congo.[69]

On the edge of Stanley Falls, amid a row of "miserable" workers' huts, Buls was struck by a few dwellings that looked nicer than the rest. He looked more closely and saw women on the verandas, dressed in necklaces and tidy smocks, rocking babies. Then he saw that the babies had a "yellow color," the telltale sign of "fraternisation among the races"—and in Buls's moral universe, of civilization gone wrong.

And the babies' white fathers, Buls was alarmed to discover, were actually proud of them! Plainly, Buls decided, it took strong inner resources to withstand "moral and physical depression" in a place like this. When weaker men, "and one unfortunately sees many in Congo, find themselves in contact with pure savagery, primitive nature, barbaric man," they give in to "brutal instincts no longer constrained by the influence of civilized society." To learn more about this social, mental, even biological contamination, Buls directed his reader to the "fine psychological analysis" of white men in the jungle by a steamship captain named Joseph Conrad, in his story "An Outpost of Progress."[70]

It was with some humor that Conrad announced the birth of his own first child, in January 1898, as the arrival of a hybrid. The boy was christened Alfred Borys, "the principle on which his name was chosen" being "that the rights of the two nations [English and Polish] must be respected. Thus, my wife representing the Anglo-Saxons chose the Saxon name Alfred," while Conrad "wanted to have a purely Slavonic name" but also one that English-speakers could pronounce, and settled on Borys.[71] Baby Borys appeared henceforth in his father's letters as another burden to carry through an especially dark and challenging year.

Conrad spent 1898 beset by financial pressures and deadlines, which while stimulating to some authors, he found debilitating. He had lost the majority of his inheritance in a bad investment (in a South African mining company), so he depended entirely on the small income he earned from writing: £20 here, £35 there—enough to cover the rent (£28 per year), but not much besides.[72] Though Conrad did manage to write "Youth" in the summer of 1898, he was supposed to be finishing his novel *The Rescue* (as he'd renamed *The Rescuer*), and it felt more impossible than ever.[73] Desperate for an escape, he even went to Glasgow to look for a ship, despite not having worked as a sailor in five years. "To get to sea would be salvation. I am really in a deplorable state, mentally. I feel utterly wretched. I haven't the courage to tackle my work."[74]

A £250 contract for serial rights to *The Rescue* promised to bail him out financially, but the deadline terrified him. "Gone are alas! those fine days of 'Alm: Folly' when I wrote with the serene audacity of an unsophisticated fool."[75] Unable to make headway on the novel, in December 1898 Conrad started a fresh story to fulfill a commission from the prestigious *Blackwood's Magazine*.[76] He turned to the same subject that had engaged him during his honeymoon. "It is a story much as my *Outpost of Progress* was," Conrad explained to the publisher, "but, so to speak 'takes in' more—is a little wider—is less concentrated upon individuals." "The title I am thinking of is '*The Heart of Darkness*' but the narrative is not gloomy. The criminality of inefficiency and pure selfishness when tackling the civilizing work in Africa is a justifiable idea."[77]

"Kayerts" was just a diphthong away from "Kurtz." Many people would interpret *Heart of Darkness* the same way Buls read "An Outpost of Progress." Edward Garnett, whom Conrad praised as "the Seer of the Figures in the Carpet" in his work, described *Heart of Darkness* as "the acutest analysis of the deterioration of the white man's *morale*, when he is let loose from European restraint, and planted down in the tropics as an 'emissary of light' armed to the teeth, to make trade profits out of the 'subject races.'"[78] Both made Africa the backdrop, if not the agent, of white men's psychological collapse.

Yet as acts of literary creation, both African stories actually helped save Conrad from a psychological collapse induced by his rather ironically entitled novel *The Rescue*. The same way Conrad's 1890 trip to Congo was a brief anomaly in a maritime career spent overwhelmingly on long-haul sailing ships, *Heart of Darkness* was a brief anomaly amid years of writing about the sea and Southeast Asia. Not only had Conrad composed it on the heels of "Youth" and in the middle of *The Rescue*. When it was finished, still unable to face *The Rescue* ("which seems to have no end and whose beginning I declare I've forgotten. . . . The African nightmare feeling I've tried to put into *H of D* is a mere trifle to it"), Conrad resumed a story he'd begun earlier in the year, in the blank pages of an old poetry album of his grandmother's, which he'd called "Jim: A Sketch."[79] Now Conrad introduced the character of Marlow, fresh from *Heart of Darkness*, transforming "Jim: A Sketch" into the novel *Lord Jim*.

Where, in Conrad's imagination, did Borneo end and Congo begin? Maybe, when Conrad wrote about the heads on stakes around Kurtz's house, he had read about the Stanley Falls station chief who had placed severed heads around his garden. Or maybe he had read, in one of the only English books then available about Congo, about an upriver village "surrounded by a palisade," "the top of every tree" of which "was crowned with a human skull."[80] Then again, maybe Conrad had been thinking of the place where head-hunting was the "savage" practice that Europeans most wanted to stamp out—namely Borneo.[81] Perhaps he remembered how on his first voyage east in 1881, his uncle Tadeusz passed on a request from a well-known Kraków anthropologist "to collect during your voyages skulls of natives, writing on each one whose skull it is and the place of origin."[82] While Kurtz's stockade evoked head-hunting, the archetypal "savage" practice of Borneo, when Conrad later wrote a story ("Falk") about the archetypal "savage" practice of Congo—cannibalism—he set it in Asia. In both stories, the savages were white.

You can't tell a river's source by standing midstream, but you can take the measure of its flow. Conrad's imagination, like his experience, coursed over continents. It may have been that interplay of influences, the global range of his experience, that let Conrad take the book's essential turn, from Africa to Europe. For as the rivers of Borneo flowed into the Congo, the Congo flowed in and out of the Thames. Conrad bent the narrative line of Marlow's river journey into a loop.

When the Thames reminded Marlow of the Congo, he wasn't simply saying: Look, Africa is more primitive than England. He was saying that history is like a river. You can go up or you can go down. You can ride the current to get ahead, but the same force can push you back. By nesting Marlow's experience in Africa inside the telling of his story in England, Conrad warned his readers against any complacent notion that savagery was as far from civilization as there was from here. What happened there and what happened here were fundamentally connected. Anyone could be savage. Everywhere could go dark.

PART FOUR

EMPIRE

Map of the American empire, 1904.

TEN

A NEW WORLD

BOXING DAY AT Pent Farm, Kent, 1903. Presents unwrapped, fowl digested, Nellie Lyons the housemaid busily tidied their "sort of one-horse existence" into well-scrubbed respectability.[1] The cold this winter had sapped Jessie, who rested upstairs. Five-year-old Borys tinkered with his mechanical toys. Escamillo the dog slumped in a shaggy white heap on the floor. Conrad wrote Christmas letters. Thank you for the pencil case you sent to Borys. Thank you for the book you gave him. Borys says "that the pistol is first rate."[2]

The Pent lived up to its name, an old Kentish word for "slope," with a pitched roof drawn like an oilskin hat down an old man's face.[3] From the back of the house Conrad could see the sloping Downs zigzagging toward the sea. He worked in the front, facing the farm. Winter made black-edged widows of the outbuildings—rook-infested tithe barn, granary, wagon shed—squired for most of a generation by the Finn brothers. Borys told them apart by the color of their aging beards, Brown Finn and Grey Finn.[4]

Conrad had sublet the Pent in 1898 from another writer, Ford Madox Ford. Ford came with a distinguished cultural inheritance—he was the

Pent Farm, Kent, the house where the Conrads lived from 1898 to 1907.

grandson of the painter Ford Madox Brown, and nephew of the pre-Raphaelite painter Dante Gabriel Rossetti and poet Christina Rossetti—and so did the Pent. "The whole old place is full of rubbishy relics of Browns and Rossettis," said Conrad. He set himself up at "Christina Rossetti's writing table" to work.[5]

Moving into the Pent was like moving into the profession of being a writer. Just a few years earlier, Conrad had been a bachelor and a jobbing sailor looking for a captaincy. He arrived at the Pent in 1898 as a critically acclaimed writer, with Jessie and baby Borys, to join a circle of fellow writers who all lived within easy visiting distance. Henry James was the fulcrum, revered among younger authors as "the Master." James had gratefully received an inscribed copy of *An Outcast of the Islands* and given Conrad his imprimatur by reciprocating with a book of his own. Also nearby was H. G. Wells, one of the most popular writers in England, with whom Conrad had seized an acquaintance after Wells favorably reviewed *An Outcast*.[6] Still closer was Stephen Crane, the precocious American author of *The Red Badge of Courage*. He had judged *The Nigger of the 'Narcissus'* "crackerjack," and bonded with Conrad over a lunch arranged by their publisher. Closest of all, in body and spirit, was Ford. Half a generation younger than Conrad, Ford was a disciple, an amanuensis, and, at Conrad's suggestion, a collaborator. In 1903 they had published their second coauthored novel together, *Romance*, though judging by the first, *The Inheritors* (1901)—an overwrought stab at popular science fiction—one talent plus another came out closer to zero than to two.[7]

It was at the Pent that Conrad had also become a professional writer in a material respect. Everyone in his circle was represented by the same literary agent, James Brand Pinker, who placed their writing with the best publishers for the best price. In 1901, following the completion of *Lord Jim*, Conrad had signed up with Pinker too. Pinker quickly became more than just Conrad's agent; he was banker, mentor, taskmaster, friend. Conrad never looked for a berth at sea again.

The first thing Conrad had written at the Pent, in December 1898, was *Heart of Darkness*. Now, five Decembers later, in walked Roger Casement to discuss it. For a day and a night, Conrad listened to Casement describe fresh horrors from the Congo Free State. Bodies smeared in rubber, baskets filled with hands. Though he couldn't bring himself to join an organized reform movement, he did know one small way he might help Casement. Conrad took out a fresh sheet of notepaper and addressed it to the writer and social activist Robert Bontine Cunninghame Graham.

"I send you two letters I had from a man called Casement," Conrad wrote to Graham. Read them, Conrad urged, and see what horrors had been unleashed in Africa. A horde of "modern Conquistadores" was plundering the continent. "Leopold is their Pizarro, Thys their Cortez." Conrad suspected that Casement himself had "a touch of the Conquistador" about him, "for I've seen him start off into an unspeakable wilderness swinging a crookhandled stick for all weapons, with two bull-dogs . . . at his heels and a Loanda boy carrying a bundle for all company." But Casement had the conscience and the courage of a saint. "I have always thought that some particle of Las Casas' soul had found refuge in his indefatigable body," Conrad concluded, likening Casement to the conquistadors' fiercest critic.[8]

Conrad knew that Graham would instantly seize the analogies between Latin America and Africa. They had become friends in 1897 when Graham had read "An Outpost of Progress" and, impressed by Conrad's unflinching critique of the "civilizing mission," had written to him to tell him so. In his armchair by the fire Conrad had just finished reading Graham's latest book, a biography of the conquistador Hernando de Soto. Britons would come to such a book well aware of the "Black Legend" that demonized the Spanish invaders of the New World. But Graham opened with a warning to his readers. Before you condemn the conquistadors, he said, take a look around. That greed and violence the conquistadors unleashed in South America? "The massacres in German Africa may be put beside the worst deeds of Cortes, and the inhuman bringing in of basketfuls of human hands in Belgian Congoland excels the atrocities of any Spaniard in the whole conquest of America."[9]

And there was another reason that Conrad thought of Latin America when he heard about Africa. He had been exploring it all year himself, in a manuscript of a novel thickening beside him.

From his desk Conrad could practically see Sulaco. Notched in a crook of the South American coast, you reached the port city by cruising between a pair of rocky islands and over a serene, sheltered bay. In the days of sail, few vessels could cross the windless Golfo Placido, but now Sulaco was a regular port of call for the liners of the Occidental Steam Navigation Company. Passengers would see the Republic of Costaguana unfold before them, a sunbaked plain stretching east, and the cloud-crowned mountains of the Cordillera towering over the west. Behind the mountains resided a silver mine, the driver of Costaguana's economy. Behind the silver mine lay a web of political and business interests that determined Costaguana's fate.

In real life, nobody would ever see Costaguana, because Conrad had made the whole country up. And Costaguana was a New World creation in more ways than one. Until now Conrad had woven his fictions from the threads of his own experience, based on voyages he'd taken, regions he'd seen, people he'd met. But of South America, he told Graham, "I just had a glimpse 25 years ago—a short glance" when his ship had stopped for a day or two off Venezuela in 1875 or 1876.[10] For the very first time Conrad was writing a novel about a part of the world he had never actually visited himself.

The invention of Costaguana was Conrad's declaration of independence as a writer. Conrad had an agent to steward his income, critical acclaim to bolster his confidence, a circle of writer friends who reminded him that he had actually become this thing, a professional novelist. He was one of them. It set his imagination free. "I have never worked so hard before—with so much anxiety," Conrad told Pinker of the emerging book, "but the result is good." "It is a very genuine Conrad. At the same time it is more of a novel pure and simple than anything I've done since Almayer's Folly."[11] Just about the first thing Conrad settled on was its "title which shall be I think: NOSTROMO."[12]

Books can often be named, like babies, before their personalities are known. Conrad imagined *Nostromo* in the first instance to be a story about Italian immigrants in South America. Conrad didn't yet know how this novel would run through one set of sources and then through others, spiraling into the longest novel he'd ever write. He didn't yet know that his novel of the New World would chronicle the coming of a new world order.

What he did know was that to write *Nostromo* he would need to rely more heavily than ever before on other sources and other people. He'd need to rely, in the first instance, on his dear friend and informant on all things Latin American, Cunninghame Graham.[13]

WHENEVER GRAHAM CAME TO VISIT he blazed into the Pent like a struck match, strawberry blond hair bristling, bandanna flaring around his neck. Everyone lit up. Borys, his godson, adored Graham because he was so much fun; Borys would drag him into the garden and throw apples and plums into the air for Graham to shoot down with his pistol.[14] Jessie welcomed him because (unlike Ford) he always put Conrad in a good mood. The two men would sit up late into the night talking, laughing, and smoking Brazilian cigarettes till Conrad felt his throat had been "scraped . . . [with] rusty knives."[15]

Athletic, charismatic, elegant, at ease with women and at home on a horse, Graham was like the older brother (by five years) Conrad never had—or the edited version Conrad might have authored of himself. Graham claimed descent from Robert the Bruce on one side and had a

Spanish grandmother on the other, which gave him at once a sense of hereditary privilege and the sensibility of an outsider. He'd spent much of his twenties in Latin America, much of his thirties in the House of Commons, and much of his forties fighting for various radical causes outside Parliament. "Don Roberto," Graham's many friends called him, capturing his flamboyant Hispanophilia. Don Quixote, thought others, mocking his attachment to big, impossible ideas. The artist William Strang used Graham as a model for the man from La Mancha, all angles and points.[16]

R. B. Cunninghame Graham on his horse Malacarita.

What really drew Conrad to Graham, though, was what lay behind the cut and dash. A sense of ancestral loss trailed Graham of a kind Conrad knew well. Poland, for him, was Scotland for Graham, whose independence Graham campaigned to restore. Graham, too, had lost his father young, in his case to the unsettling perversions of mental illness. The elder Graham was hustled away to live in isolation under medical supervision, and the family estates—what remained of them, against soaring debts—were placed in the hands of a trustee. Like Conrad, Graham had been raised in a hollow of loss and displacement. Conrad sensed in Graham an affinity that made him an epistolary soul mate, as Marguerite Poradowska once had been, someone to whom he could confide his darkest thoughts.

Where the adolescent Conrad had yearned for the sea, Graham, with his love of horses and his semi-native Spanish, dreamed of South America.[17] In 1870, a few months shy of eighteen, he sailed to Argentina to become a cowboy. What he experienced there profoundly shaped his perspective on politics and social affairs—and, in due course, Conrad's picture of South America in *Nostromo*.

English-speakers knew the silty wash of the Rio de la Plata by the dull name "the River Plate." They ought to have called it by its literal translation, the "Silver River," urged one British diplomat, for Argentina—the silver land (from Latin *argentum*)—stood fit to become "one of the most promising countries of the globe."[18] Argentina's wealth lay in the vast grasslands of the interior, ideal for ranching. In the Andean language Quechua they were called, simply, "space": *pampas*. "All grass and sky, and sky and grass, and still more sky and grass," Cunninghame Graham wrote, the pampas stretched into the continent like a great inland ocean, brown-capped waves billowing in the wind.[19]

You took to the pampas on a horse the way you put to sea in a boat, and the eighteen-year-old Graham took instantly to the pampas horses, small as English ponies but fiery and full of stamina.[20] With a sheepskin cushioning his saddle, feet hanging gently in the metal shoe stirrups, in a day he could ride a hundred miles or more, scoping the horizon for herds of deer springing like dolphins, and inquisitive *ñandús*, New World cousins of the ostrich, poking their bald heads like periscopes over the grass line.[21] At an estancia (ranch) in the province of Entre Ríos, on the edge of Uruguay, Graham trained to be a gaucho—a pampas cowboy—herding, droving, breeding, branding. He learned to throw the *bolas*, three weighted balls on a long leather thong, which you spun over your head and hurled at a scampering animal's legs to bring it down.[22] At the *pulperías* (general stores) that doubled as social hubs, he swigged clear Brazilian *caña* with hard handed, barefooted gauchos, half in admiration, half on guard. Never sit on a gaucho's left, because he'll have the advantage when he pulls a knife on you.[23] If you play monte with a gaucho, watch out for a marked deck. Graham visited the "China" girls who called to him from the mare hide–covered doorways of their brothels: "Hey, if you want something, you'll get a good price here."[24]

This was where the great Italian nationalist Giuseppe Garibaldi had earned his freedom-fighting stripes, back in the 1840s, defending Uruguay's "Reds" (Colorados) in a civil war with the Argentinian-backed "Whites" (Blancos). Garibaldi took a touch of the gaucho back with him to Europe, where he led the Italian Risorgimento with a poncho slung over his shoulders. He left behind in South America many of his Italian followers, who nurtured his romantic ideals.[25]

But the political reality of the River Plate region, as Graham found it, had strayed far from the Garibaldini vision. Just months before Graham arrived in the province of Entre Ríos, a gaucho *caudillo* had seized power, and the president of Argentina, Domingo Sarmiento, dispatched an army to bring him into line. "Revolutions in the S. American Republics are of too frequent an occurrence," moaned Graham's Scottish ranching partner, who knew what the ensuing civil war would mean.[26] Red, White, the differences scarcely mattered when your estancia was in their way. Rival bands plundered and raided the countryside, so devastating the plains that horses starved down to their ribs and ballooning carcasses of cattle floated in the river among clumps of weeds.

From the ruin of cowboy country, Graham decided to travel into Paraguay to scope out the possibility of trading yerba maté, the local equivalent of tea. Here again he found a land choked and stymied by misrule. Paraguay's president, Francisco Solano López, had tried to reverse decades of isolation by recruiting foreign engineers, technicians, advisers, and doctors, to build up the nation's infrastructure.[27] Yet the farther into Paraguay Graham traveled, the stranger everything looked. It wasn't just the macaws that sprayed cackling from the trees, or the unfamiliar lilt of Guaraní instead of Spanish, or that everyone, even children, smoked fat green cigars. It was that nearly all the adults he saw were female. The male population of Paraguay had been practically wiped out in one of the deadliest wars the world had ever known, waged by Solano López against the Triple Alliance of Brazil, Argentina, and Uruguay. Some Europeans portrayed Paraguay under Solano López as a plucky little Poland of the west, standing up to an imperial juggernaut (Brazil).[28] Graham saw in Solano López only "sadism, an inverted patriotism, colossal ignorance of the outside world, a megalomania pushed almost to insanity, a total disregard of human life or human dignity, [and] an abject cowardice" unprecedented in the annals of barbarism. The memory of that ravaged country haunted him as long as he lived.[29]

Graham went back to Argentina only to run into a third, comprehensive assault on his ideal of freedom. It took the form of President Domingo Sarmiento's ambitious modernization plan for Argentina. In his 1845 book *Facundo: Civilization and Barbarism*, widely acclaimed by European and American liberals, Sarmiento described Argentina as a society divided between two kinds of people, one "Spanish, European, and cultivated," the other "barbarous, American, and almost wholly . . . native."[30] Barbarism, for Sarmiento, arrived on horseback, both in the "savage horde" of Indians who preyed on intruders "like packs of hyenas" and in the "white-skinned savage" gauchos, "at war with society and proscribed by the laws."[31] It flew red flags and flaunted red ribbons, "because red is the symbol of violence, blood, and barbarism."[32] Civilization, by contrast, traveled by steamboat, lived in cities, went to school, and worked in offices and shops. Civilization wore a frock coat. When Sarmiento and his successors deemed necessary, civilization wielded state-of-the-art weapons and exterminated the Indians or gauchos who stood in its way.[33]

If Konrad Korzeniowski in his sailing days had gotten a berth on one of the swish transatlantic steamers ferrying emigrants to the River Plate, he'd have seen for himself the Argentina of Sarmiento's dreams taking shape. Europe, especially Italy, poured in the people. From Argentina's

first census in 1869 to the second in 1895, the population more than doubled to four million. Britain, in particular, pumped in capital, financing
government loans, railways, factories, and utilities.[34] Telegraph wires
strung together the cities. Train lines girded the pampas. Buenos Aires
started to look like a New World Paris, with stately public buildings, a
fine network of trams, and cafés bustling with "a perfect *macédoine* [fruit
salad] of races."[35]

As it was, Conrad saw Spanish-speaking America through the filter
of Graham—and Graham, in turn, saw Latin America through a filter of
mounting distaste for everything that passed in the name of "progress."
Conrad and Graham both returned from their travels on the far side of
the world with eyes softened and heads hardened, more romantic, more
cynical. Based in Britain from the early 1880s, Graham channeled his
beliefs into the burgeoning socialist movement. For six years he served as
a member of Parliament—the first socialist in the House—where he became no less memorable for his radical speeches than for his habit of
riding into Westminster on a black Argentinian horse named Pampa. In
1887 Graham gained national notoriety as one of the ringleaders of a pro-
worker, pro-Irish demonstration in Trafalgar Square, known as "Bloody
Sunday" because of clashes between protesters and police. By the time he
met Conrad, Graham had helped found both the Scottish Labour Party
and the forerunner of the Scottish National Party (of which he'd later be
the first president), and become a die-hard enemy of capitalism and imperialism alike.[36]

In a string of books and sketches published from 1895 onward,
Graham portrayed South America as a place ruined by greed. He
mourned *A Vanished Arcadia* in the Jesuit missions of colonial Paraguay,
where priests protected Guaraní Indians from near-certain enslavement
by Spanish settlers, and formed "a semi-communistic settlement," sharing products of ranch and field.[37] He grieved for "A Vanishing Race" of
gauchos, rugged individualists who were getting shoved aside "by the

heavy-footed Basque, the commonplace Canary Islander, and the Italian in his greasy velveteen suit." In the free, open pampas of his youth, Graham could already see trains "snort and puff" where once "the ostrich scudded," capitalists who "rob[bed] in counting-houses and on exchange with pen and book, instead of on the highway" at knifepoint. He saw "civilization . . . plant its empty sardine tin as a mark on the earth's face . . . and the hideous pall of gloom and hypocrisy which generally accompanies it" blight the pampas.[38]

In his brightest moments Graham hoped that there would come a day when "common-sense" would "dawn upon the world" and people would "recognise that it is better to let others follow their destiny as it best pleases them." But to force "progress—which to them means tramways and electric light" on other people—"that," Graham determined, "is a crime against humanity." Every champion of civilization might end up another imperialist, every imperialist could become a conquistador. Capitalism was extraction, extraction was plunder. Someday "posterity . . . will . . . hold us up to execration, as we to-day in our hypocrisy piously curse the memories of Pizarro and Cortés."[39]

"I WANT TO TALK TO YOU of the work I am engaged on now. I hardly dare avow my audacity—but I am placing it in Sth America in a Republic I call Costaguana," Conrad confessed to Graham in the spring of 1903. "It is however concerned mostly with Italians."[40] In the beginning, Conrad used his colorful new setting as a backdrop to a recurring theme in his work: the futility of nationalist ideals.

Conrad introduced the reader to an old, white-haired innkeeper named Giorgio Viola, "often called simply 'the Garibaldino.'" Viola had fought with Garibaldi and admired him for his "spirit of self-forgetfulness, the simple devotion to a vast humanitarian idea." Fed up with Old World monarchies, Viola decided to settle in the Americas with his wife and daughters because he wanted to live in a republic. He chose Costaguana because of the strong British economic presence in the country. Viola "had a great consideration for the English . . . because they loved Garibaldi" too.[41]

Next Conrad introduced another Genoese, who worked for the steamship company as its head longshoreman (Capataz de Cargadores), managing an "outcast lot of very mixed blood, mainly Negroes." His given name was Gian' Battista Fidanza—*fidanza* meaning "trust"—but just about everyone called him Nostromo, a nickname given to him by his English employers. "What a name! What is that? Nostromo?" scoffed Viola's wife. There was something pompous in it. "All he cares for" is "to be first somewhere—somehow," she grumbled, "to be first with these English. . . . He would take a name that is properly no word from them." Perhaps her Italian ear heard an echo between "Nostromo" and *nemo*, or "no man." In fact "Nostromo" was what a clumsy English mouth did to the Italian words *nostro uomo*, "our man."[42]

Conrad sketched these scenes assuming that "it will end in something silly and saleable." He envisioned a short story of 35,000 words, organized around the tension between Viola the romantic and Nostromo the pragmatist.[43] He took some inspiration for the character of Viola from a figure in Graham's anecdotes, a Garibaldino innkeeper on the border of Paraguay, who liked to break up bar fights by hurling empty bottles into the fray. To help fill out the Italians' background, Conrad asked Ford Madox Ford to send him a biography of Garibaldi, and "some book that would give me picturesque locutions idioms, swear words—suggestive phrases on Italy."[44]

But as Conrad's pages multiplied, so did the plotlines. No doubt guided by Graham, Conrad read Sarmiento, or people like him, who were busy building a steam-powered neo-Europe. He reread Graham's *A Vanished Arcadia*, with its elegy for the lost world of Europeans and Indians living in communal peace. He explored the writings of another friend, the Anglo-Argentine writer W. H. Hudson, who celebrated in the plains of Uruguay a freedom more honest, moral, and natural than "British civilisation" or its ersatz Latin American cousins could ever offer.[45] He delved into books about the River Plate and deepened his portrayal of the history and significance of Costaguana's defining asset, a silver mine. In one of his readings Conrad paused over the story of a sailor who made off with a lighter (a kind of small boat) filled with silver—an episode he'd co-opt for *Nostromo*.[46]

The more he read, the more he wrote. The more he wrote, the more his story about romantic nationalism became a story about "progress" and its discontents. Conrad shoved the concept between quotation marks and delivered it to the reader in chapter 5, which described the ground-breaking ceremony for a new, British-built railroad between Sulaco and the capital city. Costaguana's self-styled president-dictator heralded the project as a "progressive and patriotic undertaking" and praised "the great body of strong-limbed foreigners who dug the earth, blasted the rocks, [and] drove the engines." The chairman of the railroad company promised to transform this "out-of-the-way place" into a global hub. "You shall have more steamers, a railway, a telegraph-cable—a future in the great world."[47]

In just five chapters, Conrad doubled his cast of characters and themes. His projected short story lengthened apace; he now anticipated a short novel of 80,000 words.[48] And as *Nostromo* grew, so did the imaginative effort required. "I am dying over that cursed Nostromo thing," he groaned to Graham in July 1903. "All my memories of Central America seem to slip away."[49] Graham steered Conrad to still more books that could help.[50] Conrad started reading about the war in Paraguay. In the memoir of a British apothecary caught up in the war, titled *Seven Eventful Years in Paraguay*, Conrad noted spine-tingling tales of the dictator Solano López's sadism: graphic accounts of how he murdered rivals, tortured suspects, and dragged his prisoners behind him in chains when he marched. Conrad took down names that all made their way into *Nostromo*: a turncoat Italian sailor named Captain Fidanza, a tortured young lover named Decoud, an upstanding British envoy named Charles Gould.

Conrad had turned to South America in the first instance in part for the local color. What he came to discover in these accounts, and under Graham's tutelage, was far more than that. He absorbed a sense of the South American republics as victims of a unique political trajectory. He saw them hurtling through history like carts on wheels of dictatorship and revolution. A well-meaning few, British investors mostly, tried to set a brake. Others, power-hungry strongmen or the craven foreigners who supported them, just pushed them faster downhill.

The sixth chapter of *Nostromo*, as long as the previous five combined, turned into a lesson on the history of Latin America. Conrad invented a political past for Costaguana that was heavily informed by his reading on Paraguay. A generation or so before the novel's present day, he wrote, Costaguana had suffered under a ruthless autocrat. A reminder of those violent days lurched down Sulaco's avenues every day in the broken form of an Irish doctor disfigured in body and mind by torture and the falsehoods to which, in agony, he had confessed.[51] Another veteran of those years was a white-haired grandee called Don José Avellanos, "a statesman, a poet," and a diplomat, who also "had suffered untold indignities as a state prisoner" in the tyrant's time. Since then, Don José had witnessed too many regimes in Costaguana to count. Most didn't last eighteen months before some "casual colonel of the barefooted army of scarecrows" slashed and burned his way into power. He chronicled his despair in a history of Costaguana he entitled *Fifty Years of Misrule*.[52]

In the same chapter, Conrad introduced one of the novel's central characters. The Anglo-Costaguanan Charles Gould (a name plucked from *Seven Eventful Years in Paraguay*) resembled Cunninghame Graham right down to his initials. "With a flaming moustache, a neat chin, clear blue eyes, auburn hair, and a thin, fresh, red face, he looked like a new arrival from over the sea," wrote Conrad. "He looked more English than the last arrived batch of young railway engineers," and he "went on looking thoroughly English even on horseback." Yet "no one could be more of a Costaguanero than Don Carlos Gould." His grandfather had fought with Simón Bolívar, an uncle had been president, and he himself, born in Costaguana, "rode like a centaur," wore a sombrero with his Norfolk coat, and spoke Spanish and "the Indian dialect of the country-people" without a trace of an English accent. Gould accepted as normal "the continuous political changes, the constant saving of the country," which struck his appalled English-born wife Emilia as "a puerile and bloodthirsty game of murder and rapine played . . . by depraved children." "My dear," he gently reminded her, "you seem to forget that I was born here."[53]

Gould (like Graham) struggled with a troubled inheritance. His father had been given the San Tomé mine to run by the government, but it came at an impossible price, as Gould was required to deliver massive royalties—well in excess of what the mine could feasibly produce. The mine bound the elder Gould in silver shackles. "Everybody around him was being robbed by grotesque and murderous bands that played their game of governments and revolutions. . . . But to be robbed under the forms of legality and business was intolerable to his imagination." "God looked wrathfully at these countries," he muttered, "or else He would let some ray of hope fall through a rift in the appalling darkness of intrigue, bloodshed, and crime."[54] The pronouncement echoed Cunninghame Graham's bitter satire of imperialism, "Bloody Niggers," in which a white man sarcastically jeered that God "must have . . . created [Africa] in sheer ill-humour," for "no-one can think it possible that an all-wise God . . . would create a land and fill it full of people destined to be replaced by other races from across the seas."[55]

By this point in the book Conrad knew that the story he had begun writing about Italian nationalists (chapters 1–4) was also a meditation on so-called progress (chapter 5)—and the story about so-called progress was also a story about "the tearing of the raw material of treasure from the earth" (chapter 6).[56] Conrad had folded into *Nostromo* more major characters and plotlines than in any of his other books. Yet for all its difference in structure from anything Conrad had written before, *Nostromo*, thematically, was the natural sequel to *everything* he'd written. The flimsiness of ideals he'd encountered among the nationalists of his youth, the perils of modernization he'd seen at sea, the malignancy of greed he'd witnessed in Africa—all of it landed in Costaguana. Poles into Italians; steamships into trains, telegraphs, and more steamships; ivory into silver.

By pouring his experiences from Europe, Asia, and Africa into Latin America, Conrad turned the past into prologue. The main storyline of *Nostromo* was only just beginning. It concerned competing visions for the world—British and American—and it was unfolding even as Conrad wrote.

THE ONLY PLACE you can go from a summit is down. At the turn of the twentieth century, the Scramble for Africa complete, the British Empire covered a quarter of the world. It was three times the size of the French Empire, its nearest imperial rival, five times that of the Roman Empire.[57] It didn't take much imagination to predict decline. Rudyard Kipling, the empire's most popular poet, warned of impending decay in his poem for Queen Victoria's Diamond Jubilee in 1897, "Recessional." Someday Britain's empire too, he intoned, would lie in ruins, like those of "Nineveh and Tyre." "Judge of the nations, spare us yet, / Lest we forget, lest we forget!"[58]

Conrad began writing *Nostromo* just as Britain was concluding a costly, difficult, politically divisive war against the Boer republics of South Africa. Among the Boer War's many critics was Cunninghame Graham, who saw it as a thinly disguised landgrab promoted by capitalists in cahoots with the state. (He labeled Rhodesia, named for the millionaire expansionist Cecil Rhodes, "Fraudesia.")[59] Economist J. A. Hobson cited the war as a premier case of what he called, in a 1902 book of that title, "imperialism"—a term popularized by his work. Imperialism, for Hobson, was racist, "aggressive," "cut-throat," "calculating, greedy," and "cynical," egged on by industrialists and financiers cloaked in talk of a "mission to civilize."[60] Alongside the socialist critique of the war, many others condemned the brutal counterinsurgency tactics adopted by the British military, which included herding civilians into so-called concentration camps. Surveying the scene in South Africa, Conrad quipped cynically to Graham about God's view of Britain. "Here's His very own chosen people (of assorted denominations) getting banged about and not a sign from the sky but a snowfall and a fiendish frost," he wrote. "Perhaps Kipling's Recessional (if He understood it—which I doubt) had offended Him?"[61]

Champions of British imperialism, meanwhile, left the war deeply concerned about Britain's military preparedness. Boer War hero Robert Baden-Powell, for one, sought to address perceived deficiencies in manpower by founding the Boy Scouts. Worries about the nation's capacity appeared especially acute in light of a rising new rival, Germany. Fired up by Alfred Thayer Mahan's hugely influential 1890 book *The Influence of Sea Power upon History*, Kaiser Wilhelm II sponsored a massive buildup of the German fleet, challenging Britain's dominance at sea. While Conrad was working on *Nostromo*, an avid yachtsman named Erskine Childers published a spy novel called *The Riddle of the Sands* (1903), in which two British friends on a sailing trip stumbled upon a German fleet gathering to invade Britain. A new genre of fiction took off. Popular writers churned out thrillers about German forces overrunning a prone, unprepared Britain. The notion of a German invasion seemed silly enough for the humorist P. G. Wodehouse to spoof in *The Swoop! Or, How Clarence Saved England* (1909), where the Germans were driven away by Boy Scouts wielding slingshots and hockey sticks.[62] But it was serious enough for the British government to undertake a thorough overhaul of national defense and to realign the nation's diplomatic alliances.[63]

As Conrad's peers scribbled frantically about Germany, he looked the other way and saw a second rival rising in the west: the United States. In 1898, the United States went to war with Spain and came away with nearly all Spain's colonies for its own. A new overseas empire was born. Kipling composed another poem for the occasion, urging Americans to join Britain in the thankless, necessary work of "civilizing": "Take up the white man's burden— / Send forth the best ye breed— / Go bind your sons to exile / To serve your captives' need."[64]

Many Britons toasted the United States' arrival as an imperial power. Champions of British imperialism such as Cecil Rhodes saw the United States as the ideal partner in a so-called Greater Britain of white, English-speaking people.[65] That's why he endowed scholarships for white American men to study at Oxford. Critics of British imperialism such as the influential journalist W. T. Stead also welcomed a stronger United States, albeit for a different reason. He hoped the United States would replace British hegemony with a better, more democratic alternative. In the prophetically entitled book *The Americanization of the World: Or, the Trend of the Twentieth Century* (1902), Stead presented Britons with a choice. Either they could sit back and wait for the United States to supersede Britain, reducing it "to the status of an English-speaking Belgium"—or they could work toward an outright merger with the United States (in which Britain would be the smaller partner) and "continue for all time to be an integral part of the greatest of all World Powers."[66]

Plenty of others, though, fired back at rosy portrayals of American might. "Pile on the Poor Man's Burden," retorted an American labor activist: "Your Monopolistic rings / Shall crush the serf and sweeper / Like iron rule of Kings."[67] "Pile on the Black Man's Burden," charged an African-American clergyman: "Your Jim-Crow laws and customs . . . /

Will some day trouble breed."[68] Cunninghame Graham wrote of sitting in a Paris hotel amid a crowd of vulgar, overdressed "Yankees" who were celebrating their victories over Spain. "England's turn was coming next," they sneered. "'We'll show Victoria in a cage for a picayune a peep, and teach the Britishers what to do with their Union Jack.'"[69]

Written in the face of anxieties about British decline, with Latin America as its setting, and with Graham as its chief informant, Conrad's *Nostromo* became a novel about the new, hard fact of American imperialism. It coalesced around the story of the San Tomé silver mine, Charles Gould's ill-starred inheritance.

Gould studied mining and engineering to prepare for the job and concluded that the best way to stave off the ruin that had wrecked his father was to invest heavily in modernizing the mine. The best place to get that investment, he realized, was the United States. "I pin my faith on material interests," Gould announced. He traveled to San Francisco to meet with a mining magnate named Holroyd.

All Europe had gone into the making of Mr. Holroyd: a blend of German, Scottish, English, French, and Danish made him into the quintessential American, with "the temperament of a Puritan and an insatiable imagination of conquest." Holroyd thought Costaguana was a risky investment proposition—you could lose your money every time a revolution blew up—but he was impressed enough by Gould to take a chance. As long as Gould could keep the silver flowing and keep the peace, Holroyd agreed to back him. The minute anything changed, Holroyd warned, "we shall know how to drop you." "Under no circumstances will we consent to throw good money after bad."[70]

For Holroyd the San Tomé mine was just a glancing "hobby," a "great man's caprice." For Costaguana, the American investment was a lifeline. Under Gould's management the mine became an *imperium in imperio*, an empire within an empire. Gould bought machines and men: three villages' worth of Indian laborers and a roster of government officials were put on the San Tomé payroll for their compliance. People started calling him the uncrowned "King of Sulaco" (much as Cunninghame Graham had been jestingly called the uncrowned "King of Scotland"). They said he'd financed the ascent of Costaguana's president, a man of "unblemished character, invested with a mandate of reform." Every three months, "an increasing stream of treasure" wound down in convoy from San Tomé to Sulaco and got loaded onto a steamer (under Nostromo's watchful eye) for shipment north. Gould's wife Emilia handled the first, warm ingot from the mine and knew she was touching more than mere money. She was touching "something far-reaching and impalpable, like the true expression of emotion or the emergency of principle." She was touching peace.[71]

Conrad concluded Part I of *Nostromo* by circling back to the groundbreaking for the railroad. Sulaco's grandees, the Goulds foremost among them, gathered on board one of the O.S.N.'s steamships for a celebratory lunch. The president gave his toasts. The British railroad chairman surveyed his investments—the train line, the "loan to the state, and a project for systematic colonisation of the Occidental Province"—and pictured a future for Costaguana marked by "good faith, order, honesty, peace." Emilia Gould couldn't help feeling some regret that "the future means change," and the loss of traditional ways of life. But even she acknowledged that "all this brings nearer the sort of future we desire for the country." She got the railroad company to agree not to tear down Giorgio Viola's inn, which lay in the construction path. This was British power at its best, protecting well-meaning liberals and their values.

At least that was one way to interpret the scene. Another was that the British-backed aspirations for Costaguana might be just as outmoded as the dreams of the old Garibaldino. For as against the Goulds' vision for Costaguana, committed to stability and justice, the American investor Holroyd offered a different "theory of the world's future." Costaguana was "the bottomless pit of 10 per cent loans and other fool investments.

European capital had been flung into it with both hands for years," he'd told Gould. Americans were prepared to "sit and wait" till everyone else went bust. "There's no hurry. Time itself has got to wait on the greatest country in the whole of God's universe." But "of course, some day we shall step in. We are bound to. . . . We shall be giving the word for everything," he concluded, "industry, trade, law, journalism, art, politics, and religion. . . . We shall run the world's business whether the world likes it or not." And Costaguana would pay the price.[72]

ELEVEN

————— · —————

MATERIAL INTERESTS

In August 1903 Conrad sent Part I of *Nostromo* to his agent. The novel had grown bigger and more involved than any of his previous meditations on nationalism, imperialism, and capitalism. It had outgrown Conrad's personal travels and observations, something he'd recognized when he chose to write about South America in the first place. By introducing the United States as a player, it had outgrown all the reading he had done on Argentina, Uruguay, Paraguay, Venezuela. It had even begun to outgrow the picture of South America Conrad had received from his friend Cunninghame Graham, with its passionate denunciations of so-called progress.

Conrad certainly hadn't intended such complexity at the outset. Yet six chapters in, the story of the San Tomé mine, and the "material interests" invested in it, had only just begun. Conrad had gotten trapped in the net of his own plot, and he couldn't escape without drawing the lines out. But for better or worse, events unfolding in Latin America that year offered Conrad a real-time, real-world example of precisely the type of story he was now trying to tell. It was a tale of U.S. intervention on behalf of a valuable asset: a long-dreamed-of project to build a canal in Panama.[1]

Gold, not silver, kicked the whole thing off. Fifty years earlier, the California gold rush of 1849 had brought millions of prospectors from the Atlantic to the Pacific. To reach California, they could spend weeks trekking overland across the United States; spend weeks sailing around the whole of South America; or, thanks to a package put together by the transport magnate Cornelius Vanderbilt, they could nip down on a steamer to Nicaragua, dart across the isthmus, board another steamer, and reach San Francisco in a matter of days. Soon Vanderbilt and other entrepreneurs plotted a permanent shipping canal across Central America, consummating the relationship of Atlantic and Pacific.

Throw in the ambitions of the nations that had a stake in the project, and the canal had the potential to reshape international affairs. The United States had claimed, by the 1823 Monroe Doctrine, that the Americas "are henceforth not to be considered as subjects for future colonization by any European powers."[2] But Britain was still a major American power, with territory in Canada, the Caribbean, and in Central and South America (Belize, Guyana, the Falkland Islands). As a canal project gained momentum, Britain and the United States signed a preemptive treaty agreeing that neither power would have "exclusive control" of a Central American waterway nor use undue influence to try to obtain it.[3]

That was partly why it was a French company, not a British or American one, that actually commenced building a canal in 1881. Using plans laid by the man who'd designed the Suez Canal (which had opened in 1869), the French consortium chose to dig at the narrowest point of the isthmus, in Panama, a province of Colombia. But the French engineers hadn't adequately considered how plans developed for the Egyptian desert might have to be modified for the Central American tropics. After billions of francs invested, millions of cubic meters of earth moved, tens of thousands of laborers dead from disease—and no viable canal remotely

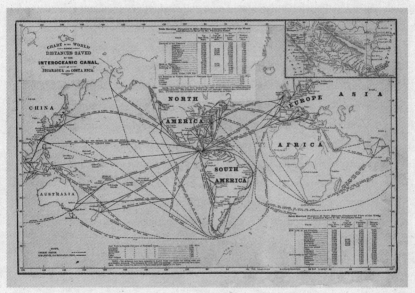

Map of sailing distances reduced by a canal in Central America, 1901.

in sight—the French Panama Canal Company went bust in 1888, taking the fortunes of millions of French citizens with it.

Meanwhile, the balance of power in the region realigned. Colombia dissolved into a bitter civil war. The succession to the U.S. presidency in 1901 of a new man with ambitious plans, Theodore Roosevelt, put a canal in Central America at the top of America's foreign policy wish list. Britain, already stretched beyond expectation in South Africa and worried about a rising Germany, agreed to repeal the earlier treaty and concede ascendancy in Central America to the United States.

Any British newspaper reader could follow what happened next. In January 1903, just as Conrad started writing *Nostromo*, the U.S. and Colombian secretaries of state signed a treaty granting the United States a one-hundred-year renewable lease on a six-mile strip flanking the canal. Colombia would get a $10 million lump sum plus a $250,000 annuity in return. "The United States disavows any intention of impairing the sovereignty of Colombia," the treaty insisted, "or of increasing her territory at the expense of Colombia."[4] *The Times* in London congratulated "our kinsmen of the great English-speaking Republic . . . on this decisive step towards the realization of a project they have long had very earnestly to heart."[5]

In the spring of 1903, as Conrad sketched out the backstory for Costaguana, President Roosevelt set off on a national lecture tour promoting a version of the Monroe Doctrine updated for the twentieth century. "We have no choice as to whether or not we shall play a great part in the world," Roosevelt told his audiences.[6] "There is a homely old adage which runs, 'Speak softly, but carry a big stick, and you will go far,'" he continued. "If the American nation will speak softly, and yet build and keep at a pitch of the highest training a thoroughly efficient navy, the Monroe doctrine will go far."[7] This interventionist stance came to be called the "Roosevelt Corollary" to the Monroe Doctrine. In essence, it was the same as Holroyd's assertion in *Nostromo*: "We shall run the world's business whether the world likes it or not."

However eager or wary European imperial powers felt about American interventionism, the Roosevelt Corollary didn't look so great to those on the receiving end. In the summer of 1903, as Conrad expanded the story of the mine and its American investor, the Colombian Senate voted to reject the canal treaty, which had been negotiated under duress during Colombia's civil war, by a government no longer in power. The senators considered the treaty downright unconstitutional—no government had the right to give away territory like that—to say nothing of too cheap.[8] "Panama is bone of the bone and blood of the blood of Colombia, . . . the patrimony of all future generations of Colombians," declared the treaty's opponents. "It seems more patriotic to feel that no compensation at all would be preferable" than "to kill the goose that lays the golden eggs."[9] The deal was off. No canal in Panama, at least not according to Bogotá.

In September 1903, rumors reached the pages of *The Times* that, "disgusted with the attitude of the Colombian Congress in the matter of the Canal Treaty, the people on the isthmus are likely to start an insurrection in the hope of forming a separate State of Panama." If Panama could break free and become an independent country, then it could strike a fresh deal with the United States, granting the Americans rights to the canal zone and letting the Panamanians pocket the payout for themselves—a win-win. Pundits in Washington foresaw Panama's "secession from Colombia" as "inevitable sooner or later."[10]

While the papers murmured about revolution in Colombia, Conrad opened a fresh section of *Nostromo* with hints of dissent in Costaguana. On the face of it, the American investor Holroyd backed the mine management under Charles Gould; Charles Gould, "the visible sign of the stability that could be achieved on the shifting ground of revolutions," backed the current president of Costaguana; and the president backed progress and peace. But none of them could brake the spinning cartwheel of dictatorship and revolution. A disaffected general named Pedro Montero, a pantomime villain with drooping black-dyed mustaches and gold epaulettes bookending his fat shoulders, rasped darkly about "the national honour" getting "sold to foreigners." Montero and his brother led a successful coup in Costaguana's capital, "with secret promises of support given by 'our sister Republic of the North' against the sinister land-grabbing designs of European powers."[11] They set their sights next on Sulaco and the San Tomé treasure.

Meanwhile in Panama, a conspiracy was fully under way. It was hatched over lunch one summer Sunday by a group of Panama City businessmen and civic leaders, under the auspices of the U.S. consul general. "Plans for the revolution were freely discussed," the consul said. The secessionists dispatched a representative to New York to secure money, weapons, and the backing of the U.S. federal government. They were right to expect it. President Roosevelt had already told his secretary of state "that the Bogotá lot of jack rabbits should [not] be allowed permanently to bar one of the future highways of civilization." What they didn't expect was that one of the conspirators would turn around and reveal the plot to the Colombian ambassador.[12] Thus both the U.S. and Colombian governments knew a revolution in Panama was in the works.

Back in Costaguana, Conrad plotted a revolution in the fictional Sulaco that mirrored the real-life secessionist movement brewing in Panama. Its architect was a young Costaguanero, just returned from Paris, named Martin Decoud. "Frenchified" from his plump, blond-fuzzed face to the lacquered shine of his shoes, Decoud, a journalist by trade and "nondescript dilettante" in spirit, slid as naturally into a salon as the Anglo-Costaguanan Charles Gould onto a saddle. With a fashionable air of ennui, Decoud used to describe Costaguana to his French friends as an opéra bouffe of "farcical stealing, intriguing, and stabbing" all "done in deadly earnest." "We convulsed a continent for our independence only to become the passive prey of a democratic parody . . . our institutions a mockery, our laws a farce," he said with a sigh, regretfully repeating a lament attributed to the great liberator Simón Bolívar: "'America is ungovernable. Those who worked for her independence have ploughed the sea.'" Decoud saw only one way to secure his country's future against General Montero. "Separation, of course . . . Yes; separation of the whole Occidental province from the rest of the unquiet body." "The Occidental territory is large enough to make any man's country. Look at the mountains! Nature itself seems to cry to us 'Separate!'"[13]

The fight for Sulaco was on. The railroad engineers and the shipping company *cargadores* put up barricades to stop the advance of Montero and his men. Nostromo helped the old president escape capture and slip safely out of the country. Decoud wrote up a "Separationist proclamation" to deliver when the forces of order regained power, tucked it into his pocket, and headed to the barricades.[14]

What would become of the country's greatest asset? Whoever had possession of the San Tomé mine had *de facto* possession of Costaguana. The secessionists decided to dispatch Charles Gould to San Francisco to "present the affair to Holroyd (the Steel and Silver King) in such a manner as to secure his financial support" and retain the mine for Sulaco. Moments later, they learned of a decisive Montero victory nearby. If Montero seized Sulaco, the secessionists would be in trouble enough. If he took the silver, their revolution would be finished. Decoud arranged with Nostromo to smuggle the silver out of the warehouse and hide it on an island in the gulf, the Great Isabel.[15]

Conrad ended Part II with a scene inspired by his Latin American reading. Decoud and Nostromo slipped away from shore in a lighter filled with silver. Ingots safely unloaded on the Great Isabel, Decoud stayed with the treasure while Nostromo scuttled the boat and swam back to shore. Nobody in Sulaco would ever know what happened. They would assume the silver had sunk to the bottom of the gulf, and both men drowned with it.

Conrad had scarcely finished sketching these episodes in *Nostromo* when the real-life plot in Panama kicked into action.[16] As Panama City awoke from its siesta on the afternoon of November 3, 1903, a brigade of secessionist national guardsmen turned their rifles on a party of Colombian generals and marched them off into prison. A crowd gathered in the plaza shouting, "*Viva el Istmo Libre!*" A Colombian battleship lobbed a few shells at the city to try to restore order, but got chased away by a barrage of return fire. Meanwhile a U.S. warship had arrived at Colón, on the Caribbean coast, and soon a veritable American fleet had assembled offshore with instructions to prevent any Colombian troops from landing.[17] Bribes (funneled through American financiers) took care of the rest. The standing force of Colombians in Colón evacuated, and four hundred American marines landed as occupiers in their place.

On November 6, 1903, the new government of the new state of Panama sent a telegram to Washington declaring its independence. The United States recognized Panama by return cable. "Today we are free," proclaimed Panama's president beneath the nation's first, home-stitched flag. "President Roosevelt has made good. . . . Long live President Roosevelt!"[18]

What would become of the country's greatest asset? Twelve days later, a Panamanian emissary signed an agreement for the canal with the U.S. secretary of state. On terms still more generous to the United States than the ones offered by Colombia, the new nation of Panama granted the United States "in perpetuity the use, occupation and control" of a ten-mile zone flanking the canal (rather than the earlier six), along with a host of associated privileges.[19] President Roosevelt celebrated the deal in his year-end message to Congress. With fifty-three "disturbances" in Panama in fifty-seven years, he said, "Colombia was incapable of keeping order." "The people of Panama rose literally as one man" against their distant rulers, and "the duty of the United States in the premises was clear." By helping the secessionists the United States advanced the "honor," "commerce and traffic" of "our own people . . . , the people of the Isthmus of Panama and the people of the civilized countries of the world."[20]

The Times of London saluted the Roosevelt administration's "firm, luminous, and convincing" stand. "Whatever may have been the action of individual American partisans of the Panama Canal in fomenting the rebellion," the editors averred, "there is no reason whatever to suppose that President Roosevelt's Government took the least part in working for the overthrow of Colombian rule upon the Isthmus."[21] But the *Manchester Guardian* was more suspicious, and accused the United States of having torn off by force what it had failed to acquire by legitimate diplomacy.[22]

What outsiders had surmised about American complicity in the revolution, insiders could prove. One such insider was a Colombian intellectual and diplomat named Santiago Pérez Triana. The son of one of Colombia's leading liberals, he had fled to Europe after a revolution in 1893 and was then living in London.[23] When contacts in Bogotá told him about the American shenanigans in Panama, Pérez Triana shared what he knew with British liberals—including his friend R. B. Cunninghame Graham. When Cunninghame Graham introduced Pérez Triana to others, including Joseph Conrad, that's how the cynical truth of the Panama story came to Conrad's attention just as he was sketching out the final section of *Nostromo*.

Reading Pérez Triana's travelogue of his escape from Bogotá, *Down the Orinoco in a Canoe* (published in English with a preface by Graham in 1902), Conrad might have been struck by the way Pérez Triana led his reader into Colombia as if on the trail of the conquistadors—the same way Marlow had imagined the Romans arriving in England in *Heart of Darkness*. "The land of Bogotá was really the land of El Dorado," Conrad read. It lured foreign prospectors deeper and deeper on a "bootless quest" for rumored treasure.[24] With a spot of literary alchemy Conrad could turn gold into silver, Colombia into Costaguana.

From Pérez Triana, Conrad would have heard both the facts leading to the secession of Panama and a compelling interpretation of them. Pérez Triana had little tolerance for the instability of his home country—but the alternative, an influx of Americans as "wolves in sheep's clothing under cover of the Monroe doctrine," appeared far worse.[25] "As a rule," Pérez Triana believed, "the citizens of the United States in their dealings . . . with Latin Americans are either patronising or overbearing." When Americans said "that America should be for the Americans, they mean America for the citizens of the United States."[26]

Every Colombian knew whom to blame for Panama's secession. A mob in the coastal city of Baranquilla stoned the American vice-consul's house, shouting, "Death to the Americans!" The American legation in Bogotá had to be secured against protesters. Colombia's president called on other Latin American republics to support him in putting down the insurrection and vowed to fight the United States–backed regime as fiercely as the Boers had fought Britain.[27] Colombia's consul in Cardiff raged that such "conduct is so discreditable that it far surpasses the most atrocious spoliations which have disgraced the history of even unscrupulous conquerors."[28]

Pérez Triana, for his part, reviewed what had happened through a scrim of despair. It was bad enough that Colombians had had to suffer at America's hands. Much worse was what U.S. intervention portended for the future of international affairs. Pérez Triana remembered wistfully the time when the great American republic "carried in her womb the hopes of all humanity," and everybody knew that the United States promised a "homeland, home, and justice." In those days, he felt, a Latin American liberal might have been right to think that the United States, with its rejection of Old World imperialism, was an even better friend to liberty than Britain. With its behavior in Panama, the United States showed that it too had been "infected with the virus of imperialism, contaminated with the leprosy of militarism," and disfigured by a grandiose sense of superiority. "The second hundred years of the Republic will not compare in true national greatness to its first," Pérez Triana moaned, and the world would be the loser.[29]

Listening to his Colombian acquaintance, Joseph Conrad knew one thing for sure. The future would be American. He didn't like it one bit.

BOXING DAY AT PENT FARM, 1903. Conrad was writing letters at his desk. He worked with the manuscript of *Nostromo* before him, his back bowed by the toil of a difficult year. He couldn't keep the weariness out of his thank-you letters. "This year has been bad for me as far as my work is concerned." "My mind struggles with a strange sort of torpor, struggles desperately while the sands are running out." "If I had written each page with my blood I could not feel more exhausted at the end of this twelvemonth."[30] He desperately needed a rest. "Perez Triana heard . . . of my longing to get away south and has written me the kindest letter imaginable," Conrad told Cunninghame Graham. "And à propos what do you think of the Yankee Conquistadors in Panama? Pretty, isn't it?"[31]

Nostromo had been taken up for serialization by the leftist magazine *T. P.'s Weekly* starting in January 1904, which meant Conrad would have to deliver the remaining chapters on a tight schedule. He thought he had only a little more of the book left to write, but the story just kept on coming; the book's final section, "The Lighthouse," would end up being its longest.

Nostromo, having hidden the silver and swum back to shore, "woke up from a fourteen hours' sleep" like "a man just born into the world." He walked into Sulaco to find the city turned upside down. A renegade colonel had seized power and was trawling the harbor in search of the missing silver. The colonel confronted the British captain of the

Occidental Steam Navigation Company's vessel. "You arrogant English-man!" he spat. "You foreigners come here to rob our country of its wealth. You never have enough!"[32] The old regime loyalists massed in the plaza and fled the city in convoy, before Sulaco fell entirely to the forces of the rebellion.

Charles Gould watched the refugees drain away and a "close-meshed net of crime and corruption" ensnare Sulaco. "The words one knows so well have a nightmarish meaning in this country," he fumed. "Liberty, democracy, patriotism, government—all of them have a flavor of folly and murder." General Montero dreamed of ruling Costaguana as an "Emperor—why not as an Emperor?" and "demand[ing] a share in every enterprise—in railways, in mines, in sugar estates, in cotton mills, in land companies, in each and every undertaking—as the price of his protection." Maybe we're not so different, the villains and I, realized Gould, "equals before the lawlessness of the land," clutching at silver to secure our power. Gould planned to write to Holroyd in San Francisco, asking him to "take up openly the plan of a provincial revolution as the only way of placing the enormous material interests . . . of Sulaco in a position of permanent safety." If that failed, or if the enemy got to the mine first, Gould would trigger the last resort. He'd ask his deputy to dynamite the whole precinct and "blow up . . . the famous Gould Concession into fragments, flying sky high out of a horrified world."[33]

By this point in the manuscript, Conrad, too, was reaching his limit. He'd already pushed the novel through some of the hardest months of his writing life. Then a New Year's visit to London upended his household when Jessie slipped on the street and wrenched both her knees so badly it seemed she might never walk properly again. On top of that, the doctors discovered she had a heart condition and needed dangerous, expensive surgery. On top of that, Conrad's bank failed. "Two fifty [pounds] gone in one fell swoop. I am nearly out of my mind with worry and overwork."[34]

On top of *Nostromo*, desperate for more money, Conrad started an-other writing project to bring in some cash, the essays that would form *The Mirror of the Sea*. All day he'd write *Nostromo*, till his hands hurt so badly he couldn't hold a pen. Every night from eleven P.M. to one A.M. Conrad sat up dictating *The Mirror* to Ford Madox Ford, like a bearded Scheherazade, staving off ruin by telling stories.[35] "Half the time I feel on the verge of insanity," he said. Other times the only way he knew he was still alive was because of the pain.

And then, over a chapter break, the revolution was over. Conrad hired a typist to help him, "a most good-natured, useful girl" named Lil-lian Hallowes. He dictated the remaining chapters to her.[36]

Flash forward in narrative time. The steamship captain Joseph Mitch-ell tours visitors around postwar Sulaco proud as a new grandfather, clucking over shops fronted in French plate glass, showing off its social clubs, swinging his arm expansively toward the new quays in the harbor. Between the sights Mitchell reminisces about the revolution: how the Monterists had seized Gould and prepared to execute him; how Don José Avellanos had died in the woods when the city residents had fled; and how, just in time, Nostromo had saved the city by riding to the govern-ment camp and persuading them to recapture Sulaco. The government marched in, Gould was rescued, General Montero was assassinated, and "an international naval demonstration" of warships appeared in the harbor to support the independence of Sulaco as a breakaway state. "The United States cruiser, *Powhattan*, was the first to salute the Occidental flag," with a sun-colored flower in a green laurel wreath—the color of American money. "The 'Treasure House of the World,' as *The Times* man calls Sulaco in his book, was saved intact for civilisation," Mitchell beams. He loved that phrase, "the Treasure House of the World." He owned seventeen $1,000 shares in the Consolidated San Tomé Mines himself.[37]

"Finished!" Conrad declared on September 1, 1904.[38] He left Sulaco in the condition of Panama. As Panama had gotten its independence instantly recognized by the United States and its economy bolstered by American investment in the canal, so Sulaco had *its* independence instantly recognized by the United States, and its economy underwritten by American investment in the San Tomé mine. The ending for Sulaco could have been far worse. The tyrant could have consolidated power in Costaguana, pillaged the whole country, and the wheel of dictatorship and revolution turned again.

But Conrad seeded the conclusion of *Nostromo* with disquiet. He had gotten his information about Panama from a Colombian who opposed independence, after all, not from a Panamanian who welcomed it. Beneath the polished surface of peace and prosperity in Sulaco, the concluding chapters of *Nostromo* sounded a depressing and ominous reality.

"The young apostle of Separation" Decoud, who had gone with Nostromo to hide the silver from the revolutionaries, had never been seen in Sulaco again. Though many assumed he'd been drowned in the gulf while trying to save the treasure—that he'd "died striving for his idea"— "the truth was that he died from solitude . . . and want of faith in himself and others." Alone on the island of Great Isabel, Decoud had become overwhelmed by a sense of emptiness. The "sustaining illusion" of action collapsed. Hope, love, purpose, sunk. He rowed his boat into the Golfo Placido, shot himself in the chest, and fell into the sea, "swallowed up in the immense indifference of things."[39] Into his pockets he had stuffed four silver ingots, the better to weigh his body down.

The "possessing, consuming" demon of the mine tormented Charles Gould as badly as it had his father. He spent most of his time at the mine, feeding the maw of "material interests to which he had pinned his faith in the triumph of order and justice." "There is no peace and rest in the development of material interests," the crippled Irish doctor warned Gould's wife Emilia. "The time approaches when all that the Gould Concession stands for shall weigh as heavily upon the people as the barbarism, cruelty, and misrule of a few years back." The mine, once the country's bright shining hope, had stifled "the whole land, feared, hated, wealthy, more soulless than any tyrant, more pitiless and autocratic than the worst Government." Emilia saw her life flash before her, "the degradation of her young ideal of life, of love, of work," and as if talking in a nightmarish sleep, "she stammered out aimlessly the words, 'Material Interests.'"[40]

Nostromo preferred now to go by his given name, Captain Fidanza, "Captain Trust." He "grew rich slowly" and prudently, taking away just one ingot at a time from his stash of silver on the Great Isabel and trading it far away from Sulaco.[41] The silver made him feel like a thief. As cover for his visits to the hoard he paid court to Giorgio Viola's daughters; the elderly innkeeper, now a widower, had gone to the Great Isabel to keep a new lighthouse. Nostromo's deceit would be his undoing. One night, mistaking Nostromo for another, less reputable suitor, Viola fatally shot him.

"The silver has killed me," Nostromo told Emilia Gould on his deathbed. He offered to tell her where he'd hidden it. "Isn't there enough treasure without it to make everybody in the world miserable?" she cried. "No, Capataz. . . . No one misses it now. Let it be lost forever." Everyone and everything who'd ever come near it had been tarnished. Conrad ended the novel with a parting glimpse of Sulaco as one might see it while sailing away. It hunched over the gulf as if compressed beneath "a big white cloud shining like a mass of solid silver."[42]

THE MAGAZINE SERIAL COMPLETE, Conrad made some quick revisions and published *Nostromo* in book form in October 1904. The novel's subtitle, "A Tale of the Seaboard," a tale of the coast, signaled a departure for Conrad. A coast was something new in Conrad's work.

The border of land and sea, a coast could be both barrier and meeting place—a voyager's point of departure, the place where an invader lands. In *Nostromo* the stories Conrad had set on land about outsiders, conspiracies, and families met the themes of honor, community, and isolation he had set at sea.

It was a "wonderful" novel, Cunninghame Graham felt, but the title was all wrong.[43] "The book ought to have been called Costaguana" and should have ended with Captain Mitchell's tour of the newly independent Sulaco. The character of Nostromo only distracted from "the affairs of Costaguana," Graham thought, and "the last two chapters are a mistake." Edward Garnett and book reviewers agreed. The novel seemed all "topsy-turvy," the structure "formless," the language "tortuous," the subplots exasperatingly involved. "The story of the regeneration, the revolution, and the creation of the Occidental Republic is the compelling interest of the book," they judged. "Nostromo comes in only as a handy *deus ex machina*."[44]

The critics were onto something, and Conrad knew it. The agonized composition process of *Nostromo* and the piling up of sources—Graham's recollections of the River Plate, a stray anecdote about a lighter filled with silver, the American-backed revolution in Panama—made for a tough uphill trek. Conrad backtracked. "I don't defend Nostromo generally. Fact is he does not take *my* fancy either," he told Graham. "Truly N is nothing at all—a fiction—embodied vanity of the sailor kind—a romantic mouthpiece of 'the people' which (I mean 'the people') frequently experience the very feelings to which he gives utterance."[45]

For all its flaws, everyone recognized *Nostromo* as a work of genius. "It is a book which will well repay those who give it the close attention which it deserves," concluded its most insightful reviewer, the young diplomat John Buchan, who was making a name for himself by writing political thrillers. *Nostromo* convinced Buchan that Conrad "has a greater range of knowledge . . . of the strange ways of the world than any contemporary writer."[46] Conrad had managed to create "the world in miniature" said another reviewer.[47] "One leaves *Nostromo* with a memory as intense and lucid as that of a real experience."[48]

It's ironic if not surprising that a place Conrad had totally fabricated felt so stunningly real to readers. Conrad had fashioned his ideas of Latin America from precisely the same kinds of books and newspapers his audience might have read. *Nostromo* thus confirmed their stereotypes. Conrad's reviewers in the United States, in particular, read *Nostromo* as a vindication of all their prejudices about Latin America. "Conrad knows this continent of half-baked civilizations; life grows there like rank vegetations," wrote the critic James Huneker.[49] H. L. Mencken admired its "extraordinarily brilliant and incisive study of the Latin-American temperament . . . of the perverse passions and incomprehensible ideals which provoke presumably sane men to pursue one another like wolves."[50]

For Conrad's British readers, however, *Nostromo* presented a more worrying picture of the world. The novel's prophecy of American dominance—"we shall run the world's business whether the world likes it or not"—tapped into persistent and evolving anxieties about British decline.

Nostromo appeared on the heels of a prediction about international affairs issued by the influential geographer Halford Mackinder. A new age was dawning in geopolitics, Mackinder announced. For centuries, European powers had played out their ambitions in other parts of the world. Now, suddenly, the world was full up. Africa partitioned, the center of Asia staked out, North America bound by coast-to-coast railroads, there was "scarcely a region left for the pegging out of a claim of ownership." Almost overnight, international relations had become a zero-sum game: what one nation-state claimed, another would lose. Mackinder forecasted more violent, wider-ranging wars, and a reorientation of the great

W. A. Rogers, "The Great American Durbar," *ca. 1905. This cartoon portrays Theodore Roosevelt in the pompous guise of a Viceroy of India, flanked by representatives of "material interests," and a Panamanian spade-carrier leading the procession.*

powers.[51] "Other empires have had their day, and so may that of Britain. . . . The European phase of history is passing away . . . and a new balance of power is being evolved."[52]

Mackinder's vision already appeared to be coming true. Concerned about fending off rising Germany, Britain scaled back its commitments in the Western Hemisphere in favor of American interests. In the Far East, Japan trounced Russia in a war in the Pacific, and the tsar had to cede power to a newly formed parliament. (Conrad crowed over the corpse of his childhood bogeyman, "part ghoul, part Djinn, part Old Man of the Sea, with beak and claws and a double head.")[53] A 1905 pamphlet by Elliott Evans Mills called *The Decline and Fall of the British Empire*, purportedly written for the use of Tokyo schools in 2005, imagined Japan coming for Britain next. "They were too busy with their commerce and their cargoes, their professional athletes and their race-horses, to study the past and the unalterable decrees of Heaven."[54]

To casual readers *Nostromo* offered another illustration of the changing balance of power. But Conrad pulled back the curtain of geopolitics to reveal a deeper logic at work. "*Il n'y a plus d'Europe*," he growled— something he'd already muttered when Casement told him about the Congo abuses.[55] There's no more Europe. "There is only an armed and trading continent, the home of slowly maturing economical contests for life and death, and of loudly proclaimed world-wide ambitions." More fool all those free traders who hoped that people who did business together would live together in peace. "Industrialism and commercialism . . . stand ready, almost eager, to appeal to the sword."[56] Henceforth, he predicted, "no war will be waged for an idea." Money was everything.[57]

The problem for Costaguana wasn't that the United States eclipsed Britain. It was that Americans and Britons joined forces in the service of "material interests." Through characters like Captain Mitchell, Conrad channeled the confident ideas of capitalists who believed that the global expansion of Western finance and industry was good for everybody. They looked at maps of the world that showed steamship, train, and telegraph lines bursting like fireworks and basked in the glow of "progress." The only people who walked out of *Nostromo* alive and happy were the steamship captain, the railroad entrepreneur, and the financier—globalization's three Fates, spinning and snipping the thread of Costaguana's destiny. "Silver," Conrad explained, "is the pivot of the moral and material events, affecting the lives of everybody in the tale."[58]

Conrad directed the reader's sympathies toward Emilia Gould, who peered into the shadows and assessed the damage. She understood that the things designed to make Costaguana more prosperous, more stable, more "civilized," came at a moral and social cost. They wiped out indigenous ways of life, hollowed out liberal principles, subordinated good to greed. *Nostromo*'s cynicism about "material interests" picked up where *Heart of Darkness* and *Lord Jim* left off. Jim had fled into the distant corner of Asia "beyond the end of telegraph cables and mail-boat lines" where "the haggard utilitarian lies of our civilisation wither and die." *Nostromo* showed what happened when the lines—and the lies—encroached.[59]

Conrad was far from alone in his critique of "material interests." *Nostromo* sat squarely alongside the idea of imperialism launched by Hobson. In fact, though Conrad would have shivered at the comparison, it illustrated imperialism as defined by Hobson's follower V. I. Lenin in his 1917 pamphlet *Imperialism: The Highest Stage of Capitalism*, namely "the exploitation of an increasing number of small or weak nations by a handful of the richest or most powerful nations."[60]

Conrad shared the ideals of Cunninghame Graham, who wanted to restore vanished Arcadias where a sense of fairness and common good prevailed over grasping materialism. But where Cunninghame Graham used politics to hold power brokers to account, Conrad never had faith in organized action and steered clear of signing on to any movement.

That may explain why he stuck to the title *Nostromo*, rather than

Costaguana, as Graham preferred. Nostromo had the stolid look of a man who'd never let you down. Like Lord Jim he approached the world with a "glance fixed upon nothing from under a forced frown." "Our man"— or as Charles Marlow might put it, "one of us"—Nostromo broke faith with his British employers the moment he hid the silver and lied about it. Like Jim, he sealed his fate with a jump from a boat, plunging into the Golfo Placido from the sinking lighter. But when Nostromo made his comeback, he did so not in the white clothes of a hero, as Jim had done, but in the hide of "a magnificent and unconscious wild beast."[61] Nostromo was "one of us" in the most general sense: an everyman consumed by self-interest.

Nostromo wasn't just Conrad's only novel about a place he'd never been. It was a novel about *every* place he'd been. It exuded the political cynicism of the Pole who'd seen his parents wrecked by unattainable nationalist ideals. It projected the nostalgia of the man of sail who saw the craft he admired displaced by industrial technology. It trembled with the shock and revulsion of the white European who saw values of "civilization" and "progress" turned into weapons of mass destruction in Africa and beyond.

The secret to *Nostromo*'s extraordinary prescience was that Conrad folded between its covers his own "theory of the world's future." In the world to come, the better values that Conrad associated with British power would become as obsolete as the romantic dreams of Garibaldi. Instead he anticipated the ascent of an American-led consortium of "material interests." "Material interests" would dictate the fortunes of new nations. They would make imperialism continue to thrive whether or not it had the word "empire" attached to it. The real question for the world's future, in Conrad's theory, wasn't *what* would happen. It was when and how.

TWELVE

WHETHER THE WORLD
LIKES IT OR NOT

"THIS IS A CRITICAL TIME in the history of advancement of men," warned the American intellectual W. E. B. Du Bois in 1910, in the inaugural issue of *The Crisis*, the magazine put out by the National Association for the Advancement of Colored People. "All mankind is becoming one people." If humanity is headed in the right direction, "tolerance, reason and forebearance can to-day make the old-world dream of human brotherhood approach realization." But if people didn't keep striving toward unity, they'd find that "bigotry and prejudice . . . can repeat the awful history of the contact of nations and groups in the past."[1]

More than thirty years since Joseph Conrad first walked out of Liverpool Street Station, the paths he'd traced in the late nineteenth century as an immigrant and a sailor had broadened into avenues. Tens of millions of migrants boarded cheap steamers and trains to richer possibilities in North and South America, north and Southeast Asia. "Material interests" drilled oil in the East Indies for German-designed diesel engines, planted oil palms in Congo for British-manufactured washing powder, and extracted rubber from South America for American-made automobile tires.

Ships at sea sailed over a web of submarine telegraph cables while beaming messages by wireless to shore. There were more Londons and more Singapores, international cities whose polyglot populations wore similar styles of clothes to similar kinds of jobs and spent their free time in similar forms of fun.

There had never been such global interconnection—and never such manifest division.[2] An age of mass migration was also an age of regulated movement, with the introduction of passport controls and exclusionary immigration laws. An era of unprecedented free trade was also a time of mounting calls for protectionism. Some saw world peace guaranteed by global economic integration; others saw surging militant nationalism (in crises in Morocco and the Balkans) and feared the outbreak of war. Democracy increased, as liberal revolutions challenged autocracy in China, Russia, Persia, and the Ottoman Empire; and women's suffrage movements gained ground worldwide. But imperialism intensified as a handful of Western powers consolidated their rule over the majority of the world's people. Rising prosperity went with increasing inequality. More conversation across cultures came with more elaborate theories of racial difference. The same year Du Bois launched *The Crisis*, American academics started the world's first journal of international relations and gave it a title they thought described the crux: the *Journal of Race Development*. It would go on to be better known under a second title, *Foreign Affairs*.[3]

Younger men than Conrad now crossed oceans and challenged the inequities of an entangled world. A Vietnamese ship's steward called Ho Chi Minh worked between berths in Marseille and San Francisco, where he learned about the revolutionary potential of socialism. An Indian lawyer named Mohandas Gandhi holed up in his cabin on a sea voyage from London to South Africa and wrote a treatise about how India could become free from British rule. A Chinese doctor raised in Hawaii named Sun Yat-sen traveled to Europe, Japan, and Singapore, plotting how to overthrow China's Manchu emperor. An Anglo-Irish diplomat who'd campaigned against labor abuses in Africa and the Amazon resigned his position to join the fight for Irish independence. That was Roger Casement.

But Conrad's experience of the world had made him skeptical that you could change systems, or redirect fate. He kept his focus on the individuals bound up in those systems and pegged his hopes for good outcomes on a sense of human solidarity that encouraged individuals to be just and true. He traipsed into the 1910s with the weariness of late middle age. "Illusions get tarnished a bit and one's imaginative machinery begins to show signs of wear. It works, but it creaks—which is annoying."[4]

The Conrad family had expanded to include John, born in 1906. Conrad's debts also increased. Though Conrad cut costs by moving the family from the Pent to a cramped four-room cottage in Kent, by 1910 he owed his agent an almost unimaginable (and surely unrepayable) £2,700—one hundred times the average fee for one of his stories.[5] Pinker kept pressing him to deliver; Conrad replied in aggrieved, defensive letters that might almost have been sent to his uncle Tadeusz decades earlier. The cottage backed onto a slaughterhouse, and to the squeal of dying pigs Conrad worked on his novel *Under Western Eyes*. Narrated by "a teacher of languages" in Geneva, it told of a Russian student who'd informed on a revolutionary friend. Engaged with themes of betrayal, guilt, and dislocation, against a backdrop of eastern European intrigue, Conrad drew the book from some of the darkest corners of his experience. He felt like he was "quarrying my English out of a black night, working like a coalminer in his pit."[6]

In January 1910, Conrad finally finished *Under Western Eyes* and went up to London to deliver the last installment to Pinker in person. He came back to the cottage, crawled into his tiny room, curled up in a ball on the couch, and wouldn't budge.[7] Jessie found him trembling and babbling, his neck and tongue alarmingly swollen. Nobody could understand what Conrad said—because he was speaking Polish. For weeks he remained delirious, "convers[ing] with the characters" of his novels and lapsing into English only to curse Pinker or recite the service for burial at sea.[8] Four-year-old John, who'd seen his father sick so often he used to play at "being ill" by wrapping himself in a blanket and groaning, was so frightened that he never played the game again.[9] Jessie finally discovered what had triggered her husband's breakdown. Conrad and Pinker had gotten into a fight about money, and the furious agent said something the author couldn't forget. As Conrad would write to him, "You told me that I 'did not speak English' to you."[10]

Conrad would rarely ever write fiction with the same passion and insight again. He crept back to work "more crippled mentally than physically" and resumed a novel called *Chance*, which he'd started in 1907.[11] Even as he wrote it he knew it wasn't his best. Although it featured Marlow once again, Conrad deliberately made it less "complicated" than *Lord Jim*, "English in personages and locality, much easier to follow and understand."[12] Marlow in his older age had grown jaded, grumpy, and almost comically misogynistic. Conrad contrasted Marlow's dyspeptic rants with the only fully rounded heroine he'd ever written, Flora de Barral, the spirited daughter of a ruined banker. A picture of her adorned the dust jacket of the finished novel, which was published in January 1914.

And just like that, the fifty-six-year-old author had his first bestseller. *Chance* went into five printings in as many months. Edward Garnett attributed the book's success to the cover design, others to its appealing heroine and its relative narrative simplicity. Conrad could only smirk at the irony of fortune shining into the twilight of his imagination. "How I would have felt about it ten or eight years ago I can't say. Now I can't even pretend I am elated," he confessed to John Galsworthy. "If I had Nostromo, The Nigger or Lord Jim in my desk or only in my head I would feel differently no doubt."[13] On the heels of his *Chance* success, Conrad

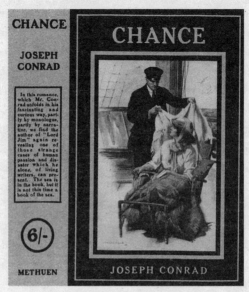

The first-edition dust jacket of Chance.

sold serial rights to his next book to the American *Munsey's Magazine* for $6,000 (approximately £1,225)—an order of magnitude higher than anything he'd ever earned before.[14] He had a jolly meeting in London with his new American book publisher, Frank Doubleday, who was preparing an edition of Conrad's *Complete Works* to take the booming American market by storm.

In the glow of this newfound material and emotional comfort, some young Polish friends, Józef and Otolia Retinger, invited the Conrads to visit their family's country house near Kraków. Jessie was thrilled by the idea of seeing her "husband's native country for the first time," despite the 1903 injury that made walking painful for her. The timing worked well for Conrad, who had just finished another novel, and it seemed a good time to travel with the boys, too. Seven-year-old John was an enthusiastic builder of Meccano, rider of motorcars, and sailor of model ships; with his father's help he'd constructed a miniature Malay archipelago and "'native village' of Patusan" in the garden pond.[15] Borys, nearly sixteen, had just finished a cadetship on the officers' training vessel *Worcester* and, if he passed the entrance exam, would soon be off to Sheffield University for an engineering course.[16]

The prospect of the trip to Poland "caused such an excitement in the household that if I had not accepted immediately I would have been torn to pieces by my wife and children," Conrad wrote to Galsworthy on the morning of their departure. John "yelled from morning till night," Borys

"rushed about in the car on errands of his own contriving," Jessie, as usual, kept everything organized, while Conrad, equally characteristically, managed to muddle things up: he'd failed "to put his full name, Korzeniowski," on the passport application, and the correct documents had arrived only the day before.[17]

"As to this Polish journey I depart on it with mixed feelings," Conrad confessed. He welcomed the idea of showing and sharing the sites of his youth, yet he worried that places once so familiar to him might now feel foreign. "In 1874 I got into a train in Cracow (Vienna express) on my way to the sea, as a man might get

The Conrad family's passport for their 1914 trip to Poland.

into a dream. And here is the dream going on still. Only now it is peopled mostly by ghosts and the moment of awakening draws near."[18]

The date at the top of the page was July 25, 1914. He had no idea what an awakening was in store.

THEY ARRIVED IN KRAKÓW three evenings later, after a rough passage over the North Sea and a night in Berlin. Jessie had to rest her bad leg, and John was running a temperature, but Conrad was too excited to go to bed.

"I am going out for a look round," he said to Borys. "Coming?" Father and son walked down the narrow street from the hotel and entered the great moonlit basin of the Rynek. The lopsided spires of St. Mary's loomed overhead, and the unfinished paving and the trees, which he'd always thought an unnecessary ornament, looked exactly the same as when he had left. Ghosts flickered in the moonlight. Conrad glimpsed the shadow of a little boy darting across the square to school, and a boy dressed in black, following his father's hearse.

That world was no more. He was just a "grizzled foreigner holding forth in a strange tongue" to the son by his side.

"Let's go back," he said to Borys. "It's getting late."

That's how Conrad described his first night in Poland, a few months later—but by then another layer of nostalgia had settled over the experience.[19]

On July 31, after a couple of days of sightseeing in Kraków, the Conrads went to visit the country house of Conrad's old schoolmate Konstantin Buszczyński. They were having tea when a rap at the door announced the arrival of "a troop of Austrian cavalry," who "proceeded to commandeer every horse and vehicle on the premises." The soldiers were prevented from driving away with the Conrads' hired car only by the poignant appearance of Jessie hobbling out of the house on her two walking sticks.[20] The Conrads drove back to Kraków through fields that seemed to have been sown with dragon's teeth: soldiers had sprung up everywhere and were stopping carts and carriages on the road and leading the horses away. The Grand Hotel in Kraków, which just that morning had been a temple of serenity, teemed with "fully armed officers and men staggering under enormous bundles of kit."[21] While the Conrads were out, somebody had started a war.

Conrad said he had paid no attention earlier in July when a friend asked him what he thought about the assassination in Sarajevo of Archduke Franz Ferdinand, heir to the Hapsburg throne. It hadn't seemed any different to Conrad from all the other political assassinations he'd read about over the years—the U.S. president, the president of France, two Spanish prime ministers, the empress of Austria-Hungary, the king of Italy, and the king of Greece—most of them committed by anarchists. But this one actually was different: it was the act of a Serbian nationalist and touched off a strong reaction from Austria-Hungary, which was keen to suppress such anti-imperial dissent. Austria-Hungary determined to retaliate and received a "blank check" of support from Germany to do so. But Serbia, in turn, had the protection of Russia—and Russia was part of a Triple Entente with Britain and France. What that meant was that if Austria declared war on Serbia, then Russia would declare war on Austria; if Russia went to war with Austria, then Germany would go to war with Russia; if Germany fought Russia, then France would fight Germany; and if France was attacked by Germany, via Belgium, then Britain would attack Germany.

In the space of one week, every "if" became a when. The day the Conrads crossed the North Sea, Austria-Hungary rejected Serbia's response to its ultimatum.[22] The day the Conrads passed through Berlin, Austria declared war on Serbia. (Now the Conrads understood why the city had seemed uncomfortably tense.)[23] The days the Conrads went sightseeing in Kraków, Russia mobilized for war. The day the Conrads visited Buszczyński, Austria, Germany, and France mobilized. On August 3 Germany declared war on France; on August 4 Britain declared war on Germany. And the Conrads—British citizens all—were in Austrian territory, on the wrong side of enemy lines.

It was as if Conrad and his family had suddenly become characters in one of his books, forced into a corner by fate. Conrad described Kraków thrown into "a state of siege," telegraph and telephone lines shut down, newspapers censored, and the place crawling with soldiers, albeit "the mildest behaved of any I have seen."[24] He knew his Polish name would offer some protection against sudden internment as an enemy alien, but exiting Austria-Hungary would now require special passes, to say nothing of considerable logistical effort. Conrad took up a cousin's suggestion to get out of the army's way in the meantime by going to stay at her pension in the Tatra Mountains resort of Zakopane, a four-hour train ride to the south.

John spent his eighth birthday on the train, darting from one window to another to catch a glimpse of the engine as it curled around the hills. Zakopane looked like a town sprouted from the forest, into pointy timber chalets with shingle roofs, steeped in the dark, clean smell of pines. For all that the Conrads joined a throng of "refugees of various nationalities . . . cut off from all news and expecting to have a very hungry time of it before long," the resort surroundings gave their retreat the whiff of a summer holiday. Borys, who spoke good French and so could communicate with many of the Poles of the sort to be holidaying in Zakopane, joined hiking parties and flirted with a girl in the pension. Jessie went shopping in town with Conrad's cousin Aniela, and on scenic country drives with John. Conrad caught up on a generation's worth of recent Polish fiction, loaned to him by Aniela, and with a generation's worth of Polish politics, described to him by new friends around the café tables of Zakopane.[25]

The war trapped Poland, in Conrad's words, between "Russian barbarism" and "Germany's superficial, grinding civilization."[26] Polish

Conrad and his cousin Aniela Zagórska.

nationalists who'd already endured the partition of their country now watched it become a battleground among the three partitioning powers. Some nationalists hoped that allying themselves with the winning side would yield Polish independence as a reward; others saw the war as a deadly new stage in a great power struggle that would go on ravaging their country. "The sheer despair of these people seeing nothing but ruin and ultimate extinction," Conrad told Cunninghame Graham, was "very hard to bear."[27] More refugees arrived by the week, tumbling out of horse carts with little more than the clothes on their back; in one shopwindow Jessie saw "hundreds of wedding rings offered for sale" by cash-strapped migrants.[28] Conrad threw himself into the challenge of organizing the family's exit. He wrote to Galsworthy and Pinker to arrange transfers of money. He got his American publisher to ask the American ambassador in Vienna to issue transit papers. He mapped out possible routes they could follow west: Vienna, Switzerland, Bordeaux; Vienna, Italy, Marseille.

Pine-scented summer veered into dank, frost-nipped autumn. The Russians occupied eastern Galicia in September and advanced ever westward in the direction of Zakopane. Conrad's hand and knee stiffened with gout. At last in early October, the family received official permission to depart. Even as they escaped the war there was no escaping the war. They left Zakopane in a heavy snow, riding to a nearby railway station in a trap lined with bug-infested sheepskins, shivering in spite of hot-water bottles and borrowed furs. A journey to Kraków that should have taken less than four hours lasted eighteen "in a train smelling of disenfectants* and resounding with groans" of wounded soldiers. At Kraków's central station they waited another twelve hours for an onward train to Vienna. Jessie led John to the bathroom down corridors lined with wounded soldiers; passing a dressing station, she whipped her hand over the little boy's eyes so he wouldn't catch sight of "a huge pail full of human scraps." The journey to Vienna that should have taken less than seven hours lasted twenty-six, as the train stopped again and again to load and unload sick and injured soldiers.[29]

From Vienna, where Jessie remembered a heroic quest through the city's stations to locate a missing trunk, they took a train to Italy (John remembered the big, bright red car they rode to the station), crossed a frontier guarded by German soldiers (Borys remembered his father seeming suddenly to muster "great fluency" in German to fight their way through), and continued on to Genoa.[30] A timely infusion of cash from Pinker let them buy passage on a Dutch mail boat—homeward bound from Java—and they returned to England in early November, more than four months after they had left. Conrad had spent almost his entire trip in Poland figuring out how to get home.

EVEN WHEN YOU CAN TRACE the fault lines, there's no knowing where or when an earthquake will strike. The Conrads' experience in the summer of 1914 illustrated in dramatic fashion a central feature of the Great War: almost nobody saw it coming, at least not on that scale. Stories of getting trapped by the war became something of a continental genre. Conrad wryly recalled some people assuring him that war was "a material impossibility . . . because it would mean the complete ruin of all material interests"—an argument made by British peace activist Norman Angell.[31] Once the fighting did start, most Europeans imagined it would be over by Christmas. But by winter 1915, when Conrad wrote an essay about the family's trip, the conflict had become a man-eating war of attrition with no obvious end in sight.

Conrad's essay "Poland Revisited" played on a widely held perception that the war changed everything. He described the journey as if it were a dream within a dream, nesting recollections of his distant youth within a haze of prewar innocence. "What I had started on was a journey in time, into the past," and every step came with memories. When they boarded the boat train at Liverpool Street Station, Conrad thought of the day he'd arrived at that station in 1878, "the year of 'Peace with Honour,'" and walked through the Dickensian streets to find his shipping agent.[32] "It was like the closing of a thirty-six-year cycle." As they crossed the North Sea, he remembered his earliest voyages on those waters and recognized it as "the same old thing" it had been before: "a grey-green expanse of smudgy waters" under a sky "made of wet blotting paper."[33] He walked his son around Kraków and recalled his dead father.

The war dropped a veil over memory's face. There was "the London before the war," twinkling with electric light, versus wartime London in the blackout. There was the North Sea at peace, that "same old thing," versus the North Sea at war, "one great minefield, sown thickly with the seeds of hate." There was the previous pan-European war (Napoleonic), when even bitter enemies had a sense of honor and mutual respect, versus the "stealthy, murderous contrivance" of today's war, equipped with the technology of twisted "progress." In the essay's final scene Conrad described coming within sight of the Downs on the homeward passage, "thick with memories of my sea-life," only to be jerked out of reverie by the shock of a shell bursting on the Continent. He caught Jessie's eye and saw that "she also had felt profoundly . . . the faint boom of the big guns at work on the coast of Flanders—shaping the future."[34]

Like Conrad's book-length memoir *A Personal Record*, "Poland Revisited" featured plenty of autobiographical invention and omission. Conrad hadn't walked through the Kraków Rynek with just Borys, feeling like a "grizzled foreigner"; his Polish friends the Retingers had been with him, and they described joining hands with Conrad in patriotic solidarity outside St. Mary's Church to listen to the bugler play the *hejnał*. Conrad wrote of wanting to escape the "shadows" of his parents' generation, "in their clinging air of the grave that tasted of dust and of the bitter vanity of old hopes"—but he didn't write of visiting Apollo Korzeniowski's grave, where Borys remembered seeing Conrad, for the first and only time, get down on his knees and pray.[35] Nor did Conrad mention looking at Apollo's papers in the Jagiellonian library, which in *A Personal Record* he had described having watched his father burn.

One obvious effect of these literary maneuvers was to turn "Poland Revisited" into an affirmation of Conrad's Englishness—at a moment when some Poles were fighting Britain's ally Russia, at that. In a passage virtually draped in the Union Jack, Conrad described looking back on his house as they left, "nestled in, perhaps, the most peaceful nook of Kent," and taking with him in his mind's eye "this tiny fragment of Great Britain; a few fields, a wooded rise . . . and here and there a gleam of red wall and tiled roof . . . wrapped up in a soft mist and peace. And I felt that all this had a very strong hold on me . . . that it was dear to me not as an inheritance, but as an acquisition"—like falling in love.[36] It was no coincidence that Conrad made these professions at the same time that he was more involved in Polish affairs than ever before. At Józef Retinger's instigation, Conrad broke with his normal practice of staying out of politics by writing a "Note on the Polish Problem" to the Foreign Office in 1917, arguing that western Europe had a "moral obligation" to defend Poland from Germany and Russia, and advocating "an Anglo-French protectorate" as "the ideal form of moral and material support."[37]

A subtler effect of Conrad's essay, though, was to fold the coming of the war into a quire of reminiscences, so that it turned out to be a new page, rather than a new story altogether. He said almost nothing about the long homeward journey (which dominated his relatives' accounts), which was entwined at every stage with the danger and damage of combat. Instead, the war emerged in "Poland Revisited" the same way that critical events—like an explosion at Greenwich, or a jump from a ship—so often happened in Conrad's novels: that is, offstage. Conrad cared less about what actually happened than about how people reacted to it. Conrad's choice, within the essay, not to tell Borys about the ghosts he saw flitting through the Kraków Rynek echoed Marlow's lie to Kurtz's fiancée, an action undertaken to preserve someone's innocence. It resonated with the way so many soldiers would be unable to describe "the horror" of the front.

The war opened a new chapter in Conrad's relationship to memory, age, and the past. An evening stroll in that peaceful Home Counties nook might now be interrupted by "the hum of an airship's engines filling the still night air," and tea in the garden with "the constant faint thudding of the guns in Flanders."[38] Borys, who had been mad about motorcars since boyhood, didn't go to Sheffield University after all (he failed the entrance exam), but into the army's Mechanical Transport Corps. Conrad drove with him to the camp "on the day he had to put his boyhood definitely behind him. . . . I saw him wriggle between a bus and a van, and then I hobbled across the road feeling more old than I have ever felt before."[39]

Conrad went back to the manuscript he was writing, a novella called *The Shadow-Line*. It told a coming-of-age story, based loosely on Conrad's captaincy of the *Otago*, about a young captain in the Gulf of Siam on his first command—the same setting Conrad had adopted for his 1909 story "The Secret Sharer." The crew had been afflicted by a mysterious tropical disease, and the quinine in the medicine chest turned out to have been swapped for a useless powder. Guiding the ship to port pushed the captain over the "shadow-line" from youth to adulthood. Exceptionally among Conrad's longer works, the novella involved no major flashbacks or leaps forward: once you cross the line, he seemed to say, there's no going back. So haunting and ominous was it that some people read the dedication—"to Borys and all others who like himself have crossed in early youth the shadow-line of their generation"—and concluded that Borys had been killed.

In fact, the teenage Lieutenant Conrad was deployed to the Western Front in early 1916 and wrote "cheerful boyish letters" home. His parents replied by sending "a tuck box now and again. It's as if he were still in school."[40] That autumn, the sexagenarian Captain Conrad relived a bit of his youth, too, when he accepted an assignment to write some propaganda pieces for the Admiralty. He visited the naval base at Lowestoft and spent two days on a minesweeper, then went up to Scotland for a twelve-day cruise on a decoy destroyer disguised as a merchant ship to attract German U-boats.

Conrad's daily bulletins to Jessie— his "Dear Chica," "Dearest Kitty-wick," his "own woman and best of chums"—doubled as the most intimate written record of their now twenty-year-old marriage.[41] Less fresh were the actual articles he wrote—"'Well Done,'" "Confidence," "Tradition"— which offered warmed-over versions

Conrad on board HMS Ready *in 1916.*

of his peacetime praise for those "British men whose material and moral existence is conditioned by their loyalty to each other and their faithful devotion to a ship."[42] They read like period pieces. And Conrad suspected he was becoming a bit of one himself. In another wartime essay, "Flight," Conrad described a trip in an airplane that he'd been treated to by one of the navy pilots. For eighty magical minutes, Conrad felt as if he'd been frozen "in a block of suspended marble," transfixed by the shadow of the plane inching across the crinkled foil of the sea. He disembarked, he said, certain that he "would never go flying again." Not because he hadn't liked it, but because he couldn't bear to get seduced by the new craft of aviation when he knew himself to be "a man too old for its glory."[43]

Wrong-footed though he had been by the start of the war, Conrad didn't miss a step when it came to assessing the challenges of the peace.

Friends had lost brothers and sons. Borys had been gassed and shell-shocked in the very last weeks of fighting and came home to convalesce. The Conrads' long-serving housemaid Nellie Lyons died of flu, one of the millions killed in the worldwide pandemic. On Armistice Day 1918, Conrad surveyed a continent flanked on the east by the Bolsheviks, who had taken over Russia in 1917, and on the west by the United States, which had entered the war in 1917 and stood poised to "take the head of the table at the Peace Conference" at Versailles, while "Europe generally" would "take a back seat."[44] "The great sacrifice is consummated, and what will come of it to the nations of the earth the future will show," Conrad told the novelist Hugh Walpole. "I can not confess to an easy mind. Great and very blind forces are set free catastrophically all over the world."[45]

In *Nostromo*, fifteen years earlier, Conrad had advanced a "theory of the world's future" that forecasted the ascent of the United States. Now here it was. President Woodrow Wilson arrived in Versailles with "Fourteen Points," or principles, around which the Allies would structure the peace. "The day of conquest and aggrandizement is gone by," Wilson announced, and henceforth national self-determination—not imperialism—should form the basis of international relations. The Ottoman, German, and Austro-Hungarian empires were carved up into putative nation-states and mandate territories, to be managed by Allied powers under the supervision of the League of Nations.[46]

Point Thirteen called for the establishment of "an independent Polish state," something Conrad welcomed, but with a remarkable absence of sentiment. "The only justification for the reestablishment of Poland is political necessity." (Though even then, he was more sympathetic than the economist John Maynard Keynes, who snapped that "Poland is an economic impossibility, with no industry but Jew-baiting.")[47] Conrad suspected that "American influence in European affairs cannot possibly be good on account of those people's crudeness and ignorance backed by great material strength and an awakened sense of their power."[48] As far as he was concerned, Wilson was shaping a world of Costaguanas: countries whose independence would endure only as long as the bigger powers thought it worthwhile. Conrad was on to something. The League of Nations mandates clothed a form of imperialism in the language of internationalism—not wholly unlike the Congo Free State of 1885.[49]

It became a commonplace to see the Great War as the crisis of an old order. To peoples around the world, especially beyond Europe, nationalism and democratic socialism promised liberation from even more restrictive imperial regimes. Wilsonian principles were invoked by people as varied as Koreans seeking independence from Japanese rule, Egyptians demanding independence from the British, Arabs hoping to establish a state in the Hejaz and Levant, and Zionists looking for recognition of a Jewish state in Palestine.[50] Ho Chi Minh signed a letter to Wilson and French prime minister Georges Clemenceau in search of greater rights for Vietnam within the French Empire. Mohandas Gandhi organized his first all-India protest against British rule. Chinese radicals, in the republic set up by Sun Yat-sen, sought to overturn the Western-imposed "Unequal Treaties."

But Conrad's assessment pointed out the ways in which the peace marked a reaction to the emerging *new* order of globalization. As Conrad judged it, perhaps the blindest force to be feared was Bolshevism, despite its promise to lift the stranglehold of "material interests." His friendship with Cunninghame Graham and other socialists notwithstanding, Conrad described "international socialism" as "the sort of thing to which I cannot attach any definite meaning," let alone hope.[51] He railed against the rise of the labor movement in Britain. "Class for me is by definition a hateful thing. The only class really worth consideration is the class of honest and able men to whatever sphere of human activity they may belong."[52] He was equally skeptical of an emerging world order organized around nationalism. The creation of new states licensed a surge in ethnic nationalism, which had already been savagely expressed in the Armenian genocide. Among the war's victorious powers, the spirit of revanchism seemed to obstruct sensible policies of reconstruction.

That was how Roger Casement, once more, crossed Conrad's path. Casement had been arrested for gunrunning from Germany in the lead-up to the Easter Rising of 1916. He was convicted of high treason and sentenced to death. Many of Conrad's friends signed a petition seeking clemency, but Conrad refused to add his name. Not only did Conrad believe Irish republicanism to be "a stab in the back," especially because his travels in the empires of Russia, Austria-Hungary, France, the Netherlands, and Belgium had left intact Conrad's romanticized faith in the British Empire as something better and different.[53] "Already in Africa I judged that he was a man, properly speaking, of no mind at all," Conrad said. "I don't mean stupid. I mean that he was all emotion. By emotional force (Congo report Putumayo—etc.) he made his way, and sheer emotionalism has undone him."[54] It was as if the ghost of his uncle Tadeusz had taken hold of Conrad's pen to launch a parting shot at Apollo Korzeniowski.

Conrad knew firsthand about the oppressions of imperialism, about immigration, about the appeal and peril of nationalism, and about the power of economic and technological change. He also knew that tribalism offered no cure for their ills.[55] "I have never been able to find in any man's book or any man's talk anything convincing enough to stand up for a moment against my deep-seated sense of fatality governing this man-inhabited world," he told the pacifist philosopher Bertrand Russell. "But I know you wouldn't expect me to put faith in *any* system."[56] The only prescriptions Conrad wrote were for individuals. The captain in *The Shadow-Line*, with no medicine available to treat his ailing crew, looks instead for support in that inherited wisdom of his "dynasty; continuous not in blood, indeed, but in experience, in its training, in its conception of duty, and in the blessed simplicity of its traditional point of view on life."[57] Conrad promoted the values (as he imagined them) of the *szlachta* and the sailing ship; the dreams of the depressive who at once depended on and doubted them; and the self-critical awareness of the white man who traveled overseas and saw the limits of his own society, even if he didn't enter into the possibilities of others.

For all that Conrad had been caught off guard by the mistimed trip to Poland, the novel he had finished two months earlier acquired fresh resonance with the war. Combining elements of *Nostromo*'s realm of "material interests" with the Patusan sequence of *Lord Jim*, the novel told the story of a Swede in the East Indies named Axel Heyst, who was persecuted by a jealous German hotel keeper and sinister adventurer named Mr. Jones. Like Brown in *Lord Jim*, Jones, a "gentleman at large," invaded Heyst's hideaway like a devil from another world. "I am the world itself, come to pay you a visit," he said menacingly.[58] All the novel's major characters were killed or killed themselves. The title Conrad gave to this deadly convergence? *Victory*.

A BEST-SELLING AUTHOR on the eve of the war, Conrad emerged in the peace as something of an institution. The first book-length analysis of his work had been published in 1914 by a young Scottish critic named Richard Curle, who declared Conrad to be one of the greatest, least appreciated, and most misunderstood writers alive. "Conrad's work actually does mark a new epoch" in literature, Curle declared. Though "to read Conrad calls for exertion, and nowadays that is enough to damn anyone," Curle was "sure that Conrad's day is at hand and that once his sun has risen it will not set. I do not mean, of course, that he will ever be popular. . . . But I mean that he will be genuinely revered."[59]

Conrad regarded the blossoming of his fortune with ambivalence, finding it both too late and perhaps too much. "You have no idea how much these second rate efforts have brought in," he complained to

Portrait of Joseph Conrad by
Alvin Langdon Coburn, 1916.

Galsworthy of a 1915 story that "earned eight times as much as Youth, six times as much as Heart of Darkness. It makes one sick."[60] To a rumor that he was to be put up for the prestigious Order of Merit, Conrad replied: "I feel strongly that K[ipling] is the right person, and that the O. M. would not perhaps be an appropriate honour for me who, whatever my deepest feelings may be, can't claim English literature as my inheritance." He went on to reject honorary degrees from Oxford, Edinburgh, Cambridge, and Yale—as well as the offer of a knighthood. The only award he'd want to accept, he told his agent, was the Nobel Prize, "as it is an international thing, and less in the nature of an honour than of mere reward."[61]

Conrad had earned critical success with his earlier fiction (Curle was the first to make the case for *Nostromo*, in particular, as Conrad's greatest novel), but his biggest sales came with a series of works, beginning with *Chance*, that were structurally simpler, largely set in Europe, and featured female central characters. When Conrad was writing *Lord Jim*, no other major writers had been experimenting the same way with narrative form—but when James Joyce was writing *Ulysses*, Conrad was writing *The Arrow of Gold*, an awkwardly plotted melodrama centering on a Spanish femme fatale and a gunrunning ring in Marseille. (E. M. Forster's mother cracked that it might better have been titled *The Arrow of Lead*.)[62] When D. H. Lawrence was writing *Women in Love*, Conrad at last completed *The Rescue*, dormant since 1898, which became an ungainly hybrid of ponderous romance and flaccid adventure. When E. M. Forster was writing *A Passage to India*, Conrad wrote *The Rover*, a determinedly historical novel about an old French seaman coming home to his village during the Napoleonic wars. Perhaps not surprisingly, Conrad had next to no contact with the new generation of British avant-garde writers, though he enjoyed a good friendship with André Gide—who supervised the translation of many of his works into French—and once entertained Paul Valéry and Maurice Ravel to lunch. (Several of Conrad's novels had also been translated into Polish, and somebody even offered to translate him into Esperanto. ("A monstrous jargon," he thought it, but if they wanted to do it, he had no objection.)[63]

There was no question where Conrad's biggest fan base resided. That, ironically enough, was in the capital of the coming world, the United States.[64] In 1919, *The Arrow of Gold* was the second-best-selling novel in the country.[65] Newspapers reported "that in 1920 the sales of the books of Joseph Conrad amounted to 36 times what they did in 1911," and "that the sales of Conrad in '21 (June) have reached 300,000 copies."[66] Conrad's American publisher Frank Doubleday kept urging Conrad to do a lecture tour in the United States, which would further boost his sales. Plagued with gout, uneasy about public speaking because of his accent, and reluctant to visit a country whose ethos he was so dubious about, Conrad, at last, agreed.

In April 1923, Conrad boarded the spiffy new Anchor Line steamship *Tuscania* for his first ocean crossing since his seafaring days ("that I should want a ticket in order to go on board a ship on a foreign voyage seems to me the most absurd thing in the world")—his first westbound Atlantic passage since that "short glance" at Latin America almost fifty years earlier.[67] He arrived in New York City ten days later to find himself, to his alarm, a celebrity. The moment he stepped off the boat he was mobbed by journalists and "aimed at by forty cameras held by forty men that looked as if they came out of the slums." The next thing he knew a delegation of Polish-Americans "rushed me on the wharf and thrust enormous nosegays into my hands."[68] Doubleday hustled Conrad into a waiting car and whisked him out to the Doubleday estate at Oyster Bay.

Conrad's visit had been heralded on the cover of *Time* magazine; newspapers hailed him as "the greatest living writer in the English language." He gave a private reading in New York, talked to reporters, dined with politicians, and visited the campuses of Columbia, Yale, and

Harvard (where he "laughed outright at the Germanic Museum," a pastiche of medieval German architecture, "being amused that the Kaiser should give anything to Harvard").[69] He returned to Kent after one month in the States surprised by the "overwhelmingly kindly" and "very human" people he'd met.[70]

He left his besotted American fans "drunk on Conrad."[71] Conrad's most sophisticated American readers appreciated his stylistic innovation and the way in which, as H. L. Mencken put it, "he sees . . . not merely this man's aspiration or that woman's destiny, but the overwhelming sweep and devastation of universal forces."[72] Those were the gifts that made one young admirer—F. Scott Fitzgerald—so eager to crash a party that Doubleday held for Conrad that he performed a jig on the front lawn, hoping to be invited in.[73]

The socialites who swooned over Conrad, though, were surely responding to the image skillfully cultivated by Doubleday, of a "rover of the seven seas" come to discover the New World.[74] Conrad had to some extent encouraged the making of his legend—letting stand, for instance, the false idea that he had been involved in gunrunning to Spain, and volunteering a host of autobiographical episodes in author's notes for Doubleday's collected edition of his works.

But the trip left Conrad more desperate than ever "to get freed from that infernal tale of ships, and that obsession of my sea life which has about as much bearing on my literary existence, on my quality as a writer, as the enumeration of drawing-rooms which Thackeray frequented could have had on his gift as a great novelist. After all," he grumbled to Richard Curle, "I may have been a seaman, but I am a writer of prose."[75]

Conrad turned to Curle as his conduit to future readers. Twenty-five years younger, Curle had become Conrad's amanuensis, and almost a surrogate son. On the one hand, Conrad fed anecdotes and interpretations to Curle, knowing the younger man would be a guardian of his legacy; on the other, Conrad warned him off literal-minded interpretations. "Didn't it ever occur to you, my dear Curle, that I knew what I was doing in leaving the facts of my life and even my tales in the background. Explicitness, my dear fellow, is fatal to the glamour of all artistic work, robbing it of all suggestiveness, destroying all illusion."[76] It was as if Conrad was playing Marlow to Curle, constantly narrating versions of his story, while simultaneously questioning which account was actually true.

Conrad recognized that being able to annotate an essay Curle was writing in 1923 called "The History of Mr. Conrad's Books" presented "an opportunity, if not unique then not likely to occur again in my lifetime" to correct the record of his life. Another record of his life, though, needed no editing. It arrived in the letters that crossed his desk. Conrad's correspondence in the months after his return from the United States seemed to replay his life before him in reverse. Here was Ford Madox Ford writing from Paris to organize reprintings of their coauthored works. There was his "querido amigo" Cunninghame Graham, thanking him for a copy of The Rover, "almost worthy of being a twin brother of your immortal Nostromo."[77] A letter from Edward Garnett reminded Conrad that it was "thirty years now (almost to a day) since I came ashore for good. And the very next year our friendship began! Straight from the sea into your arms, as it were."[78] An elderly anarchist sent Conrad a pamphlet about the 1894 Greenwich explosion.[79] He received a letter from Captain James Craig and the second engineer of the Vidar, who assumed he wouldn't remember them, offering their congratulations on his success.[80] "You could not really have believed that I had forgotten my time in the Vidar," Conrad replied. "It is part of my sea life to which my memory returns most often."[81] He even heard, after a silence of decades, from one of the daughters of the family with whom he'd lodged on Dynevor Road, during his earliest years in London. "I remember how good you all were to me," he replied, "and how on my voyage, I looked forward to the unfailing warm welcome awaiting me in your home."[82]

Conrad's own family all came home to Oswalds, a Georgian house near Canterbury Conrad had rented since 1919, for the Bank Holiday weekend in August 1924. August 2 was John's eighteenth birthday—ten years to the day since they'd taken that wartime train to Zakopane—and he traveled to Kent from Le Havre, where he'd been studying French. Jessie had just gotten home herself after several weeks in a Canterbury nursing home, recuperating from

Conrad in the garden at Oswalds in 1924. His right hand is bandaged for gout.

another operation on her knee. Curle, practically a member of the family, joined the group, and more unusually Borys too—a rapprochement all around, for after years of struggling with shell shock, trouble finding a job, and running up debts (like father like son), Borys had gotten secretly married in 1922 to a woman his parents disapproved of. "Not even of a good working class," said Jessie.[83] Happily Borys had recently found a new job, and came not only with his wife Joan but baby Philip, the Conrads' first grandson.

Conrad spent the Saturday morning with Curle, talking about his new novel, *Suspense*, set in Italy during the Napoleonic wars. They went out together to look at a nearby house Conrad was considering moving to, with a view of the sea, but Conrad had a bout of chest pains in the car and they turned back. He went to bed with what the doctor diagnosed as indigestion, though soon his breathing grew troubled and he was placed on oxygen. By evening he'd recovered enough to chat with the children in his room, "propped up by pillows with the inevitable cigarette smouldering between his fingers."[84] The following morning, Conrad felt well enough to get into his chair and holler greetings to Jessie (laid up in the next room). Then everyone in the house heard a thump. Conrad had fallen dead from his chair, alone in his room, in a houseful of family and friends.

A light rain fell on the morning of Conrad's funeral, in the Catholic church of the ancient cathedral town of Canterbury. There was a cricket festival going on, and as the funeral procession wound through streets filled with bunting and men dressed in cricketing whites, Robert Cunninghame Graham found himself wishing it would never end, so he could linger in these last moments with Conrad. But as the car crunched up the gravel to the cemetery gates, Graham saw the sun break through, felt a good sea breeze whip up, and prepared to say goodbye. They carried the casket to the grave site and lowered it to the murmur of English prayers. Graham left his friend "with his sails all duly furled, rope flemished down, and with the anchor holding truly in the kind Kentish earth." Over Conrad's resting place the gulls would forever screech news from the sea.[85]

TO MAKE YOU SEE

A PIPED-IN SOUND TRACK of "Let It Snow" and "Winter Wonderland" played as the airplane descended into the thick pile of forest around Kisangani. It was a dry, bright day in the "Inner Station," at the uppermost navigable point of the great Congo River. A huge mosque on the outskirts of town showed the influence of the Zanzibaris who'd once ruled this spot. The riverfront was lined with Belgian colonial bungalows with rusted roofs, and abandoned brick factories crumbling back into the red earth.

Aside from a handful of flights, prohibitively expensive for Congolese, the only way to get between Kisangani and Kinshasa is by boat—or rather, by barge. Vessels about the size of tugboats push flotillas of barges downriver, and passengers camp on them in the open air for weeks, equipped with their own sleeping mats, washing buckets, and charcoal stoves. Given how few boats make the trip at all, I was lucky to find one departing within a week. It belonged to Congo's biggest brewery, Bralima, and was heading downriver with four barge loads of Primus beer. Stacked high with yellow plastic bottle crates, *Primus I* looked like a miniature version of the container ship I had sailed on across the Indian Ocean, CMA CGM *Christophe Colomb*.

I settled into a small cabin for the one-thousand-mile trip. I batted away tsetse flies as I reread *Heart of Darkness*. The silhouette of forest scrolled past, interrupted now and then by villages of thatched huts on poles. Above me on the bridge, the captain navigated the same way Conrad had, by experience and by eye, his only other aid a book of bird's-eye drawings of the river in ten-kilometer strips, its pages worn soft as flannel by hundreds of thumbs. In shallow reaches, two men sat on the bow turning sounding poles through the water to gauge depth, as Conrad's crew had done.

But the jungle wasn't closing in, there was no sense of menace, and rather than feeling alienated by my surroundings, I was embraced into a veritable floating village. Where Marlow had had scarcely any interaction with the African crew, I spent all day every day with my fellow travelers, gossiping and talking politics, preparing food, playing *ngola* (a mankala board game), babysitting, and listening to music. Where Conrad and his peers feared attacks from shore (and vice versa), barely an hour passed without pirogues approaching us from the riverbanks. Villagers sold fish, plantains, cassava, and a menagerie of bushmeat—from fat white grubs to smoked monkeys on stakes—and bought urban luxuries from the passengers in turn: toothpaste, salt, biscuits, and batteries. Sensationalists had led me to expect disorder, menace, even danger in Congo, whereas all I saw were a lot of extremely enterprising people minding and finding business. Even the river itself looked different from in Conrad's day, dappled by floating clumps of water hyacinth, an invasive species introduced in the 1950s.

I had come to Congo to find Conrad, yet he had never felt further away. It was an abrupt reminder that, for all the analogies, the early twenty-first century *isn't* the late nineteenth. I had read Conrad after Chinua Achebe's resonant critique, which made me aware of Conrad's dated prejudices, and the risks of using my own outsider's voice to say anything about what Congo was "really" like. I followed lines of globalization that have linked up even more people and places than in Conrad's era—witness the fact that most of us on board spoke a common language (French), and that the boat stopped one evening so everyone could crowd around a small generator-powered television to watch Champions League football. I also saw how economic and technological advances have sustained the gaps between haves and have-nots. None of the towns we stopped in had viable electricity or running water, let alone access to modern health care, roads, or the Internet. Conrad's Congo story had always been about more than one specific place. His insistence on the universal potential for savagery, and the hollowness of civilization, explains why *Heart of Darkness* lends itself so well to transposition. (In light of Conrad's own influences, Francis Ford Coppola's relocation of the story to Southeast Asia in *Apocalypse Now* was unusually apt.)

Conrad famously described the purpose of the artist as being "by the power of the written word to make you hear, to make you feel—it is, before all, to make you see." What Conrad had made me see, I realized, was a set of forces whose shapes may have changed but whose challenges have not. Today's hearts of darkness are to be found in other places where civilizing missions serve as covers for exploitation. The heirs of Conrad's technologically displaced sailors are to be found in industries disrupted by digitization. The analogues to his anarchists are to be found in Internet chat rooms or terrorist cells. The material interests he centered in the United States emanate today as much from China.

It's no coincidence, given the global compass of Conrad's fiction, that his literary heirs have been scattered around the world. When Conrad died in 1924 Robert Cunninghame Graham had been appalled by the silence of the British press on the passing of one of the country's greatest writers; he even had trouble finding a publisher for his own remembrance.[1] Of the few obituaries that did appear in British journals, the longest was by Virginia Woolf in the *Times Literary Supplement*. Though she praised Conrad's seafaring works as enduring classics, she judged his later novels unconvincing and his appeal greatest to "boys and young people."[2] In terms that would have enraged Conrad, Woolf also emphasized his foreignness. "Our guest," she called him, highlighting his "air of mystery," his alien appearance, and his "strong foreign accent."[3]

But in another obituary tribute, the twenty-five-year-old Ernest Hemingway recalled staying up all night reading Conrad "like a drunkard," gulping down four novels so fast he felt "like a young man who had blown his patrimony." Some people, scoffed Hemingway, said that T. S. Eliot was a great writer and that Conrad was not. But if you could mince up Eliot, sprinkle him on Conrad's grave, and bring Conrad back to life, "I would leave for London early tomorrow morning with a sausage grinder."[4] Hemingway may not have known that Eliot was a Conrad fan too. He used a line from *Heart of Darkness*—"Mistah Kurtz—he dead"—as an epigraph for his 1925 poem "The Hollow Men."

Woolf and her circle sniffed, but Hemingway, Eliot, F. Scott Fitzgerald, and William Faulkner all embraced Conrad. These young Americans, outsiders to the British literary establishment, were among the first in a long line of unusually international authors—along with André Gide and Thomas Mann—who claimed Conrad as an inspiration. As an immigrant, a traveler, and, not least, a writer in his nonnative language, Conrad has been at once a model and a bête noire to postcolonial authors from Achebe to V. S. Naipaul. He has turned up in the pages of Latin American writers from Jorge Luis Borges to Gabriel García Márquez, Mario Vargas Llosa, and Juan Gabriel Vásquez. He's been cited as an influence by Robert Stone, Joan Didion, Philip Roth, and Ann Patchett; by W. G. Sebald and John le Carré. Graham Greene even chose his biographer, Norman Sherry, after reading Sherry's work on Conrad.[5]

Conrad himself might be bemused to know that, a century after World War I, Poles are the largest foreign-born group in Britain. In

Lowestoft, where he first touched down in England, there's a Polish shop on the High Street, and a pub opposite the train station called "The Joseph Conrad." This part of England voted heavily for Brexit in 2016, which might not have surprised the immigrant who had seen earlier waves of xenophobia follow from a period of global openness.[6]

One blustery English summer day, I visited Conrad in his patch of Kentish ground. Two Polish women had come to pay their respects, and someone had left a votive candle before Conrad's rough-hewn granite headstone. The block bore a couplet from Edmund Spenser's *Faerie Queene*, which Conrad had used as an epigraph to his last published novel, *The Rover*:

> *Sleep after toyle, port after stormy seas,*
> *Ease after warre, death after life, doth greatly please.*

Above the verse was inscribed, in small black letters, "Joseph Teador Conrad Korzeniowski." It spliced the English "Joseph Conrad" into the Polish name he was baptized by, "Józef Teodor Konrad Korzeniowski," and spelled the "Teodor" wrong.

ACKNOWLEDGMENTS

I first met Joseph Conrad in my eleventh-grade English Class, when my teacher Heidi Dawidoff assigned *Lord Jim*, and I deepened the acquaintance by reading *Heart of Darkness* in AP English with James Pullman. My initial thanks go to them for opening the door to Conrad's world.

I went to college expecting to major in English, but a history course taught by Mark Kishlansky awakened me to the power of historical narrative. I concentrated instead in Harvard's History and Literature program, and when I next read Conrad (*The Secret Agent*) it was in a history course. It's no coincidence that the idea for a book about Conrad and his times—a quintessential History and Literature topic—arrived in 2007 just as I was returning to Harvard to teach. This book has matured in step with my years here.

My greatest intellectual debts fall due to my faculty colleagues, beginning with Mark himself, who died in 2015, but whose advocacy for writing history *as* literature remains an inspiration. Sunil Amrith, David Armitage, Caroline Elkins, and Emma Rothschild have consistently sharpened my perspective on British imperial and global history. Peter Gordon, Alison Johnson, Mary Lewis, and Charles Maier have enriched my understanding of continental European history. I've learned much from conversations with Niall Ferguson and Jill Lepore about the purpose of history and how to write it. From Amanda Claybaugh, Luke Menand,

Leah Price, and Martin Puchner, I've gotten indispensable lessons in how to read literature like a critic.

Two terrific cohorts of undergraduates in my seminar on "The Worlds of Joseph Conrad" gave me new ways of interpreting and presenting this material. I've also been lucky to work with superb graduate students—notably Barnaby Crowcroft, Erik Linstrum, and Mircea Raianu—and learn from their fresh questions and original research.

Staff at the History Department and Center for European Studies—Paul Dzus, Elizabeth Johnson, Ann Kaufmann, Elaine Papoulias, and Anna Popiel—have made going into the office seem almost a pleasure. I also want to acknowledge Deans Michael D. Smith and Nina Zipser of the Faculty of Arts and Sciences for their generous material and moral support.

I had the chance to test out portions of this project before a number of audiences who gave me extremely helpful feedback. My thanks to those who invited and listened to me at Columbia University, Davidson College, Duke University, Johns Hopkins University, the Mahindra Humanities Center at Harvard, the National History Center, the New York Institute for the Humanities, New York University, Northwestern University, Pomona College, Princeton University, the University of California at Berkeley, the University of Konstanz, the University of Maryland-Baltimore County; and at meetings of the Joseph Conrad Society (UK), the New Zealand Historical Association, and the North American Conference on British Studies. I'm particularly grateful to Peter Brooks, Sarah Cole, Susan Pedersen, Philip Stern, and Judith Surkis for their responses.

In the summer of 2013, David Miller took me on a walk around Conrad's London haunts and we began a conversation about Conrad that continued until David's sudden death, just weeks before I completed this manuscript. Among the many things for which I am indebted to David are introductions to Keith Carabine, Laurence Davies, and Allan

Simmons, without whose meticulous scholarship on Conrad I simply could not have written this book. Special appreciation goes to Allan for agreeing to look over the manuscript, and to Keith for taking me to Conrad's grave.

My research for this book was supported by a Guggenheim Fellowship, and I also benefited from a short-term research fellowship at St. John's College, Oxford. Tomasz Blusiewicz and Michael Tworek provided invaluable assistance with Polish sources; and Robert Foulke, Janet Polasky, Debora Silverman, and Eric Tagliacozzo gave valuable pointers on aspects of maritime, Belgian, and Malay history. I couldn't round out a reckoning of scholarly debts without acknowledging Linda Colley for her ongoing mentorship and the model of her own scholarship, and David Cannadine for his enthusiasm and encouragement.

Although I began this project in archives in Britain and Singapore, assuming that the research process would resemble that of my earlier books, I ended up coming closest to Conrad on board ships. Three journeys profoundly shaped my sense of Conrad's world and how to write about it. To Captain Thierry Robin and the welcoming crew of CMA CGM *Christophe Colomb* I'm immensely grateful for an unforgettable ocean crossing; their good company ensured that this long voyage had scarcely a longueur along the way. To Captain Doug Nemeth, Daniel Brayton, and the crew and students on *Corwith Cramer* C261, I'm indebted for a crash course in seamanship. My sincere thanks go, too, to the Sea Education Association for allowing me to join the vessel, and to Joyce Chaplin for suggesting it.

I deeply appreciate the advice and assistance of those many people who generously fielded my out-of-the-blue queries about the logistics of a Congo River journey, including Philip Gourevitch, Nancy Rose Hunt, Michael Kavanagh, Jocelyn Kelly, Max McClellan, Arlette Nyembo, Chris Rosenkrans, Aaron Ross, and Anjan Sundaram. Ote Mbili and Gerry Mulcaire were able and genial guides. To Captain Moïse, to the crew, and to the many passengers who shared with me the trip of a lifetime on board the floating village of *Primus I*, I owe far more than a simple word like "thanks" can possibly convey.

It took a long time to figure out how actually to structure and compose this book. I've taken much from discussions with some of the most inspiring authors I know: William Dalrymple, Nicholas Dawidoff, Geoff Dyer, and Phyllis Rose. It was Geoff who paved the way for my first piece of writing about Conrad, as part of a collaboration between Artangel and A Room for London. I'm also grateful to the late Robert Silvers and to Stéphanie Giry for giving me space in their pages to ruminate on Conrad. I wrote large chunks of the book at Yaddo and the MacDowell Colony (as a Stanford Calderwood Fellow), whose extraordinary support for the arts seems little short of miraculous.

Numerous friends and colleagues read portions of the manuscript and offered vital suggestions for improvement, including Jason Harding, Alison Johnson, Luke Menand, Martin Puchner, Marco Roth, Emma Rothschild, Kirsten Weld, and Larry Wolff. Deborah Cohen and Rachel Cohen braved my earliest drafts and responded with an ideal blend of advice and encouragement. Amanda Claybaugh read the entire manuscript, in some places twice, and told me what I was trying to say better than I had managed to do myself. Martin Quinn provided the most thorough, perceptive line editing I've ever had the privilege of receiving. Phyllis Rose saw me over the finish line with an indispensable vetting of the final draft.

Though writing this book has been challenging, seeing it into print has been seamless, beginning with the expert stewardship of Andrew Wylie and Sarah Chalfant. It has been a true pleasure to work with Scott Moyers, who has been nothing but engaged, responsive, thoughtful, and wise. Likewise it has been wonderful to do another book with Arabella Pike, the best champion I could hope for, and a source of unstinting encouragement and advice. I'm also grateful to the tremendous editorial, production, and publicity teams at Penguin Press—including Kiara

Barrow, Beena Kamlani, and Christopher Richards—and at William Collins for their commitment to this book.

"Writing," Conrad once said, takes place "in a solitude almost as great as that of the ship at sea." Yet even in the loneliest moments, he conceded, a writer, like a sailor, can draw support from those "few friends, and relations" who remain "always distinct, indubitable, the only ones who matter." I've been fortunate to have within just a few square miles what Conrad so early lost, namely the support and companionship of my immediate family. My parents Jay and Sheila, my brother Alan, Luba, and no-longer-so-little Nina, have each contributed to the realization of this book with everything from erudite conversation and professional advice to home-cooked meals, airport pickups, and forays into the adventures of Tintin.

In spending time with Conrad, though, whose wonderful capacity for making close friends meant that he was never truly alone, I've become especially aware of the sustaining power of friendship in my own life. Many of my friends have by now traveled with me over decades and across continents, including Duncan Chesney, Anna Dale, Michael Dresser, Josiah Osgood, Bahare Rashidi, Marco Roth, Neil Safier, Jesse Scott, Stephanie Snider, Kirk Swinehart, Nasser Zakariya, and Julie Zikherman. Others have helped turn Cambridge into home, including Nir Eyal, Healan Gaston, Crate Herbert, Andy Jewett, Ian Miller, Kate Monaghan, Megan O'Grady, Leah Price, Martin Quinn, Lisa Randall, Dana Sajdi, Sharmila Sen, and Heidi Voskuhl. With Rachel Cohen and Matt, Sylvia, and Tobias Boyle I have enjoyed a spectacular combination of warmth, intelligence, and delight in toy tigers. And with Amanda Claybaugh, Sam Haselby, and Martin Puchner I've discovered a "social family" of tremendous companionability and insight. I dedicate this book to you, my friends—my anchors and my sails.

NOTES

ABBREVIATIONS USED IN NOTES:

CL: Joseph Conrad, *The Collected Letters of Joseph Conrad*, eds. Frederick R. Karl and Laurence Davies, 9 vols. (Cambridge, UK: Cambridge University Press, 1983–2008). Vols. 1–6 edited by Laurence Davies, Frederick R. Karl, and Owen Knowles. Vol. 7 edited by Laurence Davies and J. H. Stape. Vol. 8 edited by Laurence Davies and Gene M. Moore. Vol. 9 edited by Laurence Davies, Owen Knowles, Gene M. Moore, and J. H. Stape.

CPB: Zdzisław Najder, ed., *Conrad's Polish Background: Letters to and from Polish Friends*, trans. Halina Carroll (London: Oxford University Press, 1964).

CUFE: Zdzisław Najder ed., *Conrad Under Familial Eyes: Texts*, trans. Halina Carroll-Najder (Cambridge, UK: Cambridge University Press, 1983).

PROLOGUE: ONE OF US

1. Tom Burgis, *The Looting Machine: Warlords, Oligarchs, Corporations, Smugglers, and the Theft of Africa's Wealth* (New York: PublicAffairs, 2015), chapter 2; Jason K. Stearns, *Dancing in the Glory of Monsters: The Collapse of the Congo and the Great War of Africa* (New York: PublicAffairs, 2012); United Nations Development Program, *Human Development Report 2015: Work for Human Development* (New York: UNDP, 2015), pp. 208–11.

2. Sean Rorison, *Congo: Democratic Republic, Republic*, 2nd ed. (Chalfont St. Peters, Buckinghamshire, UK: Bradt Travel Guides, 2012), p. 3.

3. "Democratic Republic of the Congo Travel Warning," September 29, 2016. https://travel.state.gov/content/passports/en/alertswarnings/democratic-republic-of-the-congo-travel-warning.html; Jeffrey Gettleman, "Kinshasa, Congo, Is Locked Down as Protests Erupt Against Joseph Kabila," *The New York Times*, September 19, 2016; www.nytimes.com/2016/09/20/world/africa/congo-protests-joseph-kabila.html; Robin Emmott, "European Union Prepares Sanctions over Congo Vote Delay," October 17, 2016, www.reuters.com/article/us-congo-politics-eu-idUSKBN12G0X9; Aaron Ross, "Congo Security Forces Killed Dozens of Anti-Government Protestors: U.N.," October 21, 2016, www.reuters.com/article/us-congo-politics-un-idUSKCN12L13D.

4. Joseph Conrad [henceforth JC] to Karol Zagórski, May 22, 1890, *CL*, vol. 1, p. 52.

5. Chinua Achebe, "An Image of Africa," *The Massachusetts Review* 18, no. 4 (December 1, 1977): 788, 790.

6. Barack Obama, *Dreams from My Father*, rev. ed. (New York: Three Rivers Press, 2004), pp. 102–3.

7. Cf. Juan Gabriel Vásquez, "Remember the Future," in *A London Address: The Artangel Essays* (London: Granta, 2013).

8. V. S. Naipaul, "Conrad's Darkness," *The New York Review of Books*, October 17, 1974.

9. "Cosmic Purposes: Whitman's 'Passage to India,'" http://exhibitions.nypl.org/treasures/items/show/103.

10. I base this paragraph on, among others: Eric Hobsbawm, *The Age of Empire* (New York: Vintage Books, 1989); A. G. Hopkins, ed., *Globalization in World History* (New York: W. W. Norton, 2002); C. A. Bayly, *The Birth of the Modern World, 1780–1914: Global Connections and Comparisons* (Malden, MA: Blackwell Publishing, 2004); Adam McKeown, "Global Migration, 1846–1940," *Journal of World History* 15, no. 2 (June 2004): 155–89; Jürgen Osterhammel and Niels P. Petersson, *Globalization: A Short History* (Princeton, NJ: Princeton University Press, 2005), trans. Dona Geyer; John Darwin, *After Tamerlane: The Rise and Fall of Global Empires, 1400–2000* (New York: Bloomsbury, 2009); Mark Mazower, *Governing the World: The History of an Idea* (New York: Penguin Press, 2012); Jürgen Osterhammel, *The Transformation of the World: A Global History of the Nineteenth Century*, trans. Patrick Camiller (Princeton, NJ: Princeton University Press, 2014); Charles S. Maier, *Once Within Borders: Territories of Power, Wealth, and Belonging Since 1500* (Cambridge, MA: Harvard University Press, 2016).

11. Quoted in Edward Garnett, "Introduction" to Joseph Conrad, *Conrad's Prefaces to His Works* (New York: Haskell House, 1971), p. 28.

12. JC to Marguerite Poradowska, August [18?], 1894, *CL*, vol. 1, p. 171.

13. I draw this example from Rose George, *Ninety Percent of Everything: Inside Shipping, the Invisible Industry That Puts Clothes on Your Back, Gas in Your Car, and Food on Your Plate* (New York: Metropolitan Books, 2013), p. 18. See also Marc Levenson, *The Box: How the Shipping Industry Made the World Smaller and the World Economy Bigger* (Princeton, NJ: Princeton University Press, 2008).

14. JC to Kazimierz Waliszewski, December 5, 1903, *CL*, vol. 3, p. 89.

15. Edward W. Said, *Joseph Conrad and the Fiction of Autobiography* (New York: Columbia University Press, 2008); Ian P. Watt, *Conrad in the Nineteenth Century* (Berkeley: University of California Press, 1979).

16. Norman Sherry, *Conrad's Eastern World* (Cambridge, UK: Cambridge University Press, 1966); Norman Sherry, *Conrad's Western World* (Cambridge, UK: Cambridge University Press, 1971).

17. Jocelyn Baines, *Joseph Conrad: A Critical Biography* (Westport, CT: Greenwood Press, 1975); Frederick Robert Karl, *Joseph Conrad: The Three Lives* (New York: Farrar, Straus and Giroux, 1979); Zdzisław Najder, *Joseph Conrad: A Life*, 2nd ed. (Rochester, NY: Camden House, 2007); John Stape, *The Several Lives of Joseph Conrad* (New York: Pantheon Books, 2007). As readers will see, I draw most heavily in this book on Najder, thanks to his unparalleled research on Conrad's early life.

18. Karl Marx, *The Eighteenth Brumaire of Louis Bonaparte*, trans. Daniel De Leon (Chicago: Charles H. Kerr & Company, 1907), p. 5.

19. "Henry James: An Appreciation," in Joseph Conrad, *Notes on Life and Letters* (Garden City, NY: Doubleday, Page & Co., 1924), p. 17.

20. JC to Humphrey Milford, January 15, 1907, *CL*, vol. 3, p. 408.

21. JC to F. N. Doubleday, May 19, 1916, *CL*, vol. 5, p. 589.

CHAPTER ONE: NO HOME, NO COUNTRY

1. Many of the sites of Conrad's childhood were known by various names, spellings, and alphabets to their linguistically diverse inhabitants (Polish, Ukrainian, Yiddish, German, Russian), and he may

have known by Polish names towns that are rendered differently under the politico-linguistic boundaries of today. I have chosen to use the spellings of these locations as they currently appear on the map—with the exception of locations that have an accepted English equivalent (e.g., Lviv for Lwów/L'viv, and Warsaw instead of Warszawa).

2. "The Order of Baptism," *The Offices of the Old Catholic Prayer-Book* (Oxford and London: James Parker and Co., 1876), p. 13; "Conrad's Certificate of Baptism," *CUFE*, p. 31. For an extensive discussion of Conrad's place of birth, see Zdzisław Najder, *Joseph Conrad: A Life*, 2nd ed. (Rochester, NY: Camden House, 2007), pp. 10–12n.

3. Piotr Stefan Wandycz, *The Lands of Partitioned Poland, 1795–1918*, 2nd printing, with corrections (Seattle: University of Washington Press, 1996 printing, 1984), p. 17.

4. Apollo Korzeniowski, "To my son born in the 85th year of Muscovite oppression," *CUFE*, pp.32–33. Czesław Miłosz, "Apollo N. Korzeniowski: Joseph Conrad's Father," *Mosaic* 6, no. 4 (1973): 125.

5. On the meaning of the Polish phrase "*pisz na Berdychiv*," see Julian Krzyżanowski, ed., *Nowa księga przysłów i wyrażeń przysłowiowych polskich* (Warsaw: PIW, 1969), vol. 1, p. 75. I am grateful to Tomasz Blusiewicz for the citation and his explication of this phrase.

6. Charles W. Calomiris and Larry Schweikart, "The Panic of 1857: Origins, Transmission, and Containment," *The Journal of Economic History* 51, no. 4 (December 1991): 807–34.

7. "Chronicle," *The Annual Register, or a View of History and Politics of the Year 1857* (London: Printed for F. & J. Rivington, 1858), p. 228.

8. The month of the Haj that year ended in late August: www.muslimphilosophy.com/ip/hijri.htm.

9. Jan Vansina, *Paths in the Rainforests: Toward a History of Political Tradition in Equatorial Africa* (Madison:.University of Wisconsin Press, 1990), chapter 7.

10. Robert Louis Gilmore and John Parker Harrison, "Juan Bernardo Elbers and the Introduction of Steam Navigation on the Magdalena River," *The Hispanic American Historical Review* 28, no. 3 (August 1948): 335–59; Jason McGraw, *The Work of Recognition: Caribbean Colombia and the Post-emancipation Struggle for Citizenship* (Chapel Hill: University of North Carolina Press, 2014), chapter 3.

11. Cf. Alfred Jarry's 1896 play *Ubu Roi*, which opens in "Poland—that is to say nowhere." Kate Brown portrays the region of Conrad's childhood as "no place" in *A Biography of No Place* (Cambridge, MA: Harvard University Press, 2004).

12. Wandycz, *Lands of Partitioned Poland*, pp. 4–5; Patrice M. Dabrowski, *Poland: The First Thousand Years* (DeKalb, IL: NIU Press, 2014), pp. 132–35; Tadeusz Bobrowski, *A Memoir of My Life*, trans., ed., and intro. Addison Bross (Boulder, CO: East European Monographs, 2008), pp. 14–19; Andrzej Walicki, *Poland Between East and West: The Controversies over Self-definition and Modernization in Partitioned Poland* (Cambridge, MA: Harvard Ukrainian Research Institute, 1994), pp. 10–11.

13. Wandycz, *Lands of Partitioned Poland*, pp. 105–26; Norman Davies, *God's Playground: A History of Poland* (New York: Columbia University Press, 1982), vol. 2, pp. 202–3, 232–45; Dabrowski, *Poland: The First Thousand Years*, pp. 319–21.

14. Bobrowski, *Memoir*, pp. 114–15, 148.

15. Ibid., pp. 272–73.

16. Ibid., p. 10.

17. Adam Mickiewicz, *The Books and the Pilgrimage of the Polish Nation* (London: James Ridgway, 1833), pp. 15–20.

18. Jerzy Zdrada, "Apollo Korzeniowski's Poland and Muscovy (translated by Ewa Kowal—revised by REP)," *Yearbook of Conrad Studies (Poland)* IV (2008): 25, 28. An early photograph of Apollo has his name written below in Arabic script, testament perhaps to his time as a language student in St. Petersburg. (Box 16, Joseph Conrad Collection, Beinecke Library, Yale University.)

19. Ibid., pp. 27–31.

20. Bobrowski, *Memoir*, pp. 240–41; Najder, *Joseph Conrad: A Life*, pp. 5, 580–81.

21. Bobrowski, *Memoir*, p. 237.

22. Ibid., pp. 18–24.

23. Roman Taborski, *Apollo Korzeniowski, ostatni dramatopisarz romantyczny* (Wrocław: Zakład im Ossolińskich, 1957), chapter 2.

24. Apollo Korzeniowski [henceforth AK] to Tadeusz Bobrowski [henceforth TB], May 11, 1849, *CUFE*, p. 22.

25. Buszczyński, quoted in Miłosz, "Apollo N. Korzeniowski," p. 123; Bobrowski, *Memoir*, pp. 280–81.

26. Bobrowski, *Memoir*, pp. 238–39, 280–81, 311.

27. Ibid., pp. 300–303, notes pp. 304–5; Miłosz, "Apollo N. Korzeniowski," pp. 131–32. When Ukrainian peasants launched their own rebellion in 1855, *szlachta* scurried ignominiously to the safety of towns, leaving the serfs to be gunned down by Russian troops.

28. Bobrowski, *Memoir*, pp. 311–12.

29. Adam Mickiewicz, *Konrad Wallenrod: An Historical Poem*, trans. Maude Ashurst Biggs (London: Trübner & Co., 1882), p. 82. This particular translation was made by an almost exact contemporary of Conrad's and reflects contemporary British support for Polish nationalism: the translator grew up in a family of prominent reformers and translated Mickiewicz as part of a lifelong involvement in Polish affairs. ("Maude Ashurst Biggs," in Jonathan Spain, "Biggs, Matilda Ashurst [1816/17–1866]," *Oxford Dictionary of National Biography*, Oxford University Press, 2004; online ed., May 2011 [www.oxforddnb.com.ezp-prod1.hul.harvard.edu/view/article/59172].)

30. Adam Mickiewicz, Dorothea Prall Radin, and George Rapall Noyes, "Part III, Sc. II–V, Forefathers' Eve," *The Slavonic Review* 4, no. 10 (1925): 48–49.

31. The estate belonged to the Sobański family. Bobrowski, *Memoir*, pp. 239, 326.

32. Quoted in Zdrada, "Apollo Korzeniowski's Poland and Muscovy," p. 33.

33. Wandycz, *Lands of Partitioned Poland*, p. 156.

34. Najder, *Joseph Conrad: A Life*, p. 14.

35. Quoted in Taborski, *Apollo Korzeniowski*, p. 95.

36. Ibid., p. 66.

37. Miłosz, "Apollo N. Korzeniowski," p. 126.

38. Wandycz, *Lands of Partitioned Poland*, pp. 159–61; Dabrowski, *Poland: The First Thousand Years*, pp. 332–33.

39. Bobrowski, *Memoir*, pp. 384–89.

40. JC to AK, [May 23, 1861], *CL*, vol. 1, p. 3.

41. Ewa Korzeniowska [henceforth EK] to AK, May 23/June 4, 1861, *CUFE*, p. 43; EK to AK, July 5/17, 1861, *CUFE*, p. 53. Conrad's son John later noted that his father "was inclined to be too generous, particularly to tramps and people down on their luck." John Conrad, *Joseph Conrad: Times Remembered, 'Ojciec Jest Tutaj'* (Cambridge, UK: Cambridge University Press, 1981), p. 201.

42. EK to AK, May 28/June 9, 1861, *CUFE*, p. 44; EK to AK, June 20/July 2, 1861, *CUFE*, p. 51.

43. EK to AK [n.d.], *CUFE*, p. 37; EK to AK, May 23/June 4, 1861, *CUFE*, p. 41; Taborski, *Apollo Korzeniowski*, pp. 98–104. Bobrowski, *Memoir*, pp. 378–95.

44. EK to Antoni Pietkiewicz, July 27/August 8, 1861, *CUFE*, p. 57.

45. Stefan Buszczyński, *Mało Znany Poeta [A Little-Known Poet]* (Kraków: Drukarnia "Czas" W. Kirchmayera, 1870), p. 37. I am grateful to Tomasz Blusiewicz for his notes on and translation of this work.

46. Najder, *Joseph Conrad: A Life*, pp. 16–19; Taborski, *Apollo Korzeniowski*, p. 104. The so-called *chłopomani*, "peasant-lovers," made a point of wearing peasant clothes, reviving peasant folklore, etc. Bobrowski, *Memoir*, p. 442n.

47. Davies, *God's Playground*, pp. 258–59; Taborski, *Apollo Korzeniowski*, p. 104; Najder, *Joseph Conrad: A Life*, p. 18; Zdrada, "Apollo Korzeniowski's Poland and Muscovy," pp. 36–37.

48. EK to AK, June 20/July 2, 1861, *CUFE*, p. 51; EK to AK, [n.d.], *CUFE*, p. 37.

49. EK to AK, June 9/21, 1861, *CUFE*, pp. 45–46.

50. EK to AK, July 5/17, 1861, *CUFE*, p. 53.

51. EK to AK, June 19/July 1, 1861, *CUFE*, pp. 48–49.

52. Wandycz, *Lands of Partitioned Poland*, pp. 166–67.

53. Najder, *Joseph Conrad: A Life*, p. 18; Zdrada, "Apollo Korzeniowski's Poland and Muscovy," p. 39.

54. EK to Mr. and Mrs. Antoni Pietkiewicz, November 19, 1861, *CUFE*, p. 59; Apollo Korzeniowski, "Poland and Muscovy," *CUFE*, p. 87.

55. "The investigation and the court's verdict in the case of Apollo and Ewa Korzeniowski," *CUFE*, pp. 62–63. See also Zdrada, "Apollo Korzeniowski's Poland and Muscovy," pp. 42–44.

56. Buszczyński, *Mało Znany Poeta*, p. 37. Quotes from Apollo Korzeniowski, "Poland and Muscovy," *CUFE*, pp. 76–88.

57. Najder, *Joseph Conrad: A Life*, p. 20.

58. EK to Antoni Pietkiewicz, January 7, 1862, *CUFE*, p. 61.

59. I quote from and base my description of this scene on EK to Antoni Pietkiewicz, January 7, 1862, *CUFE*, pp. 60–61.

60. JC to Wincenty Lutosławski, June 9, 1897, *CL*, vol. 1, p. 358.

61. "The Investigation and the Court's Verdict in the Case of Apollo and Ewa Korzeniowski," *CUFE*, pp. 62–63. Korzeniowski described the scene in "Poland and Muscovy," *CUFE*, pp. 76–83. Cf. Buszczyński, *Mało Znany Poeta*, p. 37: "The exile sentence to Perm was pronounced. Since the sentence was too long, the judges interrupted the reading and told him to sign. 'I will sign where you, Sirs, stopped reading.'"

62. Zdrada, "Apollo Korzeniowski's Poland and Muscovy," p. 44.

63. In his fervently patriotic biography *Mało Znany Poeta* [*A Little-Known Poet*], Stefan Buszczyński said: "Korzeniowski's passage through Lithuania was a true triumph. In Białystok crowds gathered to greet him, dispersed by gendarmes and Cossacks with whips." (38)

64. Bobrowski, *Memoir*, p. 396; AK to Gabriela and Jan Zagórski, June 15/27, 1862, *CUFE*, p. 66.

65. AK to Gabriela and Jan Zagórski, June 15/27, 1862, *CUFE*, pp. 66–67; AK to Gabriela and Jan Zagórski, October 2/14, 1862, *CUFE*, p. 70.

66. AK to Gabriela and Jan Zagórski, June 15/27, 1862, *CUFE*, p. 67.

67. Apollo mentions the photographer, Stanisław Kraków, in his June letter to the Zagórskis. The name of the studio is printed on the back.

68. Wandycz, *Lands of Partitioned Poland*, pp. 197–99; Davies, *God's Playground*, pp. 259–66.

69. Bobrowski, *Memoir*, p. 401.

70. He mentions twenty wards in his memoir, including Konrad Korzeniowski. Ibid., p. 442.

71. AK to Gabriela and Jan Zagórski, March 15/27, 1863, *CUFE*, p. 89.

72. Richard Niland, *Conrad and History* (Oxford: Oxford University Press, 2010), pp. 27–32.

73. Apollo Korzeniowski, "Poland and Muscovy," *CUFE*, pp. 75–84.

74. AK to Gabriela and Jan Zagórski, October 2/14, 1862, *CUFE*, p. 70. Najder dates the family's move to Chernihiv in January 1863 on the basis of a police file (pp. 22, 583n). But in a letter of mid-March 1863, enclosing a photograph of himself with two Vologda friends, Apollo mentions that they are about to celebrate the name day of a Polish priest in Vologda, proof they were still there in March. (AK to Gabriela and Jan Zagórski, March 15/27, 1863, *CUFE*, p. 90.) This also squares with Bobrowski's recollection that they arrived in Chernihiv "in the summer of 1863." (Bobrowswki, *Memoir*, p. 397.) See Zdrada, "Apollo Korzeniowski's Poland and Muscovy," p. 47n.

75. AK to Kazimierz Kaszewski, [February 26, 1865] and AK to Kazimierz Kaszewski, February 28, 1865, *CUFE*, pp. 90–94.

76. Buszczyński, *Mało Znany Poeta*, p. 40.

77. AK to Kazimierz Kaszewski, May 29/June 10, 1865, *CUFE*, pp. 95–96.

78. AK to Gabriela and Jan Zagórski, January 6/18, 1866, *CUFE*, p. 102.

79. AK to Kazimierz Kaszewski, September 6/18, 1865, *CUFE*, p. 97.

80. AK to Kazimierz Kaszewski, October 19/31, 1865, *CUFE*, p. 100.

81. AK to Gabriela and Jan Zagórski, January 6/18 1866, *CUFE*, p. 102.

82. AK to Kazimierz Kaszewski, November 10/22, 1866, *CUFE*, p. 105.

83. AK to Kazimierz Kaszewski, October 19/31, 1865, *CUFE*, p. 100.

84. AK to Kazimierz Kaszewski, January 20/February 1, 1866, *CUFE*, p. 103.

85. AK to Kazimierz Kaszewski, November 10/22, 1866, *CUFE*, pp. 105–7.

86. AK to Kazimierz Kaszewski, February 7/19, 1867, *CUFE*, p. 111.

87. AK to Kazimierz Kaszewski, November 10/22, 1866, *CUFE*, p. 105.

88. An 1868 photograph of Apollo is reproduced in Najder, *Joseph Conrad: A Life*, between pp. 360 and 361.

89. Reminiscences of Jadwiga Kałuska, quoted in Roman Dyboski, "From Conrad's Youth," *CUFE*, p. 138.

90. AK to Kazimierz Kaszewski, June 24, 1868, *CUFE*, pp. 118–19.

91. "Morze-Lud" in Taborski, *Apollo Korzeniowski*, p. 158. My thanks to Tomasz Blusiewicz for the translation.

92. AK to Stefan Buszczyński, March 5/17, 1868, p. 113. The line paraphrases the poet Wincenty Kasiński (Taborski, *Apollo Korzeniowski*, p. 129). Apollo disdained the political scene in Lviv, though the city was in fact twice as large as Kraków and far more politically and culturally significant. See Larry Wolff, *The Idea of Galicia: History and Fantasy in Habsburg Political Culture* (Stanford, CA: Stanford University Press, 2010), pp. 229–30; Lawrence D. Orton, "The Formation of Modern Cracow (1866–1914)," *Austrian History Yearbook* 19, no. 1 (January 1983): 107.

93. Buszczyński, *Mało Znany Poeta*, p. 51.

94. AK to Kazimierz Kaszewski, January 20,/February 1, 1866, *CUFE*, pp. 103–4. Many decades later, Buszczyński's son Konstantin said that Stefan had put the inscription "I will rise, Lord, when you call me; But let me rest, for I am very weary" on Apollo's gravestone. In fact the grave reads, "A victim of Muscovite martyrdom." George Palmer Putnam, "Conrad in Cracow," *CUFE*, p. 143. (See illustration in Najder, *Joseph Conrad: A Life*, between pp. 360 and 361.)

95. "Description of Apollo Korzeniowski's funeral," *CUFE*, pp. 129–30.

96. Teofila Bobrowska to Kazimierz Kaszewski, June 12, 1869, *CUFE*, p. 131.

CHAPTER TWO: THE POINT OF DEPARTURE

1. AK to Kazimierz Kaszewski, December 24, 1868, *CUFE*, p. 123.

2. Teofila Bobrowska to Kazimierz Kaszewski, June 12, 1869, *CUFE*, p. 131.

3. Ibid. Tadeusz was not officially appointed one of Konrad's guardians in Kraków because he lived in another country, Russia. His only child, a daughter about Conrad's age, died in 1871.

4. TB to JC, September 8/20, 1869, *CUFE*, pp. 34–35.

5. AK, "To my son born in the 85th year of Muscovite oppression," *CUFE*, p. 32.

6. "Tadeusz Bobrowski's 'Document,'" *CPB*, p. 183.

7. Biographers debate whether or not Conrad attended St. Anne's Gymnasium in Kraków. Conrad himself said he did, and provided a few corroborating details about the school, but Najder found no evidence of his name in the student registers, nor does it appear anywhere in Bobrowski's "Document." Either the otherwise well-preserved registers failed to note his enrollment and Bobrowski didn't pay for it—or, more likely, Conrad found it easier (and more distinguished) to explain his education this way. Zdzisław Najder, *Joseph Conrad: A Life*, 2nd ed. (Rochester, NY: Camden House, 2007), pp. 38–39n.

8. "Tadeusz Bobrowski's 'Document,'" *CPB*, pp. 188–93.

9. Reminiscences of Tekla Wojakowska, quoted by Stefan Czosnowski, "Conradiana," *CUFE*, p. 136.

10. George Palmer Putnam, "Conrad in Cracow," *CUFE*, pp. 142–43.

11. Lawrence D. Orton, "The Formation of Modern Cracow (1866–1914)," *Austrian History Yearbook* 19, no. 1 (January 1983): 105–17; Jerzy Dobrzycki, *Hejnał Krakowski* (Kraków: PWM, 1983). I am grateful to Michael Tworek for his assistance with this Polish source.

12. The photographer was Walery Rzewuski. John Stape, *The Several Lives of Joseph Conrad* (New York: Vintage, 2007), p. 22.

13. Najder, *Joseph Conrad: A Life*, p. 49.

14. JC to Stefan Buszczyński, August 14, 1883, *CL*, vol. 1, pp. 7–8. Gustav Morf points out that Buszczyński may have been referring to a poem by Juliusz Słowacki: "For I well know that my vessel, / Sailing through the wide world, / Will *not* sail to my country." Gustave Morf, *The Polish Shades and Ghosts of Joseph Conrad* (New York: Astra Books, 1976), p. 84.

15. "Poland Revisited," in Joseph Conrad, *Notes on Life and Letters* (Garden City, NY: Doubleday, Page & Co., 1921), pp. 168–69.

16. "Geography and Some Explorers," in Joseph Conrad, *Last Essays*, ed. and intro. Richard Curle (London: J. M. Dent & Sons, 1926), pp. 10–17.

17. Joseph Conrad, *A Personal Record* (New York: Harper & Brothers, 1921), pp. 126–27.

18. Ibid., pp. 80–81.

19. Ibid., pp. 82–83.

20. Ibid., p. 10.

21. "To make Polish life enter English literature is no small ambition. . . . And yet it presents itself easily just because of the intimate nature of the task, and of the 2 vols of my uncle's Memoirs which I have by me, to refresh my recollections and settle my ideas." JC to J. B. Pinker, October [7], 1908, *CL*, vol. 4, p. 138.

22. Conrad, *A Personal Record*, pp. 52–53, 60, 104; Bobrowski, *Memoir*, pp. 280–81.

23. Joseph Conrad, "Author's Note" (1919), in Joseph Conrad, *A Personal Record*, eds. Zdzisław Najder and J. H. Stape (Cambridge, UK: Cambridge University Press, 2008), p. 7.

24. AK, "Poland and Muscovy," *CUFE*, p. 80.

25. JC to R. B. Cunninghame Graham, December 20, 1897, *CL*, vol. 1, p. 425. For a reading of this passage, see Edward Said, *Joseph Conrad and the Fiction of Autobiography* (New York: Columbia University Press, 2008), ch. 2. At much the same time Conrad characterized the artist, in the preface to *The Nigger of the 'Narcissus,'* as someone who "speaks to . . . the subtle but invincible, conviction of solidarity that knits together the loneliness of innumerable hearts to the solidarity in dreams, in joy, in sorrow, in aspirations, in illusions, in hope, in fear. . . ." Joseph Conrad, *The Nigger of the 'Narcissus': A Tale of Forecastle* (Garden City, NY: Doubleday, Page & Co., 1914), pp. viii–ix.

26. I draw this description from Simon Bense, *Les Heures Marseillaises* (Marseille, 1878) and Franciszek Ziejka, "Conrad's Marseilles," *Yearbook of Conrad Studies (Poland)*, VII (2012): 51-67. Tadeusz Bobrowski said that Conrad was called "Monsieur Georges," a nickname Conrad later gave the protagonist of *The Arrow of Gold*. TB to Stefan Buszczyński, March 12/24, 1879, *CPB*, p. 178.

27. TB to JC, September 27 [old style], 1876, *CPB*, pp. 37–38.

28. TB to JC, October 14/26, 1876, *CPB*, pp. 39–45. "Tadeusz Bobrowski's 'Document,'" *CPB*, pp. 194–95.

29. TB to JC, September 2/14, 1877, *CPB*, p. 51.

30. TB to JC, July 28/August 8, 1877, *CPB*, p. 48.

31. The entanglement with the ship captain, Jean-Prosper Duteil, represents the only documentable truth to one of the tales Conrad most often repeated about his Marseille years, namely that he participated in gunrunning to Carlists in Spain. The absence of many records about his time in Marseille encourages some to interpret his 1919 novel *The Arrow of Gold* as heavily autobiographical.

32. TB to Stefan Buszczyński, March 12/24, 1879, *CPB*, p. 176.

33. Decades later, Conrad's son John noticed scars on his father's chest that "looked as though they had been made with a sword or cutlass." Conrad told him he had fought in a duel. John Conrad, *Joseph Conrad: Times Remembered, 'Ojciec Jest Tutaj'* (Cambridge, UK: Cambridge University Press, 1981), p. 181.

34. TB to Buszczyński, March 12/24, 1879, *CPB*, pp. 176–77.

35. "Tadeusz Bobrowski's 'Document,'" *CPB*, p. 198; Najder, *Joseph Conrad: A Life*, pp. 70–71.

CHAPTER THREE: AMONG STRANGERS

1. See among others: J. Thomson and Adolphe Smith, *Street Life in London: With Permanent Photographic Illustrations Taken from Life Expressly for This Publication* (London: Sampson Low, Marston, Searle & Rivington, [1877]); "Cleopatra's Needle," *Illustrated London News*, September 21, 1878, p. 286; William John Gordon, *The Horse-World of London* (London: The Religious Tract Society, 1893).

2. *The Times* (London, England), September 25, 1878.

3. TB to JC, June 26/July 8, 1878, *CPB*, pp. 54–55.

4. Bernard Porter, "The Asylum of Nations: Britain and the Refugees of 1848," and Andreas Fahrmeir, "British Exceptionalism in Perspective: Political Asylum in Continental Europe," in Sabine Freitag, ed., *Exiles from European Revolutions: Refugees in Mid-Victorian England* (New York: Berghahn Books, 2003), pp. 40, 43.

5. Andrea Zemgulys, *Modernism and the Locations of Literary Heritage* (Cambridge, UK: Cambridge University Press, 2008), p. 81.

6. Population figures from [London County Council], *County of London. Census of London, 1901 . . .* (London: London County Council, 1903), p. 17.

7. Herbert Fry, *London in 1880: Illustrated with Bird's Eye Views of the Principal Streets* (London: David Bogue, 1880), pp. 306–10.

8. Joseph Conrad, *A Personal Record* (New York: Harper & Brothers, 1921), p. 71.

9. Joseph Conrad, "Poland Revisited," in *Notes on Life and Letters* (Garden City, NY: Doubleday, Page & Co., 1921), pp. 152–54. Deliberate or not, there are several factual errors in Conrad's account: he did not arrive in London in early September but in late September; it was not his first visit to London but his second; he was not nineteen at the time but nearly twenty-one.

10. JC to Spiridion Kliczkewski, October 13, 1885, *CL*, vol. 1, p. 12.

11. British National Archives: HO 144/177/A44314.

12. "Author's Note," in Joseph Conrad, *The Secret Agent* (London: Penguin Classics, 2007), p. 250. (All subsequent citations drawn from this edition.) "Five millions" approximated the population of Greater London in the early 1880s. When Conrad wrote this note, in 1920, the population of Inner London alone was 4.5 million, and Greater London had passed 7 million.

13. Conrad, *The Secret Agent*, p. 12.

14. Ibid., pp. 3–7.

15. Ibid., pp. 35, 38, 40, 52–54, 56.

16. Ibid., pp. 14, 22. The Russian embassy at this time was in fact at Chesham House, in Chesham Place.

17. Ibid., pp. 23–30.

18. Ibid., pp. 56–57.

19. Ibid., p. 68.

20. Ibid., pp. 110–11.

21. Ibid., pp. 117–18.

22. Ibid., p. 148.

23. Ibid., p. 166.

24. Ibid., pp. 167, 179.

25. Ibid., p. 175. This "Personage," as Conrad calls him, Sir Ethelred, has been likened to Lord Salisbury, but the physical description ("a long white face, which, broadened at the base by a big double-chin, appeared egg-shaped in the fringe of thin grayish whisker") more closely resembles Sir William Harcourt, who was home secretary during the Fenian bombings of the 1880s. (Andrew Roberts, *Salisbury: Victorian Titan* [London: Weidenfeld & Nicolson, 1999], p. 520.)

26. Conrad, *The Secret Agent*, p. 183.

27. Ibid., pp. 195–97.

28. Ibid., pp. 208–9.

29. Ibid., p. 214.

30. Ibid., pp. 216, 235.

31. Ibid., pp. 244–46.

32. Conrad, *A Personal Record*, p. 110.

33. Hugh Epstein, "*Bleak House* and Conrad: The Presence of Dickens in Conrad's Writing," in Gene M. Moore, Owen Knowles, and J. H. Stape, eds., *Conrad: Intertexts & Appropriations: Essays in Memory of Yves Hervouet* (Amsterdam: Rodopi, 1997), pp. 119–40.

34. "The Assassination of the Emperor of Russia," *Reynolds's Newspaper* (London, England), Sunday, March 20, 1881, p. 1.

35. TB to JC, September 11/23, 1881, *CPB*, p. 79.

36. Mikhail Bakunin, "Critique of the Marxist Theory of the State," in Sam Dolgoff, ed., trans., and intro., *Bakunin on Anarchy: Selected Works by the Activist-Founder of World Anarchism* (New York: Random House, 1971), p. 330.

37. Mikhail Bakunin, "Letters to a Frenchman on the Present Crisis," in ibid., pp. 195–96.

38. The fullest account of the congress is given in Max Nettlau, *Anarchisten und Sozial-Revolutionäre: Die historische Entwicklung des Anarchismus in den Jahren 1880–1886* (*Geschichte der Anarchie*, vol. 3) (Glashütten im Taunus, Germany: D. Auvermann, 1972 [1931]), pp. 187–231.

39. Quoted in Richard Bach Jensen, "Daggers, Rifles and Dynamite: Anarchist Terrorism in Nineteenth Century Europe," *Terrorism and Political Violence* 16, no. 1 (January 1, 2004): 116–53. For anarchism in London in this period, see: Pietro Di Paola, "The Spies Who Came In from the Heat: The International Surveillance of the Anarchists in London," *European History Quarterly* 37, no. 2 (2007): 192; Matthew Thomas, *Anarchist Ideas and Counter-Cultures in Britain, 1880–1914: Revolutions in Everyday Life* (Aldershot, Hampshire, UK: Ashgate, 2005), p. 6; Alex Butterworth, *The World That Never Was: A True Story of Dreamers, Schemers, Anarchists and Secret Agents* (New York: Pantheon Books, 2010), pp. 164–69; Bernard Porter, "The Freiheit Prosecutions, 1881–1882," *The Historical Journal* 23, no. 4 (1980): 833–56.

40. Jensen, "Daggers, Rifles, and Dynamite": 129–30.

41. James Joll, *The Anarchists*, 2nd ed. (Cambridge, MA: Harvard University Press, 1980), p. 109. Most's manual was an inspiration for William Powell's 1971 *The Anarchist Cookbook*.

42. John M. Merriman, *The Dynamite Club: How a Bombing in Fin-de-Siècle Paris Ignited the Age of Modern Terror* (Boston: Houghton Mifflin Harcourt, 2009), p. 75.

43. "Extraordinary Outrage in Salford," *Glasgow Herald* (Scotland), Saturday, January 15, 1881, p. 4.

44. "Alleged Discovery of Infernal Machines," *The Pall Mall Gazette* (London, England), Monday, July 25, 1881, p. 8.

45. "Terrific Explosion on the Underground Railway," *Reynolds's Newspaper* (London, England), Sunday, November 4, 1883, p. 4.

46. John Sweeney, *At Scotland Yard: Being the Experiences During Twenty-Seven Years' Service of John Sweeney* (London: Grant Richards, 1904), pp. 21–22.

47. "Dynamite Outrages," *Illustrated Police News* (London, England), Saturday, January 31, 1885, Issue Supplement.

48. Quoted in Deaglán Ó Donghaile, "Anarchism, Anti-imperialism and 'The Doctrine of Dynamite,'" *Journal of Postcolonial Writing* 46, nos. 3–4 (July 2010): 293.

49. Fenian bombers also targeted sites in Canada: "Attempt to Blow Up the Court House at Montreal," *The Pall Mall Gazette* (London, England), Monday, December 5, 1881, p. 8; "The Dynamite Explosions at Quebec," *The Pall Mall Gazette* (London, England), Monday, October 13, 1884, p. 8.

50. Haia Shpayer-Makov, *The Ascent of the Detective: Police Sleuths in Victorian and Edwardian England* (Oxford: Oxford University Press, 2011), pp. 52–56. Both the Explosive Substances Act and a version of Special Branch (merged into Counter Terrorism Command in 2006) remain in force.

51. Sweeney, *At Scotland Yard*, pp. 31–32; Robert Anderson, *The Lighter Side of My Official Life*

(London: Hodder and Stoughton, 1910), p. 109; Robert Anderson, *Sidelights on the Home Rule Movement* (London: John Murray, 1906), p. 127.

52. *The Daily News* ran an interview with a Polish anarchist in Switzerland, who hinted at a vast conspiracy of terror. "You may call us Anarchists, Nihilists, Socialists, Fenians, Dynamiters—what you will," the anarchist told the reporter, "but we are linked together in a stupendous brotherhood" committed to "equality and freedom." The Pole supported the Fenians because "England treats Ireland as badly as Russia treats Poland; and the Irish, like the Poles, are justified in resorting to any means to obtain their freedom." "An Interview with a Dynamitard," *The Daily News* (London, England), Tuesday, March 17, 1885, p. 7. This was one of the biggest London dailies, and it's perfectly possible Conrad would have read it on occasion. In the early 1900s, he both read and contributed to *The Daily News*, and was friends with some of its reporters. See "The Daily News & Leader (London, UK)," www.conradfirst.net/view/periodical?id=91.

53. Butterworth, *World That Never Was*, p. 323.

54. Merriman, *Dynamite Club*, pp. 77–86.

55. Charles Malato, *Les joyeusetés de l'exil* (Mauléon, France: Acratie, 1985), pp. 170–75.

56. Matthew Thomas, *Anarchist Ideas and Counter-Cultures in Britain, 1880–1914: Revolutions in Everyday Life* (Burlington, VT: Ashgate, 2005), pp. 10–11; Malato, *Les joyeusetés de l'exil*, p. 59; Sweeney, *At Scotland Yard*, pp. 36, 219; W. C. Hart, *Confessions of an Anarchist* (London: E. Grant Richards, 1906), pp. 91–94.

57. Robert Hampson, *Conrad's Secrets* (Basingstoke, UK: Palgrave Macmillan, 2012), pp. 89–91.

58. Isabel Meredith, *A Girl Among the Anarchists* (London: Duckworth, 1903), chapter 6.

59. "The Anarchists in London," *The Pall Mall Gazette* (London, England), Tuesday, February 13, 1894, p. 1.

60. Edward Douglas Fawcett, *Hartmann the Anarchist: Or, The Doom of the Great City* (London: E. Arnold, 1893), p. 148. (Fawcett was the elder brother of Amazon explorer Percy Fawcett.) It's possible Fawcett took the name from the actual anarchist Lev Hartmann, a member of the People's Will, who had been an exile in England since 1880 (Butterworth, *World That Never Was*, p. 156). Fawcett may also conceivably have run into the half-German, half-Japanese poet Carl Sadakichi Hartmann, who visited London in 1888 (where he associated with the Rossettis, among others) and went on to launch the American anarchist newspaper *Mother Earth* with Emma Goldman. (George Knox, "Sadakichi Hartmann's Life and Career," www.english.illinois.edu/maps/poets/g_l/hartmann/life.htm.)

61. This image appears as the frontispiece to the published book, and in serial in *The English Illustrated Magazine*, vol. 10 (London: Edward Arnold, 1893), p. 741. The illustrator, Fred Jane, went on to publish *All the World's Fighting Ships* in 1898, the first production in what grew into the military intelligence firm Jane's Information Group.

62. Meredith, *Girl Among the Anarchists*, chapter 5; Hart, *Confessions of an Anarchist*, p. 18.

63. Sweeney, *At Scotland Yard*, pp. 35–36.

64. Ernest Alfred Vizetelly, *The Anarchists, Their Faith and Their Record, Including Sidelights on the Royal and Other Personages Who Have Been Assassinated* (London: John Lane, 1911), p. 165.

65. See, among others, "Explosion in Greenwich Park," *The Times* (London, England), Friday, February 16, 1894, p. 5; "The Explosion in Greenwich Park," *The Daily News* (London, England), Saturday, February 17, 1894, p. 5; "Anarchists in London," *The Standard* (London, England), Saturday, February 17, 1894, p. 3.

66. Norman Sherry, *Conrad's Western World* (Cambridge, UK: Cambridge University Press, 1971), pp. 230–31; David Nicoll, *The Greenwich Mystery: Letters from the Dead* (London: David Nicoll, 1898), p. 379.

67. Conrad, Author's Note (1920), *The Secret Agent*, p. 248.

68. He later said he hadn't even been in England at the time, though he had been. On Conrad's evasiveness, see Jacques Berthoud, "The Secret Agent," in J. H. Stape, ed., *The Cambridge Companion to Joseph Conrad* (Cambridge, UK: Cambridge University Press, 1996), pp. 101–3.

69. Marie Corelli, *The Sorrows of Satan: Or, the Strange Experience of One Geoffrey Tempest, Millionaire: a Romance* (London: Methuen, 1895); Hall Caine, *The Christian: A Story* (London: W. Heinemann, 1897).

70. Meredith, *Girl Among the Anarchists*, chapter 2.

71. "Bourdin's Funeral," *The St. James Gazette*, reprinted in Mary Burgoyne, "Conrad Among the Anarchists: Documents on Martial Bourdin and the Greenwich Bombing," *The Conradian* 32, no. 1 (2007): 172–74.

72. Judith Walkowitz, *Nights Out: Life in Cosmopolitan London* (New Haven, CT: Yale University Press, 2012), chapter 1.

73. JC to R. B. Cunninghame Graham, October 7, 1907, *CL*, vol. 3, p. 491.

74. JC to Algernon Methuen, November 7, 1906, *CL*, vol. 3, p. 371.

75. JC to John Galsworthy, September 12, 1906, *CL*, vol. 3, p. 354.

76. Conrad, Author's Note (1920), *The Secret Agent*, p. 249.

77. He repeated the characterization several times. To R. B. Cunninghame Graham: "a new departure in *genre* and . . . a sustained effort in ironical treatment of a melodramatic subject" (October 7, 1907, *CL*, vol. 3, p. 491). To Marguerite Poradowska: "I think I have succeeded there in treating an essentially melodramatic subject by means of irony. That was the artistic goal that I set for myself, for, you are right, anarchy and the anarchists scarcely concern me; I know almost nothing of the doctrine and nothing at all of the men. It is all made up" (June 20, 1912, *CL*, vol. 5, p. 76). And in the Author's Note: "Even the purely artistic purpose, that of applying an ironic method to a subject of that kind, was formulated . . . in the earnest belief that ironic treatment alone would enable me to say all I felt I would have to say in scorn as well as in pity." (251)

78. Wayne Booth, *The Rhetoric of Irony* (Chicago: University of Chicago Press, 1974), p. 33; Aaron Matz, *Satire in an Age of Realism* (Cambridge, UK: Cambridge University Press, 2010), pp. 142–45, 166–72.

79. Author's Note (1919) to Joseph Conrad, *A Personal Record*, ed. Zdzisław Najder and J. H. Stape (Cambridge, UK: Cambridge University Press, 2008), p. 8.

80. JC to Kazimierz Waliszewski, December 5, 1903, *CL*, vol. 3, p. 89.

81. JC to R. B. Cunninghame Graham, October 7, 1907, *CL*, vol. 3, p. 491.

82. JC to Edward Garnett, January 20, 1900, *CL*, vol. 2, p. 246.

83. Board of Trade, *(Alien Immigration): Reports on the Volume and Effects of Recent Immigration from Eastern Europe into the United Kingdom* (London: H. M. Stationery Office, 1894). The investigators found no clear evidence that Jewish immigration lowered wages, showed that sanitary conditions were improving, and dismissed complaints about Jewish criminality. "Prejudices of race, religion, or custom" might be responsible for the negative "attitude of the non-Jewish population towards the foreign immigrants, quite apart from any question of economic or social interference" (p. 136).

84. Sweeney, *At Scotland Yard*, pp. 235–38, 279.

85. Caroline Shaw, *Britannia's Embrace: Modern Humanitarianism and the Imperial Origins of Refugee Relief* (Oxford: Oxford University Press, 2015), p. 234. See also Commons Sitting of Monday, July 10, 1905, House of Commons Hansard, Fourth Series, vol. 149, cols. 171–82; Commons Sitting of Monday, July 17, 1905, cols. 966–71; Alison Bashford and Jane McAdam, "The Right to Asylum: Britain's 1905 Aliens Act and the Evolution of Refugee Law," *Law and History Review* 32 (2014): 309–50.

86. JC to Marguerite Poradowska, January 5, 1907, *CL*, vol. 4, p. 401.

87. JC to J. B. Pinker, May 6, 1907, *CL*, vol. 3, p. 434.

88. JC to H.-D Davray, November 8, 1906, *CL*, vol. 3, p. 372.

89. JC to Edward Garnett, [October 4, 1907], *CL*, vol. 3, p. 488.

90. JC to John Galsworthy, January 6, 1908, *CL*, vol. 5, p. 9.

91. JC to John Galsworthy, [August 23, 1908], *CL*, vol. 5, p. 110.

92. JC to Edward Garnett, August 21, 1908, *CL*, vol. 5, pp. 107–8.

93. For a perceptive reading of Conrad's Englishness and *The Secret Agent*, see Rebecca Walkowitz,

Cosmopolitan Style: Modernism Beyond the Nation (New York: Columbia University Press, 2006), pp. 40–49.

94. JC to Wincenty Lutosławski, June 9, 1897, *CL*, vol. 1, p. 359.

CHAPTER FOUR: FOLLOWING THE SEA

1. Richard Henry Dana, *The Seaman's Manual* (London: Edward Maxon & Co., 1863), p. 163.

2. For the purposes of this reconstruction I have assigned Konrad Korzeniowski to this watch schedule. I owe information about the ship's itinerary, crew, and cargo to the assiduous research of Allan Simmons, "Conrad and the *Duke of Sutherland*," *The Conradian* 35, no. 1 (Spring 2010): 101–25.

3. For the rat problems on the *Duke of Sutherland*, see G. F. W. Hope and Gene Moore, "Friend of Conrad," *The Conradian* 25, no. 2 (Autumn 2000): 25. On tender heels, William Caius Crutchley, *My Life at Sea* (London: Brentano's, 1912), p. 69.

4. Hope and Moore, "Friend of Conrad," p. 18.

5. Joseph Conrad, *The Mirror of the Sea* (New York: Harper & Brothers, 1906), p. 60.

6. Simmons, "Conrad and the *Duke of Sutherland*," p. 106.

7. "My husband often lamented his inability to appreciate verse and his indifferent sense of smell." Jessie Conrad, *Joseph Conrad as I Knew Him* (Garden City, NY: Doubleday, Page & Co., 1926), p. 149; David Miller, "Conrad and Smell: Life, and the Limit of Literature," paper presented at the Joseph Conrad Society (UK) 41st Annual Conference, London, July 4, 2015.

8. Dana, *Seaman's Manual*, pp. 31–32, 155.

9. The provision of antiscorbutics was mandated under the Merchant Shipping Acts, and scale of provisions itemized in Agreement and Crew Lists. Board of Trade, *A Digest of Statutes Relating to Merchant Shipping* (London: HMSO, 1875), pp. 150–52.

10. Descriptions of these ceremonies are a staple of contemporary travel accounts. See, e.g., Hope and Moore, "Friend of Conrad," pp. 12–13.

11. Conrad invested his earliest British wages in volumes of Shakespeare and Byron: Hope and Moore, "Friend of Conrad," p. 36; Martin Ray, *Joseph Conrad: Memories and Impressions: An Annotated Bibliography* (Amsterdam: Rodopi, 2007), p. 101.

12. "They regarded Conrad as a foreigner because of his difficulties with the language and were therefore inclined to be against him." Hope and Moore, "Friend of Conrad," p. 35.

13. British National Archives: BT 100/21: Agreements and Crew Lists, *Duke of Sutherland*, 1865–1882.

14. On Baker, see Conrad, *The Mirror of the Sea*, pp. 209–15. On the crew of the ship, see Simmons, "Conrad and the *Duke of Sutherland*."

15. Frank Bullen, *The Men of the Merchant Service: Being the Polity of the Mercantile Marine for Longshore Readers* (New York: Frederick A. Stokes, 1900), p. 266.

16. Richard Henry Dana, *Two Years Before the Mast: A Personal Narrative of Life at Sea* (New York: Harper & Brothers, 1842), pp. 406–7.

17. Bullen, *Men of the Merchant Service*, pp. 261–63.

18. Joseph Conrad, *A Personal Record* (London: Harper & Brothers 1912), p. 199.

19. Ibid., pp. 76–78.

20. Ibid., pp. 212–29.

21. JC to R. B. Cunninghame Graham, February 4, 1898, *CL*, vol. 1, pp. 35–36. See also the description in Hope and Moore, "Friend of Conrad," p. 35.

22. TB to JC, July 8, 1878, *CPB*, pp. 54–56.

23. "The sailing ship may be said to have been at its best at the moment when the great economies, and the greater regularity connected with steam, had pronounced the doom of the more picturesque, and, perhaps, one may say, the more lovable, type of ship." Adam W. Kirkaldy, *British Shipping, Its History, Organisation and Importance* (London: K. Paul, Trench, Trübner & Co., 1914), p. 25.

24. Into the early 1900s many oceangoing steamships still carried sailing rigs, to help balance the vessel and provide emergency or auxiliary power. Gerald Peter Allington, "Sailing Rigs and Their Use on Ocean-Going Merchant Steamships, 1820–1910," *International Journal of Maritime History* 16, no. 1 (June 2004): 125–52. The maritime historian R. J. Cornewall-Jones mused in 1898 that "in these days of South Wales coal strikes it is a pleasant thing to be able to contemplate the fact that it is sometimes possible to do without coals altogether, and that there are still many branches of commerce in which sailing-ships may yet be more profitably employed than steamers"—a thought that resonates in an age of anxiety over fossil fuel consumption. R. J. Cornewall-Jones, *The British Merchant Service: Being a History of the British Mercantile Marine from the Earliest Times to the Present Day* (London: S. Low, Marston & Company, 1898), p. 237.

25. Richard Woodman, *Masters Under God: Makers of Empire, 1816–1884* (Stroud, UK: History Press, 2009), p. 319.

26. See the chart of "Exports Plus Imports as Share of GDP in Europe, 1655–1913—Our World in Data, with Data from Broadberry and O'Rourke (2010)," in Esteban Ortiz-Ospina and Max Roser, "International Trade," published online at OurWorldInData.org, https://ourworldindata.org/international-trade.

27. In 1870 it was the United States and in 1880 it was Norway. Table 11 in Great Britain Board of Trade, *Merchant Shipping, Tables Showing the Progress of Merchant Shipping in the United Kingdom and the Principal Maritime Countries* . . . (London: H. M. Stationery Office, 1908), pp. 46–47.

28. Woodman, *Masters Under God*, p. 360.

29. Shipbuilding was the one heavy industry in which Britain retained a lead over the United States and Germany well into the twentieth century. Nonstandardized and requiring a range of specialists, it represented the ne plus ultra of "archaic structure and technique" in the era of mass production. Eric Hobsbawm, *Industry and Empire: From 1750 to the Present Day* (Harmondsworth, Middlesex, UK: Penguin, 1969), pp. 178–79.

30. "A Brief History," www.lr.org/en/about-us/our-heritage/brief-history.

31. *Lloyd's Register of British and Foreign Shipping, from 1st July, 1866, to the 30th June, 1867* (London: Cox & Wyman, 1866), n.p.

32. Bullen, *Men of the Merchant Service*, p. 29.

33. Hope and Moore, "Friend of Conrad," pp. 18–34.

34. Joseph Conrad, *The Nigger of the 'Narcissus' and Other Stories* (London: Penguin Classics, 2007), pp. 7, 12, 16, 21. Cf. Conrad, *The Mirror of the Sea*, p. 216: "'Ships!' exclaimed an elderly seaman in clean, shore togs. . . . 'ships are all right; it's the men in 'em. . . . '"

35. Samuel Plimsoll, *Our Seamen: An Appeal* (London: Virtue & Company, 1873), p. 30.

36. Woodman, *Masters Under God*, pp. 344–46; A. H. Millar, "Leng, Sir William Christopher (1825–1902)," rev. Dilwyn Porter, *Oxford Dictionary of National Biography* (Oxford: Oxford University Press, 2004), www.oxforddnb.com/view/article/34495.

37. Plimsoll, *Our Seamen*, pp. 85, 87.

38. Leon Fink, *Sweatshops at Sea: Merchant Seamen in the World's First Globalized Industry, from 1812 to the Present* (Chapel Hill: University of North Carolina Press, 2011), chapter 3; Anita McConnell, "Plimsoll, Samuel (1824–1898)," *Oxford Dictionary of National Biography* (Oxford: Oxford University Press, 2004), online ed., September 2013, www.oxforddnb.com/view/article/22384; "Parliament–Breach of Order (Mr. Plimsoll)," July 22, 1875, hansard.millbanksystems.com/commons/1875/jul/22/parliament-breach-of-order-mr-plimsoll.

39. He was also immortalized in the name of a rubber-soled canvas shoe, the "plimsoll." A black line around the rubber showed the level below which the wearer's feet couldn't get wet.

40. Plimsoll, *Our Seamen*, p. 85.

41. "Replies by Certain of Her Majesty's Consuls to a Circular Letter from the Board of Trade," Command Paper 630 (London: H. M. Stationery Office, 1872), p. 3.

42. Thomas Brassey, *British Seamen, as Described in Recent Parliamentary and Official Documents* (London: Longmans, Green & Co., 1877), pp. 4–8. A similar circular was issued in 1843: W. S.

Lindsay, *History of Merchant Shipping and Ancient Commerce*, 4 vols. (London: Sampson Low, Marston, Low, and Searle, 1876), vol. 3, pp. 42–43.

43. Royal Commission on Unseaworthy Ships, *Final Report of the Commissioners, Minutes of the Evidence, and Appendix*, 2 vols. (London: H. M. Stationery Office, 1874), vol. 2, p. xii; Cornewall-Jones, *British Merchant Service*, p. 265; Lindsay, *History of Merchant Shipping*, p. 351.

44. Lindsay, *History of Merchant Shipping*, pp. 51–52.

45. Ibid., p. 298.

46. JC to R. B. Cunninghame Graham, February 4, 1898, *CL*, vol. 1, pp. 35–36.

47. [Board of Trade], *Report of the Committee Appointed to Inquire into the Manning of British Merchant Ships*, 2 vols. (London: H. M. Stationery office, 1896), vol.1, p. 50.

48. Brassey, *British Seamen*, pp. 54–58, 69.

49. "Table 19. Predominant Rates of Wages Paid per Month to Able Seamen for Certain Voyages . . . ," [Board of Trade], *Tables Showing the Progress of Merchant Shipping* (London: H. M. Stationery Office, 1908), pp. 60–63.

50. A Glasgow coal hewer in 1880 made an average of about 25 shillings per week, and a male Huddersfield spinner 30 shillings. "Average Rates of Wages Paid in Huddersfield and Neighborhood During the Year 1880," "Average Rates of Wages Paid in Glasgow and Neighborhood During the Year 1880," [Board of Trade], *Returns of Wages, Published Between 1830 and 1886* (London: H. M. Stationery Office, 1887), pp. 99, 145. These wages were for fifty-six- and sixty-hour weeks, respectively; sailors were on duty fourteen hours per day, with no weekend breaks.

51. Brassey, *British Seamen*, p. 170.

52. Edward Blackmore, *The British Mercantile Marine* (London: C. Griffin and Co., 1897), p. 169; *Report . . . into the Manning of British Merchant Ships*, vol. 1, p. 12; Cornewall-Jones, *British Merchant Service*, p. 271.

53. *Report . . . into the Manning of British Merchant Ships*, vol. 1, p. 11.

54. Lascars signed contracts that restricted their service in European waters, and required that they be engaged and discharged only in Asian ports, thus preventing them from settling in Europe. Captain W. H. Hood, *The Blight of Insubordination: The Lascar Question, and Rights and Wrongs of the British Shipmaster . . .* (London: Spottiswoode & Co., 1903), p. 84. See also G. Balachandran, *Globalizing Labour?: Indian Seafarers and World Shipping, c. 1870–1945* (New Delhi: Oxford University Press, 2012).

55. Cornewall-Jones, *British Merchant Service*, pp. 270–71.

56. [Board of Trade], *Report . . . to the Royal Commission on the Loss of Life at Sea on the Supply of British Seamen . . .* (London: H. M. Stationery Office, 1886), p. 4.

57. Cornewall-Jones, *British Merchant Service*, p. 272.

58. *Report . . . into the Manning of British Merchant Ships* (1896), vol. 1, pp. 10–11.

59. Hood, *Blight of Insubordination*, p. 12. A 1902 Board of Trade inquiry into the increase of Asian and European sailors took evidence directly from Asian sailors, through Hindustani interpreters, who by and large pronounced themselves satisfied with their working conditions and confirmed that they would be happy to serve on British warships if necessary. The committee thus concluded: "We think that in addition to their claim as British subjects, they have also some claim to employment, because British vessels have displaced the native trading vessels." [Board of Trade], *Report of the Committee Appointed by the Board of Trade to Inquire into Certain Questions Affecting the Mercantile Marine*, 2 vols. (London: H. M. Stationery Office, 1903), vol. 1, p. vi; vol. 2, pp. 335–341.

60. Bullen, *Men of the Merchant Service*, pp. 324–25.

61. Questions 6258, 6298, 6308, *Report . . . into the Manning of British Merchant Ships* (1896), vol. 2, pp. 147–50. They also asked whether he had "been in any foreign ships." He said no—which wasn't strictly true, though "I know something about French manning, because . . . I speak French, and have been visiting French ships."

62. Cornewall-Jones, *British Merchant Service*, p. 261.

63. Zdzisław Najder, *Joseph Conrad: A Life*, 2nd ed. (Rochester, NY: Camden House, 2007), pp. 80–82; John Stape, *The Several Lives of Joseph Conrad* (New York: Pantheon Books, 2007), pp. 39, 45, 47.

64. TB to JC, November 14/26, 1886, *CPB*, p. 113.

65. JC to Karol Zagórski, May 22, 1890, *CL*, vol. 1, p. 52.

66. JC to Kazimierz Waliszewski, December 5, 1903, *CL*, vol. 2, p. 89.

67. TB to JC, May 18/30, 1880, *CPB*, p. 62.

68. TB to JC, September 11/23, 1881, *CPB*, p. 79.

69. On the discharge certificate, the captain rated Conrad "Very Good" in ability, but under "Character for Conduct" he wrote "Decline." Beinecke Library: "Original Discharges Issued," Joseph Conrad Collection, Gen. Mss. 1207, Box 16.

70. For ships of fifty tons or higher. Blackmore, *British Mercantile Marine*, p. 168.

71. Joseph Conrad, *Chance* (Oxford: Oxford World's Classics, 2002), p. 9. Cf. "What . . . is the young newly passed officer to do when, with his creamy new certificate in his pocket, he finds nothing before him in his old firm but a voyage before the mast as an able seaman?" lamented Frank Bullen. "I know of no more depressing occupation than that of a capable seaman looking for a ship as officer." Bullen, *Men of the Merchant Service*, pp. 10–12.

72. This may explain why or how Conrad spent more time onshore between berths, on average, than his peers. Alston Kennerley, "Global Nautical Livelihoods: The Sea Careers of the Maritime Writers Frank T. Bullen and Joseph Conrad, 1869–1894," *International Journal of Maritime History* 26, no. 1 (February 1, 2014): 13.

73. TB to JC, August 3/15 1881, *CPB*, pp. 72–73. Najder, *Joseph Conrad: A Life*, pp. 86–87.

74. "POLICE: At the MANSION-HOUSE, Yesterday, Mr. WILLIAM SUTHERLAND," *The Times*, February 28, 1878; "Police Intelligence," *Reynolds's Newspaper*, September 26, 1880; "Police," *The Times*, April 5, 1881; "Hughes, Appelant v. Sutherland, Respondent," *The Justice of the Peace*, vol. 46 (London: Richard Shaw Bond, 1882), pp. 6–7.

75. Blackmore, *British Mercantile Marine*, pp. 76–79.

76. Kennerley, "Global Nautical Livelihoods," p. 17.

77. Najder, *Joseph Conrad: A Life*, p. 185.

78. See, e.g., Crutchley, *My Life at Sea*; Captain John D. Whidden, *Ocean Life in the Old Sailing Ship Days* (Boston: Little, Brown and Company, 1909); Walter Runciman, *Windjammers and Sea Tramps* (London and Newcastle-on-Tyne: Walter Scott Publishing Company, 1905); and the many nautical books by Frank Bullen, beginning with *The Cruise of the Cachalot Round the World After Sperm Whales* (London: Smith, Elder & Co., 1899); and Basil Lubbock, beginning with *Round the Horn Before the Mast* (New York: E. P. Dutton, 1903). In Lubbock's pungent formulation: "Wood and hemp were things of the past; canvas was on its last legs; the old breed of sea-dog, who lived hard and died hard, was all but extinct, and his place filled by a mongrel crowd of weak-kneed, know-nothing, dare-nothing, fit-for-nothing skulkers." Basil Lubbock, *Deep Sea Warriors* (New York: Dodd, Mead and Company, 1910), p. 254. For the historical ramifications of this transition, see Robert D. Foulke, "Life in the Dying World of Sail, 1870–1910," *Journal of British Studies* 3, no. 1 (November 1, 1963); and Frances Steele, *Oceania Under Steam: Sea Transport and the Cultures of Colonialism, c. 1870–1914* (Manchester, UK: Manchester University Press, 2011), chapter 3.

79. Conrad, *Nigger of the 'Narcissus'* (2007 ed.), p. 39.

80. JC to Messrs. Methuen & Co., May 30, 1906, *CL*, vol. 3, p. 332.

81. "The Mirror of the Sea," in Owen Knowles and Gene M. Moore, eds., *Oxford Reader's Companion to Conrad* (Oxford: Oxford University Press, 2000), pp. 262–63.

82. JC to J. B. Pinker, April 18, 1904, *CL*, vol. 3, p. 133.

83. Conrad, *The Mirror of the Sea*, p. 218.

84. Ibid., pp. 59, 105.

85. I owe my understanding of "craft" in part to Margaret Cohen, *The Novel and the Sea* (Princeton, NJ: Princeton University Press, 2010), chapter 1.

86. Conrad, *The Mirror of the Sea*, pp. 47–48.

87. Joseph Conrad, *The Nigger of the 'Narcissus': A Tale of the Forecastle* (Garden City, NY: Doubleday, Page & Co., 1914), p. xi.

88. The phrase or close variations on it ("fellowship of seamen") appears in "Youth," *Lord Jim*, *The Mirror of the Sea*, and *The Shadow-Line*, among others.

89. Conrad, *The Mirror of the Sea*, p. 29.

90. Conrad, *Nigger of the 'Narcissus'* (2007 ed.), p. 22.

91. Ibid., p. 11.

92. JC to Spiridion Kliszczewski, December 19, 1885, *CL*, vol. 1, p. 16.

93. "Youth," in Joseph Conrad, *Youth/Heart of Darkness/The End of the Tether* (London: Penguin Books, 1995), p. 9.

94. Conrad, "Author's Note" (1917), p. 5. Not long after it was published he professed surprise that "some critics . . . called it a short story!" JC to David Meldrum, January 7, 1902, *CL*, vol. 2, p. 368.

95. Najder, *Joseph Conrad: A Life*, p. 94; Conrad, "Youth," p. 21.

96. Quotes in this paragraph from Conrad, "Youth," pp. 28, 31.

97. "What spirit was it that inspired the unfailing manifestations of their simple fidelity? No outward cohesive force of compulsion or discipline was holding them together. . . . It was very mysterious. At last I came to the conclusion that it must be something in the nature of the life itself; the sea-life chosen blindly, embraed for the most part accidentally. . . ." "Well Done," in Joseph Conrad, *Notes on Life & Letters* (Garden City, NY: Doubleday, Page & Co., 1921), p. 183.

98. Quotes in this paragraph from Conrad, *The Nigger of the 'Narcissus'* (2007 ed.), pp. 123, 128.

99. Conrad, *A Personal Record*, p. 192.

100. Ibid., p. 196.

101. John Newton, *Newton's Seamanship Examiner of Masters and Mates at the Board of Trade Examinations*, 18th ed. (London: J. Newton, 1884), p. 94.

102. William Culley Bergen, *Seamanship*, 6th ed. (North Shields, UK; W. J. Potts, 1882), pp. 148–49.

103. Conrad, *A Personal Record*, pp. 198–99.

104. Ibid., p. 201.

105. Ibid., p. 203. Cf. JC to Kazimierz Waliszewski, December 5, 1903, *CL*, vol. 2, p. 89: "I never sought for a career, but possibly, unaware of it, I was looking for sensations."

106. Conrad, *A Personal Record*, p. 197.

CHAPTER FIVE: GOING INTO STEAM

1. Joseph Conrad, *The Mirror of the Sea* (New York: Harper & Brothers, 1906), pp. 81–82.

2. Robert White Stevens, *On the Stowage of Ships and Their Cargoes*, 5th ed. (London: Longmans, Reader & Dyer, 1871), pp. 67–68, 77–78, 108–9, 380–81, 643. Conrad refers to this book in *The Mirror of the Sea*, p. 76.

3. Quotes from *The Mirror of the Sea*, pp. 87–89.

4. Conrad described to his uncle symptoms that suggested sciatica, rheumatism, and paralysis. TB to JC, August 8/20, 1887, *CPB*, p. 117.

5. Conrad later suggested that his story "The Black Mate" had first been drafted in 1886 for *Tit-Bits*. (Jocelyn Baines, *Joseph Conrad: A Critical Biography* [Westport, CT: Greenwood Press, 1975], pp. 84–85.) The coincidence of these three episodes prompted Conrad's first biographer, Gérard Jean-Aubry, to note that "1886 marks what amounts to a triple adoption by the country of his choice." Gérard Jean-Aubry, *Joseph Conrad: Life and Letters*, 2 vols. (Garden City, NY: Doubleday, 1927), vol. 1, p. 90.

6. JC to Spiridion Kliszczewski, November 25, [1885], *CL*, vol. 1, p. 15.

7. TB to JC, August 8/20, 1887, *CPB*, p. 117.

8. Cf. "The End of the Tether," in Joseph Conrad, *Youth/Heart of Darkness/The End of the Tether* (London: Penguin Books, 1995), p. 168.

9. Conrad, *Lord Jim*, p. 12. For the hillside location of the Singapore hospital, see Norman Sherry, *Conrad's Eastern World* (Cambridge, UK: Cambridge University Press, 1966), pp. 28–29.

10. JC to Spiridion Kliszczewski, November 25, 1885, quoted in Jean-Aubry, *Joseph Conrad: Life and Letters*, vol. 1, p. 83.

11. Sherry, *Conrad's Eastern World*, p. 182; Roland St. John Braddell, Gilbert Edward Brooke, and Walter Makepeace, *One Hundred Years of Singapore: Being Some Account of the Capital of the Straits Settlements from Its Foundation by Sir Stamford Raffles on the 6th February 1819 to the 6th February 1919*, 2 vols. (London: Murray, 1921); vol. 1, p. 459.

12. Joseph Conrad, *The Shadow-Line* (Oxford: Oxford World's Classics, 2009), pp. 8–9. On the superintendent, Charles Phillips, see Walter Makepeace, "Concerning Known Persons," in Braddell, Brooke, and Makepeace, *One Hundred Years of Singapore*, vol. 1, p. 459.

13. The Thian Hock Keng Temple, dedicated to the Tao goddess of the sea, was finished in 1842 by Fujian Chinese on Telok Ayer Street, not far from the Masjid Jamae, established in 1826 by Tamil Muslims on South Bridge Road.

14. I draw these observations from William Temple Hornaday, *Two Years in the Jungle* (New York: C. Scribner's Sons, 1885), pp. 293–94; Baroness Annie Alnutt Brassey, *A Voyage in the "Sunbeam": Our Home on the Ocean for Eleven Months* (London: Belford, Clarke, 1884), pp. 408–12; Ada Pryer, *A Decade in Borneo* (London: Hutchinson, 1894), pp. 135–38. Conrad's most detailed impressions of Singapore appear in "The End of the Tether," where Captain Whalley takes a walk through the city that has been historically reconstructed by Sherry, *Conrad's Eastern World*, pp. 175–81.

15. Cf. "The End of the Tether," in which Captain Whalley pauses on the Cavanagh Bridge to see "a sea-going Malay prau floated half hidden under the arch of masonry, with her spars lowered down." Conrad, "The End of the Tether," p. 171.

16. Stephen Dobbs, *The Singapore River: A Social History, 1819–2002* (Singapore: Singapore University Press, 2003), Appendix 1.

17. My understanding of Singapore as a hub of Indian Ocean trade and migration has been informed by: Sunil S. Amrith, *Crossing the Bay of Bengal: The Furies of Nature and the Fortunes of Migrants* (Cambridge, MA: Harvard University Press, 2013); Sugata Bose, *A Hundred Horizons: The Indian Ocean in the Age of Global Empire* (Cambridge, MA: Harvard University Press, 2006); Engseng Ho, *The Graves of Tarim: Genealogy and Mobility Across the Indian Ocean* (Berkeley and Los Angeles: University of California Press, 2006); Rajat Kanta Ray, "Asian Capital in the Age of European Domination: The Rise of the Bazaar, 1800–1914," *Modern Asian Studies* 29, no. 3 (July 1, 1995): 449–554; Eric Tagliacozzo, *Secret Trades, Porous Borders: Smuggling and States Along a Southeast Asian Frontier, 1865–1915* (New Haven, CT: Yale University Press, 2005). For the most thorough treatment of late-nineteenth-century European shipping in the archipelago, see J. F. N. M. à Campo, *Engines of Empire: Steamshipping and State Formation in Colonial Indonesia* (Hilversum, Netherlands: Verloren, 2002).

18. Andrew Carnegie, *Round the World* (New York: Charles Scribner's Sons, 1884), pp. 152–54.

19. Conrad, "Youth," pp. 41–42.

20. Conrad, "The End of the Tether," p. 154.

21. George Bogaars, "The Effect of the Opening of the Suez Canal on the Trade and Development of Singapore," *Journal of the Malayan Branch of the Royal Asiatic Society* 28, no. 1 (March 1, 1955): 99–143.

22. *The Singapore and Straits Directory for 1881* (Singapore: Printed at the 'Misson Press', 1881), pp. 57–58, N21–26.

23. Hornaday, *Two Years in the Jungle*, p. 291.

24. As late as World War I, it was cheaper to send freight between Europe and the Pacific coast of America by sail. C. Knick Harley, "Ocean Freight Rates and Productivity, 1740–1913: The Primacy of Mechanical Invention Reaffirmed," *The Journal of Economic History* 48, no. 4 (December 1, 1988): 863–65; Charles K. Harley, "The Shift from Sailing Ships to Steamships, 1850–1890: A Study in Technological Change and Its Diffusion," in Donald N. McCloskey and Alfred D.

Chandler, eds., *Essays on a Mature Economy: Britain After 1840* (London: Methuen, 1971), pp. 223–29.

25. Wong Lin Ken, "Singapore: Its Growth as an Entrepot Port, 1819–1941," *Journal of Southeast Asian Studies* 9, no. 1 (March 1, 1978): 63–66.

26. W. A. Laxon, *The Straits Steamship Fleets* (Kuching, Malaysia: Sarawak Steamship Co. Berhad, 2004).

27. Woodman, *More Days, More Dollars*, p. 125.

28. Conrad, "The End of the Tether," p. 179.

29. Sir John Rumney Nicholson, "The Tanjong Pagar Dock Company," in Braddell, Brooke, and Makepeace, *One Hundred Years of Singapore*, vol. 2, pp. 1–19; Pryer, *A Decade in Borneo*, p. 143.

30. Norman Sherry, "Conrad and the S. S. Vidar," *The Review of English Studies* 14, no. 54 (May 1, 1963): 157–63.

31. Conrad, *The Shadow-Line*, p. 4. Conrad wrote that description in 1917, not long after an all-Muslim regiment of the Indian army mutinied in Singapore, in part responding to calls for jihad launched by the Ottoman sultan. To mark the suppression of the mutiny, a member of the ship-owning Al Sagoff family made a public appearance with Singapore's colonial secretary to demonstrate his support for the regime. See Nurfadzilah Yahaya, "Tea and Company: Interactions Between the Arab Elite and the British in Cosmopolitan Singapore," in Ahmed Ibrahim Abushouk and Hassan Ahmed Ibrahim, eds., *The Hadhrami Diaspora in Southeast Asia: Identity Maintenance or Assimilation?* (Leiden, Netherlands: Brill, 2009), p. 63.

32. Sherry, *Conrad's Eastern World*, p. 31. J. H. Drysdale, who worked as chief engineer on the *Vidar* in the 1870s, estimated that 90 percent of engineers in the Straits were Scots (like him). J. H. Drysdale, "Awakening Old Memories," in Braddell, Brooke, and Makepeace, *One Hundred Years of Singapore*, vol. 1, p. 539.

33. Woodman, *More Days, More Dollars*, p. 24.

34. Najder notes that the crew consisted of twelve Malays and one Chinese stoker (Najder, *Joseph Conrad: A Life*, 2nd ed. [Rochester, New York: Camden House, 2007], p. 115). In *A Personal Record*, Conrad mentions a Malay Serang and "Jurumudi Itam, our best quartermaster," but implied there were more Chinese on board including a "Chinaman carpenter" and "Ah Sing, our chief steward" (143–45). Captain Craig later claimed that Conrad "had learned to speak Malay fluently, though with a peculiar guttural accent, in an incredible short time" (quoted in Woodman, *More Days, More Dollars*, p. 128), but many of Craig's recollections of Conrad and the *Vidar* have been shown to be unreliable.

35. Sherry, *Conrad's Eastern World*, pp. 29–30.

36. For Anglo-Dutch rivalry in this period, see L. R. Wright, *The Origins of British Borneo* (Hong Kong: Hong Kong University Press, 1988); and J. Thomas Lindblad, "Economic Aspects of the Dutch Expansion in Indonesia, 1870–1914," *Modern Asian Studies* 23, no. 1 (1989).

37. See JC to Lady Margaret Brooke, July 15, 1920: "The first Rajah Brooke has been one of my boyish admirations. . . . For all my admiration for and mental familiarity with the Great Rajah the only concrete object I ever saw connected with him was the old steamer 'Royalist' which was still in 1887 running between Kuching and Singapore." *CL*, vol. 7, p. 137.

38. See James Francis Warren, *The Sulu Zone, 1768–1898: The Dynamics of External Trade, Slavery, and Ethnicity in the Transformation of a Southeast Asian Maritime State* (Singapore: Singapore University Press, 1981), chapter 10; and James Francis Warren, "The Structure of Slavery in the Sulu Zone in the Late Eighteenth and Nineteenth Centuries," *Slavery & Abolition* 24, no. 2 (August 1, 2003): 111–28.

39. James Francis Warren, "Saltwater Slavers and Captives in the Sulu Zone, 1768–1878," *Slavery & Abolition* 31, no. 3 (September 1, 2010): 429–49.

40. Warren, *The Sulu Zone*, pp. 197–200.

41. J. F. N. M. à Campo, "A Profound Debt to the Eastern Seas: Documentary History and Literary Representation of Berau's Maritime Trade in Conrad's Malay Novels," *International Journal of Maritime History* 12, no. 2 (December 2000): 116–17.

42. Beinecke Library, Yale University: Syed Mohsin bin al Jaffree Co., Joseph Conrad Collection, Gen. Mss. 1207, Box 39.

43. Conrad, *The Mirror of the Sea*, p. 76.

44. JC to William Blackwood, [September 6, 1897], *CL*, vol. 1, p. 382.

45. À Campo, "A Profound Debt," p. 117; Gene M. Moore, "Slavery and Racism in Joseph Conrad's Eastern World," *Journal of Modern Literature* 30, no. 4 (2007): 20–35.

46. Conrad, "The End of the Tether," p. 152.

47. Cf. Conrad's description of Sambir in *The Outcast of the Islands*, chapter 6; Conrad, *A Personal Record*, p. 130.

48. À Campo, "A Profound Debt," pp. 95, 97.

49. Sherry, *Conrad's Eastern World*, pp. 96–110. The quote is from John Dill Ross's fictionalized memoir *Sixty Years: Life and Adventure in the Far East*, 2 vols. (London: Hutchinson & Co., 1911), vol. 1, p. 82.

50. Norman Sherry has carefully traced the movements of these historical figures (see *Conrad's Eastern World*, esp. chapter 5), but à Campo, "A Profound Debt," provides a few important correctives on the basis of Dutch documents: see esp. pp. 111–15.

51. Conrad, *A Personal Record*, pp. 131–42.

52. All four of these ships arrived within three days of the *Vidar* in September 1887: *Straits Times Weekly Issue*, October 5, 1887, p. 13.

53. JC to W. G. St. Clair, March 31, 1917, *CL*, vol. 6, p. 62.

54. Conrad, "The End of the Tether," pp. 151–52. Najder, *Joseph Conrad: A Life*, p. 121. À Campo suggests that Conrad may have felt uneasy about the *Vidar*'s covert trade: "A Profound Debt," pp. 124–25.

CHAPTER SIX: WHEN YOUR SHIP FAILS YOU

1. Gérard Jean-Aubry, *Joseph Conrad: Life and Letters*, 2 vols. (Garden City, NY: Doubleday & Company, 1927), vol. 1, p. 98.

2. Edward Douwes Dekker, *Max Havelaar: Or, The Coffee Auctions of the Dutch Trading Company, by Multatuli*, trans. Baron Alphonse Nahuÿs (Edinburgh: Edmonston and Douglas, 1868). Conrad didn't seem to know of the Italian author Emilio Salgari, who in 1883 began publishing an enduringly popular series of adventures featuring a Malay pirate called Sandokan.

3. *Literary World* (Boston), May 18, 1895, in Keith Carabine, ed., *Joseph Conrad: Critical Assessments*, 4 vols. (Mountfield, East Sussex, UK: Helm Information, 1992), vol. 1, p. 243.

4. *The Critic*, May 9, 1896, in Carabine, ed., *Critical Assessments*, p. 246.

5. *The Spectator*, October 19, 1895, in ibid., p. 245. Cf. a review in the *National Observer* of *An Outcast of the Islands*: "Mr. Conrad does not possess Mr. Kipling's extraordinary faculty of making his natives interesting. . . . It is like one of Mr. Stevenson's South Sea stories, grown miraculously long and miraculously tedious." Quoted in *CL*, vol. 1, p. 276n.

6. JC to T. Fisher Unwin, April 22, 1896, *CL*, vol. 1, p. 276. Scholars have counted sixty-five different Malay words in his writing: Florence Clemens, "Conrad's Malaysia" (1941), in Robert D. Hamner, ed., *Joseph Conrad: Third World Perspectives* (Washington, DC: Three Continents Press, 1990), p. 25.

7. JC to William Blackwood, December 13, 1898, *CL*, vol. 2, p. 130. Conrad and Clifford went on to become good friends.

8. Hugh Charles Clifford, *Studies in Brown Humanity, Being Scrawls and Smudges in Sepia, White, and Yellow* (London: G. Richards, 1898), p. ix.

9. JC to William Blackwood, [September 6, 1897], *CL*, vol. 1, p. 382. He was referring here to *The Rescue*, which he put aside to work on *Lord Jim*.

10. Joseph Conrad, *Lord Jim* (London: Penguin Classics, 2007), pp. 7–8. All quotes drawn from this edition.

11. Ibid., pp. 16–18, 20.

12. Ibid., pp. 15, 23–25, 68.

13. Ibid., p. 82.

14. I draw details of the *Jeddah* case from the original documents reprinted as Appendix C, "The 'Jeddah' Inquiry," in Norman Sherry, *Conrad's Eastern World* (Cambridge, UK: Cambridge University Press, 1966), pp. 299–312. See also Eric Tagliacozzo, *The Longest Journey: Southeast Asians and the Pilgrimage to Mecca* (Oxford: Oxford University Press, 2013), chapter 5; Michael B. Miller, "Pilgrims' Progress: The Business of the Hajj," *Past & Present* 191, no. 1 (May 2006): 189–228; Valeska Huber, *Channelling Mobilities: Migration and Globalisation in the Suez Canal Region and Beyond* (Cambridge, UK: Cambridge University Press, 2013), chapter 6.

15. Sherry, *Conrad's Eastern World*, pp. 57, 62.

16. See the report on the action for salvage brought by the *Antenor*'s owners against the *Jeddah*'s owners, in the *Straits Times Overland Journal*, October 22, 1881, p. 3. The Vice-Admiralty Court awarded the plaintiffs £6,000, £2,000 of which was to be apportioned among the *Antenor*'s officers and crew.

17. Sherry, *Conrad's Eastern World*, pp. 302–5.

18. Ibid., pp. 304–5, 309.

19. Quoted in Ibid., p. 62.

20. Commons Sitting of Thursday, March 9, 1882, House of Commons Hansard, 3rd ser., vol. 267, cols. 454–55.

21. Sherry, *Conrad's Eastern World*, p. 80.

22. Conrad, *Lord Jim*, p. 87.

23. Ibid., pp. 24, 41.

24. Ibid., pp. 61, 26.

25. Ibid., pp. 12, 34.

26. Gene M. Moore suggests that this is because Conrad had in mind the small crew of the *Vidar* when writing about the *Patna*. Gene M. Moore, "The Missing Crew of the 'Patna,'" *The Conradian* 25, no. 1 (2000): 83–98.

27. Conrad, *Lord Jim*, pp. 37, 64.

28. Ibid., pp. 6, 150, 169, 273.

29. Ibid., pp. 179, 182, 193, 290.

30. Ibid., pp. 209, 250, 187, 245.

31. Ibid., p. 270.

32. Ibid., pp. 312, 317–18.

33. On Conrad's relationship to this tradition, see Linda Dryden, *Joseph Conrad and the Imperial Romance* (New York: St. Martin's Press, 2000).

34. JC to J. B. Pinker, August 14, 1919, *CL*, vol. 6, p. 465.

35. Conrad, *Lord Jim*, pp. 6, 317, 203, 257, 206, 200, 276, 212, 217, 290.

36. Reviews in *The Pall Mall Gazette*, December 5, 1900; *Manchester Guardian*, October 29, 1900; *Critic* 28, May 1901, in Carabine, ed., *Critical Assessments*, vol. 1, pp. 281–82, 285–86.

37. Conrad, *Lord Jim*, p. 10.

38. I draw my sense of narratorial functions from Gérard Genette, *Narrative Discourse: An Essay in Method* (Ithaca, NY: Cornell University Press, 1980), pp. 255–56. Genette cites *Lord Jim* as a notable example of metadiagesis, or the entangling of events (what happened) with narrative (telling what happened). In *Lord Jim* such "entanglement reaches the bounds of general intelligibility" (p. 232).

39. Ford Madox Ford, *Joseph Conrad: A Personal Remembrance* (London: Duckworth & Co., 1924), p. 180. See also Ian P. Watt, *Conrad in the Nineteenth Century* (Berkeley: University of California Press, 1979), p. 290.

40. The essential book on this topic is Edward Said's *Orientalism* (New York: Pantheon Books, 1978). Said wrote his Ph.D. dissertation and first book on Joseph Conrad.

41. On Conrad's debt to Schopenhauer, see, e.g., Owen Knowles, "'Who's Afraid of Arthur Schopenhauer?': A New Context for Conrad's Heart of Darkness," *Nineteenth-Century Literature* 49, no. 1 (June 1, 1994): 76–78. In the late 1920s John Galsworthy wrote of Conrad that "Schopenhauer used to give him satisfaction twenty years and more ago, and he liked both the personality and the writings of William James." Quoted in Carabine, ed., *Critical Assessments*, vol. 1, p. 141.

42. Marlow's faith in "the deep hidden truth of works of art" chimed with Conrad's paean to the artist's purpose, in the 1897 preface to *The Nigger of the 'Narcissus,'* to identify and represent "the very truth" of the "visible universe."

43. Conrad, *Lord Jim*, pp. 200, 215, 246–47, 318.

44. *The Critic* 28 (May, 1901), in Carabine, ed., *Critical Assessments*, vol. 1, pp. 281–82, 285–86.

45. Quoted in F. R. Leavis, *The Great Tradition: George Eliot, Henry James, Joseph Conrad* (New York: George W. Stewart, 1950), p. 173.

46. Conrad, *Lord Jim*, p. 309.

CHAPTER SEVEN: HEART TO HEART

1. Joseph Conrad, *The Shadow-Line* (Oxford: Oxford World's Classics, 2009), pp. 24, 26.

2. Mark Twain, *Following the Equator* (Hartford, CT: American Publishing Company, 1898), p. 619.

3. Reminiscences of Paul Langlois, quoted in Zdzisław Najder, *Joseph Conrad: A Life*, 2nd ed. (Rochester, NY: Camden House, 2007), pp. 129–30.

4. This questionnaire is described and reproduced in Savinien Mérédac, "Joseph Conrad chez nous," *Le Radical* (Port-Louis, Mauritius), August 7, 1931.

5. Joseph Conrad, "A Smile of Fortune," in *'Twixt Land and Sea* (New York: Hodder & Stoughton, 1912), p. 46.

6. Members of the family told Mérédac that "Joseph Conrad Korzeniowski spent many afternoons there, always charming, meticulously courteous, but alas, they admitted, alas! often 'absent' from the conversation."

7. Joseph Conrad, *Chance* (Oxford: Oxford World's Classics, 2002), p. 91.

8. TB to JC, December 22/January 3, 1889, *CPB*, p. 127.

9. G. F. W. Hope and Gene M. Moore, "Friend of Conrad," *The Conradian* 25, no. 2 (Autumn 2000): 35. Krieger has been variously described as "born in Prussia" (John Stape, *The Several Lives of Joseph Conrad* [New York: Pantheon Books, 2007], p. 45) and "an American of German origin" (Owen Knowles and Gene M. Moore, eds., *Oxford Reader's Companion to Conrad* [Oxford: Oxford University Press, 2000], p. 219). Barr, Moering & Co. (sometimes Mohring) specialized in imports from Germany, especially silver, on which see John Culme, *The Directory of Gold and Silversmiths, Jewellers, and Allied Traders, 1838–1914: From the London Assay Office Registers*, 2 vols. (Woodbridge, Suffolk, UK: Antique Collectors Club, 1987), vol. 2, p. 32. It also acted as an agent for at least one Belgian company. (*The Law Journal Reports for the Year 1897*, vol. 66 [London: Law Journal Reports, 1897], pp. 23–24.)

10. On Conrad's financial affairs during this period, see TB to JC, August 19/31, 1883; TB to JC, March 24/April 5, 1886; TB to JC, April 12/24, 1886; TB to JC, July 8/20, 1886, *CPB*, pp. 94, 101, 103, 106–7.

11. Hope and Moore, "Friend of Conrad," pp. 34–35.

12. Joseph Conrad, *A Personal Record* (London: Harper & Brothers, 1912), pp. 128–34.

13. Najder, *Joseph Conrad: A Life*, p. 118n.

14. On Antwerp's port facilities and monuments, see *Notice sur le Port d'Anvers* (Brussels: E. Guyot, 1898); Paul Salvagne, *Anvers Maritime* (Antwerp: J. Maes, 1898), pp. 62–84; Karl Baedeker (Firm), *Belgium and Holland: Handbook for Travellers* (Leipzig: K. Baedeker, 1888), pp. 129–31, 138, 158–60. I am indebted to Debora Silverman for alerting me to the connection between Antwerp's

founding legend and the practice of hand severing that became notorious in the Congo Free State. See Debora L. Silverman, "Art Nouveau, Art of Darkness: African Lineages of Belgian Modernism, Part III," *West 86th* 20, no. 1 (2013): 26–29.

15. JC to Albert Thys, November 4, 1889, *CL*, vol. 1, p. 25.

16. G. C. de Baerdemaecker to Albert Thys, September 24, 1889, in J. H. Stape and Owen Knowles, eds., *A Portrait in Letters: Correspondence to and About Conrad* (Amsterdam: Rodopi, 1996), pp. 5–6. The letter of introduction noted that *"son instruction générale est supérieure à celle qu'ont habituellement les marins et c'est un parfait* gentleman."

17. The company HQ was on the Rue Brédérode; see *The Congo Railway from Matadi to the Stanley Pool* (Brussels: P. Weissenbruch, 1889).

18. Guy Vanthemsche, *Belgium and the Congo, 1885–1980* (Cambridge, UK: Cambridge University Press, 2012), p. 37.

19. JC to Albert Thys, November 4/28, 1889, *CL*, vol. 1, pp. 25–27. In 1902, "The old and well-known firm of Walford & Co., of Antwerp," would be "turned into a 'Société Anonyme,' with a capital of £200,000" and "Col. Thys, the Belgian Cecil Rhodes, of Congo fame" made its chairman. *The Syren and Shipping Illustrated* 24, no. 311 (August 13, 1902): 279.

20. Anne Arnold, "Marguerite Poradowska as Conrad's Friend and Adviser," *The Conradian* 34, no. 1 (2009): 68–83.

21. Kazimierówka was burned down in the October Revolution of 1917. It was located in Vinnyts'ka Oblast, near the village of Orativ.

22. Conrad, *A Personal Record*, pp. 49–50.

23. JC to Marguerite Poradowska, February 14 [15-16?], 1890, *CL*, vol. 1, p. 39.

24. On this relationship, see especially Susan Jones, *Conrad and Women* (Oxford: Clarendon Press, 1999) and Arnold, "Marguerite Poradowska." Both emphasize Poradowska's significance as Konrad's premier contact to the literary world, at just the time that he was beginning *Almayer's Folly*.

25. Najder, *Joseph Conrad: A Life*, pp. 140–43.

26. Conrad, *A Personal Record*, p. 36. Cf. Joseph Conrad, "Geography and Some Explorers," in *Last Essays* (Garden City, NY: Doubleday, Page & Co., 1926), p. 16: "One day, putting my finger on a spot in the very middle of the then white heart of Africa, I declared that some day I would go there."

27. JC to Marguerite Poradowska, May 15, 1890, *CL*, vol. 1, p. 51.

28. JC to Marguerite Poradowska, June 10, 1890, *CL*, vol. 1, p. 55.

29. JC to Karol Zagórski, May 22, 1890, *CL*, vol. 1, p. 52.

30. Makulo Akambu, *La Vie de Disasi Makulo: Ancien Esclave de Tippo Tip et Catéchiste de Grenfell* (Kinshasa: Editions Saint Paul Afrique, 1983), pp. 15–16. I owe my awareness of this source to the splendid work of David van Reybrouck, *Congo: The Epic History of a People*, trans. Sam Garrett (New York: Ecco, 2014), pp. 29–45.

31. Akambu, *Vie de Disasi Makulo*, p. 18. A variant on Matambatamba: Jan Vansina, *Paths in the Rainforests: Toward a History of Political Tradition in Equatorial Africa* (Madison: University of Wisconsin Press, 1990), p. 240; Osumaka Likaka, *Naming Colonialism: History and Collective Memory in the Congo, 1870–1960* (Madison: University of Wisconsin Press, 2009), p. 102.

32. Stanley described his visit to the camp in *The Congo and the Founding of Its Free State: A Story of Work and Exploration*, 2 vols. (New York: Harper & Brothers, 1885), vol. 2, pp. 146–50.

33. Akambu, *Vie de Disasi Makulo*, pp. 20–25.

34. Similar forms of this word mean "white man" in various languages around the Great Lakes region, e.g., Swahili *muzungu*. The Lingala word for foreigner is, by contrast, *mundele*.

35. Akambu, *Vie de Disasi Makulo*, pp. 29–31.

36. Ibid., pp. 32–36.

37. David Livingstone, *Dr. Livingstone's Cambridge Lectures* (Cambridge, UK: Deighton, Bell & Co., 1858), p. 18.

38. Henry M. Stanley, *Through the Dark Continent*, (New York: Harper and Brothers, 1879) vol. 2, pp. 95–114.

39. Ibid., p. 190.

40. Ibid., pp. 158, 174, 272. Tim Jeal, *Stanley: The Impossible Life of Africa's Greatest Explorer* (London: Faber, 2007), p. 155. Jeal notes throughout that Stanley deliberately exaggerated his violent encounters to win readers, having observed that Americans lapped up reports of fights with Indians. It backfired.

41. Alexandre Delcommune, *Vingt années de vie africaine, 1874–1893, récits de voyages d'aventures et d'exploration au Congo Belge*, 2 vols. (Brussels: Ferdinand Larcier, 1922), vol. 1, p. 89; Stanley, *Through the Dark Continent*, vol. 2, pp. 454, 466–67.

42. Stanley, *Through the Dark Continent*, vol. 2, p. 466; Patrick Brantlinger, *Rule of Darkness: British Literature and Imperialism, 1830–1914* (Ithaca, NY: Cornell University Press, 1988), chapter 6.

43. Jeal, *Stanley*, pp. 221–28.

44. Adam Hochschild, *King Leopold's Ghost: A Story of Greed, Terror, and Heroism in Colonial Africa* (Boston: Houghton Mifflin, 1999), p. 39.

45. Vanthemsche, *Belgium and the Congo*, p. 18; Hochschild, *King Leopold's Ghost*, pp. 37–38. On the Sarawak overture, see John Brooke to Sir James Brooke, August 4, 1861, in Rhodes House, Oxford: Basil Brooke Papers, Mss. Pac s90, vol. 5. Steven Press brilliantly excavates the connections between European interventions in Borneo and the Scramble for Africa in *Rogue Empires: Contracts and Conmen in Europe's Scramble for Africa* (Cambridge, MA: Harvard University Press, 2017).

46. Émile Banning, *Africa and the Brussels Geographical Conference*, trans. Richard Henry Major (London: Sampson Low, Marston, Searle & Rivington, 1877), p. 152.

47. Ibid., p. 109.

48. H. M. Stanley, *The Congo and the Founding of Its Free State: A Story of Work and Exploration*, 2 vols. (London: Sampson Low, Marston, Searle & Rivington, 1886), vol. 1, p. 26.

49. Ibid., pp. 59–60.

50. As Eric D. Weitz points out, this had a significant impact on twentieth-century conceptions of minority rights and protection. Eric D. Weitz, "From the Vienna to the Paris System: International Politics and the Entangled Histories of Human Rights, Forced Deportations, and Civilizing Missions," *The American Historical Review* 113, no. 5 (December 1, 2008): 1313–43.

51. Vanthemsche, *Belgium and the Congo*, p. 29; Hochschild, *King Leopold's Ghost*, pp. 80–87. For an overview of the Berlin Conference, see H. L. Wesseling, *Divide and Rule: The Partition of Africa, 1880–1914*, trans. Arnold J. Pomerans (Westport, CT: Praeger, 1996).

52. Banning, *Africa and the Brussels Geographical Conference*, p. 153.

53. Jeal, *Stanley*, chapter 19; Hochschild, *King Leopold's Ghost*, p. 81; Stanley, *The Congo and the Founding of Its Free State*, vol. 1, pp. 51, 462.

54. Anonymous "ancien diplomat" quoted in Jesse Siddall Reeves, *The International Beginnings of the Congo Free State* (Baltimore: Johns Hopkins University Press, 1894), p. 70.

55. Stanley, *The Congo and the Founding of Its Free State*, vol. 2, p. 196.

56. Delcommune, *Vingt années*, vol. 1, p. 64. European breech-loading rifles were substantially more accurate than African muskets.

57. George Washington Williams, "George Washington Williams's Open Letter to King Leopold on the Congo, 1890 | The Black Past: Remembered and Reclaimed," www.blackpast.org/george-washington-williams-open-letter-king-leopold-congo-1890.

58. Sabine Cornelis, Maria Moreno, and John Peffer, "L'Exposition du Congo and Edouard Manduau's La Civilisation au Congo (1884–1885)," *Critical Interventions* 1, no. 1 (January 1, 2007): 125–40.

59. Delcommune, *Vingt années*, vol. 1, p. 194.

60. A. J. Wauters, *L'état indépendant du Congo; historique, géographie physique, ethnographie, situation économique, organisation politique* (Brussels: Librairie Falk fils, 1899), p. 431. Recent histories have traced the ways in which the colonial exploitation in Congo became a broadly Belgian undertaking. See esp. Vincent Viaene, "King Leopold's Imperialism and the Origins of the Belgian Colonial Party, 1860–1905," *Journal of Modern History* 80, no. 4 (December 2008): 741–90.

61. Delcommune, *Vingt années*, vol. 1, p. 56.

62. Jean Stengers and Jan Vansina, "King Leopold's Congo, 1886–1908," in R. Oliver and G. N. Sanderson, eds., *The Cambridge History of Africa* (Cambridge, UK: Cambridge University Press, 1985), p. 330.

63. Norman Sherry, *Conrad's Western World* (Cambridge, UK: Cambridge University Press, 1971), pp. 376–77.

64. Hochschild, *King Leopold's Ghost*, pp. 133–35.

65. This is the account given by Johannes Scharffenberg, a Norwegian officer on the *Florida*; see Espen Waehle, "Scandinavian Agents and Entrepreneurs in the Scramble for Ethnographica During Colonial Expansion in the Congo," in Kirsten Alsaker Kjerland and Bjørn Enge Bertelsen, eds., *Navigating Colonial Orders: Norwegian Entrepreneurship in Africa and Oceania* (London: Berghahn Books, 2015), pp. 348–49. Grenfell was told something more picturesque (and more likely to seem "savage"). Taken by the sight of a child and its mother bathing in the river, Freiesleben gave the woman a couple of *mitakos*, and the gift touched off the scuffle. (Sherry, *Conrad's Western World*, pp. 18–19.)

66. Quoted in Sherry, *Conrad's Western World*, p. 17.

CHAPTER EIGHT: THE DARK PLACES

1. "Harou (Prosper-Félix-Joseph)," *Biographie coloniale belge*, vol. 3 (Brussels: Librairie Falk fils, 1952), p. 418; Henry Morton Stanley, *The Congo and the Founding of Its Free State: A Story of Work and Exploration* (New York: Harper & Brothers, 1885), vol. 2, p. 298.

2. Adam Hochschild, *King Leopold's Ghost: A Story of Greed, Terror, and Heroism in Colonial Africa* (Boston: Houghton Mifflin, 1999), p. 115; David van Reybrouck, *Congo: The Epic History of a People*, trans. Sam Garrett (New York: Ecco, 2014), p. 61.

3. A.-J. Wauters, *L'état indépendant du Congo: historique, géographie physique, ethnographie, situation économique, organisation politique* (Brussels: Librairie Falk fils, 1899), pp. 431–32.

4. There is some disagreement about whether this was the only diary Conrad kept. Najder points to Captain Craig of the *Vidar*'s much later statement that he "usually found [Conrad] writing" (see chapter 6) as evidence that Conrad may have kept notes on other journeys. (Zdzisław Najder, "Introduction" to Joseph Conrad, *Congo Diary and Other Uncollected Pieces* [Garden City, NY: Doubleday, 1978], pp. 3–4.) But no actual diaries of this sort survive, nor does any other corroborating evidence they once existed, so the speculation is based on evidence from absence. A passage in *The Shadow-Line* (which Conrad, admittedly with considerable exaggeration, called "exact autobiography") tends to support the notion that diary keeping was not his usual practice: "It's the only period of my life in which I attempted to keep a diary. No, not the only one. Years later, in conditions of moral isolation, I did put down on paper the thoughts and events of a score of days. But this was the first time. I don't remember how it came about or how the pocket-book and the pencil came into my hands." Joseph Conrad, *The Shadow-Line* (Oxford: Oxford World's Classics, 2009), p. 87.

5. Oscar Michaux, *Au Congo: Carnet de campagne: épisodes & impressions de 1889 à 1897* (Brussels: Librairie Falk fils, 1907), p. 67.

6. Louis Goffin, *Le chemin de fer du Congo (Matadi-Stanley-Pool)* (Brussels: M. Weissenbruch, 1907), pp. 37–38.

7. Conrad, *Congo Diary*, p. 7.

8. Wauters, *L'état indépendant du Congo*, p. 334. Given that an African elephant tusk weighs 23 kilograms on average, 75,000 kilograms could represent the tusks of more than 1,600 elephants; www.britannica.com/topic/ivory.

9. E. J. Glave, "The Congo River of To-Day," *The Century Magazine* 39, no. 4 (February 1890): 619.

10. Henry M. Stanley, *The Congo and the Founding of Its Free State: A Story of Work and Exploration*, 2 vols. (London: Sampson Low, Marston, Searle & Rivington, 1886), vol. 1, p. 401.

11. Albert Thys, *Au Congo et au Kassaï: Conférences Données À La Société Belge Des Ingénieurs et Des Industriels* (Brussels, 1888), p. 7.

12. Wauters, *L'état indépendant du Congo*, pp. 348–49. Wauters estimated that 50,000 porters worked the route in 1893; Lemaire offered the more modest number of 25,280. Charles Lemaire, *Congo & Belgique (à propos de l'Exposition d'Anvers)* (Brussels: C. Bulens, 1894), p. 162.

13. Conrad, *Congo Diary*, p. 9.

14. Ibid., pp. 7, 10, 14.

15. Ibid., pp. 8–9, 12.

16. Ibid., pp. 8–9, 13.

17. Ibid., p. 15.

18. TB to JC, October 28/November 9, 1890, *CPB*, p. 133. Bobrowski's line "*Tu l'as voulu*, Georges Dandin" referred to Molière's 1668 comedy *George Dandin ou le mari confondu*.

19. Norman Sherry, *Conrad's Western World* (Cambridge, UK: Cambridge University Press, 1971), p. 56.

20. Conrad, *Youth/Heart of Darkness/The End of the Tether* (London: Penguin Books, 1995), p. 98. Henceforth cited as *Heart of Darkness*.

21. Conrad, *Congo Diary*, pp. 17, 20–21, 34, 36.

22. Conrad, *Heart of Darkness*, p. 88.

23. For the composition history of the manuscript, see the Cambridge critical edition: Joseph Conrad, *Almayer's Folly*, eds. Floyd Eugene Eddleman and David Leon Higdon (Cambridge, UK: Cambridge University Press, 1994), pp. 159–65. Quotes from chapter 5, pp. 52–57. Five pages of chapter 5 are also written in pencil, like the "Up-River Book" but unlike most of the rest of the *Almayer's Folly* manuscript.

24. Conrad, *Heart of Darkness*, p. 90.

25. Zdzisław Najder, *Joseph Conrad: A Life*, 2nd ed. (Rochester, NY: Camden House, 2007), p. 156.

26. Herbert Ward, *Five Years with the Congo Cannibals* (London: Chatto & Windus, 1891), pp. 196–214.

27. John Rose Troup, *With Stanley's Rear Column* (London: Chapman and Hall, 1890), p. 178. See also Henry Morton Stanley, *In Darkest Africa: The Quest, Rescue, and Retreat of Emin, Governor of Equatoria*, 2 vols. (New York: Scribner, 1891), vol. 1, pp. 64–65.

28. Sherry, *Conrad's Western World*, pp. 64–66.

29. Wauters, *L'état indépendant du Congo*, p. 401.

30. Stanley's officers commented more or less critically on the unholy alliance between the Congo Free State and the most famous of slavers. "The man of civilization condemns with indignation the barbarism of the Arab slaver, but let the white man pause and think for but one moment and he will realize how deeply he himself is implicated. By whom are the guns and ammunition supplied with which this persecution is carried on, and who is the purchaser of the costly elephant tusk?" E. J. Glave, *Six Years of Adventure in Congo-Land* (London: S. Low, Marston, Limited, 1893), p. 231. See also Ward, *Five Years with the Congo Cannibals*, pp. 216–21.

31. "The subdued thundering mutter of the Stanley Falls hung in the heavy night air of the last navigable reach of the upper Congo." "Geography and Some Explorers," in Joseph Conrad, *Last Essays*, ed. and intro. Richard Curle (London: J. M. Dent & Sons, 1926), p. 17.

32. Camille Delcommune to JC, September 6, 1890, in J. H. Stape and Owen Knowles, eds., *A Portrait in Letters: Correspondence to and About Conrad* (Amsterdam: Rodopi, 1996), p. 10.

33. Sherry, *Conrad's Western World*, pp. 78–80.

34. Marguerite Poradowska to JC, June 9, 1890, in Stape and Knowles, eds., *Portrait in Letters*, p. 8.

35. JC to Marguerite Poradowska, September 26, 1890, *CL*, vol. 1, pp. 61–63. Conrad wrote to Poradowska in French; nonetheless one hears an echo with *Almayer's Folly*, whose first chapter ends with Nina looking at "the upper reach of the river whipped into white foam by the wind." Joseph Conrad, *Almayer's Folly* (Garden City, NY: Doubleday, Page & Co., 1915), p. 17.

36. TB to JC, October 28/November 9, 1890, *CPB*, p. 133.

37. Najder, *Joseph Conrad: A Life*, p. 162.

38. TB to JC, June 12/24, 1890, *CPB*, pp. 128–29.

39. Conrad, *Heart of Darkness*, pp. 54, 56–57.

40. Ibid., p. 67.

41. Ibid., pp. 68–69, 76, 84, 106, 126.

42. Ibid., p. 88.

43. Ibid., p. 90.

44. John Thomas Towson (1804–81) was the author of several reference works on navigation, including *Practical Information on the Deviation of the Compass: For the Use of Masters and Mates of Iron Ships* (1863), which was used as a manual for the Board of Trade examinations Conrad took. C. W. Sutton, "Towson, John Thomas (1804–1881)," rev. Elizabeth Baigent, *Oxford Dictionary of National Biography*, (Oxford: Oxford University Press, 2004), online ed., May 2010, www.oxforddnb.com .ezp-prod1.hul.harvard.edu/view/article/27642.

45. Conrad, *Heart of Darkness*, p. 94.

46. Ibid., p. 103.

47. Louis Menand, *Discovering Modernism: T. S. Eliot and His Context*, 2nd ed. (New York: Oxford University Press, 2007), p. 111; Conrad, *Heart of Darkness*, p. 113.

48. Conrad, *Heart of Darkness*, pp. 120–21.

49. Ibid., pp. 111, 123, 125.

50. Ibid., pp. 132–37.

51. Ibid., pp. 139–47.

52. Ibid., pp. 49, 148. Cf. the end of *The Nigger of the 'Narcissus'* (written about a year earlier), where a vision of Britain rising from the waves as a ship in full sail degenerates into industrial squalor as the *Narcissus* goes up the Thames to dock: "A mad jumble of begrimed walls loomed up vaguely in the smoke, bewildering and mournful, like a vision of disaster . . . and a swarm of strange men, clambering up her sides, took possession of her in the name of the sordid earth." (Joseph Conrad, *The Nigger of the 'Narcissus' and Other Stories* [London: Penguin Classics, 2007], p. 130.) In a 1904 essay about the Thames, Conrad recapitulated the opening of *Heart of Darkness*, once again imagining a Roman entering the river to face its savage denizens, and likening the stretch of Thames from London Bridge to the Albert Docks to "a jungle," "like the matted growth of bushes and creepers veiling the silent depths of an unexplored wilderness." (Joseph Conrad, *The Mirror of the Sea* [New York: Harper & Brothers, 1906], pp.178–79.) Nicholas Delbanco notes a parallel between Conrad's opening description of the Thames and Ford Madox Ford's *The Cinque Ports* in *Group Portrait: Joseph Conrad, Stephen Crane, Ford Madox Ford, Henry James, and H. G. Wells* (New York: Morrow, 1982), pp. 103–4.

53. Wauters, *L'état indépendant du Congo*, pp. 336, 448, 460, 463; A.-J. Wauters, *Histoire politique du Congo Belge* (Brussels: P. Van Fleteren, 1911), p. 75.

54. Wauters, *L'état indépendant du Congo*, pp. 402–3; Guy Vanthemsche, *Belgium and the Congo, 1885–1980* (Cambridge, UK: Cambridge University Press, 2012), pp. 147–49.

55. Wauters, *Histoire politique*, pp. 93–96, 120–24; Vincent Viaene, "King Leopold's Imperialism and the Origins of the Belgian Colonial Party, 1860–1905," *Journal of Modern History* 80, no. 4 (December 2008): 761–62.

56. Michaux, *Au Congo*, p. 218. Michaux admitted that he still, twenty years later, felt uneasy about the taking of Nyangwé because he could never quite convince himself that the Force Publique had been attacked first (pp. 223–24). A British doctor attached to the expedition hailed another achievement: the elimination of Islam as a political force. "This great struggle is, without doubt, a turning-point in African history. It is impossible even to surmise what would have been the effect on the future of Africa had another great Mohammedan Empire been established in the Congo Basin." Sidney Langforde Hinde, *The Fall of the Congo Arabs* (New York: Thomas Whittaker, 1897), pp. 24–25.

57. Sir Harry Johnston, *George Grenfell and the Congo . . .* , 2 vols. (New York: D. Appleton & Company, 1910), vol. 1, p. 428. He blamed it on the "frantic cannibals" who accompanied Dhanis as irregulars.

58. Jan Vansina, *Paths in the Rainforests: Toward a History of Political Tradition in Equatorial Africa* (Madison: University of Wisconsin Press, 1990), pp. 244–45.

59. E. D. Morel, *The Congo Slave State* (Liverpool: John Richardson & Sons, 1903), pp. 13–18; Jean Stengers and Jan Vansina, "King Leopold's Congo, 1886–1908," in R. Oliver and G. N. Sanderson, eds., *The Cambridge History of Africa* (Cambridge, UK: Cambridge University Press, 1985), pp. 339–40, 344. Reybrouck, *Congo*, p. 86.

60. Henry Richard Fox Bourne, *Civilisation in Congoland: A Story of International Wrong-Doing* (London: P. S. King and Co., 1903), pp. 178–79; Hochschild, *King Leopold's Ghost*, p. 162.

61. Glave, quoted in Fox Bourne, *Civilisation in Congoland*, p. 181.

62. Wauters, *L'état indépendant du Congo*, p. 447.

63. Makulo Akambu, *La Vie de Disasi Makulo: Ancien Esclave de Tippo Tip et Catéchiste de Grenfell* (Kinshasa: Editions Saint Paul Afrique, 1983), pp. 59–60.

64. Wauters, *L'état indépendant du Congo*, pp. 334–41.

65. Ibid., pp. 104–5; Wauters, *Histoire politique*, pp. 120–27; Vanthemsche, *Belgium and the Congo*, pp. 38–39; Viaene, "King Leopold's Imperialism," 770.

66. The British had already started cultivating rubber trees in Southeast Asia, which, once they matured, would outproduce wild rubber and displace Congo (and Brazil) on the international market. See Zephyr Frank and Aldo Musacchio, "The International Natural Rubber Market, 1870–1930," EH.Net Encyclopedia, ed. Robert Whaples, March 16, 2008, http://eh.net/encyclopedia/the-international-natural-rubber-market-1870-1930/.

67. Charles Lemaire, *Congo & Belgique (à propos de l'Exposition d'Anvers)* (Brussels: C. Bulens, 1894), pp. 37–38; Morel, *Congo Slave State*, p. 62.

68. Robert Harms, "The End of Red Rubber: A Reassessment," *The Journal of African History* 16, no. 1 (January 1, 1975): 78–81.

69. E. J. Glave, "Cruelty in the Congo Free State," *The Century Magazine* 54, no. 5 (September 1897): 709; Reybrouck, *Congo*, 87–96.

70. Testimony of Murphy and Sjöblom, quoted in Fox Bourne, *Civilisation in Congoland*, pp. 210, 213–14. Cf. Glave, quoted on pp. 198–99.

71. See Debora L. Silverman, "Art Nouveau, Art of Darkness: African Lineages of Belgian Modernism, Part I," *West 86th: A Journal of Decorative Arts, Design History, and Material Culture* 18, no. 2 (2011): 143–50; Debora L. Silverman, "Art Nouveau, Art of Darkness: African Lineages of Belgian Modernism, Part III," *West 86th* 20, no. 1 (2013): 8–11.

72. Hochschild, *King Leopold's Ghost*, pp. 206–7.

73. Unsigned review by Hugh Clifford in *The Spectator*, in Keith Carabine, ed., *Joseph Conrad: Critical Assessments*, vol. 1 (Mountfield, East Sussex, UK: Helm Information, 1992), p. 295. Clifford and Conrad were already friends.

74. Conrad, *Heart of Darkness*, p. 84.

75. Glave, "Cruelty in the Congo Free State," 706. Hochschild points out that Conrad might well have read this.

76. JC to Roger Casement, December 21, 1903, *CL*, vol. 3, p. 96.

77. JC to R. B. Cunninghame Graham, December 26, 1903, *CL*, vol. 3, p. 102.

78. Hunt Hawkins, "Joseph Conrad, Roger Casement, and the Congo Reform Movement," *Journal of Modern Literature* 9, no. 1 (1981): 65–80. Conrad wrote Casement a letter condemning the outrages, which Morel quoted in *King Leopold's Rule in Africa* (New York: Funk and Wagnalls, 1905), p. 117.

79. JC to Roger Casement, December 17, 1903, *CL*, vol. 3, p. 95.

80. Conrad, *Heart of Darkness*, p. 50.

81. JC to Edward Garnett, December 22, 1902, *CL*, vol. 2, pp. 467–68. Conrad's most important early academic champion, F. R. Leavis, was "exasperated" by *Heart of Darkness* due to Conrad's "adjectival insistence upon inexpressible and incomprehensible mystery." F. R. Leavis, *The Great Tradition: George Eliot, Henry James, Joseph Conrad* (New York: George W. Stewart, 1950), p. 177.

82. Ian Watt influentially explained this technique as "delayed decoding" in *Conrad in the Nineteenth Century* (Berkeley: University of California Press, 1979), pp. 176–77.

CHAPTER NINE: WHITE SAVAGES

1. JC to Marguerite Poradowska, March 30, 1890; April 14, 1891; May 1, 1891; May 10, 1891, *CL*, vol. 1, pp. 74–75, 77, 79.

2. TB to JC, March 30/April 12, 1891, *CPB*, p. 139.

3. TB to JC, May 25/June 6, 1891, *CPB*, p. 141.

4. TB to JC, March 30/April 12, 1891, *CPB*, p. 140.

5. JC to Marguerite Poradowska, August 26, 1891, *CL*, vol. 1, p. 91.

6. Joseph Conrad, *Almayer's Folly* (Garden City, NY: Doubleday, Page & Co., 1915), pp. 129–30.

7. Ibid., p. 108.

8. Ibid., pp. 146, 151.

9. Ibid., pp. 87, 132.

10. JC to Marguerite Poradowska, July 8, 1891, *CL*, vol. 1, p. 86.

11. TB to JC, July 18/30, 1891, *CPB*, pp. 147–48.

12. TB to JC, August 14/26, 1891, *CPB*, p. 149.

13. Joseph Conrad, *Youth/Heart of Darkness/The End of the Tether* (London: Penguin Books, 1995), p. 79.

14. JC to Marguerite Poradowska, October 16, 1891, *CL*, vol. 1, p. 99.

15. JC to Marguerite Poradowska, August 26, 1891, *CL*, vol. 1, p. 92.

16. JC to Marguerite Poradowska, November 14, 1891, *CL*, vol. 1, p. 102.

17. Quoted in Zdzisław Najder, *Joseph Conrad: A Life*, 2nd ed. (Rochester, NY: Camden House, 2007), p. 182.

18. John Stape, *The Several Lives of Joseph Conrad* (New York: Pantheon, 2007), p. 73.

19. TB to JC, February 9/21, 1894, in J. H. Stape and Owen Knowles, eds., *A Portrait in Letters: Correspondence to and About Conrad* (Amsterdam: Rodopi, 1996), p. 12.

20. JC to Marguerite Poradowska, February 18, 1894, *CL*, vol. 1, p. 148.

21. JC to Marguerite Poradowska, [March 29 or April 5, 1894], *CL*, vol. 1, p. 151.

22. Joseph Conrad, *Almayer's Folly* (Garden City, NY: Doubleday, Page & Co., 1915), p. 259.

23. JC to Marguerite Poradowska, April 24, 1894, *CL*, vol. 1, pp. 153–54.

24. JC to Marguerite Poradowska, [August 18?, 1891], *CL*, vol. 1, p. 170.

25. JC to Marguerite Poradowska, [July 25?, 1894], *CL*, vol. 1, pp. 163–64.

26. JC to Marguerite Poradowska, [August 18?, 1894], *CL*, vol. 1, p. 171.

27. JC to Marguerite Poradowska, October 23, 1894 to [February 23?, 1895], *CL*, vol. 1, pp. 182, 189, 191, 202.

28. JC to Marguerite Poradowska, [March 29 or April 4, 1894] to May 13, [1895], *CL*, vol. 1, pp. 150, 156, 185, 192, 210, 215, 219.

29. JC to Marguerite Poradowska, October 4, 1894, *CL*, vol. 1, p. 178.

30. JC to Marguerite Poradowska, October 10, 1894, *CL*, vol. 1, p. 180.

31. JC to W. H. Chesson, [mid-October to mid-November 1894], *CL*, vol. 1, p. 186.

32. JC to W. H. Chesson, [early January?, 1895], *CL*, vol. 1, p. 199.

33. The preface wasn't included in the first edition, likely because Unwin rarely published prefaces except by well-known authors.

34. Conrad, *Almayer's Folly*, p. 3. It refers to the essay "Decivilized" by Alice Meynell (which doesn't use African analogies), www.gutenberg.org/files/1434/1434-h/1434-h.htm.

35. See, e.g., Herbert Ward, *Five Years with the Congo Cannibals* (London: Chatto & Windus, 1891), p. 270.

36. Conrad, *Heart of Darkness*, pp. 90–91.

37. Conrad may well have read the "Note on Cannibalism" in Sidney Langford Hinde, *The Fall of the Congo Arabs* (New York: Whittaker, 1897), pp. 282–85. Congolese also suspected whites of the practice: see Osumaka Likaka, *Naming Colonialism: History and Collective Memory in the Congo, 1870–1960* (Madison: University of Wisconsin Press, 2009), p. 96.

38. Conrad, *Heart of Darkness*, p. 107.

39. For a summary of what is—and, more often, isn't—known about Conrad's sex life, see Robert Hampson, *Conrad's Secrets* (Basingstoke, UK: Palgrave Macmillan, 2012), pp. 4–11.

40. JC to E. B. Redmayne, May 23, 1895, quoted in J. H. Stape and Hans Van Marle, "'Pleasant Memories' and 'Precious Friendships': Conrad's *Torrens* Connections and Unpublished Letters from the 1890s," *Conradiana* 27, no. 1 (1995): 30.

41. JC to Edward Garnett, June 7, 1895, *CL*, vol. 1, p. 224.

42. JC to Marguerite Poradowska, June 11, 1895, *CL*, vol. 1, p. 229.

43. JC to Mme. Briquel, March 7, 1896, *CL*, vol. 1, pp. 264–65.

44. JC to Karol Zagórski, March 10, 1896, *CL*, vol. 1, pp. 265–66.

45. JC to E. B. Redmayne, February 23, 1896, Stape and Van Marle, "'Pleasant Memories'": 32.

46. JC to Nita Wall, March 22, 1896, Stape and Van Marle, "'Pleasant Memories'": 35.

47. Zdzisław Najder, *Joseph Conrad: A Life*, 2nd ed. (Rochester, NY: Camden House, 2007), pp. 223–24.

48. Jessie Conrad, *Joseph Conrad as I Knew Him* (Garden City, NY: Doubleday, Page & Co., 1926), pp. 101–5.

49. Ibid., pp. 25, 102.

50. J. H. Stape, "Jessie Conrad in Context: A George Family History," *The Conradian* 34, no. 1 (April 1, 2009): 84–110.

51. Jessie Conrad, *Joseph Conrad as I Knew Him*, p. 106.

52. JC to Edward Garnett, April 9, 1896, *CL*, vol. 1, p. 272.

53. JC to Edward Sanderson, April 14, 1896, *CL*, vol. 1, p. 274.

54. Jessie Conrad, *Joseph Conrad as I Knew Him*, pp. 30–31.

55. JC to Edward Garnett, June 2, 1896, *CL*, vol. 1, p. 283.

56. JC to Edward Garnett, August 5, 1896, *CL*, vol. 1, pp. 295–96.

57. On Conrad's tendency to avoid one work by writing another, see John Batchelor, "Conrad's Truancy," in John Batchelor, ed., *The Art of Literary Biography* (Oxford: Clarendon Press, 1995), pp. 115–27.

58. Sherry, *Conrad's Western World*, pp. 126–31.

59. "An Outpost of Progress" in Joseph Conrad, *Tales of Unrest* (Garden City, NY: Doubleday, Page & Co., 1920), p. 161.

60. Conrad, "An Outpost of Progress," pp. 150, 163, 171, 183, 185, 197–98.

61. Jessie Conrad, *Joseph Conrad as I Knew Him*, pp. 109, 139.

62. Ibid., pp. 153–54. Sven Lindqvist also points to the fact that Charles Dilke's satirical essay "Civilisation in Africa" appeared in the July 1896 number of *Cosmopolis*, to which Conrad submitted "An Outpost of Progress" for publication. But it's not clear whether or not Conrad read the journal at that time. Sven Lindqvist, *"Exterminate All the Brutes": One Man's Odyssey into the Heart of Darkness and the Origins of European Genocide*, trans. Joan Tate (New York: The New Press, 2007), pp. 25–27.

63. Conrad, "An Outpost of Progress," pp. 178–79.

64. Louis Goffin, *Le chemin de fer du Congo (Matadi-Stanley-Pool)* (Brussels: M. Weissenbruch, 1907), 73.

65. On Buls's connection to Poradowska, see Anne Arnold, "Marguerite Poradowska as Conrad's Friend and Adviser," *The Conradian* 34, no. 1 (2009): 72–76.

66. Goffin, *Le chemin de fer*, pp. 19, 43–44, 65; Henry Richard Fox Bourne, *Civilisation in Congoland: A Story of International Wrong-Doing* (London: P. S. King and Co., 1903), pp. 122–26, 245–46; A.-J. Wauters, *L'état indépendant du Congo: historique, géographie physique, ethnographie, situation économique, organisation politique* (Brussels: Librairie Falk fils, 1899), pp. 360–66; A.-J. Wauters, *Histoire politique du Congo Belge* (Brussels: P. Van Fleteren, 1911), p. 162.

67. Charles François Gommaire Buls, *Croquis congolais [par] Charles Buls. Illustrés de nombreuses photogravures et dessins* (Brussels: G. Balat, 1899), p. 77.

68. Buls to JC, May 11, 1895, *Portrait in Letters*, p. 16.

69. Buls singled out p. 97 "the dazzling splendor of tropical nature." On page 92 of the novel's first edition, Conrad described "plants shooting upward, entwined, interlaced in inextricable confusion, climbing madly and brutally over each other in the terrible silence of a desperate struggle towards the life-giving sunshine above—as if struck with sudden horror at the seething mass of corruption below; at the death and decay from which they sprang." Compare Buls's description of "The Equatorial Forest": "All these parasitic plants struggle to see which will be the first to reach the light; they tangle and climb over one another by the most ingenious means: with hooks, spirals, spears, suckers, and give the impression of a fierce fight for air. . . . Around us we see the fatal consequence of this assault by climbing plants. Crushed under their shroud, the trees have no room to grow; they die suffocated, rotting on their trunks, devoured by ants and centipedes." (Buls, *Croquis Congolais*, pp. 88–89, my translation.)

70. Buls, *Croquis Congolais*, pp. 204–10.

71. JC to R. B. Cunninghame Graham, January 14–15, *CL*, vol. 2, 1898, p. 17. Cf. JC to Aniela Zagórska, January 21, 1898, *CL*, vol. 2, pp. 23–24. Conrad knew Borys to be a Russian name, but "remember[ed] that my friend Stanisław Zaleski gave this name to his eldest son, so that apparently a Pole may use it."

72. Stape, *Several Lives of Joseph Conrad*, pp. 95, 99.

73. JC to David Meldrum, June 4, 1898, *CL*, vol. 2, p. 65.

74. JC to R. B. Cunninghame Graham, August 26, 1898, *CL*, vol. 2, p. 88.

75. JC to E. L. Sanderson, November 21, 1896, *CL*, vol. 1, p. 319. On the loan and advance: Najder, *Joseph Conrad: A Life*, pp. 236, 252, 261.

76. JC to Edward Garnett, [December 18, 1898], *CL*, vol. 2, pp. 132–33.

77. JC to William Blackwood, December 31, 1898, *CL*, vol. 2, pp. 139–40.

78. Unsigned review by Edward Garnett, *Academy and Literature* 63, no. 1596 (December 6, 1902): 606.

79. JC to William Blackwood, February 8, 1899, *CL*, vol. 2, p. 162.

80. Sidney Langford Hinde, *The Fall of the Congo Arabs* (London: Whittaker, 1897), p. 91. This was one of the only English books available about Congo. Hinde has a particular obsession with cannibalism, a topic treated at some length in *Heart of Darkness*—unlike Stanley's obsession, slavery, which figures rather less in *Heart of Darkness*. Traveling on the Congo River in 2016 I was approached by vendors of monkeys smoked on stakes, whose wizened heads resembled the human trophies imagined by Conrad.

81. The rajahs of Sarawak made a particular point of suppressing head-hunting, as Conrad would have known from reading books such as Alfred Russel Wallace's *The Malay Archipelago* (1869).

82. TB to JC, August 3/15, 1881, *CPB*, p. 74. In *Heart of Darkness* Marlow's skull gets measured by a European doctor fascinated by "the first Englishman coming under my observation." (Conrad, *Heart of Darkness*, p. 58.)

CHAPTER TEN: A NEW WORLD

1. JC to Roger Casement, December 1, 1903, *CL*, vol. 3, p. 87.

2. JC to Harriet Mary Capes, December 26, 1903; JC to Mariah Hannah Martindale, December 26, 1903, *CL*, vol. 3, pp. 98–99; JC to Catherine Hueffer, December 26, 1903, *CL*, vol. 9, p. 95.

3. John Stape, *The Several Lives of Joseph Conrad* (New York: Pantheon Books, 2007), p. 109.

4. JC to Aniela Zagórska, December 12, 1898, *CL*, vol. 2, p. 131; Borys Conrad, *My Father Joseph Conrad* (New York: Coward-McCann, 1970), pp. 21–24.

5. JC to David Meldrum, October 12, 1898, *CL*, vol. 2, p. 101. Born Ford Hermann Hueffer, son of a German émigré, the author went by Ford Madox Hueffer when Conrad met him. In 1919 he changed his name to Ford Madox Ford, under which he has been called ever since. To avoid confusion I refer to him as Ford Madox Ford throughout.

6. JC to H. G. Wells, November [25] 1898, *CL*, vol. 2, p. 123.

7. Nicholas Delbanco, *Group Portrait: Joseph Conrad, Stephen Crane, Ford Madox Ford, Henry James, and H. G. Wells* (New York: Morrow, 1982). The relationship between Conrad and Ford has attracted much critical attention. Conrad scholars generally mistrust Ford's many claims about their relationship made after their friendship cooled in 1909. A stylometric analysis has confirmed the sense that, of their three major collaborations, Conrad was the dominant author of *Romance* (1903). See Jan Rybicki, David Hoover, and Mike Kestemont, "Collaborative Authorship: Conrad, Ford and Rolling Delta," *Literary and Linguistic Computing* 29, no. 3 (September 1, 2014): 422–31.

8. JC to R. B. Cunninghame Graham, December 26, 1903, *CL*, vol. 3, pp. 101–2.

9. R. B. Cunninghame Graham, *Hernando de Soto* (London: William Heinemann, 1903), p. x.

10. JC to R. B. Cunninghame Graham, July 8, 1903, *CL*, vol. 3, p. 45.

11. JC to J. B. Pinker, August 22, 1903, *CL*, vol. 3, p. 55.

12. JC to John Galsworthy, [October 23, 1902?], *CL*, vol. 2, p. 448.

13. For a succinct treatment of the literary dimensions of this relationship, see Cedric Watts, "Conrad and Cunninghame Graham: A Discussion with Addenda to Their CL," *The Yearbook of English Studies* 7 (1977): 157–65.

14. Laurence Davies and Cedric Thomas Watts, *Cunninghame Graham: A Critical Biography* (Cambridge, UK: Cambridge University Press, 1979), p. 269.

15. JC to John Galsworthy, July 2, 1904, *CL*, vol. 3, p. 148.

16. Davies and Watts, *Cunninghame Graham*, pp. 127, 134.

17. Ibid., pp. 3–14.

18. Sir Horace Rumbold, *The Great Silver River: Notes of a Residence in Buenos Ayres in 1880 and 1881*, 2nd ed. (London: John Murray, 1890), pp. 6–7.

19. "La Pampa," in R. B. Cunninghame Graham, *The South American Sketches of R. B. Cunninghame Graham*, ed. John Walker (Norman: University of Oklahoma Press, 1978), p. 23.

20. "Paja y Cielo," in Graham, *South American Sketches*, p. 31.

21. "The Pampas Horse," in Graham, *South American Sketches*, pp. 46–49.

22. "A Vanishing Race," in Graham, *South American Sketches*, pp. 38–39.

23. "A Silhouette," in Graham, *South American Sketches*, p. 106.

24. "Cruz Alta," in R. B. Cunninghame Graham, *Thirteen Stories* (London: W. Heinemann, 1900), p. 12. "La Pulpería," and "Gualeguaychú," in Graham, *South American Sketches*, pp. 63–64, 146.

25. Lucy Riall, *Garibaldi: Invention of a Hero* (New Haven, CT: Yale University Press, 2007), pp. 43–45.

26. Ogilvy, quoted in Davies and Watts, *Cunninghame Graham*, p. 18.

27. John Hoyt Williams, *The Rise and Fall of the Paraguayan Republic, 1800–1870* (Austin: University of Texas Press, 1979), chapter 11.

28. Sir Richard Francis Burton, *Letters from the Battlefields of Paraguay* (London: Tinsley Brothers, 1870).

29. R. B. Cunninghame Graham, *Portrait of a Dictator, Francisco Solano Lopez (Paraguay, 1865–1870)* (London: W. Heinemann, 1933), p. 241.

30. Domingo Faustino Sarmiento, *Life in the Argentine Republic in the Days of the Tyrants: Or, Civilization and Barbarism*, trans. Mary Tyler Peabody Mann (New York: Hurd and Houghton, 1868), p. 54. Richard Burton dedicated his *Letters from the Battlefields of Paraguay* to Sarmiento "and the homage which he pays to progress."

31. Ibid., pp. 2, 40.

32. Ibid., pp. 138–39.

33. Ibid., pp. 13, 18, 65–66, 187–88, 213–14.

34. D. C. M. Platt, *Latin America and British Trade 1806–1914* (London: Adam & Charles Black, 1972); Rory Miller, *Britain and Latin America in the Nineteenth and Twentieth Centuries* (London: Longman, 1993), esp. pp. 149–59.

35. Rumbold, *Great Silver River*, p. 8; E. R. Pearce Edgcumbe, *Zephyrus: A Holiday in Brazil and on the River Plate* (London: Chatto & Windus, 1887), pp. 181–89.

36. Davies and Watts, *Cunninghame Graham*, chapters 2–5.

37. R. B. Cunninghame Graham, *A Vanished Arcadia: Being Some Account of the Jesuits in Paraguay 1607–1767* (London: W. Heinemann, 1901), p. 179.

38. "A Vanishing Race," in Graham, *South American Sketches*, pp. 35–42.

39. Graham, *A Vanished Arcadia*, pp. 225, 287.

40. JC to Cunninghame Graham, May 9, 1903, *CL*, vol. 3, p. 34.

41. Joseph Conrad, *Nostromo* (London: Penguin Classics, 2007), p. 26.

42. Ibid., pp. 13, 20, 36.

43. JC to Ford Madox Ford, January 2, 1903, *CL*, vol. 3, pp. 3–4; JC to J. B. Pinker, January 5, 1903, *CL*, vol. 3, p. 6.

44. JC to Ford Madox Ford, March 23, 1903, *CL*, vol. 3, pp. 27–28.

45. JC to R. B. Cunninghame Graham, March 19, 1903, p. 25; JC to R. B. Cunninghame Graham, [June 9?, 1903], p. 41; W. H. Hudson, *The Purple Land: Being the Narrative of One Richard Lamb's Adventures in the Banda Oriental, in South America, as Told by Himself* (New York: Dutton, 1916), pp. 332–38.

46. Norman Sherry, *Conrad's Western World* (Cambridge, UK: Cambridge University Press, 1971), p. 162.

47. Conrad, *Nostromo*, pp. 28, 30.

48. JC to J. B. Pinker, March 16, 1903, *CL*, vol. 3, p. 22.

49. JC to R. B. Cunninghame Graham, July 8, 1903, *CL*, vol. 3, p. 45.

50. On Conrad's sources, see Sherry, *Conrad's Western World*, chapters 15–18.

51. For a description of the *cepo uruguayano*, see George Frederick Masterman, *Seven Eventful Years in Paraguay* (London: Sampson Low, Son, and Marston, 1869), p. 321.

52. Conrad, *Nostromo*, pp. 37, 41, 43, 46, 90, 293.

53. Ibid., pp. 38–40, 58, 68.

54. Ibid., pp. 43–45, 68.

55. R. B. Cunninghame Graham, "Bloody Niggers," *The Social Democrat: A Monthly Socialist Review* 1, no. 4 (April, 1897): 109.

56. Conrad, *Nostromo*, p. 49.

57. Niall Ferguson, *Empire* (New York: Basic Books, 2003), pp. 201–2; James Bryce, "The Roman Empire and the British Empire in India," in *Studies in History and Jurisprudence*, 2 vols. (Oxford: Clarendon Press, 1901), vol. 1, p. 5.

58. Rudyard Kipling, "Recessional" (1897), www.poetryfoundation.org/poems-and-poets/poems/detail/46780.

59. Graham, "Bloody Niggers," 109.

60. J. A. Hobson, *Imperialism: A Study* (London: James Nisbet & Co., 1902).

61. JC to R. B. Cunninghame Graham, December 19, 1899, *CL*, vol. 2, p. 228.

62. P. G. Wodehouse, *The Swoop! Or, How Clarence Saved England: A Tale of the Great Invasion* (London: Alston Rivers, 1909).

63. Paul M. Kennedy, *The Rise and Fall of British Naval Mastery* (New York: Scribner, 1976), pp. 216–18.

64. Rudyard Kipling, "The White Man's Burden" (1899), http://sourcebooks.fordham.edu/halsall/mod/kipling.asp.

65. On the range of positions captured by the concept, see Duncan Bell, *The Idea of Greater Britain: Empire and the Future of World Order, 1860–1900* (Princeton, NJ: Princeton University Press, 2007).

66. William Thomas Stead, *The Americanization of the World: Or, The Trend of the Twentieth Century* (London: H. Markley, 1902), pp. 2, 396.

67. "The Poor Man's Burden," http://historymatters.gmu.edu/d/5475. For the context and consequences of Kipling's poem, see Patrick Brantlinger, "Kipling's 'The White Man's Burden' and its Afterlives," *English Literature in Translation, 1880–1920* 50, no. 2 (2007), pp. 172–191.

68. H. T. Johnson, "The Black Man's Burden," *Christian Recorder* (March 1899), http://nationalhumanitiescenter.org/pds/gilded/empire/text7/johnson.pdf.

69. "Victory," in Graham, *Thirteen Stories*, p. 214.

70. Conrad, *Nostromo*, pp. 62, 64.

71. Ibid., pp. 67, 86, 94, 193.

72. Ibid., pp. 62–63.

CHAPTER ELEVEN: MATERIAL INTERESTS

1. For a vivid fictional exposition of the relationship between the plotting of *Nostromo* and the building of the Panama Canal, see Juan-Gabriel Vásquez, *The Secret History of Costaguana*, trans. Anne McLean (New York: Riverhead, 2011).

2. "Monroe Doctrine, December 2, 1823," http://avalon.law.yale.edu/19th_century/monroe.asp.

3. "Clayton-Bulwer Treaty, 1850," http://avalon.law.yale.edu/19th_century/br1850.asp.

4. "The Panama Canal Treaty," *The Times*, January 24, 1903, p. 7; January 26, 1903, p. 5.

5. Leader, *The Times*, March 19, 1903, p. 7. I have focused on the coverage in *The Times* since this was the newspaper that members of Conrad's social milieu would have been most likely to read on a regular basis.

6. Quoted in David McCullough, *The Path Between the Seas: The Creation of the Panama Canal, 1870–1914* (New York: Simon and Schuster, 1977), p. 380.

7. "President Roosevelt on the Monroe Doctrine," *The Times*, April 4, 1903, p. 7.

8. Abelardo Aldana et al., *The Panama Canal Question: A Plea for Colombia* (New York: [n.p.], 1904), pp. 9–10.

9. Raúl Pérez, "A Colombian View of the Panama Canal Question," *The North American Review* 177, no. 560 (1903): 63–68.

10. "Panama Canal Treaty," *The Times*, September 24, 1903, p. 3.

11. Joseph Conrad, *Nostromo* (London: Penguin Classics, 2007), pp. 96, 116, 152.

12. McCullough, *Path Between the Seas*, pp. 340–42.

13. Conrad, *Nostromo*, pp. 120–21, 135, 145, 147, 170.

14. Ibid., pp. 177, 220.

15. Ibid., pp. 189, 247.

16. JC to J. B. Pinker, [October 7 or 14?, 1903], *CL*, vol. 3, p. 67. "I don't send you P II^d yet. I simply can't spare time to look it over; the drama of the P III^d filling my mind. I don't like to send P II^d if I can help it." It's not clear how much of Part II Conrad had actually written by then. Only six months later did he actually send a chunk of Part II to Pinker for serialization, saying that "The next set to follow in a few days shall contain the end of P. II. Part Third will not take long." (JC to J. B. Pinker, April 5, 1904, *CL*, vol. 3, p. 129.)

17. McCullough, *Path Between the Seas*, pp. 359–60; Philippe Bunau-Varilla, *Panama: The Creation, Destruction, and Resurrection* (New York: McBride, Nast, 1914), p. 318.

18. McCullough, *Path Between the Seas*, pp. 370–79.

19. "Convention for the Construction of a Ship Canal (Hay-Bunau-Varilla Treaty), November 18, 1903," http://avalon.law.yale.edu/20th_century/pan001.asp.

20. Quotes from "The United States Congress," *The Times*, December 8, 1903, p. 5. See also Theodore Roosevelt, "Third Annual Message," December 7, 1903, online by Gerhard Peters and John T. Woolley, *The American Presidency Project*, www.presidency.ucsb.edu/ws/?pid=29544.

21. Leader, *The Times*, November 10, 1903, p. 9.

22. Quoted in Abelardo Aldana et al., *The Panama Canal Question: A Plea for Colombia* (New York: n. p., 1904), p. 68.

23. Eduardo Zuleta, "Elogio de Santiago Pérez Triana" (1919), www.bdigital.unal.edu.co/426/1/elo gio_de_santiago_perez_Triana.pdf; Charles W. Bergquist, *Coffee and Conflict in Colombia, 1886–1910* (Durham, NC: Duke University Press, 1978), pp. 44–45.

24. Santiago Pérez Triana, *Down the Orinoco in a Canoe* (London: W. Heinemann, 1902), pp. 18, 22.

25. Ibid., p. 247.

26. Santiago Pérez Triana, "The Partition of South America," *The Anglo-Saxon Review* 10 (September 1901): 110, 115.

27. "The United States and Panama," *The Times*, November 12, 1903, p. 3; "The United States and Panama," *The Times*, November 14, 1903, p. 7; "The United States and Panama," *The Times*, November 16, 1903, p. 6.

28. Aldana et al., *Panama Canal Question*, pp. 15, 18.

29. Santiago Pérez Triana, "Canal de Panamá," *La Lectura: Revista de Ciencias y de Artes* 3, no. 36 (December 1903): 447-48.

30. JC to Harriet Mary Capes, December 26, 1903; JC to Mariah Hannah Martindale, December 26, 1903; JC to David Meldrum, December 26, 1903, *CL*, vol. 3, pp. 98-100.

31. JC to R. B. Cunninghame Graham, December 26, 1903, *CL*, vol. 3, p. 102.

32. Conrad, *Nostromo*, p. 262.

33. Ibid., pp. 279, 283, 298, 305, 314, 320.

34. JC to Adolf Krieger, March 15, 1904, *CL*, vol. 3, p. 122.

35. JC to H. G. Wells, February 7, 1904, *CL*, vol. 3, pp. 111-12.

36. JC to David Meldrum, April 5, 1904, *CL*, vol. 3, pp. 128-29.

37. Conrad, *Nostromo*, pp. 376, 379, 382, 385.

38. JC to John Galsworthy, September 1, 1904, *CL*, vol. 3, pp. 158-59.

39. Conrad, *Nostromo*, pp. 393, 396.

40. Ibid., pp. 403-4, 412.

41. Ibid., p. 427.

42. Ibid., pp. 440, 442, 447.

43. American newspapers grumbled that "*Nostromo* is the unenlightening title Joseph Conrad has chosen for his new romance." "Gossip for Readers of Books," *Kansas City Star*, February 18, 1904, p. 7.

44. R. B. Cunninghame Graham to Edward Garnett, October 31, 1904, in J. H. Stape and Owen Knowles, eds., *A Portrait in Letters: Correspondence to and About Conrad* (Amsterdam: Rodopi, 1996), p. 45. Garnett had the same reaction in his review, published two weeks later: "We regret the last two chapters describing Nostromo's death. . . . The narrative should have ended with the monologue of Captain Mitchell." See Edward Garnett, "Mr. Conrad's Art," *Speaker* 11 (November 12, 1904), and John Buchan, *Spectator* 93 (November 19, 1904), quoted in Keith Carabine, ed., *Joseph Conrad: Critical Assessments*, 4 vols. (Mountfield, East Sussex, UK: Helm Information, 1992), vol. 1, pp. 310-11, 314-15.

45. JC to R. B. Cunninghame Graham, October 31, 1904, *CL*, vol. 3, p. 175. Many years later he admitted to André Gide "that you will find *Nostromo* badly made and difficult to read—boring even. It was an utter frost, you know. I have a sort of tenderness for that vast contrivance. But it does not work. It's true." JC to André Gide, June 21, 1912, *CL*, vol. 5, p. 79.

46. Buchan, in Carabine, ed., *Critical Assessments*, p. 310.

47. Wilson Follett, *Joseph Conrad: A Short Study* (Garden City, NY: Doubleday, Page & Co., 1915), p. 58.

48. Henry Louis Mencken, *A Book of Prefaces* (New York: A. A. Knopf, 1917), pp. 46-47.

49. James Huneker, "The Genius of Joseph Conrad," *The North American Review* 200, no. 705 (August 1, 1914): 278.

50. Mencken, *Book of Prefaces*, p. 46. Reviewers also saw an affinity with O. Henry's *Cabbages and Kings*, set in a "comic opera" version of a Latin American republic like Costaguana. "South American Tales," *Springfield Republican*, January 1, 1905, p. 19.

51. H. J. Mackinder, "The Geographical Pivot of History," *The Geographical Journal* 23, no. 4 (April 1, 1904): 421-37.

52. H. J. Mackinder, *Britain and the British Seas* (London: W. Heinemann, 1902), p. 350.

53. "Autocracy and War," in Joseph Conrad, *Notes on Life and Letters* (Garden City, NY: Doubleday, Page & Co., 1921), p. 93.

54. Elliott Evans Mills, *The Decline and Fall of the British Empire* . . . (Oxford: Alden & Co., Bocario Press, 1905), pp. 55-56.

55. JC to Roger Casement, 21 December 1903, *CL*, vol. 3, p. 96. The line is a quote from Adolphe Thiers.

56. Conrad, "Autocracy and War," pp. 107, 112. An "ell," or cubit, was a measurement of forty-five inches used in the tailoring industry, now obsolete.

57. Ibid., pp. 106–7.

58. JC to Ernst P. Bendz, March 7, 1923, *CL*, vol. 8, p. 37.

59. Conrad, *Lord Jim*, p. 215.

60. V. I. Lenin, *Imperialism: The Highest Stage of Capitalism*, chapter 10, www.marxists.org/archive/lenin/works/1916/imp-hsc/.

61. Conrad, *Nostromo*, p. 323.

CHAPTER TWELVE: WHETHER THE WORLD LIKES IT OR NOT

1. W. E. B. Dubois et al., "Editorial," *The Crisis* 1, no. 1 (November 1910): 9–10.

2. For a succinct account of the tensions of this era, see Eric Hobsbawm, *The Age of Empire, 1875–1914* (New York: Vintage Books, 1989), chapter 1.

3. Mark Mazower, *Governing the World: The History of an Idea* (New York: Penguin Press, 2012), p. 165.

4. JC to John Quinn, July 1, 1912, *CL*, vol. 5, p. 81.

5. John Stape, *The Several Lives of Joseph Conrad* (New York: Pantheon Books, 2007), p. 173. See also Zdzisław Najder, *Joseph Conrad: A Life*, 2nd ed. (Rochester, NY: Camden House, 2007), p. 424.

6. JC to Arthur Symons, August 29, 1908, *CL*, vol. 4, p. 114.

7. Jessie Conrad, *Joseph Conrad as I Knew Him* (Garden City, NY: Doubleday, Page & Co., 1926), pp. 57–58.

8. I paraphrase here the eloquent description in Laurence Davies's introduction to *CL*, vol. 4, p. xxiv; Jessie Conrad quoted in Stape, *Several Lives of Joseph Conrad*, p. 174.

9. John Conrad, *Joseph Conrad: Times Remembered, 'Ojciec Jest Tutaj'* (Cambridge, UK: Cambridge University Press, 1981), pp. 3–4.

10. JC to J. B. Pinker, May 23, 1910, *CL*, vol. 4, p. 334.

11. JC to Stephen Reynolds, August 20, 1912, *CL*, vol. 5, p. 104.

12. JC to Austin Harrison, March 28, 1912, *CL*, vol. 5, p. 45.

13. JC to John Galsworthy, March 19, 1914, *CL*, vol. 5, p. 365.

14. Stape, *Several Lives of Joseph Conrad*, p. 195. For the dollar/pound conversion, www.measuringworth.com/datasets/exchangepound/result.php.

15. John Conrad, *Joseph Conrad: Times Remembered*, pp. 26–27.

16. He was disqualified from a maritime career because of nearsightedness. Borys Conrad, *My Father Joseph Conrad* (New York: Coward-McCann, 1970), p. 70.

17. JC to Harriet Mary Capes, July 21, 1914; JC to Warrington Dawson, [late July 1914], *CL*, vol. 5, pp. 398–401; Jessie Conrad, *Joseph Conrad as I Knew Him*, p. 63.

18. JC to John Galsworthy, July 25, 1914, *CL*, vol. 5, p. 407. Cf. JC to Harriet Mary Capes, July 21, 1914, *CL*, vol. 5, pp. 400–401.

19. "Poland Revisited," in Joseph Conrad, *Notes on Life and Letters* (Garden City, NY: Doubleday, Page & Co., 1921), pp. 164–70.

20. Borys Conrad, *My Father Joseph Conrad*, p. 86.

21. Jessie Conrad, *Joseph Conrad as I Knew Him*, pp. 71–72. See also "First News," in Conrad, *Notes on Life and Letters*, pp. 174–78.

22. Conrad had noted "an interminable procession of steamers" and attributed it to "the great change of sea life since my time." In fact, the merchant fleet had been summoned back to German waters, and the navy was already massing. Conrad, "Poland Revisited," p. 161.

23. Jessie Conrad, *Joseph Conrad as I Knew Him*, p. 66.

24. JC to John Galsworthy, August 1, 1914, *CL*, vol. 5, p. 409.

25. John Conrad, "Some Reminiscences of My Father" (London: Joseph Conrad Society, 1976), pp. 11–12. Borys Conrad, *My Father Joseph Conrad*, p. 90.

26. "The Crime of Partition," in Conrad, *Notes on Life and Letters*, p. 124.

27. JC to R. B. Cunninghame Graham, February 25, 1915, *CL*, vol. 5, p. 446. Cf. "Poland Revisited," p. 171: "a figure of dread, murmuring with iron lips the final words: Ruin—and Extinction."

28. Jessie Conrad, *Joseph Conrad as I Knew Him*, p. 78.

29. JC to Mrs. Aniela and Miss Aniela Zagórska, October 9, 1914, *CL*, vol. 5, p. 415; JC to Ada and John Galsworthy, November 15, 1914, *CL*, vol. 5, p. 424; Jessie Conrad, *Joseph Conrad as I Knew Him*, pp. 82–85.

30. Jessie Conrad, *Joseph Conrad as I Knew Him*, pp. 88–89; John Conrad, *Joseph Conrad: Times Remembered*, p. 13; Borys Conrad, *My Father Joseph Conrad*, p. 97.

31. Conrad, "First News," p. 173.

32. Prime Minister Benjamin Disraeli used the phrase "Peace with Honour" to describe the outcome of the 1878 Berlin Conference, which established borders in the Balkans following the Russo-Turkish War. Conrad's readers would have caught the connection between the 1878 settlement and the Balkan crises that touched off World War I. In 1938, Neville Chamberlain infamously invoked the phrase upon returning from his meeting with Hitler in Munich.

33. Conrad, "Poland Revisited," pp. 156, 163.

34. Ibid., p. 173.

35. Ibid., p. 170; Najder, *Joseph Conrad: A Life*, pp. 460–61.

36. Conrad, "Poland Revisited," p. 148.

37. "Note on the Polish Problem," in Conrad, *Notes on Life and Letters*, pp. 137–39. Najder, *Joseph Conrad: A Life*, p. 482.

38. JC to Eugene F. Saxton, August 17, 1915, *CL*, vol. 5, p. 500; JC to F. N. Doubleday, July 3, 1916, *CL*, vol. 5, p. 614. On such ironic juxtapositions, see Paul Fussell, *The Great War and Modern Memory* (New York: Oxford University Press, 1975).

39. JC to John Galsworthy, September 23, 1915, *CL*, vol. 5, pp. 512–13.

40. JC to John Galsworthy, March 29, 1916, *CL*, vol. 5, p. 572.

41. JC to Jessie Conrad, September 14, and October 1, 1916, *CL*, vol. 5, pp. 661–67.

42. "Well Done," in Conrad, *Notes on Life and Letters*, p. 192; "Confidence," in Conrad, *Notes on Life and Letters*, p. 203.

43. "Flight," in Conrad, *Notes on Life and Letters*, pp. 211–12.

44. JC to Sir Sidney Colvin, September 9, 1918, *CL*, vol. 6, p. 265.

45. JC to Hugh Walpole, November 11, 1918, *CL*, vol. 6, p. 302.

46. "President Woodrow Wilson's Fourteen Points," http://avalon.law.yale.edu/20th_century/wilson14.asp.

47. J. M. Keynes, *The Economic Consequences of the Peace* (London: Harcourt, Brace & Howe, 1920), p. 291.

48. JC to Sir Hugh Clifford, January 25, 1919, *CL*, vol. 6, p. 449.

49. For a definitive assessment of the League of Nations mandates, see Susan Pedersen, *The Guardians: The League of Nations and the Crisis of Empire* (Oxford: Oxford University Press, 2015).

50. See Erez Manela, *The Wilsonian Moment: Self-determination and the International Origins of Anticolonial Nationalism* (Oxford: Oxford University Press, 2007).

51. JC to Bertrand Russell, October 23, 1922, *CL*, vol. 7, p. 543.

52. JC to Elbridge L. Adams, November 20, 1922, *CL*, vol. 7, p. 595.

53. JC to John Quinn, July 15, 1916, *CL*, vol. 5, p. 620.

54. JC to John Quinn, May 24, 1916, *CL*, vol. 5, pp. 596–98. The government was publicizing Casement's homosexuality in an effort to smear him, but it's unlikely this would have turned Conrad against him. Conrad had several friends he knew to be homosexual, including the writer Norman Douglas, who fled England after a charge of indecent assault in 1916, and for whose younger son

the Conrads subsequently acted as guardians. J. H. Stape, "'Intimate Friends': Norman Douglas and Joseph Conrad," *The Conradian* 34, no. 1 (Spring 2009): 144–62.

55. JC to John Quinn, October 16, 1918, *CL*, vol. 6, pp. 284–86. "I . . . also spring from an oppressed race where oppression was not a matter of history but a crushing fact in the daily life of all individuals." He went on to predict that "the League of Nations will have their hands full with the pacification of Ireland. It will be the only state that will be not weary of fighting, on the whole round earth."

56. JC to Bertrand Russell, October 23, 1922, *CL*, vol. 7, p. 543.

57. Conrad, *The Shadow-Line*, p. 45.

58. Joseph Conrad, *Victory: An Island Tale* (Oxford: Oxford University Press, 2004), p. 285.

59. Richard Curle, *Joseph Conrad: A Study* (Garden City, NY: Doubleday, Page & Co., 1914), pp. 1–3, 13.

60. JC to John Galsworthy, [March? 1915], *CL*, vol. 5, p. 455.

61. JC to J. B. Pinker, February 15, 1919, *CL*, vol. 6, p. 362.

62. Quoted in Stape, *Several Lives of Joseph Conrad*, p. 227.

63. JC to J. B. Pinker, March 10, 1913, *CL*, vol. 5, p. 188.

64. For a definitive treatment of Conrad's reception by American contemporaries, see Peter Lancelot Mallios, *Our Conrad: Constituting American Modernity* (Stanford, CA: Stanford University Press, 2010).

65. Statistics compiled from *Publisher's Weekly*. See www.ocf.berkeley.edu/~immer/books1910s.

66. JC to J. B. Pinker, July 4, 1921, *CL*, vol. 7, pp. 310–11.

67. JC to Edward Garnett, March 10, 1923, *CL*, vol. 8, p. 47.

68. JC to Jessie Conrad, May 4, 1923, *CL*, vol. 8, p. 88.

69. Now the Minda de Gunzburg Center for European Studies, this building houses my office.

70. JC to Borys Conrad, May 6, 1923, *CL*, vol. 8, p. 89; Najder, *Joseph Conrad: A Life*, pp. 553–57.

71. "Conrad Visits Boston," *The New York Times*, May 21, 1923, p. 15.

72. H. L. Mencken, *A Book of Prefaces* (New York: A. A. Knopf, 1917), p. 63. Conrad appreciated the American critic Wilson Follett's book *Joseph Conrad: A Short Study* (Garden City, NY: Doubleday, Page & Co., 1915).

73. Stape, *Several Lives of Joseph Conrad*, p. 271. For Fitzgerald's debt to Conrad, see most recently Jessica Martell and Zackary Vernon, "'Of Great Gabasidy': Joseph Conrad's *Lord Jim* and F. Scott Fitzgerald's *The Great Gatsby*," *Journal of Modern Literature* 38, no. 3 (2015): 56–70.

74. Mallios, *Our Conrad*, p. 41.

75. JC to Richard Curle, July 14, 1923, *CL*, vol. 8, p. 130.

76. JC to Richard Curle, April 24, 1922, *CL*, vol. 8, p. 456.

77. R. B. Cunninghame Graham to JC, December 4, 1923, in J. H. Stape and Owen Knowles, eds., *A Portrait in Letters: Correspondence to and About Conrad* (Amsterdam: Rodopi, 1996), p. 227.

78. JC to Edward Garnett, [September 1, 1923], *CL*, vol. 8, p. 167.

79. JC to Ambrose G. Barker, September 1, 1923, *CL*, vol. 8, p. 165.

80. JC to Harald Leofurn Clarke, January 2, 1923, *CL*, vol. 8, p. 4; John C. Niven to JC, December 3, 1923, *Portrait in Letters*, p. 226.

81. JC to John C. Niven, [December 5, 1923], *CL*, vol. 8, pp. 240–41.

82. JC to Amelia Ward, May 24, 1924, *CL*, vol. 8, pp. 363–64.

83. Jessie Conrad, quoted in Stape, *Several Lives of Joseph Conrad*, p. 252.

84. Borys Conrad, *My Father Joseph Conrad*, p. 162. See also John Conrad, *Joseph Conrad: Times Remembered*, pp. 213–15. On Conrad's sons' memories of their father more generally, see David Miller, "His Heart in My Hand: Stories from and About Joseph Conrad's Sons," *The Conradian* 35, no. 2 (Autumn 2010): 63–95. David Miller's novel *Today* (London: Atlantic, 2011) exquisitely recreates Conrad's final weekend.

85. R. B. Cunninghame Graham, "Inveni Portum: Joseph Conrad," *Saturday Review* 137, August 16, 1924, in Keith Carabine, ed., *Joseph Conrad: Critical Assessments*, 4 vols. (Mountfield, East Sussex, UK: Helm Information, 1992), vol. 1, pp. 425–29.

EPILOGUE: TO MAKE YOU SEE

1. R. B. Cunninghame Graham to Edward Garnett, August 13, 1924, in J. H. Stape and Owen Knowles, eds., *A Portrait in Letters: Correspondence to and About Conrad* (Amsterdam: Rodopi, 1996), pp. 249–50.
2. As Susan Jones points out, the critical establishment enhanced this reputation by diminishing the literary value of Conrad's later works, which featured more prominent female characters. (Susan Jones, *Conrad and Women* [Oxford: Clarendon Press, 1999], pp. 6–7, 24–26.) Richard Curle, by contrast, had included a chapter on "Conrad's Women" in his 1914 study.
3. Virginia Woolf, "Joseph Conrad," *Times Literary Supplement*, August 14, 1924, in Keith Carabine, ed., *Joseph Conrad: Critical Assessments*, 4 vols. (Mountfield, East Sussex, UK: Helm Information, 1992), vol. 1, pp. 420–21. She advanced a similar assessment in "Mr. Conrad: A Conversation," *Nation* (London), September 1, 1921, in Carabine, ed., *Critical Assessments*, vol. 1, pp. 526–29.
4. Ernest Hemingway, "Conrad, Optimist and Moralist," *The Transatlantic Review* 2 (October 1924): 341–42.
5. For a partial summary, see Jeffrey Meyers, "Conrad's Influence on Modern Writers," *Twentieth Century Literature* 36, no. 2 (July 1, 1990): 186–206.
6. "Poland Overtakes India as Country of Origin, Studies Show," August 25, 2016, www.bbc.com/news/uk-politics-37183733. "EU Referendum: The Result in Maps and Charts," June 24, 2016, www.bbc.com/news/uk-politics-36616028.

FURTHER READING

The endnotes to *The Dawn Watch* provide a running bibliography of primary and secondary sources—but given the vast amount of published scholarship on Conrad and his times, these pages provide a few suggestions for readers who want to know more about the topics covered in this book.

Nearly all of Conrad's fiction is still in print and widely available in paperback. Definitive scholarly versions of the texts are published by Cambridge University Press in the series *The Cambridge Edition of the Works of Joseph Conrad*, general editors J. H. Stape and Allan Simmons. The Web site Conrad First (www.conradfirst.net/conrad/home), sponsored by the Department of English at the University of Uppsala, provides an authoritative account of Conrad's serial publication history.

There is no better place to meet Joseph Conrad outside of his fiction than in the nine volumes of the superbly produced *The Collected Letters of Joseph Conrad* (Cambridge: Cambridge University Press, 1983–2008), edited by Frederick R. Karl and Laurence Davies. Each of its meticulously annotated volumes has a superb introduction by Laurence Davies, which act as a wonderfully insightful running biography. Two collections edited by Zdzisław Najder and translated by Halina Carroll-Najder present Polish documents related to Conrad, including all the extant letters from Tadeusz Bobrowski to Conrad (*Conrad's Polish Background: Letters to and from Polish Friends* [Oxford: Oxford University Press, 1964]) and the correspondence between Apollo and Ewa Korzeniowski (*Conrad Under Familial Eyes* [Cambridge: Cambridge University Press, 1983]). Many of Conrad's family members and friends wrote memoirs about him, including Jessie Conrad, *Joseph Conrad as I Knew Him* (Garden City, NY: Doubleday, Page, & Co., 1926); Borys Conrad, *My Father Joseph Conrad* (New York: Coward-McCann, 1970); John Conrad, *Joseph Conrad, Times Remembered: "ojciec jest tutaj"* (Cambridge: Cambridge University Press, 1981); and Ford Madox Ford, *Joseph Conrad: A Personal Remembrance* (Boston: Little, Brown, 1924). A good selection of reminiscences by Conrad's friends—including John Galsworthy, H. G. Wells, and Bertrand Russell—can be found in the first volume of *Joseph Conrad: Critical Assessments*, edited by Keith Carabine (East Sussex, UK: Helm Information, 1992).

The first biography of Conrad was written, with Conrad's collaboration, by G. Jean-Aubry (*Joseph Conrad: Life & Letters* [Garden City, NY: Doubleday, Page, 1927]), and despite its strategic omissions and romantic elaborations, it remains an intriguing portrait of Conrad as his first generation of fans saw him. The definitive recent biography of Conrad is J. H. Stape's concise *The Several Lives of Joseph Conrad* (New York: Pantheon, 2007), which is particularly strong on the details of Conrad's literary career. Among the older biographies of Conrad (by Jocelyn Baines, Frederick Karl, and Jeffrey Meyers, among others), my favorite is Zdzisław Najder's *Joseph Conrad: A Life*, 2nd ed. (Rochester, NY: Camden House, 2007), which gives the fullest portrait of Conrad's early years and Polish milieu.

Since Richard Curle, Wilson Follett, James Huneker, and H. L. Mencken published the first assessments of Conrad's oeuvre in the 1910s, studies of Conrad have undergone a fall, rise, and reinvention—carefully surveyed by John G. Peters in *Joseph Conrad's Critical Reception* (Cambridge: Cambridge University Press, 2013). Interwar critics tended to see Conrad as either too difficult or too simplistic, too pessimistic or too romantic, too conservative or too exotic. A major reevaluation took place just after World War II, when the British critic F. R. Leavis cemented Conrad's position in the canon by naming him one of the key authors in the "great tradition" of the English novel, marked by moral depth and stylistic innovation (*The Great Tradition: George Eliot, Henry James, Joseph Conrad* [London: Chatto & Windus, 1948]). Leavis's contemporary Morton Dauwen Zabel simultaneously placed Conrad within European modernism.

For the next thirty years Conrad studies flourished with numerous examinations of the psychology, style, and politics of his work. Several critics probed the relationship between Conrad's biography and his literary oeuvre. One was Edward W. Said, later one of the founding fathers of postcolonial studies, who wrote a penetrating doctoral dissertation on Conrad's short fiction, published as *Joseph Conrad and the Fiction of Autobiography* (Cambridge, MA: Harvard University Press, 1966). Another was Ian Watt, whose *Conrad in the Nineteenth Century* (Berkeley: University of California Press, 1979) remains as well worth reading for its powerful interpretations of Conrad's early work as for its précis of his life. And in a pair of essential books for the historically inclined reader of Conrad, Norman Sherry hunted down real-life sources for Conrad's fiction in *Conrad's Eastern World* (Cambridge: Cambridge University Press, 1966) and *Conrad's Western World* (Cambridge: Cambridge University Press, 1971).

Conrad remained an important figure for critics working in the new theoretical paradigms of the 1980s, including Fredric Jameson (*The Political Unconscious: Narrative as a Socially Symbolic Act* [Ithaca, NY: Cornell University Press, 1981]) and J. Hillis

Miller (*Reading Conrad*, eds. John G. Peters and Jakob Lothe [Columbus: Ohio University Press, 2017]). But the most significant turn in the reception of Conrad came in the wake of Chinua Achebe's 1977 essay "An Image of Africa." Almost overnight Conrad went from canonical to controversial, a flashpoint in the emerging field of postcolonial studies. Key engagements with Conrad as an author of imperialism include Edward Said's *Culture and Imperialism* (New York: Knopf, 1994), and monographs by Benita Parry, *Conrad and Imperialism: Ideological Boundaries and Visionary Frontiers* (London: Macmillan Press, 1983); Andrea White, *Joseph Conrad and the Adventure Tradition: Constructing and Deconstructing the Imperial Subject* (Cambridge: Cambridge University Press, 1993); Christopher GoGwilt, *The Invention of the West: Joseph Conrad and the Double-Mapping of Europe and Empire* (Stanford, CA: Stanford University Press, 1995); and Linda Dryden, *Joseph Conrad and the Imperial Romance* (New York: St. Martin's Press, 2000). Terry Collits, *Postcolonial Conrad: Paradoxes of Empire* (New York: Routledge, 2005), provides a recent overview of critical reactions to Conrad's imperial novels.

Twenty-first-century students of English literature are highly skeptical about the notion of a canon, let alone the place of Conrad within it. Nevertheless, for every year of the last decade, at least a hundred books, articles, and dissertations treating Conrad have appeared.[1] Many of the best article-length studies of Conrad have been published in *Conradiana* (Lubbock: Texas Tech University Press, 1968–) and *The Conradian: The Journal of the Joseph Conrad Society* (Lincoln, UK: Joseph Conrad Society, 1980–). Readers seeking a general introduction to current Conrad scholarship might begin with *Joseph Conrad in Context*, edited by Allan Simmons (Cambridge: Cambridge University Press, 2009), or *The New Cambridge Companion to Joseph Conrad*, edited by J. H. Stape (Cambridge: Cambridge University Press, 2015). A good sampling of recent responses can be found in Carola M. Kaplan, Peter Lancelot Mallios, and Andrea White, eds., *Conrad in the Twenty-first Century* (New York: Routledge, 2005). *The Oxford Reader's Companion to Conrad*, edited by Owen Knowles and Gene M. Moore (Oxford: Oxford University Press, 2000), is an authoritative, indispensable reference work.

Although *Heart of Darkness* commands the lion's share of critics' attention, I have been particularly inspired by fresh approaches to other portions of Conrad's oeuvre. These include Susan Jones's *Conrad and Women* (Oxford: Oxford University Press, 1999); Margaret Cohen's innovative approach to maritime fiction in *The Novel and the Sea* (Princeton, NJ: Princeton University Press, 2010); and fresh assessments of *The Secret Agent* by Sarah Cole in *At the Violet Hour: Modernism and Violence in England and Ireland* (New York: Oxford University Press, 2012) and Rebecca L. Walkowitz in *Cosmopolitan Style: Modernism Beyond the Nation* (New York: Columbia University

---

1. According to a subject-term search for "Joseph Conrad" in the MLA International Bibliography.

Press, 2006). It seems only a matter of time before the field sees a surge of studies exploring the role of capitalism in Conrad's writing. (See e.g., Regina Martin, "Absentee Capitalism and the Politics of Conrad's Imperial Novels," *Publications of the Modern Language Association (PMLA)* 130, no. 3 (2015): 584–98.)

IN CONRAD'S ERA, MODERN history was typically written in the service of the nation-state. *The Dawn Watch*, however, fits into the burgeoning field of global history, which traces the movement of power, people, capital, and ideas across national and imperial borders. A pithy, accessible history of globalization, as I treat the concept in this book, can be found in Jürgen Osterhammel and Niels P. Petersson's *Globalization: A Short History* (Princeton, NJ: Princeton University Press, 2005)—but the preeminent synthesis of global integration in this period is certainly C. A. Bayly's *The Birth of the Modern World 1780–1914: Global Connections and Comparisons* (Malden, UK: Blackwell, 2003). Eric Hobsbawm's *The Age of Empire: 1875–1914* (New York: Vintage, 1989) presents a stupendously erudite picture of the turn-of-the-century world; while John Darwin's *The Empire Project: The Rise and Fall of the British World-System, 1830–1970* (Cambridge: Cambridge University Press, 2009) masterfully chronicles the role of the British Empire in shaping modern globalization. Excellent new monographs in global history are being published by the year; a flavor of current approaches can be found in the edited volumes *A World Connecting, 1870–1945*, edited by Emily S. Rosenberg (Cambridge, MA: Belknap Press of Harvard University Press, 2012) and *The Prospect of Global History*, edited by James Belich, John Darwin, Margret Frenz, and Chris Wickham (Oxford: Oxford University Press, 2016).

Each section of *The Dawn Watch* stands on the shoulders of giant bodies of scholarship about its sites and subjects. An excellent introduction to the history of Poland in Conrad's time is Piotr Wandycz, *The Lands of Partitioned Poland, 1795–1918*, 2nd ed., (Seattle: University of Washington Press, 1996). Timothy Snyder, *The Reconstruction of Nations: Poland, Ukraine, Lithuania, Belarus, 1569—1999* (New Haven, CN: Yale University Press, 2003), sets nineteenth-century Polish nationalism in broader context; and Kate Brown, *A Biography of No Place: From Ethnic Borderland to Soviet Heartland* (Cambridge, MA: Harvard University Press, 2005), delivers an imaginative history of the Russian-Ukrainian borderlands of Conrad's youth. A sturdy introduction to European anarchism can be found in James Joll's classic *The Anarchists* (Cambridge, MA: Harvard University Press, 1964), while Richard Bach Jensen, *The Battle Against Anarchist Terrorism: An International History, 1878–1934* (Cambridge: Cambridge University Press, 2014), provides the first history of international counterterrorist policing. Victorian asylum policy is the subject of a great (and timely) book by Caroline Shaw, *Britannia's Embrace: Modern Humanitarianism and the Imperial Origins of Refugee Relief* (Oxford: Oxford University Press, 2015).

The best introduction to nineteenth-century British maritime history—albeit naval, not commercial—is Paul M. Kennedy's *The Rise and Fall of British Naval Mastery* (New York: Scribner, 1976). There is no one-volume "go-to" history of the British merchant marine, but Richard Woodman's *Masters Under God: Makers of Empire, 1817–1884* (Stroud, UK: History Press, 1999) and *More Days, More Dollars: The Universal Bucket Chain, 1885–1920* (Stroud, UK: History Press, 2010) are informative substitutes; and for an overview of merchant shipping in and after Conrad's day, see Michael B. Miller, *Europe and the Maritime World: A Twentieth-Century History* (Cambridge: Cambridge University Press, 2012). A number of recent monographs have explored the activities of shipping magnates, firms, and labor practices, including Freda Harcourt, *Flagships of Imperialism: The P&O Company and the Politics of Empire from Its Origins to 1867* (Manchester, UK: Manchester University Press, 2006); Leon Fink, *Sweatshops at Sea: Merchant Seamen in the World's First Globalized Industry, from 1812 to the Present* (Chapel Hill: University of North Carolina Press, 2011); and Frances Steele, *Oceania Under Steam: Sea Transport and the Cultures of Colonialism, c. 1870–1914* (Manchester, UK: Manchester University Press, 2014). On the maritime world of southeast Asia, see James Francis Warren's pathbreaking work *The Sulu Zone 1768–1898: The Dynamics of External Trade, Slavery, and Ethnicity in the Transformation of a Southeast Asian Maritime State* (Singapore: Singapore University Press, 1981); and Eric Tagliacozzo, *Secret Trades, Porous Borders: Smuggling and States Along a Southeast Asian Frontier, 1865–1915* (New Haven, CN: Yale University Press, 2005). Eric Tagliacozzo's *The Longest Journey: Southeast Asians and the Pilgrimage to Mecca* (Oxford: Oxford University Press, 2013) chronicles the history of the hajj in the era of *Lord Jim*; while Valeska Huber, *Channelling Mobilities: Migration and Globalization in the Suez Canal Region and Beyond, 1869–1914* (Cambridge: Cambridge University Press, 2013) explores the Red Sea as a global crossroads.

The abuses in the Congo Free State have been the subject of one of the best historical narratives written in recent decades, *King Leopold's Ghost: A Story of Greed, Terror, and Heroism in Colonial Africa* (Boston: Houghton Mifflin, 1999) by Adam Hochschild—a must-read for anybody interested in this topic. Also well worth consulting are Hannah Arendt's reflections on *Heart of Darkness* in Part Two of *The Origins of Totalitarianism* (New York: Harcourt, Brace, Jovanovich, 1973) and Sven Lindqvist's creative meditation on Conrad and genocide, *"Exterminate All the Brutes,"* translated by Joan Tate (New York: New Press, 1996). To put the history of the Congo Free State in longer context, I recommend David Van Reybrouck's superb *Congo: The Epic History of a People*, translated by Sam Garrett (New York: Ecco, 2014) and Jan Vansina's classic

Paths in the Rainforest: Toward a History of Political Tradition in Equatorial Africa (Madison: University of Wisconsin Press, 1990). Fascinating new studies by historians of Belgium have explored the metropolitan dimensions of Belgian imperialism in Congo, including a trio of articles by Debora Silverman on "Art Nouveau, Art of Darkness: African Lineages of Belgian Modernism," *West 86th: A Journal of Decorative Arts, Design History, and Material Culture* 18–20 (2011–13); Guy Vanthemsche, *Belgium and the Congo, 1885–1990* (Cambridge: Cambridge University Press, 2012); and Vincent Viaene, "King Leopold's Imperialism and the Origins of the Belgian Colonial Party, 1860–1905," *Journal of Modern History* 80, no. 4 (December 2008): 741–90.

The phenomenon of "informal imperialism," as historians describe the nexus of commercial and political power on display in *Nostromo*, was sketched out in a foundational article by Ronald Robinson and John Gallagher, "The Imperialism of Free Trade," *Economic History Review* 6, no. 1 (August 1953): 1–15; and has since been taken up by a number of economic histories of the British Empire, including P. J. Cain and A. G. Hopkins, *British Imperialism: 1688–2000* (London: Longman, 1993); and Gary B. Magee and Andrew S. Thompson, *Empire and Globalisation: Networks of People, Goods and Capital in the British World, c. 1850–1914* (Cambridge: Cambridge University Press, 2010). For British influence in Latin America see D. C. M. Platt, *Latin America and British Trade, 1806–1914* (London: A. & C. Black, 1972); Rory Miller, *Britain and Latin America in the Nineteenth and Twentieth Centuries* (London: Longman, 1993); and Matthew Brown, editor, *Informal Empire in Latin America: Culture, Commerce and Capital* (Oxford, UK: Blackwell, 2008). The political maneuvering behind the secession of Panama has been superbly told by David McCullough in *The Path Between the Seas: The Creation of the Panama Canal, 1870–1914* (New York: Simon & Schuster, 1977). Charles Bergquist, *Coffee and Conflict in Colombia, 1886–1910* (Durham, NC: Duke University Press, 1978), delves into Colombia's "Thousand Days War." Duncan Bell, *The Idea of Greater Britain: Empire and The Future of the World Order, 1860–1900* (Princeton, NJ: Princeton University Press, 2007), gives a splendid account of British attitudes about the rise of the United States. Conrad's captivating friend R. B. Cunninghame Graham has been the subject of a terrific profile by Cedric Watts and Laurence Davies, *Cunninghame Graham: A Critical Biography* (Cambridge: Cambridge University Press, 1979).

Finally, no suggestions for further reading would be complete without mentioning at least a few of the many novels inspired by Conrad. My choices include Chinua Achebe, *Things Fall Apart* (New York: Penguin, 1994); V. S. Naipaul, *A Bend in the River* (New York: Vintage, 1989); W. G. Sebald, *The Rings of Saturn*, translated by Michael Hulse (New York: New Directions, 2016); and Juan Gabriel Vásquez, *The Secret History of Costaguana*, translated by Anne McLean (New York: Riverhead, 2011). May the list go on.

INDEX